**Civic Garden Centre
Library**

Garden Shrubs

Paeonia ludlowii

Garden Shrubs

Arthur Hellyer

MBE, FLS, VMH, AHRHS

Drawings by Nicholas Parlett

J.M. Dent & Sons Ltd
London Melbourne Toronto

First published 1982
© Text, Arthur Hellyer 1982

This book is set in 11 on 12 point VIP Sabon by
D. P. Media Limited, Hitchin, Hertfordshire

Printed in Great Britain by
Billing & Sons Limited
Guildford, London, Oxford and Worcester for
J.M. Dent & Sons Ltd
Aldine House, 33 Welbeck Street, London W1

British Library Cataloguing in Publication Data

Hellyer, Arthur George Lee
    Garden shrubs.
    1. Shrubs
    I. Title
    635.9′76   SB435
    ISBN 0-460-04474-5

Contents

List of colour plates *vi*

Introduction *vii*

1 **Shrubs through the centuries** *1*

2 **The place of shrubs in the garden** *2*

3 **Choosing and planting shrubs** *5*

4 **Pests and diseases** *7*

5 **Hedges, screens and windbreaks** *8*

6 **Pruning shrubs** *13*

7 **Propagation** *16*
Seeds *16*
Stem cuttings *17*
Leaf cuttings *18*
Root cuttings *18*
Layering *19*
Suckers and division *19*

8 **About names and terms** *20*
Abbreviations *21*

9 **Alphabetical list of shrubs** *22*

10 **Plants for special purposes** *235*
Various kinds of climbers *235*
Shrubs to grow as individual specimens *237*
Ground cover shrubs *238*
Variegated shrubs *238*
Grey and silver-leaved shrubs *239*
Pink, red, purple and bronze-leaved shrubs *240*
Berries and other ornamental fruits *240*
Shrubs for autumn colour *242*

Bibliography *243*

Index *244*

Colour plates

between pages 96 and 97

Itea ilicifolia
Daphne odora 'Aureo-marginata'
Acer palmatum 'Dissectum'
Cistus x *corbariensis*
Woodland with azaleas
Clematis armandii

between pages 160 and 161

Hydrangea 'Blue Wave'
Rhododendron 'Brocade'
Actinidia kolomikta
Embothrium coccineum
Magnolia x *soulangiana*
Datura sanguinea

all photographed by the author

Introduction

The older I get, the more I find much of my greatest gardening pleasure in shrubs. Together with trees they are the most permanent and the most undemanding plants in the garden. Many are old friends that have been with me for thirty years or more and shrubs, unlike trees, seldom become so large and overgrown that they have to be felled to make room for other residents. A little judicious thinning and shortening of branches can often preserve the status quo so that the same plants continue year after year occupying much the same space and fulfilling the same decorative role.

Yet I am also increasingly aware of the lack of comprehensive information about this and similar matters in reasonably inexpensive form. There are many splendid works on shrubs, some filling several large volumes and giving detailed accounts of vast numbers of species and varieties. Yet even some of these occasionally omit vital items of cultural information such as the eventual size of the plant, the best method of pruning it or the way in which it can be propagated should one need extra plants for extension, replacement or to distribute among friends.

This, therefore, is my excuse for adding yet one more volume to the already extensive literature on shrubs that can be grown outdoors in temperate climates. I have been at pains to keep it as short as possible. Yet I have also wanted to include as many as possible of the shrubs commonly found in gardens. Because of this the individual descriptions have been kept brief and it has been necessary to make fairly extensive use of abbreviations. My hope is that, despite these restrictions, gardeners like me who rely heavily on shrubs

(and it does appear that there are more and more of them every year) will find it a useful guide to their selection and healthy maintenance. When visiting other gardens, nurseries and garden centres they may also find that it enables them to decide quickly which shrubs they see and admire are most likely to suit their own conditions should they decide to acquire them, and if some friend or garden owner is kind enough to offer them seeds, cuttings or small plants, how these should be treated and what likelihood there is that they will succeed.

The form of the book follows closely that of Graham Stuart Thomas's excellent volume, *Perennial Garden Plants*, and I am grateful to him for providing me with such a practical model to follow. I am also greatly indebted to Nicholas Parlett, a gifted young artist, for the care and skill with which he has prepared the many line illustrations in the text. His work would scarcely have been possible without the generous and knowledgeable assistance of Mrs Violet Lort Phillips whose beautiful and well stocked garden at La Colline, Gorey, Jersey provided many of the specimens from which the drawings were prepared.

All measurements relating to plants are inevitably approximations. Plants do not grow uniformly, indeed there are often considerable variations between individuals and even with the same plant when moved to different surroundings. What one tries to do is to indicate a norm and usually to express it in round figures which may not precisely convert from one system of measurement to another.

Arthur Hellyer
Rowfant 1981

1 Shrubs through the centuries

Shrubs have been valued by gardeners since the earliest days of their art or craft (it is, in fact, an amalgam of both, with sometimes one sometimes the other in the ascendancy) but attitudes towards them have changed dramatically during the centuries. The Romans loved to trim them into artificial shapes and so invented topiary, which emerged again in Renaissance gardens as the favourite method of growing most evergreens, but in England was almost ridiculed out of existence during the eighteenth-century landscape revolution. Topiary became fashionable again, though to a more limited degree, in Victorian gardens and still finds a place in formal designs and also as a cheaper substitute for sculpture. The emphasis today, however, is on preserving as much as possible of the natural beauty of shrubs.

The greatest changes of all have been brought about by exploration and the consequent discovery of new shrub species unknown to earlier garden makers. This stream of novelty began with the opening up of eastern North America by the early settlers but grew to a flood as Asia became ever more deeply penetrated by plant hunters. Africa, South America and Australasia have also contributed large numbers of beautiful shrubs but, since land masses in the southern hemisphere do not extend as far away from the equator as they do in the northern hemisphere, there are fewer species that can be relied on as fully hardy in our climate.

Many of the new shrubs, and most notably the rhododendrons, which were discovered in great numbers in the Himalaya and the countries bordering on them, also proved highly amenable to breeding, so that natural variety was compounded many times over by man-made hybrids. The whole character of gardening was changed by this wealth of new material and by the special requirements of some of the plants. For example it was the need of many rhododendrons and camellias for a certain amount of shade, preferably intermittent shade, which was mainly responsible for the development of woodland gardening, and since this is a very economical method of growing plants in terms of maintenance and labour, it has fitted in well with the changed economic conditions of the post-war years. Even without the extra weed suppression due to a canopy of trees, shrubs are labour-saving by comparison with most other plants, and though the diminishing size of gardens has posed some problems, they have been overcome so well that shrubs have steadily risen in popularity and become the backbone of most garden planting in the British Isles.

2 The place of shrubs in the garden

Shrubs provide the foundation planting for most British gardens. They are there all the time, giving it shape and character, and in winter the evergreen varieties, which retain their leaves, emerge from among the deciduous kinds, which lose theirs, to form new patterns and colour schemes of their own. It is around this permanent framework that the rest of the planting is arranged, the annuals and biennials requiring renewal every year, the half-hardy bedding plants having to be lifted in autumn and protected during the winter and even the herbaceous perennials needing to be dug up and replanted periodically.

Shrubby climbers can be used in a similarly permanent way to clothe walls, drape arches, pergolas and screens and cover unsightly outbuildings. They, too, include both evergreen and deciduous kinds and therefore offer similar opportunities for making striking differences between summer and winter planting densities.

Climbers ascend by various means which need to be considered when selecting places for them. Some, such as ivy and the climbing hydrangeas, have aerial roots which will cling to any firm and not too shiny surface. Others, like some species of parthenocissus (Virginia Creeper and Boston Ivy) have little adhesive pads which cling even more effectively than aerial roots. Yet other climbers, the vines and clematis among them, hold on by spiralling tendrils which need firm but fairly slender supports such as trellis, wires or the stems of shrubs and trees. Wisterias, honeysuckle, jasmine and numerous other plants are twiners which lash themselves around supports and can make use of quite stout

ones, even tree trunks. Roses, brambles and some other thorny or spiny plants are not so much climbers as scramblers, pushing their fairly stiff stems upwards through shrubs and low-branched trees and holding on with their thorns.

Finally there are plants which are used in gardens as climbers though really they are self-standing shrubs. Some, like *Cotoneaster horizontalis* and *C. microphylla*, have a natural tendency to shape themselves to anything that they meet even if it happens to be a vertical wall, and others, like the pyracanthas (firethorns), chaenomeles (Japanese quinces) and ceanothuses (Californian lilacs) are not in any sense climbers but can be trained quite easily against a wall or fence. Since they are naturally stiff-stemmed they will stand up almost on their own though it is convenient to have wires or trellis to which their young stems can be trained so that the plants spread where they are required to go. Sometimes climbers can be allowed to lie flat on the soil as ground cover. The very flexibly stemmed roses known as ramblers are excellent for this purpose and so are ivies and the creeping forms of *Euonymus fortunei* which will cease to creep and start to climb if they encounter a wall or fence.

Shrubs themselves can be used in a variety of ways. Some, such as the small Japanese maples (*Acer palmatum* varieties), are so elegant in shape that it is nice to be able to view them from all sides, and so they are often grown as isolated specimens or among low-growing plants. Others, such as the varieties of *Hydrangea macrophylla* and hardy hybrid rhododendrons, have little beauty of shape to commend them but they make magnificent flower displays which can be further enhanced by planting them in groups. But the most frequent use of shrubs is to give shape and background to beds in which plants of less permanent character will also be grown. The shrubs may be arranged to form bays or sheltered places for other plants with a variety of aspects to suit their particular needs, some sunny and warm, others cool and shady. In large gardens there may even be room to grow shrubs in beds entirely devoted to them and often these are island beds of irregular outline separated by lawns or grassed walks, which provide a semi-natural yet well-ordered setting for the shrubs.

Some shrubs thrive best in woodland, especially in rather thin woodland in which sunlight filters through the leaves even in summer and so the shade is dappled rather than complete. This is the ideal situation for most rhododenrons and azaleas and it also suits camellias, pieris, enkianthus and most of the brambles (*Rubus*). Woodland gardens virtually came into existence in the late nineteenth century to accommodate the vast new array of rhododendron species and hybrids which were then being produced, and though not many new gardens are sufficiently large to contain woodlands many have small coppices or groups of trees which can be treated in a woodland manner. Shrubs are also used as hedges and windbreaks, and some, such as atriplex, escallonias, fuchias, hebes, hippophae, lycium, pittosporums, senecios and tamarix, are particularly good at withstanding salt-laden gales from the sea. Small-leaved evergreen shrubs such as yew and box can be cut into all manner of shapes. Such shapes, some of them very fanciful, may be used to adorn hedges or can be placed in the garden as ornaments, or eye-catchers or, by repetition at regular intervals, used to emphasize or exaggerate the importance and length of a path or walk.

Finally there are low-growing shrubs which make ideal ground cover. In open places none are better for this purpose than the numerous varieties of heather, whether belonging to the genera *Calluna*, *Daboecia* or *Erica*. They enjoy growing close together as they do on the moors and hillsides of Britain, but only a few of them will tolerate lime in the soil. Fortunately on this matter of soil most shrubs are obliging. They have great tolerance for soils of many different kinds and even the vexed question of acidity and alkalinity is less of a problem than it is sometimes made to appear. The real lime-haters are largely confined to the great heather family, Ericaceae, which includes not only the heathers themselves but also many very diverse relatives such as azalea, rhododendron, kalmia, pieris and vaccineum. Camellias dislike lime, though not quite so intensely as rhododendrons, and magnolias do better without it though some will put up with moderate amounts of lime or chalk. However, there are so many excellent shrubs that grow admirably in alkaline soil, particularly if fairly generously fed with manure, garden compost and suitable fertilizers, that there is really little need to complain if a few kinds must either be left out or accommodated in specially prepared beds of lime-free soil. These beds should be made a little above the level of the surrounding land so that lime is not promptly washed down into them. It is hard to think of any shrubs that positively will not grow on acid soils though some do better if the acidity is not too great. It is not difficult to rectify excessive acidity with hydrated lime or finely ground chalk or limestone, and probably if the soil is below pH5.0 it is wise to do this whatever is to be grown. The ideal soil for much ornamental gardening is between pH5.0 and 6.5. It is much more difficult to reduce the alkalinity of soils containing an excess of calcium carbonate (chalk or lime). It can be done with sulphur but this usually creates more problems than it solves, and if the natural soil is of that character it is best to learn to live with it. As explained, with good feeding the limitations are not great.

More important for most shrubs is moisture. Not all will put up with drought and rhododendrons cope with it worse than most. They need soil that remains reasonably moist even in winter but does not get waterlogged in summer, and that is why they often grow so well in valleys so long as they are not also frost pockets, in which the young rhododendron growths, as well as the rhododendron flowers, may be destroyed in spring. Bad drainage is even more of a problem than dryness for not many shrubs like it. Some of the dogwoods (*Cornus*) enjoy it and so do the elders (*Sambucus*) and the willows (*Salix*). But a boggy piece of land is easier to fill with herbaceous plants than with shrubs.

Finally when selecting shrubs do not forget that most have a fairly short flowering season, maybe no more than ten days or a fortnight. So it is important to choose some shrubs for other qualities than their flowers; for foliage, fruits, interesting shapes, stem colour and the branch patterns that the deciduous kinds can create in winter. It is the season when shrubs may be the most interesting plants in the garden.

3 Choosing and planting shrubs

The best time to select any plant is when it is doing what you specially wish it to do in the garden. If it is flowers that are important, pick out those shrubs you want when they are in bloom; if it is autumn foliage colour, select them then, or if you expect them to have berries in January, drag yourself to the nursery then, however unpleasant the weather, for only then can you be sure that the plants you have chosen really are capable of retaining their fruit so late. Catalogue descriptions may be excellent but they tend to be based on the best, not the average, still less the sub-normal and there can be some of each in every batch of plants, especially if they started life as seedlings.

If plants are being purchased in containers it will be possible to take them home directly they have been selected whatever the time of year. Container-growing is excellent for a great many shrubs, particularly if one is prepared to take them young, which is the best way since young plants nearly always establish themselves more easily than older ones. But the larger shrubs grow in containers, the more likely they are to become starved or to get their roots wrapped round into such tight balls that they have great difficulty in growing out when they are finally planted outdoors. If large plants are required it is usually best to get them from the open ground, and that means waiting for delivery until the right planting season, which will be from early November until late March for deciduous kinds and March or October for most evergreens, though they can be planted earlier and later if soil and weather conditions are specially favourable. There may be some scarce plants that have to be purchased from the open ground because they are not available in containers, and there are plenty of gardeners who actually prefer open ground plants on the score that they do not have to adjust to very different soil and conditions as container plants usually must. So if open ground plants are selected at a time of year when they cannot be lifted and taken away the thing to do is to tie labels on them so that there can be no mistake when delivery time comes.

There are differences in the techniques of planting container-grown and open ground plants. With the former it is usually wise to keep the ball of soil and roots intact; to tap plants carefully out of rigid containers or slit and strip limp bags or pots from them. This is almost essential when planting in summer since the plants must not then suffer any sudden check to growth, but when planting under less stressful conditions between October and March it may be wise to loosen some of the outer roots and lead them out into the new soil. There is always a danger with container plants that they will be reluctant to grow out of the ball of usually very porous, peaty soil in the container into the probably much more cohesive and almost certainly very different soil of the garden. Matters can also be helped by preparing a special planting mixture of garden soil, peat and sand and working a few spadesful of this around the roots of each plant when planting.

Open ground plants are either delivered bare root, which means that all soil has been shaken from the roots to reduce weight in transport, or balled, which means that a good deal of soil has been retained and held in place by wrapping hessian or polythene tightly around the roots. Balling is used for hollies and many conifers, which tend to suffer heavy losses when transplanted with bare roots, and it is wise not to remove the wrapping material until the plants are actually standing in the holes prepared for them and it can be carefully slipped off and drawn out with a minimum of soil disturbance.

Holes prepared for container-grown shrubs need to be only slightly larger than the containers. For open ground plants they usually need to be a good deal wider so that all roots can be spread out in a natural manner. They will also need to be sufficiently deep to allow the uppermost roots to be covered with 5–8cm./2–3½in. of soil, whereas container plants need only 15mm./ ¾ in. covering over the ball of soil and roots. The soil should be trodden in quite firmly all round the shrub and, if the weather is dry, it should be well watered. Further watering may be necessary when planting in spring or summer but natural rainfall is usually adequate for plants moved in autumn or winter. Tall shrubs will almost certainly need to be staked for the first few months until they have anchored themselves firmly with new roots.

Evergreens are, on average, more difficult to establish than deciduous shrubs, since even in winter they can be losing quite a lot of moisture on warm days or when there is a lot of wind. A screen of polythene or very fine mesh netting of the type sometimes used for greenhouse shading can be helpful, since it shades leaves and slows the movement of air over them. Large plastic bags of the kind used for composts and fertilizer make good screens if slit top and bottom, slipped like sleeves over the plants and held firmly in place with stakes, three or four inside each well driven into the soil.

Soil in which shrubs are to be planted should always be well cultivated a few weeks before they are to go in, and can be improved in texture with peat or leaf-mould and fed with a little bonemeal. Rich manure and fertilizers are best reserved for use later as top dressings when the shrubs are established and able to make use of them. Bonemeal helps to promote root growth but rich nitrogenous feeds can actually retard it and do harm at the outset though they may be very useful later on.

4 Pests and Diseases

In general shrubs do not suffer greatly from pests and diseases and there is certainly no need to go round spraying them indiscriminately. However, troubles do occur. Some, such as rose black spot disease, are confined to particular genera, others such as greenflies and capsid bugs, are common to many different kinds. As a rule one good general purpose insecticide, such as malathion, HCH or dimethoate, and one fungicide, such as benomyl or triforine, will suffice for most purposes and need only be used when pests or diseases appear.

More troublesome are diseases occurring in the soil, particularly honey fungus, which tends to be present in most woodlands and can be deadly to some shrubs and yet leave others unaffected. Rhododendrons and azaleas can suffer badly but camellias scarcely ever appear to be attacked. Special preparations of phenols are available for treating the soil but effective control can be difficult and expensive, and it is probably best to lift and burn affected plants as soon as noted and break up the soil with spade or fork before replanting. Deep cultivation usually destroys the disease-causing fungus, at least temporarily, and if a barrier of polythene can be installed right round the cultivated area to a depth of about 45cm./18in. there is unlikely to be any re-infection from the surrounding uncultivated soil. The symptoms of honey fungus are leaves wilting and turning brown, bark splitting and lifting from the wood beneath, which may be covered with a cobweb growth of white fungus, and roots killed and wet with decay. The disease spreads by black stringy growths rather like bootlaces (the disease is sometimes called Bootlace Fungus), which grow out laterally a little below the surface and attack those roots of trees or shrubs with which they actually make contact. This hit or miss method of infection accounts for the rather unpredictable way in which this disease spreads.

5 Hedges, screens and windbreaks

Hedges may be required to keep out intruders, to indicate the boundary of a property or simply to make a division between one part of the garden and another. For the first purpose the hedge must be substantial and difficult to penetrate but neither quality may be essential when hedges are merely used for deliniation. For this purpose it may be much more sensible to look for a hedge that is highly decorative in its own right, a flowering hedge of berberis or roses, maybe, or a berry-bearing hedge of cotoneaster or pyracantha. Or the emphasis may be on choosing a hedge-making shrub that accords well with whatever is to be grown within it; a rose hedge, for example, for a rose garden or a hedge of lavender or rosemary for a herb garden or one to be devoted largely to cottage flowers.

If privacy is a major reason for planting a hedge or screen it will probably be important that the shrub chosen is both evergreen and reasonably fast growing, and the same two qualities are required for windbreaks, though these may need to be taller and sturdier, and perhaps include some trees for extra height. The most effective windbreaks are those sufficiently wide and yet also sufficiently open to absorb the wind, gradually, slowing it down rather than stopping it so suddenly that great turbulence occurs. This is particularly important when sheltering maritime gardens from storms blowing in from the sea. In these circumstances it is also essential that at least the outer part of the windbreak is composed of trees or shrubs that are tolerant of salt.

Hedges often suffer from neglect, both in the initial preparation of the soil and in subsequent care, particularly in feeding, which may be essential to keep close-planted and therefore highly competitive plants in good condition. Before planting the site should be well dug the whole length of the hedge and for a width of at least one metre, and compost or manure should be mixed with the soil if possible. It is also beneficial to finish off with a scattering of a compound fertilizer well raked or forked into the surface.

Usually the quickest and most effective way of planting a hedge is to open a trench about 30cm./12in. wide and the same in depth the whole length, line the plants out in this at the correct spacing and then return the soil, treading it in firmly. If the hedge is in an exposed position it may be necessary to drive in posts about 3m./10ft apart, strain one or two wires between these and tie the young plants to the wires to prevent their being rocked or even blown out by wind.

Whether the tops should be removed from hedge plants at an early stage, either immediately after planting or as soon as they are well established, depends upon the relative importance of density and height. If a thick, impenetrable hedge is required it will almost certainly be wise to behead the plants early to ensure maximum branching from low down, but if it is desired to get height as quickly as possible the hedge plants are best left to grow upwards unchecked.

Time and frequency of clipping depend partly on the character of the hedge plant, partly on the kind of hedge required. Evergreens are best clipped between May and August, with any hard cutting required completed as early as possible in that period. Deciduous hedge plants can be trimmed lightly during the same period but any hard cutting required is best done between November and February. Flowering hedges are best pruned as soon as the flowers fade and berry-bearing hedges as soon as the berries can be seen so that as many as possible can be retained, or, if deciduous, in late winter after all berries have fallen or been eaten. Large-leaved hedges, e.g. *Aucuba* and cherry laurel, are best trimmed with secateurs to avoid cutting through leaves, but this is such a slow job that it may prove a counsel of perfection that has to be ignored.

Hedges will grow faster and more reliably if kept well watered at least for the first summer. All hedges will be improved in density, leaf colour and quality if fed each spring with a compound fertilizer such as National Growmore, which should be applied at 100g./4oz. per metre length of hedge. Proprietory fertilizers should be used according to makers' directions.

Although hedges are usually formed of one variety of shrub throughout, mixed hedges of two or more contrasted varieties or kinds can be attractive. Green holly can be mixed with variegated holly, green-leaved beech with copper or purple-leaved beech or *Cotoneaster simonsii* can be mixed with thorn or privet to give it greater density. It is also possible to grow informal hedges which are carefully pruned and thinned rather than clipped so that the shrubs retain much of their natural habit and elegance. *Berberis darwinii* and *B.* x *stenophylla* are two excellent shrubs to grow in this way and so are some of the cotoneasters and escallonias but such hedges inevitably take up more room than those that are neatly trimmed.

Good Shrubs for Hedges, Screens and Windbreaks

ATRIPLEX. *A. halimus* is useful as an outer windbreak or screen near the sea as it is highly tolerant of salt-laden wind. It is naturally rather straggly but is improved in habit by regular pruning. Plant 60cm./25in. apart. Trim May to August. Excellent for sandy soil.

BEECH. *Fagus sylvatica*, the common beech, is a tree, but it stands pruning so well that it can be used to form very narrow yet tall hedges or windbreaks. Both green and coloured-leaved varieties can be used singly or mixed. Plant 50cm./20in. apart. Trim in summer but leave hard pruning until winter. Excellent for chalk or limestone soils.

BERBERIS. Several species are suitable for making informal hedges. *Berberis darwinii* and *B.* x *stenophylla* are evergreen. *B. thunbergii* is deciduous and can be used in its green-leaved and purple varieties singly or mixed. Plant 60cm./25in. apart. Trim evergreens once only after flowering, deciduous kinds in autumn or winter after any berries have fallen.

BOX. *Buxus sempervirens* stands clipping exceptionally well and so is a favourite shrub for topiary. It also makes an excellent hedge and can be used either in its green-leaved or yellow variegated varieties singly or mixed. Plant 60cm./25in. apart. Trim May to August. Excellent for chalk and limestone soils. There is a naturally dwarf variety, named 'Suffruticosa', which is specially suitable for forming the tiny hedges, or edges, used to outline formal beds or patterns made in beds. It should be planted about 15cm./6in. apart.

COTONEASTER. Several kinds, including *Cotoneaster franchetii* and *C. lacteus*, make good informal hedges pruned lightly when their berries have formed. *C. simonsii* is more stiffly erect in habit and can be used by itself or with other shrubs as a formal hedge trimmed in summer. Plant the large kinds 1m./3ft. apart, *C. simonsii* 50cm./20in. apart.

CYPRESS. The most useful kinds for inland gardens are Lawson Cypress (*Chamaecyparis lawsoniana*) and Leyland Cypress (x *Cupressocyparis leylandii*). The latter is particularly useful where a tall screen or windbreak is required quickly since it is very fast-growing. So is the Monterey Cypress (*Cupressus macrocarpa*) but it is subject to frost damage inland and often dies out with age; it is much more satisfactory near the sea. The yellow-leaved varieties are hardier than the green-leaved type. Plant Lawson and Monterey Cypress 60cm./25in. apart, Leyland Cypress 1m./3ft apart. Trim all from May to August.

ESCALLONIA. All kinds make good informal hedges particularly near the sea. Plant 1m./3ft apart. Trim once annually when the flowers fade.

EUONYMUS. *E. japonicus* makes an excellent hedge particularly near the sea. Inland it is sometimes damaged by frost. It can be used in its green-leaved and variegated varieties singly or in mixture. Plant 50cm./20in. apart. Trim from May to August.

FUCHSIA. Forms of *Fuchsia magellanica*, particularly 'Riccartonii' and *gracilis*, make attractive semi-formal hedges in maritime localities. Plant 50cm./20in. apart. Trim once annually in February.

GRISELINIA. *G. littoralis* is frequently used as a hedge in maritime gardens and withstands salt-laden wind well. It also thrives in many inland places but can be damaged by hard frost. It can be used in green-leaved and variegated varieties singly or in mixture. Plant 60cm./25in. apart. Trim from May to August.

HEBE. Most kinds are rather too tender for hedge-making except in maritime localities but *Hebe brachysiphon* is sufficiently reliable to be planted in all but the coldest places, and its neat box-like leaves make a good hedge. Plant 1m./3ft apart. Trim once only as soon as the flowers fade.

HOLLY. Common holly, *Ilex aquifolium*, makes an excellent hedge, dense, impenetrable and long-lived. Variegated forms can be used with it or on their own and if both male and female varieties are mixed berries will be produced. Plant 60cm./25in. apart. Trim from May to August.

HORNBEAM. *Carpinus betulus* is a tree with leaves closely resembling those of beech. It can be used as a hedge or windbreak in exactly the same way as beech, and is to be preferred if the soil is heavy or poorly drained.

LAUREL. There are three kinds of laurel: the true laurel or bay, *Laurus nobilis*, which makes a handsome aromatic hedge near the sea but is too tender to be reliable in most inland gardens; the Cherry Laurel, *Prunus laurocerasus*, with large shining green leaves; and the Portugal Laurel, *Prunus lusitanica*, with smaller leaves. The last two are a good deal hardier and make handsome large hedges but require plenty of room. *Laurus nobilis* is also a favourite tub plant for patios and courtyards, trimmed into simple shapes such as balls and pyramids. For hedges plant all laurels 60–90cm./25–36in. apart. Trim, preferably with secateurs, May to August.

LAURUSTINUS. *Viburnum tinus* makes a fine large-flowering hedge particularly near the sea and in mild places inland. It needs plenty of space and should be planted 1m./3ft. apart. Trim from May to August.

LAVENDER. All forms of *Lavandula angustifolia* make excellent small hedges, the taller kinds growing up to 1m./3ft high. Plant 40cm./15in. apart. Trim once only as soon as the flowers fade.

LONICERA. The shrubby honeysuckle most popular for hedge-making is *Lonicera nitida* in one or other of its several forms, which include yellow-leaved as well as green-leaved varieties. It can be clipped to form a very narrow hedge but is not sufficiently sturdy for hedges much above 1.5m./5ft high. Plant 30cm./12 in. apart. Trim May to August.

MYROBALAN. This is *Prunus cerasifera*, a small-fruited plum sometimes known as the Cherry Plum. It makes a good deciduous hedge and is particularly useful as an outer screen or barrier. It is available in green and purple-leaved forms and these are often used in mixture. A purple-leaved hybrid from this species, named *Prunus* 'Cistena' is much smaller and can be used for hedges as low as 1m./3ft. Plant *P. cerasifera* 60cm./25in. and *P.* 'Cistena' 40cm./15in. apart. Trim all once annually in spring after flowering.

OSMANTHUS. The hardy hybrid between *Osmanthus x burkwoodii* has neat evergreen leaves and sweetly scented white flowers. It makes an excellent hedge. Plant 50cm./20in. apart. Trim May to August.

PITTOSPORUM. Several species are used as hedges and windbreaks in coastal regions because of their tolerance of salt-laden wind but none is fully hardy in all parts of the British Isles. The most decorative kind is *Pittosporum tenuifolium*, available in green-leaved and grey and silver variegated varieties. Plant 50cm./20in. apart. Trim from May to August.

PRIVET. The best kind for hedge-making is *Ligustrum ovalifolium* in both green and golden-leaved forms. It withstands urban conditions well but in cold and exposed places may lose most of its leaves in winter. Plant 30cm./12in. apart and behead plants immediately to ensure branching from the base. Subsequently trim from May to August.

PYRACANTHA. Most kinds can be used for hedge-making but *Pyracantha rogersiana* is one of the most suitable, because of its fairly small leaves and abundant flowers and berries. Plant 50cm./20in. apart. Trim once annually when berries are formed. Excellent for chalk and limestone soils.

ROSEMARY. Like lavender, rosemary (*Rosmarinus officinalis*) makes a pleasantly aromatic small hedge but it is not very hardy and is most suitable for warm, sunny places and well-drained soils. Plant 50cm./20in. apart and trim from May to August.

ROSES. Some shrub and species roses and a few of the more vigorous cluster-flowered (*floribunda*) varieties make attractive informal hedges, but all need to be given a good deal of freedom in growth. An alternative is to use climbing varieties trained to horizontal wires strained between posts. Plant bush varieties 40–60cm./15–25in apart, climbing varieties 1.0–1.5m./3–5ft apart. Prune in February to March and again, more lightly, in July when the first flush of flowers (it may be the only flush with species and some shrub roses) is over.

SPIRAEA. The best species for hedge-making is *Spiraea thunbergii* because its densely twiggy habit responds well to clipping. Plant 50cm./20in. apart and trim once in late spring as soon as the very numerous white flowers fade.

THORN. *Crataegus monogyna*, also known as Hawthorn, May and Quickthorn, is the most popular plant for farm hedges and can also be used as a nearly impenetrable outer barrier for gardens. It is really a small tree but for hedge-making it should be planted 30cm./12in. apart and beheaded at once to ensure branching from the base. Prune annually in winter and trim lightly in summer if a fairly formal appearance is required.

THUYA. The best species is *Thuya plicata*, which looks much like Lawson Cypress and is to be preferred for shady places or moist soils. Plant 60cm./25in. apart. Trim from May to August.

YEW. The common yew, *Taxus baccata*, makes a splendidly dense hedge and withstands the most rigorous clipping. It is a first-rate shrub for topiary and because of its rigid stems can be used for the largest specimens. Ordinary yew has very dark green leaves but there are also golden-leaved varieties which can be used with it or on their own. Plant 60cm./25in. apart. Trim from May to August.

6 Pruning shrubs

For many shrubs pruning is merely a convenience which enables them to be restricted to a predetermined size and shape. For a few it is a necessity to maintain them in good condition and ensure that they produce the best performance of which they are capable. Necessity is most apparent for those shrubs, such as brambles and roses, that have a natural tendency to renew themselves frequently with young growth. In the wild these kinds simply let their older stems die. In time they decay and return humus and plant food to the soil, but that may take years during which the dead growth looks unsightly. Nature does not bother about appearances but gardeners do and so they anticipate nature's processes by cutting out old stems before they die and consigning them to the bonfire. It may also be essential to prune shrubs that become diseased so that infected growth can be removed and burned before the trouble spreads. Such pruning is usually best done at the earliest possible moment and there is little need to worry about correct times or methods. It is an urgent surgical task which necessitates cutting right back to healthy growth and the sooner it is done the better.

Another pruning necessity arises for purely man-made reasons. It is convenient to propagate some plants by grafting them on a root-stock of a related species. Nurserymen nearly always increase garden varieties of rose in this way, since the grafting can be done with single growth buds (the process is therefore known as 'budding') and a single stem, sufficient to make only one cutting, might easily produce six or seven buds. This method is therefore economical of propagating material, and another advantage is that root-stocks can be chosen to give increased vigour to a naturally weak variety. The drawback is that a grafted plant is really two different plants, one growing on the other. All growth that comes from the scion, that is the graft or bud, will have the character of the parent from which the scion was taken, but all growth from the root-stock will have the characteristics of its parent. That is why suckers must be removed from grafted plants, for if they are left they will produce their own type of growth and flower, probably quite useless for decorative purposes and certainly not what the plant was put there to produce. Again removal is best done quickly, as soon as the suckers are observed. They have a habit of growing fast and swamping the usually less vigorous garden variety that has been grafted on the root-stock. Note well, however, that this instruction applies only to grafted plants. There is nothing wrong with suckers as such and if the plant is on its own roots, maybe raised from a seed, a cutting or a layer, it may be wise to retain suckers because they are young and vigorous and, if necessary, to remove some of the top growth to make room for them.

Quite a lot of shrub pruning is concerned with preventing plants getting quite as crowded with growth as they might do if left to their own devices. If the shrub is part of a hedge the denser it is the better, but if it is growing as an isolated specimen or in a group or border with other plants it may look more attractive if it is not overcrowded with stems. A reduction in the number of stems may also result in an improvement in performance, maybe finer leaves or larger flowers. Thinning is, in fact, the commonest form of amenity pruning, that is of pruning to make the plant more attractive in the garden. It can be carried out with almost anything, and nearly always the best method is to cut out old growth and preserve young growth. It is easy to say this but a little more difficult to put it into practice, partly because it may not be immediately obvious which stems or branches are young and which are old but far more because much of the young growth may be carried on much older branches so that to remove one would be to destroy the other.

Age of growth can be estimated by its thickness, its colour and the character of its bark or skin. Young stems tend to be more slender, greener and smoother than old stems and to have a much thinner skin. By contrast really old wood may be stout, with thick, wrinkled, brown or grey bark. These characteristics differ according to the species but a little observation will soon make it fairly plain which is really young and which is positively old growth, and this is all that really matters. But what about the old branches that are carrying young growths. If there is a lot of it and it is vigorous and healthy it is clear that the old growth is itself in good shape and may just as well be kept if there is room for it. It is a matter for discretion and commonsense.

Available space is often the crux of the matter. In a big garden all shrubs may be able to grow to their full size but in smaller ones some have to be restricted. Then the problem is how to do it without spoiling their appearance and performance. The worst way is almost always to go over them with shears or secateurs, snipping back everything indiscriminately and reducing every bush to a neat but characterless dome. Unless the aim is to train the shrub in an entirely artificial manner, as may be necessary if it is to be spread out on a wall, the first essential is usually to preserve as much as possible of its natural habit, whatever that may be. Thinning, as already described, usually does this, which is why it is such a good

rule-of-thumb method of pruning, to be applied whenever one does not know of anything more suitable, but it is not the only method, nor always the best, and even when it is, the time at which it is done may need to be adjusted to suit the growth cycle of particular species.

First one can make a broad time division between the pruning of most deciduous as opposed to evergreen shrubs. There is only one close season for pruning deciduous shrubs and that is when they are just starting to grow in spring, and even that can be ignored for those kinds that are not subject to 'bleeding'. This term is used to describe the loss of sap that can occur through wounds, and the worst time for it is when the sap is rising strongly in spring but before there are many leaves to make use of it. If stems are cut hard then some will drip sap for days or even weeks. It can be fatal. April is probably the most risky month and by May there is usually plenty of foliage to use up all the sap and even large branches can be lopped with little or no bleeding.

With evergreens the problems are different. Many of them are a little tender and none of them becomes as dormant in winter as the deciduous kinds. There is often risk that pruning after mid-August will cause late growth which will be too immature to get through the winter safely. Similarly autumn or winter pruning may cause early growth which will be damaged by spring frosts, a problem in Britain in all but the milder southern and western maritime areas. For these reasons mid-April to mid-August is the main pruning season for evergreens, and any really hard thinning or cutting back that becomes necessary is usually most safely done in May. If the shrubs are in flower then it can be delayed until June.

That is the broad picture but there is plenty of detail to be filled in. Many shrubs flower on, or from, stems made the previous year and some actually form their flower buds one year, carry them dormant through the winter, and open them the following spring or summer. Rhododendrons, azaleas and magnolias all do this and the flower buds are so prominent that it is impossible to miss them. Shrubs with this characteristic usually start to form their new flower buds very soon after the previous flower crop has faded, and so the best time to prune is between these two events. Prune immediately after flowering and you will have done nothing to impair that display, and there should be time for the new flower buds to form for the next display.

Exactly the same applies to those shrubs that, although they do not actually form their flower buds a year in advance, nevertheless flower most freely on one-year-old growth. Many of the spring and early summer-flowering shrubs come into this category and again the least damaging time to reduce them in size is as soon as they have finished flowering. By contrast a good many late-flowering shrubs, those that start to flower in July or later, do so on stems that started to grow that same spring. It is possible to prune them quite hard in winter or even as late as March and still get a good display in the summer. It is the method applied to most roses, particularly the bedding varieties, and it works well with *Buddleia davidii*, *Hydrangea paniculata*, *Caryopteris* x *clandonensis* and most of the summer and autumn-flowering varieties of clematis.

Yet another type of shrub produces its best flowers on stems or branches that are more than a year old. This kind of flowering is common with fruit trees and can be seen very clearly in apples, pears and plums. Flower buds start to appear the second year and gradually built up into clusters which are known as 'spurs'. It is not so important with shrubs but it does occur, and the pruning must be adapted so that plenty of old growth that is still healthy and vigorous is retained. Some that is failing in these respects can be removed and, if the bushes need even more reduction in size, most of the young shoots that start to grow in spring can be shortened to a few centimetres in summer. June and July are usually good months to do this kind of work, which is known as spur pruning.

Most shrub pruning can be done with sharp secateurs but lopping shears may be required for thick stems and a pruning saw for anything over 3 or 4cm./1 or 2in. Hedges formed of small-leaved shrubs, such as yew, box, privet, euonymus, *lonicera nitida* and the various cypresses and thuyas, can be trimmed with shears or mechanical hedge-trimmers, but the sliced leaves this causes can be unsightly with large-leaved shrubs such as laurels and aucuba and these are best trimmed with secateurs. It is possible to spray hedges with chemicals, of which dikegulac is one, to restrict growth and increase branching, and this reduces the need for clipping, but growth retardants of this kind are not suitable for all shrubs and label instructions should be consulted before using them.

7 Propagation

Seeds

The natural method of increase for most shrubs is by seed, and it is usually the cheapest method to use in gardens. But from the garden standpoint seedlings suffer from two disadvantages. They can take several years to reach a size at which they begin to create much effect, and they do not always exactly resemble their parents. The differences are likely to be most serious in the case of hybrids but even species can show variations which may be more important from a decorative than from a botanical viewpoint. Flower colour may vary or there may be differences in height, habit or leaf size. How much this matters depends a great deal on the purpose for which the plants are required. For those gardeners in search of novelty seedling variation can be a positive advantage.

Many shrub seeds germinate readily either outdoors or in frames or greenhouses and require treatment similar to that given to seeds in general. They need good clean soil, porous yet rather spongy so that moisture is well retained but air is not driven out completely. The best temperatures for germination are usually in the 15–20°C./59–68°F. range and, once sown, they should not be allowed to get dry at any stage.

Germination may take place quite quickly or be delayed for weeks or months. Some shrubs have a built-in mechanism developed in the wild to prevent them from germinating until the most favourable season. Since many seeds ripen in autumn and need to germinate in spring this mechanism is often controlled by cold; the seeds must have so many months at a low temperature before they will germinate. In gardens in Britain winters are usually sufficiently cold and prolonged to supply this period of vernalization, or stratification as it is called, if the seeds are sown outdoors as soon as they are ripe. Since they may be at risk from pests during the winter, it is often safer to mix them with damp sand, place this in well-drained pots or pans, wrap these around with fine mesh wire netting so that mice, voles, squirrels etc. cannot get at them, and stand them outdoors until early March when the mixture of sand and seeds can be sown in the ordinary way. However, it is possible to stratify seeds of all kinds in a domestic refrigerator. The temperature in the bottom compartment of this, usually about 3–4°C./38–40°F., is sufficient for most seeds if they are kept in it for about three months. They must be damp all this time but this is not difficult if the seeds are placed in polythene bags with some moist peat, sand or vermiculite, and the bags are then sealed with the twist closures sold for food freezing and other domestic purposes. This artificial vernalization can be carried out at any time, and after the three months the seeds are sown in the usual way in a reasonably warm temperature. With some seeds a warm period must precede the cold period.

Some shrub seeds germinate readily if sown as soon as ripe with no pre-treatment of any kind. Azaleas and rhododendrons are of this kind and so are buddleias, clethras, deutzias, diervillas, enkianthus, ericas, hypericums, hydrangeas, kalmias, kolkwitzias, leucothoe, philadelphus, pieris, potentillas, spiraeas and weigelas – quite a goodly collection.

Seed usually provides the easiest method of transmitting plants from one country to another and is often the best way of obtaining scarce plants, since other gardeners who have them may be prepared to part with seeds where they would hesitate to provide cuttings.

Stem cuttings

Next to the seeds, however, cuttings do provide the most likely method of securing scarce plants or of propagating shrubs in one's own garden. Unlike seedlings rooted cuttings are not new individuals but simply extensions in another place of the parent plants, which they resemble in every detail. It is a method of vegetative propagation and it can be carried out with various parts of the plant, stems, leaves or even, in some cases, roots, but stem cuttings are the most commonly used kind.

Cuttings can be taken at any time of the year but the most favourable period for most shrubs is in summer, usually some time in July or August, when the young stems have ceased to grow rapidly and are becoming firm but have not yet got really hard, as they will do by the autumn. Cuttings taken at this time are said to be 'half-ripe' in contrast to 'soft' cuttings taken in spring or 'hard' or 'ripe' cuttings taken in autumn.

Half-ripe cuttings may be anything from a couple of centimetres to 10cm./4in. in length according to the nature of the growth, and may be either side-shoots, pulled off with a tiny strip of older stem attached, in which case they are said to be 'heel' cuttings, or be cut off cleanly just below a joint, that is, the point where a leaf is (or was) attached to the stem, when they are called 'nodal' cuttings. It is worth trying some of each since sometimes one type proves more successful than another. It is also worth while to take cuttings from various parts of the plant and at several

different times as there may be marked differences in the readiness with which they will form roots.

Nearly all half-ripe cuttings must be kept in moist air to prevent their drying out and dying before they have time to form roots. Professional propagators often use an automatic misting system which sprays the cuttings periodically before they have a chance to get dry, and small mist-propagating units are available for amateur use. They need to be installed inside a greenhouse and they work most efficiently when combined with soil-warming, set to keep the cutting bed at a constant 18–20°C./65–68°F. The bed itself must be very porous. Some propagators use sharp sand, some a mixture of sand, vermiculite or perlite with sphagnum peat. It is wise to experiment with a few such mixtures and see which suits one's own conditions best.

However, there are other simpler ways of rooting cuttings. The best is probably to invest in a small propagator complete with its own soil-warming equipment and thermostat. These propagators are easy and economical to run and the cuttings can be inserted in compost-filled pots or pans which makes handling easy, since each batch can have a receptacle to itself. Cheaper propagators, without soil-warming, are also available and are adequate for the easier cuttings but may not be able to cope with more difficult kinds.

The simplest way of all is to insert the cuttings in pots or pans and then slip each into its own polythene bag, sealing this with a twist closure. Polythene film has the peculiar quality of being able to let a little air pass through its pores but no moisture, so cuttings inside the bag remain healthy for a considerable time but do not flag. For the home gardener who merely wants to root a few cuttings collected from a gardening friend or during excursions this can be the perfect solution.

Before cuttings are inserted, the bottom leaves should be removed, the cutting dipped in water and then the bottom of the cutting dipped in hormone rooting powder containing a fungicide. Opinions differ about the effectiveness of hormones in promoting root formation but no one disagrees that a fungicide is useful in checking disease. Cuttings should be pushed into the compost just sufficiently far to keep them erect. They should be well watered in from a watering can fitted with a fine rose and should then go immediately into their bags or propagator.

Some may start to form roots in a week, others may take months, and a proportion will die whatever one does. Differences in behaviour depend on the species, the type and ripeness of the cuttings taken and many other factors which interact in ways that are often too complex to analyse. But cuttings cost little, it is fun trying to root them, and one is learning all the time.

Cuttings will indicate when they are rooted by starting to grow again. That is the signal to remove them from mist, frame or polythene bag and start the process of weaning them, which can be the most difficult part of the whole operation. They must not be left for more than a few days in the compost in which they were rooted or they will starve, and yet they are still quite fragile, with roots that are probably brittle and growth that has become accustomed to being coddled. So they must be handled with great care, transferred singly to small pots in good peat or soil-based potting compost and kept moist, sheltered and shaded from direct sunshine for a few days while they are getting acclimatized. Only little by little can they become accustomed to outdoor conditions, and it will help a lot if a frame is available in which they can spend the last three or four weeks before they are finally planted in a nursery bed outdoors.

Cuttings taken in autumn and prepared from fully ripe stems of that year's growth are usually much longer than half-ripe cuttings, anything up to 25cm./10in. They are prepared in the same way but are rooted outdoors or in an unheated frame, inserted 8–10cm./3–4in. deep in soil with which peat and gritty sand has been mixed. Such cuttings do not usually start to root until the following spring and are unlikely to be ready for lifting until the autumn.

Leaf cuttings

Leaf cuttings work well with some shrubs, most notably camellias. Summer is the most favourable time to take them and they are prepared from healthy fully-developed leaves that are severed from the parent plant with leaf stalk and a small slip of stem complete with the growth bud contained in the angle between stem and leaf stalk. It is this bud that will eventually grow and provide the top growth of the new plant.

In other respects leaf cuttings are treated just like stem cuttings. They are dipped in rooting and fungicidal powder and are lightly pushed into a porous compost usually half and half peat and sand for camellias, and are rooted under mist, in a propagator or inside a polythene bag.

Root cuttings

The shrubs most likely to grow well from root cuttings are those that sucker freely, such as some of the *Aralia* and *Rhus* species. Unlike stem cuttings, root cuttings are usually taken when plants are fairly dormant, in late winter or early spring. It is the fairly fleshy roots that give the best results and these, cut up into lengths of 6–8cm./2½–3in. are laid on their sides in pots, pans or seed-boxes partly filled with peat and sand, with another centimetre or so of the same mixture to cover them. They are usually kept in a frame or greenhouse with at least frost protection until they are growing freely, and they must not be allowed to become dry at any time.

Layering

Layering provides an easy and safe means of increasing many shrubs at home, and might be described as a foolproof way of taking cuttings. For what one does when layering is to select a stem and, at a point where it can be buried in soil, wound it so that it has to form a healing callous, just as a cutting has to form a callous at its base before it can produce roots, but to do all this without actually severing the stem from the parent. So it continues to draw sustenance from the parent indefinitely and can be left for a year, even two years to form roots of its own if it is reluctant to do so. Stems can be layered at any time but from April to August is usually best.

The most suitable shrubs for layering are those with flexible stems that can easily be bent down to soil level. Some shrubs do it for themselves. Old rhododendrons and magnolias with branches bent so low that they lie on the ground, in time root into the soil and commence to form a thicket where originally there was only one plant. *Viburnum farreri*, more familiar to most gardeners as *V. fragrans*, does this very readily and so do all the brambles, with the peculiarity that it is the tips of their long stems that usually root best in July or August.

When layers have to be prepared artificially, there are several possible ways of wounding to hasten the process of rooting. One is to make a slit in the underside of the stem where it touches the soil, preferably through a joint because it is here that there is most likely to be an adequate concentration of the natural hormone which enables the stem to form roots. Another method is to draw a knife blade right round the stem immediately below a joint so that the bark is cut and the sap flow interrupted. A third is to give the stem a sharp twist so that it is ruptured but not torn off. Whatever the method of preparation, the layer must be held firmly to the soil with a heavy stone or a peg of some kind, and it is wise at the same time to tie the stem, beyond the layered portion, to a stake so that it cannot be blown about. It will need at least six months to form roots, maybe twice as long, and again like a cutting it will signal the fact that it has rooted by starting to grow strongly again. That is the time to sever it from the parent plant, after which it is wise to wait for the most favourable season before lifting and replanting it elsewhere.

If it is impossible to find any stem that can be bent to soil level it is still possible to layer by wounding a suitable stem, dusting it with rooting powder, and packing wet sphagnum moss or sphagnum peat around it, enclosing this within a sleeve of polythene film. This is then tied tightly at both ends so that the sleeve becomes a closed bag, and the whole operation then proceeds much like rooting cuttings inside a polythene bag. When roots can be seen curling round inside the sleeve, this can be carefully removed and the layered stem cut off and potted to grow on into a sturdy new plant. This method is known as air layering.

Suckers and division

A few shrubs sucker so freely or spread so readily by offsets that the simplest method of increasing them is by division. It may not even be necessary to lift and split up the whole plant, as one would with a herbaceous perennial. Armed with a strong sharp spade one can simply chop through some of the outlying suckers or offsets and lift them with as much root as possible. The best time to do this with deciduous shrubs is usually November or February, or at any rate while they have few leaves. For evergreens it is usually better to do the work in April or October.

8 About names and terms

This is a book for gardeners and so I have studiously avoided technical terms wherever possible. I hope that botanically erudite readers will not wince too much when they find racemes described as spikes; umbels, cymes and corymbs lumped together as clusters, and panicles reduced to the simplicity of sprays or plumes. That is the way they appear to most people and though it would be possible to have a glossary explaining these and many other terms, it is irritating to be reminded constantly of one's ignorance by having to refer to a dictionary for an explanation of what one is reading.

There is, unfortunately, no way of side-stepping botanical names in a similar way for, though popular names work quite well for many trees they fall down badly when it comes to shrubs, many of which have either never acquired any such names or do not have names that link allied kinds together in any logical way. The binomial system used by botanists does this admirably and, as it is almost universally used for shrubs in nurseries, it is clearly the method that must be used in every reference book on shrubs.

The difficulty is that botanists themselves are constantly changing names as they discover more about the relationships of plants and they do not always agree among themselves what those relationships are and therefore what the correct names should be. A flexible system, infinitely adaptable to new botanical insights, is ideal for botanists but confusing for gardeners, who need names that are stable not constantly in flux. One day some horticultural authority will have the courage to suggest a system of conserving names for garden use but that happy innovation seems a long way off yet.

So every popular writer is left with the problem which of the many names available to use. Should he go for those most commonly used in gardens, or for those which seem most acceptable to a majority of botanists at the time of writing, or should he try to make up his own mind which names are most 'correct'. For my part I am convinced that the last option is the worst and that there is not much to choose between the other two since both involve a good deal of guesswork.

What I have done in this book is to follow almost completely the names used in the four volumes comprising the eighth edition of W. J. Bean's great work *Trees and Shrubs Hardy in the British Isles*, since this has been extensively revised under the supervision of Mr Desmond Clarke, and with the general blessing and co-operation of those in authority at The Royal Botanic Gardens, Kew and The Royal Horticultural Society's garden at Wisley. I have no doubt that some of the names are already out of date since the first volume, A to C, was published ten years ago and a lot happens botanically in that length of time. But at least it gave me, and now gives my readers, a firm point of reference and throughout this book I have also attempted to give all those other names that are likely to be encountered in gardens, nurseries and books.

For the names of families I have not followed Mr Bean but Mr J.C. Willis in *A Dictionary of Flowering Plants and Ferns*, revised by H.K. Airy Shaw of the Royal Botanic Gardens, Kew, simply because this is the authority I have used in all my books for the last fourteen years and so it seemed consistent to go on doing so.

Abbreviations

Foliage
E   evergreen
D   deciduous
ED   semi-evergreen

Hardiness
W   needs a warm or sheltered place

Pruning
T   thin out old stems and remove dead wood in winter or spring
O   thin out old stems and shorten younger ones after flowering
F   remove or shorten flowering stems when the flowers fade
K   clip or shorten stems in spring or summer
C   cut back all growth in late winter or spring
P   shorten side stems to 10–15cm./4–6in. in summer, and again to 4–5cm./2in. in autumn or winter.

Propagation
S   seed
H   cuttings of half-ripe growth in summer
A   cuttings of fully-ripe growth in autumn
R   root cuttings
L   layers
V   division or removal of offsets or suckers with roots
G   grafting or budding

9 Alphabetical list of shrubs

ABELIA, Caprifoliaceae. Rather dense twiggy bushes with slender stems, neat undivided leaves and small but abundant tubular or funnel-shaped flowers. None are very hardy but those listed will withstand some frost. Abelias are not fussy about soil but do not like to be waterlogged. They flower most freely in sunny places and though for the most part unspectacular they have a quiet beauty which appeals to many gardeners. Pruning is not essential but old or damaged stems can be removed in spring. Summer cuttings root easily in a propagator.

chinensis *1.0 × 1.5m. (3 × 5ft) White Summer Autumn D W T H S*

China. This attractive shrub is uncommon in gardens and it is none too hardy. It can be trained against a sunny wall. The tubular flowers are scented and are surrounded by pink sepals which remain after the flowers have fallen.

floribunda *2 × 3m. (6 × 10ft) Rose E. Summer E W F H S*

Mexico. The handsomest species, with clusters of pendulous bright rose flowers and small shining evergreen leaves. It grows at considerable altitudes in the wild and so is not as tender as its Mexican origin might suggest, but except in mild districts it is best trained against a sunny wall.

x grandiflora *1 × 2m. (3 × 6ft) White, Pink Summer Autumn E W T*

A hybrid between A. *chinensis* and A. *uniflora* with good shining green foliage but the flowers, widely flared at the mouth and often slightly flushed with pink, are not as large as the name might suggest. The bronze-red calyx segments persist long after the flowers have fallen. It needs the same conditions as A. *floribunda*.

Abelia x *grandiflora*

schumannii *2 × 2.5m. (6 × 8ft) Pink Summer   Autumn   D W T H S*

Central China. Next to A. *floribunda* this is the most beautiful species, with a very long flowering season. The individual flowers are larger than most, almost bell-like and very freely produced. It needs a warm position but even when cut by frost is likely to shoot up from the base.

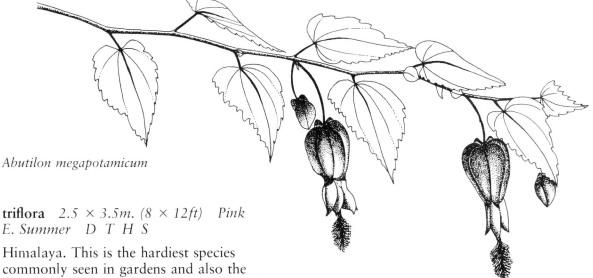

Abutilon megapotamicum

triflora   *2.5 × 3.5m. (8 × 12ft)   Pink*
E. Summer   D T H S

Himalaya. This is the hardiest species
commonly seen in gardens and also the
largest, almost tree-like in some gardens, but
it is not as showy as some and has a rather
short flowering season though the small
purplish calyx segments remain for a long
time.

ABUTILON, Malvaceae. Nearly all species
are rather tender but most are so beautiful,
flower for such a long period and are so easily
renewed by cuttings or seeds that they are
well worth planting in sheltered places and
against sunny walls. The flowers are widely
funnel-shaped in some kinds, typical of the
mallow family to which they belong, but in
others are bell-shaped or formed like little
hanging lanterns. They thrive in all
reasonably fertile, well-drained soils. Dead
branches should always be cut out in early
spring. Increase is by summer cuttings in a
propagator or species by seed in spring.

megapotamicum   *1 × 2m. (3 × 6ft)*
Yellow and red   Summer   E W T H S

Brazil. This distinctive shrub makes slender
stems which spread and sprawl unless tied to
some support. They are ideal for training
against a warm wall. The flowers are
pendulous and waisted, consisting of an
inflated red calyx from which the yellow
petals protrude like a little skirt.

ochsenii   *4 × 6m. (13 × 20ft)   Blue*
Summer   E W T H S

Chile. A species closely resembling A.
vitifolium but with deeper blue flowers. It
also appears to be a little hardier.

x suntense   *4 × 6m. (13 × 20ft)   Violet*
Summer   E W T H

A magnificent hybrid between A. *vitifolium*
and A. *ochsenii*, probably hardier than either,
making a large, well-branched shrub with soft
downy vine-shaped leaves and abundant
funnel-shaped flowers that are normally a fine
blue-violet. There is also a white-flowered
variety. Seedlings are likely to vary in
character.

vitifolium   *3 × 7m. (10 × 24ft)*
Mauve, White   Summer   E W T H S

Chile. The most popular species and a very
beautiful plant, tall to the point of being
rather gaunt but with attractive vine-shaped
leaves, soft green and downy, and with
funnel-shaped flowers which may be mauve,
pale violet or white produced for many
weeks. Despite its size stems tend to be rather
soft and plants are seldom long lived but are
easily increased from seed or summer cuttings

Abutilon vitifolium

ACACIA, Leguminosae. Wattle. Kangaroo Thorn. Mimosa. Evergreen shrubs and trees with small or feathery (pinnate) leaves and tiny flowers clustered in little balls or trails. The so-called mimosa, so popular as a cut flower, is typical of the genus, but is a tree and so is not included here. All acacias are to some degree tender but a few can be grown outdoors in sunny places and where temperatures do not fall more than a few degrees below freezing. They are attractive in foliage as well as in flower. All prefer soils that are moderately acid or neutral and are well drained. Most will even thrive where the soil is quite poor and sandy, and grow well by the sea. Old stems can be removed in spring. Plants can be grown from summer cuttings in a propagator or seed in spring.

baileyana *4 × 6m. (13 × 20ft)   Yellow E. Spring   E W T H S*

Australia. This is one of the most beautiful species, with ferny doubly-divided, blue-grey leaves and yellow flowers crowded in fluffy-looking pompom clusters. Unhappily it is distinctly tender and best trained against a sunny wall except in very mild climates.

longifolia *4 × 9m. (13 × 30ft) Yellow   Spring   E W T H S*

Australia. The leaves of this species, popularly known as the Golden Wattle, are replaced by phyllodes, really leaf stalks flattened to perform the function of leaves. The flowers are packed into little cylindrical spikes and are very pretty but the plant is distinctly tender.

pravissima *4 × 6m. (13 × 20ft)   Yellow Spring   E W T H S*

Australia. Very distinctive in appearance with angular phyllodes set closely on ribbed stems which are themselves widely and angularly branched. The bright yellow flowers are packed into short, multiple spikes. This species is hardier than many and because of its loose habit is ideal for training against a wall.

riceana *6 × 9m. (20 × 30ft)   Yellow Spring   E W T H S*

Tasmania. Though really a small tree, where there is little or no frost this elegant plant with narrow leaves, rather like those of some heathers, is usually seen as a wall-trained plant for which purpose its slender stems make it very suitable. The tiny flowers are crowded into thin spikes or trails and are freely produced.

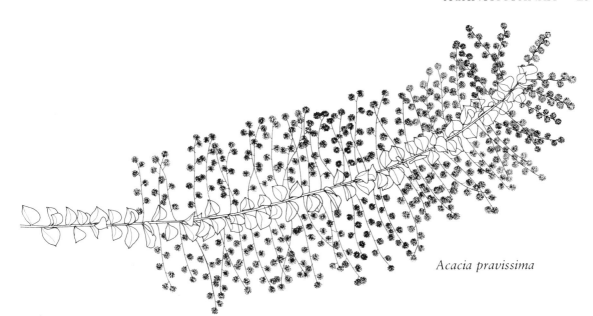

Acacia pravissima

verticillata *4 × 9m. (13 × 30ft)* *Yellow Spring E W T H S*

Australia and Tasmania. Known as the Prickly Mimosa because its very narrow phyllodes are sharp-pointed. They are arranged in whorls around the slender, much branched stems and the flowers are packed into little fluffy-looking spikes.

ACANTHOPANAX, Araliaceae. Large shrubs and small trees grown mainly for their large leaves, which are either deeply lobed or composed of several radiating leaflets. All those commonly cultivated are deciduous. The flowers, in clusters, are not attractive but they are followed by conspicuous ball-shaped clusters of black fruits similar to those of ivy. They like sunny sheltered places and fertile well drained soil. Increase is by seed or root cuttings. Little pruning is required.

lasiogyne *4 × 6m. (13 × 20ft)* *White Summer D T R S*

China. A graceful shrub with arching greyish stems and long-stalked leaves each composed of three shining light green leaflets.

leucorrhizus *2 × 3m. (6 × 10ft)* *Green Summer D T R S*

China. This is a smaller shrub than the foregoing, with yellowish stems and shorter stalked leaves composed of usually longer and narrower segments three or five in number. It is handsome in foliage and usually carries good crops of conspicuous black fruits.

sessiliflorus *3 × 4m. (10 × 13ft)* *Brown Summer D T R S*

China, Korea, Manchuria. A hardy species making a wide bush with grey stems and leaves composed of three or five leaflets. The fruits are jet black, carried in small spherical clusters. Its wild distribution guarantees its hardiness.

sieboldianus *2.5 × 3m. (8 × 10ft)* *Pale green Summer D T H A S*

China, Japan. This species has been called *Acanthopana x spinosus* because the leaf stalks often carry spines. The branches are slender and arching, rather widely spaced, the leaflets often five per leaf and bordered with cream in an attractive variety named 'Variegata'. This variegated form cannot be increased by root cuttings or by seed and is propagated by half-ripe cuttings in summer or fully ripe cuttings in autumn.

ACER, Aceraceae. Maple. All the species are trees in their native habitats but in gardens two species have produced varieties that are very slow growing, some never exceeding the dimensions of a fairly large bush. These are foliage plants of quite exceptional beauty, graceful in habit with the typical lobed leaves of the maples though in some varieties subdivided into numerous narrow segments. Some varieties have coloured leaves and even the green-leaved kinds colour brilliantly before the leaves fall in autumn. All are fairly winter hardy but are susceptible to damage by spring frosts so should not be planted in frost pockets. They like fairly fertile, well-drained but not dry soils. No pruning is required but if they grow too large it is best to remove whole branches in autumn rather than to shorten

Acer palmatum

branches and so spoil the natural habit, which varies according to variety. Seed germinates readily but seedlings of garden varieties are likely to vary considerably from their parents so are usually increased by grafting on to seedlings, sometimes of unsuitable over-vigorous kinds. It is possible, though not easy, to root cuttings in early summer or layers in spring and these, when available, are to be preferred to grafted plants.

japonicum *4 × 9m. (13 × 30ft)   Purple Spring   D T G A L S*

Japan. The species is a small tree outside the scope of this book but two varieties are so slow-growing that, for practical purposes, they can be regarded as shrubs. Aconitifolium has leaves doubly lobed and toothed and in autumn they turn crimson. Aureum has yellow leaves with up to eleven shallow lobes.

palmatum *2 × 6m. (6 × 20ft)   Purple Spring   D T G A L S*

Japan, China, Korea. This is the species commonly called Japanese Maple. In the wild it has leaves with five to seven deeply cut lobes and in gardens it has produced the most intricately cut leaves. The following are the most popular:

'**Atropurpureum**'. Leaves normally lobed, red-purple.
'**Aureum**'. Leaves normally lobed, light yellow becoming deeper yellow in autumn.
'**Dissectum**'. Leaves with up to eleven narrow lobes cut to the leaf stalk. Makes a rounded bush eventually about 2m./6 ft high.
'**Dissectum atropurpureum**'. Like the last but leaves purplish red.
'**Heptalobum**'. Leaves large, usually seven-lobed, finely toothed, green becoming crimson in autumn.
'**Heptalobum elegans**'. Like the last but leaves more deeply toothed.
'**Heptalobum lutescens**'. Like 'Heptalobum' but leaves turning yellow in autumn.
'**Heptalobum osakazuki**'. Like 'Heptalobum'

but leaves becoming scarlet in autumn.
'Heptalobum rubrum'. Like 'Heptalobum'
but leaves deep red when young, becoming
greener with age.
'Roseo-marginatum'. Leaves bright green
edged with pink.
'Senkaki'. Known as the Coral Bark Maple
because the bark of stems during their first
year is coral red. Leaves are light green
becoming yellow in autumn. Habit is erect.

ACTINIDIA, Actinidiaceae. Deciduous
twiners grown for their ornamental leaves.
They differ so greatly one from another that
without botanical knowledge it is unlikely
that they would be recognized as belonging to
the same genus. These differences apply not
only to appearance but also to cultivation.

chinensis   *9m. (30ft)   Buff   Summer*
D P T L S

China, Japan. A very rampant climber with
twining stems densely covered with red hairs
and large heart-shaped or almost round
leaves. The fruits are edible and are
sometimes imported and sold as Chinese
Gooseberries. Fruits are produced only on
plants bearing female flowers where there is a
male-flowered plant near. There is a variety
named Aureovariegata with leaves splashed
with cream. This is an excellent climber to
cover rapidly any unsightly object such as a
shed or tree stump or it can be sent up into a
tree that is of no particular value. The effect at
a short distance is not unlike that of *Vitis
coignetiae*. It will grow in any reasonably
fertile soil in sun or semi-shade.

kolomikta   *3 × 6m. (10 × 20ft)*
White   E. Summer   D P T L S

China, Manchuria. A slender twiner far less
vigorous than *A. chinensis* and with oblong
leaves remarkable for the fact that when
grown in a warm sunny place they are heavily
splashed with pink and cream particularly
when young. It will grow in all reasonably
fertile soil but to ensure maximum leaf

variegation is best grown against a sunny
wall. It requires trellis, wires or other
supports and a few ties to help it on its way.
There are male and female flowered plants
and some male forms appear to produce the
best variegation. Because of its variability this
is really a plant that should be selected in
summer when in leaf.

AESCULUS, Hippocastanaceae. Horse
Chestnut, Buckeye. With few exceptions these
are trees of great size and beauty. However,
there are a few species of shorter, more
branching habit which make large,
multi-branched shrubs with the typical horse
chestnut leaves consisting of several
finger-like leaflets, and erect, candelabra-like
clusters of flowers. They are easily grown in
any reasonably fertile soil but need plenty of
room and are emphatically not shrubs for
small gardens.

parviflora   *3 × 4m. (10 × 13ft)   White*
L. Summer   D T V S

South-east USA. W.J. Bean waxed eloquent
about this handsome plant saying that it was
of neat yet graceful habit, flowered at a time
when few shrubs were in flower and
concluding that no better plant could be
recommended as a lawn shrub. What he failed
to mention was that it spreads by suckers so
that a single plant can in time develop into a
considerable plantation. The only way to stop
this is to dig the suckers out in winter, and if
they are lifted with roots they can be planted
elsewhere or given away to friends.

pavia   *3 × 4m. (10 × 13ft)   Red*
E. Summer   D T G S

Southern USA. This is the red buckeye, a
handsome but scarce species which does not
sucker like *A. parviflora* and therefore is not a
potential hazard. However, it is not
completely hardy, its young shoots being
particularly liable to be cut by spring frosts,
so it should be planted in warm sunny
sheltered places that are not frost pockets.

AKEBIA, Lardizabalaceae. Vigorous twining plants with slender stems, attractive compound leaves composed of several small rounded leaflets, and both male and female flowers produced in the same clusters. The males are inconspicuous, the females remarkable for three coloured sepals. They can be followed by large, sausage-shaped fruits but it seems that cross-pollination is necessary with another akebia not of the same clone. All like good fertile soil and sunny places. Rather careful training is necessary to prevent a tangle of growth. They can be spread out on wires against a wall, trained over a screen or allowed to cover tripods, arbours, etc. Increase is by layering in spring or seed sown in a greenhouse in spring.

quinata *6 × 9m. (20 × 30ft)   Maroon Spring   ED T L S*

Island of Chusan. The leaves usually have five leaflets, the flowers are sweetly scented and the fruits are grey or greyish purple. The leaves are retained in winter unless it becomes very cold, when they fall.

trifoliata *6 × 9m. (20 × 30ft)   Purple Spring   D T L S*

China, Japan. Differs from *A. quinata* in having only three leaflets per leaf and pale purple fruits. It is often known as *A. lobata*.

ALBIZIA, Leguminosae. Silk Tree. The only kind cultivated outdoors in Britain is a tree in its native habitat but in our climate remains of shrub-like proportions and is usually trained against a sunny wall. It is grown for its highly ornamental foliage and is not difficult in a warm, sheltered place and well-drained soil. If one-year-old branches are shortened quite severely in spring plants can be restricted in size and kept better furnished with foliage near the ground as well as at the top. *Albizia* can be raised from seed sown in a warm greenhouse in spring or by root cuttings in winter or spring.

julibrissin *4 × 5m. (13 × 16ft)   Pink Summer   D C R S*

Near East. The leaves are a little like those of *Acacia dealbata*, compound, up to 45cm./18in. long, doubly-divided into a large number of small leaflets, the whole effect being very elegant. The flowers are mainly composed of pink stamens giving a fluffy effect, again reminiscent of acacias.

AMELANCHIER, Rosaceae. Serviceberry. Snowy Mespilus. A genus containing both small trees and large shrubs, the former making clean main stems with a head of branches, the latter suckering freely so that in time they can make a thicket of stems. The small white flowers are produced abundantly in little unbranched sprays in spring, making a fine display for a few days, and the leaves colour well before they fall in autumn. All kinds thrive in reasonably fertile soils and do not mind chalk or lime. Suckers can be dug out in autumn or winter if they spread too far, and provide a simple means of increase.

canadensis *3 × 4m. (10 × 13ft)   White Spring   D T V S*

North America. There is considerable confusion in the naming of amelanchiers and the plants cultivated as *A. canadensis* are often *A. laevis*. It does not matter greatly since the differences are not great from a garden standpoint. The slender flower sprays of *A. canadensis* are fairly compact and held erect and the branches are also slender but upright. This is the best amelanchier for damp situations. It is often called *A. oblongifolia*.

laevis *4 × 5m. (13 × 16ft)   White Spring   D T L S*

Canada, Eastern U.S.A. More tree-like in habit than *A. canadensis* with looser less erect sprays of slightly scented flowers. The young leaves are purplish bronze and most attractive. They become green in summer but colour richly in autumn.

Amelanchier laevis

lamarckii   *4 × 5m. (13 × 16ft)   White Spring   D T L S*

There is considerable confusion about this name and no certain record of it in the wild. Some authorities call it *A.* x *grandiflora* and say that it is a natural hybrid between *A. arborea*, a tree-like species, and *A. laevis*. In many respects it resembles *A. laevis* but the young leaves are covered with silky down and the flowers are a little larger. Mr Harold Hillier regards it as the best amelanchier for garden planting. There is a variety named 'Rubescens' with pink-flushed flowers.

ovalis   *3 × 5m. (10 × 16ft)   White Spring   D T L S*

Central and Southern Europe. Also known as *A. vulgaris* and notable for the relatively large size of its flowers. This is the species to which the popular name Snowy Mespilus really belongs though it is often applied to the whole genus.

stolonifera   *1.5 × 2m. (5 × 6ft)   White Spring   D T V S*

Eastern North America. The shortest species commonly grown and, as its name implies, one that suckers freely and produces thickets of erect stems. A species named *A. humilis* is very similar.

ANDROMEDA, Ericaceae. Bog Rosemary. Low-growing evergreens with narrow rosemary-like leaves, white flowers like minute dangling pitchers and a hearty dislike of lime in any form. They like damp, humus-rich soils, are ideal for peat beds and can be increased by layering or by seed sown in moist peats. Very little pruning is necessary.

polifolia   *40 × 50cm. (16 × 20in)   Pink Spring   E T L S*

North Temperate and Arctic regions. This is the species commonly grown, an attractive little shrublet which grows wild in bogs and on wet heaths in some parts of the British Isles particularly the moister and cooler districts of the north and west. There are various forms of it, some of them distinguished by names such as 'Compacta', very dwarf with clear pink flowers, 'Glaucophylla', with leaves made greyish with short hairs, and 'Latifolia' or 'Major', two similar forms with broader leaves.

ARALIA, Araliaceae. Angelica Tree. Hercules Club. Handsome foliage plants, tree-like in their native habitats but in gardens often reduced to the proportions of large suckering shrubs. Stems can be shortened in spring if it is necessary to reduce the spread of plants, and dead wood should be removed as noted. Suckers provide an easy means of increasing plants that are already growing on their own roots but nurserymen usually increase the variegated kinds by grafting onto the green-leaved type, and from such plants all suckers will be green-leaved. They can only be propagated by grafting in spring.

chinensis   *3 × 9m. (10 × 30ft)   White L. Summer E. Autumn   D T V S R*

China. A species much confused with *A. elata* from which it does not differ greatly. From a garden standpoint *A. elata* is the better plant since it has produced good decorative forms.

elata   *3 × 9m. (10 × 30ft)   White L. Summer E. Autumn   D T V S R G*

Japan and Northern Asia. This handsome plant has very large compound leaves often a full metre, 3 ft. in length, doubly divided into broadly lance-shaped, toothed leaves which are variegated in some varieties. Stems are stout but pithy, often angularly branched and sometimes wickedly spiny. The small yellowish green flowers are produced in globular clusters themselves arranged in large-branched sprays and may be followed by heavy crops of distinctive black berries. The two most ornamental varieties are 'Aureovariegata', with leaves splashed and edged with yellow, and 'Variegata', with similar marking in cream. There are no more striking deciduous foliage plants than these.

ARBUTUS, Ericaceae. Strawberry Tree. Evergreen trees and shrubs of which only one species *A. unedo* really qualifies in size for inclusion in this book. It is unusual among ericaceous plants for thriving on chalk or limestone soils. Like other species it grows well by the sea. Though regular pruning is not essential stems can be shortened in spring and plants will make new growth even if cut back severely. Seed provides the best means of increase but stems can be layered in spring,

and late summer cuttings will root in a propagator.

unedo   *4 × 9m (13 × 30ft)   White Autumn   E T S H L*

Europe including Ireland. This handsome evergreen has large, lustrous green saw-edged leaves and nodding clusters of small, pitcher-shaped flowers, white sometimes flushed with pink. This pink colouring is most marked in variety 'Rubra' and fully red-flowered forms have been recorded. The flowers are followed by strawberry-like fruits which take a year to mature, so that ripe fruits and flowers appear on the plant at the same time.

ARISTOLOCHIA, Aristolochiaceae. Dutchman's Pipe. Vigorous twiners with curious flowers shaped like a Dutchman's pipe. Most are tender but a few can be grown outdoors in Britain. They like good fertile soil, will grow in full sun or partial shade and can be used to cover old tree stumps, or be trained on walls, fences, arbours or screens. Pruning is not essential and can be difficult because of the entangled growth but dead growth should be removed in spring if possible. At the same time stems can be shortened or some of the oldest removed. Increase is by seeds under glass in spring, summer cuttings in a propagator, layering in spring or division in autumn.

heterophylla   *5 × 6m. (16 × 20ft)   Yellow E. Summer   D T L H V*

China. Less rampant in growth than some with small flowers, yellow in the throat but deep purple at the mouth.

macrophylla   *6 × 9m. (20 × 30ft) Yellow and brown   E. Summer D T L H V*

Eastern USA. This is the kind most frequently grown in Britain. It is a vigorous twiner with large heart-shaped leaves and small curled tubular flowers, yellowish green except at the mouth which spreads out in three brownish purple lobes. They are odd rather than beautiful and it is as a foliage plant that this aristolochia is chiefly valued. It is also known as *A. durior* and *A. sipho.*

moupinense   *4 × 5m. (13 × 16ft)*
Green and yellow   E. Summer
D T L H V

Western China. The leaves are smaller and narrower than those of *A. macrophylla*, the flowers are pale green and yellow with red spots on the mouth lobes.

ARONIA, Rosaceae. Chokeberry. Though these deciduous shrubs have hawthorn-like flowers followed by red or black berries neither are in the first class for beauty and it is for autumn foliage colour that aronias have the greatest appeal. They are easy to grow except on very alkaline soils. As they sucker freely, old stems can be cut out to the base in winter, and suckers dug up with roots can be planted elsewhere if desired.

arbutifolia   *2 × 3m (6 × 10ft)*
White or Pink   L. Spring   D T V A S

Eastern North America. This is the red chokeberry with clusters of white or pink-tinted flowers followed by small red berry-like fruits. The leaves can turn rich red before they fall but some forms are better than others. It is a good idea to select plants in autumn.

melanocarpa   *1 × 1.5m. (3 × 5ft)   White*
L. Spring   D T V A S

Eastern North America. Known as the Black Chokeberry because its clusters of small fruits are normally black or very deep purple, but there are forms with redder fruits not unlike those of *A. arbutifolia*, with which it is sometimes confused. It differs in having glossy instead of matt-surfaced leaves and is usually shorter in growth. Like *A. arbutifolia* some forms have better autumn leaf colour than others.

ASTER, Compositae. One shrubby member of the michaelmas daisy family has long been cultivated in gardens under the generic name microglossa now changed to aster. It is only semi-woody and its rather soft stems are often severely damaged in British winters except in the mildest places. Otherwise it is easy to grow in any reasonably fertile and well-drained soil. Damaged stems should be cut out in spring but all the previous year's growth that is in good condition should be preserved since this will produce the best flowers. Increase is by seed or summer cuttings in a propagator.

albescens   *1m. (3ft)   Blue   Summer*
D W T S H

Himalaya. Quite an attractive small shrub with grey down on stems and undersides of leaves and flattish clusters of flowers similar to those of the common michaelmas daisy.

ATRIPLEX, Chenopodiaceae. Sage Bush. Tree Purslane. Grey-leaved shrubs of rather straggly habit which have the merit of thriving in very light sandy soils close to the sea even if this means that they are exposed to

Atriplex halimus

salt spray. They are therefore useful as outer windbreaks for maritime gardens. Annual clipping or shortening of stems in spring improves their habit and increases their leaf density. Increase is by early autumn cuttings in a frame.

canescens   *1.5 × 2m. (5 × 6ft)   Yellowish Summer   E K A*

Western North America. The grey sage bush has narrow silver grey leaves and will grow in saline soils. The yellowish flowers are too small to attract attention.

halimus   *1.5 × 2.5m (5 × 8ft)   Green Summer   E W K A*

Southern Europe. This is the tree purslane, the best species to plant for shelter. It is just a little tender but rarely suffers frost damage by the sea. The leaves are oval or angled, wider than those of *A. canescens* and silvery grey. The flowers are seldom produced, which matters little since they have no beauty.

AUCUBA, Cornaceae. Spotted Laurel. These handsome evergreen shrubs were a sensation when they first arrived in Britain and were grossly overplanted in the nineteenth century, with the inevitable reaction against them later. Male and female flowers are produced on separate plants, only the females bear berries and then only if fertilized with pollen from a male. Aucubas thrive in all soils in sun or shade but the finest foliage is produced in fertile soil and a partially shaded place. They grow well in towns, are unaffected by atmospheric pollution and can be trimmed or hard-pruned at will. Cuttings root readily in a propagator or frame in summer or autumn.

japonica   *2 × 3m. (6 × 10ft)   Purplish Spring   E K C A H S*

Japan. The leaves are large, laurel-like, but lighter green, and the stems are stout but fairly soft, especially when young which makes them easy to prune. The berries, produced in clusters, are ovoid, quite large and shining scarlet. There are numerous

Aucuba japonica (female form)

variegated forms. Those with yellow spotting have the popular name Spotted Laurel. Some have larger areas of gold. The following varieties are fairly readily available:

'Crassifolia' Green-leaved male with extra large leaves.
'Crotonifolia' Female with large leaves speckled with yellow.
'Longifolia' Narrow-leaved forms some of which have been given further distinguishing names e.g. 'Lance Leaf' and 'Angustata', both male, and 'Salicifolia', female.
'Sulphurea' Leaves with a broad but irregular margin of yellow.
'Variegata' Leaves blotched with yellow. Female.

AZARA, Flacourtiaceae. Large evergreen shrub or small tree with clusters of tiny petalless flowers with tufts of yellow stamens and neat leaves. All are a little tender and need to be planted in very sheltered places except in mild localities. They thrive in the western and southern maritime gardens of the British Isles. They will grow in all reasonably fertile and porous soils and in sun or semi-shade but flower most freely with good light. Late summer cuttings will root in a propagator.

integrifolia   *3 × 6m. (10 × 20ft)   Yellow Winter   E. Spring   E W T H*

Chile, Argentina. In very mild places this species can make a small tree but it is distinctly tender and is usually trained against a wall. Leaves are up to 5cm./2in. long and half as wide, with smaller, rounded, leaf-like stipules. Flowers in good clusters, sweetly scented.

lanceolata   *3 × 6m. (10 × 20ft)   Yellow Spring   E W T H*

Chile, Argentina. The leaves are lance-shaped and toothed, the flowers are well displayed and fragrant, but the plant is distinctly tender and yet dislikes hot dry climates. It succeeds well in fairly humid coastal gardens.

Azara serrata

microphylla   *4 × 7m. (13 × 24ft)   Yellow Winter   Spring   E W T H*

Chile, Argentina. Leaves are small, rounded and often toothed, dark green and very abundantly produced so that they conceal the tiny clusters of vanilla-scented flowers. There is a very attractive variety, 'Variegata', with heavily cream-variegated leaves but it lacks vigour and is slow-growing.

serrata   *2.5 × 3m. (8 × 10ft)   Yellow Summer   E W T H*

One of the most conspicuous of azaras in flower, the clusters of flowers quite large and held well above the oval shining light green leaves. They are sweetly scented. It is much confused with *A. dentata*, which is both less hardy and less attractive.

BERBERIDOPSIS, Flacourtiaceae. Coral Plant. A genus of which only one species is known, an uncommon evergreen climber of great beauty. Its requirements are lime-free soil sufficiently porous not to become waterlogged in winter yet with sufficient humus not to dry out badly in summer, a shady place but freedom from severe frost at all times. Little or no pruning is required except for removal of old or weak stems in spring. Stems should be given an occasional tie to help them twine up vertical supports. Summer cuttings will root in a propagator and it can also be grown from layers or seeds.

corallina *4 × 6m. (13 × 20ft)   Crimson L. Summer   E   W   T   H   L   S*

Chile. A vigorous twiner that has been called the Strangle Bush, so dense can its growth become in favourable places. The dark green leaves are spiny-toothed, the flowers globose and long-stalked, hanging in clusters like very crimson currants. It is not fully hardy but trained against a north or west-facing wall it will survive a fair amount of frost.

BERBERIS. Berberidaceae. Barberry. This immense genus contains about 450 species spread widely over North and South America, Europe, North Africa and Asia. There are also innumerable garden hybrids. At one time the shrubs now know as mahonias were included with berberis, making the genus even larger. It is also very variable in character, containing evergreen and deciduous kinds, some grown primarily for their flowers, some for their leaves and some for their berries. All have yellow wood which often oozes orange-yellow sap when cut, small yellow cup-shaped flowers in clusters and with stamens which spring up when touched, so daubing visiting insects with their pollen. All are spiny, some kinds wickedly so and this, combined with their dense growth, makes them excellent for use as protective hedges. They are not fussy about soil, will grow in sun or semi-shade though they flower and fruit most freely where the light is good.

Pruning is seldom essential and usually difficult but berberis hedges can be trimmed in May–June or immediately after flowering if they are in flower then. Seed sown as soon as ripe and exposed to winter cold usually germinates well the following spring but seedlings may vary from their parents, so hybrids and selected garden varieties are increased by summer or early autumn cuttings in a propagator or frame, by layering at almost any time or by digging up the rooted suckers which appear around some kinds.

Berberis aggregata

aggregata *1 × 1.5m. (3 × 5ft)   Yellow Summer   D   T   H   S*

Western China. Forms a dense thicket of very spiny stems with narrow leaves. The pale yellow flowers are followed by coral red berries. It hybridizes so readily with some other kinds such as *B. prattii* and *B. wilsoniae* that the true species is seldom seen in gardens and would be rather difficult to identify with certainty if it were.

buxifolia *2 × 3m. (6 × 10ft)   Amber Spring   ED   T   H   V   S*

Magellan Straits. Small rounded leaves which persist in a mild winter, a dense habit, solitary flowers followed by dark purple berries. Better, as a garden foliage plant, is a dwarf variety named 'Nana' which forms a very compact bush only about 40cm./6in. high, but this rarely produces any flowers.

candidula *1m. (3ft) Yellow L. Spring E T H S*

China. This excellent species makes a dome-shaped bush with little spiny leaves, lustrous green above, milky white below. The yellow flowers are produced singly and are followed by grape-purple berries. It never grows tall but may become quite broad.

x carminea *1 × 1.5m. (3 × 5ft) Yellow E. Summer D T H*

A group name given to hybrids between *Berberis aggregata*, *B. wilsoniae* and other species. All are sold under clonal names such as 'Barbarossa', 'Buccaneer', 'Pirate King' and 'Sparkler' and are notably free-fruiting shrubs in the style of *B.* x *rubrostilla*.

concinna *1m. (3ft) Yellow E. Summer D T H S*

Himalaya, Sikkim. A distinctive shrub short and dense in habit, with small spiny leaves, white beneath, and quite large yellow berries.

darwinii *2 × 4m. (6 × 13ft) Orange Spring E T H S*

Chile. Together with its hybrid. *B. stenophylla*, this is almost certainly the most popular berberis, a very handsome evergreen with leaves like those of a holly but greatly reduced in size, clusters of orange flowers followed by grape-purple berries. It often produces self-sown seedlings, which can be transplanted when young but are more difficult to move successfully as they develop.

empetrifolia *30 × 45cm. (12 × 18in) Yellow L. Spring E H V S*

Chile. The smallest berberis, with narrow, spine-tipped leaves, yellow flowers, carried singly or in pairs, followed by black berries. It is excellent for the front of a border or a sizeable rock garden.

gagnepainii *2 × 2.5m. (6 × 8ft) Yellow L. Spring E. Summer E T H S*

China. The leaves of this attractive species are long and narrow, spine-edged and a little waved. The yellow flowers stand out distinctly on slender stalks and are followed by black berries. For a berberis the habit is fairly open. There is a variety named 'Fernspray', with lighter green, more wavy-edged leaves.

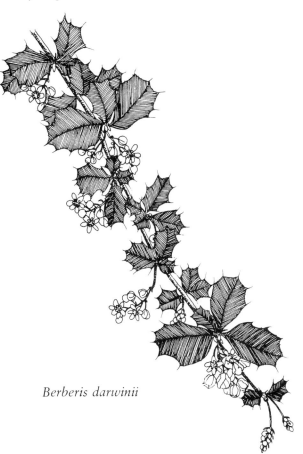

Berberis darwinii

glaucocarpa *3 × 4m. (10 × 13ft) Yellow E. Summer D T H V S*

Himalaya. This species has been confused with several others and may turn up labelled *B. aristata*. Its flowers are borne in quite stout clusters and are followed by black berries heavily powdered with white bloom. It suckers freely.

hakeoides *3 × 3.5m. (10 × 12ft)   Yellow Spring   E T L S*

Chile. The leaves are very distinctive, almost circular or kidney-shaped, and scalloped and spiny. The flowers are in clusters and are followed by bluish-black berries. Habit is loose and, as the plant is also a little tender, it is sometimes trained against a wall.

hookeri *1 × 1.5m. (3 × 5ft)   Yellow Spring   E T H S*

Himalaya. Relatively short and compact in habit with lance-shaped leaves which are sometimes white below but are green all over in variety 'Viridis'. The berries are long and almost black when ripe.

jamesiana *3 × 4m. (10 × 13ft) Yellow   Summer   D   T   H   S*

China. A tall and very handsome species, especially when the long bunches of berries are ripening from translucent green to scarlet and the foliage is colouring. It requires a lot of room.

julianae *2 × 3m. (6 × 10ft)   Yellow E. Summer   D T H S*

China. This species is similar to *B. sargentiana* for which it is often mistaken. The leaves are lance-shaped and spiny and the stems are also armed with long spines in clusters of three. The black, bloom-covered fruits can be produced in quite large clusters.

linearifolia *2 × 2.5m. (6 × 8ft) Orange-red   Spring   E T H S*

Chile. A shrub similar in many ways to *B. darwinii* but more sparse and angular in habit and with more highly-coloured flowers, which can be flushed with coppery red in some forms. The berries which follow are black, dusted with grey bloom. 'Orange King' is a selected clone.

x lologensis *2 × 2.5m. (6 × 8ft)   Orange Spring   E T H*

A hybrid between *Berberis darwinii* and *B. linearifolia*, intermediate in most of its characteristics and an excellent garden plant.

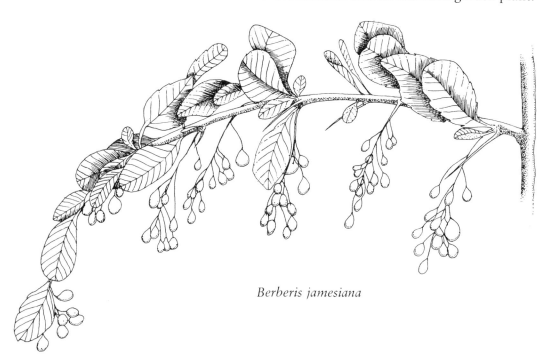

Berberis jamesiana

prattii   *2 × 3m. (6 × 10ft)   Yellow Summer   D   T   H   S*

China. A handsome late-flowering and free-fruiting barberry. The berries are pink or coral-red and hang for a long time. This fine plant is often grown as *B. polyantha*, a name which belongs to a different though allied species with more deeply-coloured berries.

pruinosa   *2.5 × 3m. (8 × 10ft)   Lemon Spring   E   T   H   S*

China. Notable for its shining light green leaves, sometimes white beneath, and lemon yellow flowers, which are followed by black fruits covered in grey bloom. From a decorative point of view it could be described as a lighter coloured *B. hookeri*.

x rubrostilla   *1 × 1.2m. (3 × 4ft)   Yellow E. Summer   D   T   H   S*

One of the most popular hybrids raised from seed of *Berberis wilsoniae* fertilized by the pollen of another species, possibly *B. aggregata*. It makes a dense thicket of spiny branches and produces heavy crops of small, translucent coral-red berries. There are numerous forms of it differing in minor details and seedlings are likely to show such variations.

sargentiana   *1.5 × 2m. (5 × 6ft)   Yellow E. Summer   E   T   H   S*

China. A handsome evergreen shrub with narrowly oval spiny leaves and stems armed with long, very sharp spines. The berries are blue-black. This is one of the hardiest evergreen barberries.

x stenophylla   *2.5 × 3.5m. (8 × 10ft) Yellow   Spring   E   T   H   V*

This fine hybrid between *Berberis darwinii* and *B. empetrifolia* is in many ways the best evergreen barberry, vigorous in growth, with arching stems well covered with narrow leaves and loaded in April and May with sweetly-scented golden yellow flowers. It forms ever-widening thickets which may need to be reduced by drastic pruning and chopping out of suckers, which can be used for propagation. It stands clipping well and can be used as a large hedge. Flowering will not be impaired if the trimming is all done in May as soon as the flowers fade. This is a variable plant and several useful forms are available, including dwarfs:

'Autumnalis'. Dwarf, and flowers a second time in autumn.
'Coccinea'. Dwarf, flower buds red opening to orange.
'Coralina Compacta'. 30cm./12in. high. Buds red but flowers yellow.
'Gracilis'. About 1m./3ft otherwise like the type.
'Gracilis Nana'. 30cm./12in. high, yellow buds and flowers.
'Irwinii'. About 1m./3ft with broader leaves and yellow flowers.
'Pink Pearl'. Some leaves variegated with pink and cream, and flowers variously pale yellow, orange, pink or multi-coloured.

temolaica   *2 × 3m. (6 × 10ft)   Yellow Summer   D   T   H   S*

Tibet. Notable for its long, arching stems, blue-grey when young but becoming purplish brown as they age. The berries are red but covered with grey bloom. In the best forms the leaves are also blue-grey but green-leaved forms exist and seedlings may be of either type, so it is wise to propagate the best forms by cuttings only.

thunbergii   *1 × 2.5m. (3 × 8ft)   Yellow Spring   D   T   H   S*

Japan. China. A densely branched and very spiny shrub inferior to many barberries in flower and fruit (the berries are small and crimson), but one of the finest for autumn leaf colour. There are also varieties with purple leaves. The following are listed:

'**Atropurpurea**'. Leaves reddish-purple but the colour can be variable.

'**Atropurpurea Nana**'. Similar to atropurpurea but only about 60cm./25in. high.

'**Bagatelle**'. Leaves red-purple, habit very dwarf and compact, forming a low dome.

'**Erecta**'. Leaves red-purple, stems erect, making a narrow column. 'Red Pillar' is similar.

'**Minor**'. Leaves green, habit dwarf and compact.

'**Rose Glow**'. Leaves purple splashed with pale pink and rose when young. 'Harlequin' is very similar.

verruculosa *1.2 × 2m. (4 × 6ft)   Yellow L. Spring   E K H S*

Western China. This fine shrub might be described as a much shorter, more compact *B. darwinii* with similar small spiny dark green leaves and deep yellow flowers followed by black berries. First class for the front or middle of a border.

vulgaris *2 × 3m. (6 × 10ft)   Yellow L. Spring   D   T   H S*

Europe, including Britain, Asia and North Africa. This native species is a very beautiful shrub, with tall arching stems laden with egg-shaped coral-red berries in autumn. It has become unpopular because it is a host for one stage of the fungus that causes the very damaging rust disease of wheat. There is a fine purple-leaved variety named 'Atropurpurea'.

wilsoniae *1 × 1.2m (3 × 4ft)   Yellow* L. Spring   D T H S

Western China. One of the best of the small, densely branched deciduous barberries, more compact in habit than most, very spiny and producing good crops of coral-red berries. The small leaves colour well before they fall. It has interbred freely with other barberries of its type. See *B.* x *carminea*.

BIGNONIA, Bignoniaceae. Cross Vine. Most of the climbers once known as bignonias are now included in other genera, particularly campsis, but one remains under the old name. It is very vigorous but not very hardy, which makes it a little difficult to place in most gardens since, if allowed to scramble up into a tree it will probably not receive sufficient warmth or shelter, yet if grown against a sunny wall it may take up too much space. One way to overcome this is to cut out a good deal of old or weak growth every summer as soon as the plant has finished flowering. Soil should be reasonably fertile and well-drained.

capreolata *12 × 15m. (40 × 50ft) Orange-red   E. Summer ED   W   T H L   S*

South-eastern USA. The leaves are unusual in being composed of two lance-shaped leaflets with a tendril from the common stalk, which enables the plant to cling to twigs, trellis, wires etc. The funnel-shaped flowers are small but brightly coloured, carried in small clusters in the leaf axils. In cold winters the leaves are likely to fall.

BILLARDIERA, Pittosporaceae. Apple Berry. Only one species appears to be cultivated in British gardens and this remains distinctly uncommon, partly because it is tender and requires a more or less frost-free site. It can be grown in west coast gardens in warm sunny places. It is a twiner which needs vertical wires or trellis for support and little pruning beyond removal of dead, damaged or weak stems in early spring. It will grow in any reasonably fertile and well drained soil.

longiflora *2m. (6ft)   Yellow   Summer E   W T S*

Tasmania. The flowers are small, greenish-yellow and bell-shaped, not very conspicuous but quite attractive in an unobtrusive way. It is the globular fruits, deep blue in the form commonly grown, which are the chief attraction. A white-fruited variety named 'Fructu-albo' is available, and it is said that purple and pink fruited varieties also occur.

BUDDLEIA, Buddlejaceae. Butterfly Bush. This is a much more varied genus of shrubs than is often realized. Some species are too tender to be reliable outdoors except in very favourable situations but others are completely hardy. Almost all grow rapidly and propagation is usually easy from cuttings, either in summer or autumn, or by seed. All like sunny places and well-drained soils, and *Buddleia davidii* thrives on chalk or limestone. It often seeds itself into crannies in walls and cliffs where there seems little roothold and yet it manages to survive.

alternifolia   *3 × 6m. (10 × 20ft)   Purple* *E. Summer   D F H A S*

China. A graceful shrub with slender, arching stems, narrow leaves placed alternately instead of in pairs opposite one another as is usual with buddleias, and small clusters of flowers set along the length of the previous year's growth, so that they appear to be wreathed in lavender purple. If flowering stems are cut out as soon as the flowers have faded the vigour of the plants will be maintained, flower production will be improved and bushes can be kept to medium size. It is possible to grow this species as a standard by training one stem of a seedling or rooted cutting up a stake, pinching out the tip at about 1.5–2m./5–6ft and removing all side-growths from the lower part of the stem so that this thickens into a bare trunk with a head of partially weeping stems on top.

auriculata   *2 × 2.5m (6 × 8ft)   Yellow* *Autumn Winter   E W T H S*

South Africa. Though not by any means the most spectacular buddleia this species is valued for its very sweet-scented cream and yellow flowers produced from September until January. In most places it needs to be trained against a sunny wall but it can be grown as a free-standing bush in some maritime gardens.

colvillei   *4 × 6m. (13 × 20ft)   Rose* *Summer   D W T H A S*

Himalaya. The purplish-rose bell-shaped flowers of this species are much larger than those of most buddleias but there are rarely enough of them to make a spectacular display. It is not very hardy and is likely to succeed best against a sunny wall.

crispa   *2 × 4m. (6 × 12ft)   Lilac* *Summer   D W C H A S*

Afghanistan, Himalaya. Rather like *Buddleia davidii* in appearance but the leaves are covered in almost white down and the flowers are always pale-coloured. It is usually trained against a sunny wall but is said to be hardy.

davidii   *3 × 4.5m. (10 × 15ft)   Purple* *L. Summer   D C H A S*

China. By far the most popular species, a very fine late-flowering shrub with small, honey-scented flowers crowded in long, conical clusters. Colour varies a great deal from pale lavender to intense violet purple with some lilac-pink and white varieties as well. Some have been selected, given distinguishing names and kept true to type by vegetative propagation. Two, named 'Harlequin' and 'Variegated Regal Red', have cream-variegated leaves. *B. davidii nanhoensis* is only 2m./6ft high. If desired all growth can be cut back to within 30–40cm./12–15in. of ground level each March or, alternatively, large plants can be formed by retaining some stems at greater length and shortening previous year's growth to within a few centimetres of these. Hard pruning improves the size but reduces the number of the flower clusters.

fallowiana   *2.5 × 3m (8 × 10ft)   Lavender*
L. Summer   D W   C   H A   S

China. Much like *Buddleia davidii* except that
the leaves are covered in white down. This
tends to disappear from the upper surface as
the leaves age but persists below. There are
white-flowered forms usually collectively
known as *B. fallowiana alba* though there
may be small differences between them. This
species is not as hardy as *B. davidii*. *Buddleia*
'Lochinch' is said to be a hybrid between *B.
davidii* and *B. fallowiana*, has grey leaves and
is reasonably hardy.

globosa   *3 × 4.5m. (10 × 15ft)   Orange*
E. Summer   ED T H A S

Chile, Peru. Very distinctive because the tiny
orange flowers are packed into globular heads
a number of which are produced in a
branched cluster. These flowers are produced
on young shoots coming from terminal buds
on the previous year's growth, so when
thinning, either after flowering or in early
spring, it is important to retain plenty of
strong young growth.

weyerana   *3 × 4.5m. (10 × 15ft)*
Yellow and purple   E. Summer
ED H A S

A hybrid between *B. globosa* and *B. davidii*
which produces ball-shaped flower clusters in
various shades of orange or yellow flushed
with purple. Some appear dull and displeasing
but the best forms are attractive and highly
distinctive.

BUPLEURUM, Umbelliferae. Buplever. Only
one kind, a semi-evergreen sub-shrub, is at all
commonly grown in British gardens. It is a
little tender but does well in mild districts
particularly near the sea on chalk or limestone
soils. It can be increased by seed or summer
cuttings.

fruticosum   *1.5 × 2.5m. (5 × 8ft)*
Yellow-green   Summer   ED W C H S

Mediterranean region. Quite a distinctive
foliage plant, with dark blue-green rather
narrow leaves and small flat-topped clusters
of yellowish-green flowers. Left to its own
devices it can become straggly but hard
pruning in early spring will restore a more
compact habit though it will mean the loss of
flower that year.

BUXUS, Buxaceae. Box. Evergreen shrubs or
sometimes small trees with small leaves and
densely branched wiry stems which make
them very suitable for clipping. All are easily
grown in most soils including those that are
markedly alkaline. Increase is usually by
cuttings, in early autumn in a propagator or
frame but the dwarf edging box is increased
by division. Clipping can be done at any time
from May to September but if hard cutting
back becomes necessary it is best done in
May. The leaves of box have a highly
distinctive, slightly fusty, aroma, particularly
marked when damp, which a few people find
objectionable.

balearica   *3 × 9m. (10 × 30ft)*
Yellow-green   Spring   E K H A

Balearic Islands, Spain. Much like *Buxus
sempervirens* but the leaves are a little larger
and not quite so shiny.

microphylla   *60 × 90cm. (2 × 3ft)*
Yellow-green   Spring   E K H A

Probably Japan. Superficially this looks like a
short and very small-leaved form of *Buxus
sempervirens* but botanists regard it as a
distinct species. It was introduced from
Japanese gardens.

sempervirens   *3 × 9m. (10 × 30ft)*
Yellow-green   Spring
E K H A V

Europe, including Britain, North Africa,
Western Asia. This is the common box, a

shrub that has produced numerous garden varieties differing in height, habit and leaf colour. The following are commonly grown:

'**Argentea**'. Leaves white-edged.
'**Aurea Pendula**'. Leaves variegated with yellow. Habit weeping.
'**Aureo Variegata**'. Leaves variegated with yellow. Also known as 'Aureo maculata'.
'**Elegantissima**'. Leaves small and edged with creamy-white.
'**Gold Tip**'. Leaves of young shoots often tipped with yellow though this is not an invariable feature.
'**Handsworthensis**'. Leaves larger than average, growth strong.
'**Longifolia**'. Leaves long in proportion to their width.
'**Myrtifolia**'. Leaves small, plant slow-growing and compact.
'**Prostrata**'. Spreading in habit but can become quite tall with age.
'**Rosmarinifolia**'. Leaves long and narrow, habit dwarf. This variety is sometimes called 'Thymifolia'.
'**Suffruticosa**'. The edging box which can be clipped to a mere 15cm./6in. or so and makes many stems from the roots so that it can be increased by division in spring or autumn.

CAESALPINIA, Leguminosae. These spectacular shrubs are nearly all too tender to be successful outdoors except in the mildest parts of Britain but *Caesalpinia japonica* will thrive trained against a sunny wall in those places where frosts are unlikely to be severe or prolonged. Previous years' stems, often very long, can be shortened to 8–10cm./3–4in. in spring if there is not room for them, and at the same time frost-damaged growth should be removed. The plant succeeds in most well-drained soils. Increase is by seed or by layering in summer or autumn.

japonica   *2.5 × 4m. (8 × 13ft)*
Yellow and red   Summer   D W C L S

Japan, China. A sprawling shrub, much wider and lower when grown as a bush than when trained against a wall. The stems are heavily armed with long thorns, the leaves are doubly divided into numerous small leaflets and the flowers are produced in large conical sprays. They are yellow with red stamens and are very showy but, unfortunately, unless the situation is really warm and sunny few, if any, may be produced.

CALLICARPA, Verbenaceae. Deciduous shrubs remarkable for their lilac or violet berries. These are most likely to be produced freely if two or more bushes are grown close together for cross-pollination and also if planted in soil that is reasonably fertile and well-drained, but not rich, nor liable to dry out severely in summer. Some of the older stems and also any that have been damaged by frost should be cut out in early spring. Summer cuttings can be rooted in a propagator.

bodinieri   *2 × 2.5m. (6 × 8ft)   Lilac*
Summer   D T H A S

China. The habit is erect and moderately branching, often with much new growth from the base, which is to be encouraged. The flowers are produced in close clusters in the axils of the leaves but it is the lilac-blue berries that follow and also the distinctive purplish-pink autumn tints of the foliage that make this a highly desirable ornamental shrub. Berry colour can vary and so it is a good idea to select plants or cuttings in autumn when the berries are ripe. One variety, named *giraldii*, is sometimes regarded as a separate species but from a garden standpoint there is little difference.

japonica   *1 × 1.5m. (3 × 4ft)   Pink*
L. Summer.   D W T H A S

Japan. This species is shorter than *C. bodinieri* and less hardy but it succeeds in warm, sunny places. The berries are violet, or white in a variety named 'Leucocarpa'. Yet another variety named 'Angustata' has narrower leaves and grows taller.

CALLISTEMON, Myrtaceae. Bottle Brush Tree. Evergreen shrubs and small trees found wild in Australia and New Zealand and mostly too tender to be grown outdoors in the British Isles, though a few species succeed near the sea and in very sheltered places. They like well-drained but not dry, moderately acid soil and a warm, sunny place. All have slender stems, narrow leaves and flowers, the most prominent feature of which are the coloured stamens. Since the flowers are crowded in cylindrical spikes this gives them a highly distinctive appearance like bottle brushes. Pruning is undesirable as it reduces flower production but if plants get too large some stems can be removed completely when the flowers fade. Summer cuttings will root in a propagator.

citrinus   *3 × 4m. (10 × 13ft)   Red Summer   E   W   T   H   S*

New South Wales, Victoria, Queensland. The species most commonly seen in maritime gardens, with long, arching stems and showy red 'bottlebrushes', which are at their finest in a variety named 'Splendens'. The leaves are lemon-scented.

rigidus   *2 × 2.5m. (6 × 8ft)   Red Summer   E   W   T   H   S*

New South Wales, Queensland. Much like C. *citrinus* but not so tall and straggly.

salignus   *2 × 2.5m (6 × 8ft)   Yellow Summer   E   W   T   H   S*

South-eastern Australia. The hardiest species but not the most beautiful since its flowers are usually a rather pale yellow. Pink, red and white forms are said to exist. In Australia it makes a small tree but is usually a medium-sized bush in Britain.

subulatus   *1 × 1.2m. (3 × 4ft)   Crimson Summer   E   W   T   H   S*

Victoria, New South Wales. Considerably smaller and more compact than C. *citrinus*

and probably hardier, at any rate if forms collected from its southern limit of distribution are obtained.

CALLUNA, Ericaceae. Heather. Ling. This is one of the major genera which provide the plants commonly known as heathers, the other being Erica. Though there are many species of erica and only one species of calluna this has produced so many good varieties that, as a hardy shrub, it is of great importance. Calluna requires an acid soil, all the better if it contains peat and is not liable to dry out in summer. Habit and flowering are best in a sunny place but plants will grow in the shade. The species and some varieties are apt to become straggly with age but this can be prevented by annual trimming in spring. Previous years' growth can be shortened quite severely but not into stems two years or more old as this hard wood is unlikely to produce new growth. Though calluna grows readily from seed, seedlings of garden varieties are unlikely to resemble their parents closely and may revert to the wild type. Garden varieties must be increased vegetatively either by layering in spring or by cuttings of firm young growth in peat and sand in a closed frame or under mist in summer.

vulgaris   *20 × 60cm. (9 × 24in.)   Purple L. Summer   Autumn   E   C   H   V*

Europe (including Britain). Common on peaty moorland and mountainsides. The leaves are very small and closely packed, the flowers are also small but numerous, arranged in slender, one-sided spikes. Habit can be straggly particularly if the soil is at all rich. However, it is not the wild species but its very numerous varieties which are valued in gardens, and these vary greatly, some quite small and compact or prostrate, some with bronze or yellow leaves, some with double flowers. The following are typical but many more will be found in the catalogues of heather specialists:

'Alba'. The white heather which is fairly common in the wild and differs from the species only in having white flowers.
'Alba Plena'. A garden variety with much larger double white flowers and a compact habit.
'Alportii'. Flowers crimson.
'Aurea'. Young leaves yellow but becoming bronze-red in winter.
'County Wicklow'. Flowers double pink. Habit short but spreading.
'C.W. Nix'. Crimson, rather tall.
'Elsie Purnell'. Double light pink, medium height.
'Foxii Nana'. Almost prostrate. Flowers purple but there are seldom many of them.
'Gold Haze'. Flowers white, foliage light yellow.
'H.E. Beale'. Flowers pink, double. Medium height.
'J.H. Hamilton'. Flowers pink, double. Semi-prostrate.
'Joan Sparkes'. Flowers pink, double. Habit of 'Alba Plena' of which it is a sport.
'Mair's Variety'. Flowers white in long spikes.
'Mullion'. Flowers light purple. Semi-prostrate.
'Peter Sparkes'. Flowers deep pink and double. Habit similar to 'H.E. Beale'.
'Robert Chapman'. Flowers light purple. Young foliage yellowish-green becoming orange-red in winter.
'Serlei'. Flowers white. Rather tall.
'Serlei Aurea'. Similar to 'Serlei' but foliage yellow.
'Sunset'. Flowers pink. Foliage yellow and orange.
'Tib'. Flowers purple, double. Rather short.

CALYCANTHUS, Calycanthaceae. Allspice. Interesting rather than beautiful deciduous shrubs, pleasantly aromatic when stems (and sometimes leaves) are bruised, and with curious, solitary flowers composed of numerous narrow petals arranged like tiny shuttlecocks. They thrive in most reasonably fertile soils that do not dry out badly in summer and they prefer open, sunny places.

Regular pruning is unnecessary but old stems can be cut out or shortened in February or March. Increase is by layering in spring or autumn, by removal of rooted suckers in autumn or by seeds, when available, sown in spring.

fertilis *2–2.5m. (6–8ft) Reddish-purple E. Summer D T S L V*

South-eastern USA. Much like C. *floridus* but not such a good garden shrub since the leaves lack the characteristic camphor-like fragrance. It makes a rather open-branched bush.

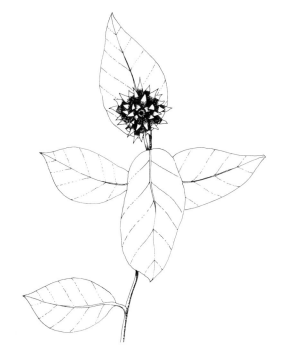

Calycanthus floridus

floridus *2–2.5m. (6–8ft) Maroon Summer D T S L V*

South-eastern USA. This is the Carolina Allspice, the best species for garden planting because of the quite marked aroma of stems and leaves. Even the flowers of this species have some fragrance but there are rarely sufficient of them to make much effect.

occidentalis   *2.4–3m. (8–10ft)   Maroon Summer   D T S L V*

California. The Californian Allspice is more strongly aromatic than either of the others and the flowers are a little larger, but the habit is even looser and less attractive.

CAMELLIA, Theaceae. Evergreen shrubs all handsome in leaf and many very beautiful in flower. All dislike lime or chalk in any quantity and thrive best in those moderately acid soils that also suit rhododendrons. The leaves are dark green with a high gloss, the flowers basically saucer-shaped like a single-rose but, like roses, camellias have a tendency to produce varieties with numerous petals, sometimes sufficient to make them fully double, sometimes only semi-double or with an outer ring of large petals and a central 'pad' of short petals, a form known as 'anemone flowered'. All grow in sun or semi-shade, flowering most freely where the light is fairly strong, but growing faster and more luxuriantly where sunshine is dappled or intermittent. They therefore make excellent shrubs for planting in thin woodland but thrive also in many other situations, including trained against walls, a useful method of providing protection for the more tender kinds. Apart from their dislike of lime they are not fussy about soil though they like best those with a fairly high humus content (leaf-mould or peat). Though they do not enjoy summer dryness they survive it far better than rhododenrons.

Pruning is not essential but old stems can be removed and others shortened in May or, if bushes have grown much too large, they can even be cut back to within 30–40cm./12–16in. of ground level, but with complete loss of flowers the following year. Seed germinates fairly readily in a cool greenhouse in spring but seedlings take some years to attain flowering size, and except for species, are likely to differ from their parents. Garden varieties are usually increased by layering at almost any time, by cuttings of firm young growth in summer in a propagator, or by mature leaves removed with a growth bud and a small piece of wood, also in summer, and rooted in a propagator.

cuspidata   *2m. (6ft)   White   Spring   E T H L S*

Western China. Quite a pretty shrub with relatively small leaves and flowers, but it is surpassed for garden planting by a hybrid between it and *Camellia saluenensis* named 'Cornish Snow'. The flowers of this are a little larger, about 4cm./2in. across, white or faintly pink-tinted and freely produced. It is quite hardy except that the flowers can be killed by frost.

japonica   *2–6m. (6–20ft) White to Crimson   E. Spring   E T H L S*

Japan. This is the most familiar camellia, a species which has produced innumerable varieties differing in habit, flower colour and form and time of flowering. When first introduced to Britain early in the nineteenth century, it was believed to be tender and was grown in glasshouses but gradually it dawned on gardeners that it was only the flowers that were at real risk, and that mainly because they commenced to open so early. Gradually camellias emerged into the open, first in the mildest parts of the south and west, but gradually all over the country. Only in the extreme north does *Camellia japonica* still appear unsatisfactory and that probably more a matter of day length in summer, which seems to inhibit flower bud production.

Whole books have been written about camellias and in all it is the varieties of C. *japonica* which occupy the greatest space. There are thousands of them and hundreds are actually available from specialist nurseries and through garden centres. Though the colour range is not great, from white and palest pink to bright red and crimson, there are infinite variations in the mixing of these colours as well as great variety in the form of the flower.

For purposes of classification six major groups are recognized. Single, with no more than eight petals completely exposing the central tuft of stamens; Semi-double, two or more rows of petals but not so many as to conceal the stamens; Anemone Form, one or more rows of the usual broad petals with a central mass of tiny petals (petaloids) mixed with the stamens; Peony Form, full but informal flowers not unlike double peonies, though considerably smaller; Double, many petals laid regularly one over the other to produce a dome-like flower, but stamens visible when the flower is fully developed; Formal Double, similar to the last but petals completely overlapping so that no stamens are visible at any stage.

A peculiarity of these camellias is that colour sometimes 'breaks', white or pink flecks and patches appearing on normally self-coloured petals. These changes may prove permanent or temporary and some named varieties have arisen by this sporting which may in some cases be caused by viruses. Yellow mottling of leaves may have a similar cause or may be an indication of iron or manganese deficiency, possibly due to an insufficiently acid soil.

maliflora *2–2.5m (6–8ft)* *Rose Winter*
E W T H L S

China. The flowers of this species are small and usually semi-double, delightful when freely produced, but because they open in winter, a particularly sheltered place is required for this little-known species.
C. rosiflora is similar but considered to be a distinct species.

reticulata *3–10m. (10–33ft)* *Rose Spring E W T H L S*

China. This magnificent but slightly tender species is notable for the size of its flowers, at least in the semi-double or fully double varieties commonly grown in gardens. The true species is of comparatively recent introduction. and in this the flowers are smaller, but variety 'Captain Rawes', so called because it was introduced in 1920 by an employee of the East India Company of that name, has semi-double, carmine flowers fully 15cm./6in. across and there are modern fully double varieties that are even bigger. The habit of the plant is loose, making a very large bush in the open, but in gardens it is usually trained against a wall or screen. 'Leonard Messel' is much like 'Captain Rawes' in appearance but is actually a hybrid between *C. reticulata* and *C. williamsii* 'Mary Christian'. Since it is hardier than *C. reticulata* it is probably the best camellia of this type for general garden planting.

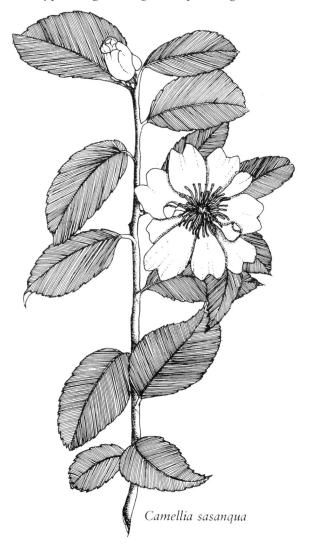

Camellia sasanqua

saluenensis   *3–4.5m (10–15ft)*   *Pink*
E. Spring   E   W   T   H   L   S

China. This species is of interest to gardeners primarily as one of the parents of the hybrid *C. x williamsii*, which combines all its good qualities of elegance and free flowering with greater hardiness.

sasanqua   *2–3m. (6–10ft)*
White or Pink   *Winter*   E   W   T   H   L   S

Japan. A lovely camellia which can be in flower by November and may continue intermittently until early spring. The flowers of the wild forms are like dog-roses but there are garden varieties with more substantial blooms, some semi-double or double. Stems and leaves are moderately hardy but flowers are destroyed by frost or spoiled by heavy rain, so if planted outdoors it should have a particularly sheltered place

x williamsii   *2–3m. (6–10ft)*
Pink or White   *Spring*   E   T   H   L   S

These are garden hybrids between *Camellia saluenensis* and varieties of *C. japonica*. Leaves are smaller than those of *C. japonica*, stems are more slender and the flowers usually drop off as they fade instead of remaining on the bushes as they commonly do with *C. japonica*. Since all varieties appear to be hardy these are excellent garden shrubs, and one variety, 'Donation', with bright pink double flowers, is rapidly becoming the most popular of all camellias. It is incredibly free-flowering. As yet the range of colour and flower shapes is less varied than those of *C. japonica* but is being steadily extended.

CAMPSIS, Bignoniaceae. Trumpet Vine. Vigorous deciduous climbing plants which have been known under the names Tecoma and Bignonia, still to be found in use in some gardens. Leaves are pinnate, composed of several leaflets, flowers are trumpet-shaped, carried in clusters, and the stems of some kinds produce sufficient aerial roots to be more to less self-clinging like ivy. They thrive in all reasonably fertile soils, require warm, sunny positions and may require some protection in severe winters. In late winter, before sap is flowing freely, the previous year's growth can be cut back to a few centimetres as flowers are produced in late summer on the young stems. Increase is by layering in spring, by cuttings in summer in a propagator or by root cuttings in winter. Seeds, if available, will germinate in a warm greenhouse in spring.

grandiflora   *6–9m. (20–30ft)*
Orange and red   *L. Summer*   *E. Autumn*
D   W   C   H   L   R   S

China. A handsome but not very hardy species with large, orange and red flowers in loose clusters. It only has a few aerial roots and must either be tied to supports or allowed to ramble through branches, trellis work or something of the kind.

radicans   *6–9m. (20–30ft)*
Orange and red   *L. Summer*   *E. Autumn*
D   W   C   H   L   R   S

South-eastern USA. This is the hardiest species and also the most self-clinging but the flowers are smaller, more closely clustered and less broadly trumpet-shaped than those of *C. grandiflora* and its hybrids.

x tagliabuana   *6–9m. (20–30ft)*
Orange and red or salmon
L. Summer   *E. Autumn*   D   W   C   H   L   R

Hybrids between *Campsis grandiflora* and *C. radicans* showing many of the characteristics of both. The most popular is 'Madame Galen', with reddish-salmon flowers as large as those of *C. grandiflora*. As it is a little hardier than that species it is probably the best trumpet vine for garden planting in Britain but it is not well supplied with aerial roots.

CARAGANA, Leguminosae. Pea Tree. Shrubs and small trees most of which have adapted themselves to live in quite poor soils and warm, sunny places. They are far less spectacular than their relatives, the Brooms, but are useful, especially in some awkward, hot and dry places. No pruning is necessary but size can be decreased by shortening young stems after flowering. Increase is by seed sown under glass in spring; by cuttings in a propagator in summer or by grafting in spring onto seedlings.

arborescens *4–6m. (13–20ft) Yellow L. Spring E. Summer D F S H G*

Siberia. Erect and rather narrow in habit, with small yellow flowers and pinnate leaves up to 15cm/6in. long. The stems are armed with spines. There are several varieties,

including 'Lorberghii', with very narrow leaflets; 'Nana', slow-growing and dwarf; and 'Pendula', with stiffly drooping stems. This is sometimes grafted onto a straight stem of the species to produce a little tree of weeping habit.

CARPENTARIA, Philadelphaceae. A genus of one species only, an evergreen shrub that is probably rather hardier than it is often supposed to be. It likes a warm, sunny place and a reasonably well-drained but not over rich soil but is not otherwise fussy. Pruning is not essential but weather-damaged stems should be removed in spring and at the same time unwanted growth can be shortened or cut out. Increase is by seed under glass in spring or by summer cuttings in a propagator.

Campsis x *tagliabuana* 'Madame Galen'

Carpentaria californica

californica *2–3m. (6–10ft) White*
Summer E W T S H

California. In its best forms this is a beautiful
shrub, well-branched with scented flowers
shaped like those of a rather flat,
broad-petalled mock-orange (philadelphus).
However, it is variable and some seedlings
may have smaller or less well-formed flowers
than others so it is worth keeping good forms
going by cuttings. The dark green leaves are
lance-shaped.

CARYOPTERIS, Verbenaceae. Blue Spiraea.
Small deciduous shrubs, mostly only
semi-woody and so tending to die back in
winter and then throw up new stems in the
spring. The small blue flowers are born in
little clusters and exerted anthers give them a
slightly fluffy look like those of some spiraeas.
All thrive in most well-drained soils and open,
preferably sunny, places. They make excellent
front row shrubs. Plants can be cut almost to
ground level each March. Increase is by
spring or summer cuttings in a propagator or
pot within a polythene bag.

x clandonensis *1m. (3ft) Blue*
L. Summer E. Autumn D C H

A group of hybrids between *Caryopteris
incana* and *C. mongolica* and probably the
best for general planting. All have greyish
leaves and flowers in some shade of blue.
Several have been given distinguishing names
e.g. 'Arthur Simmonds', bright blue;
'Ferndown', darker violet blue; and 'Kew
Blue', also a darker blue.

incana *1–1.5m. (3–5ft) Blue Autumn*
D W C H S

China and Japan. This species was for long
known as *C. mastacanthus*. Its leaves are
small and grey with down, flowers are violet
blue, but this species is probably not quite as
hardy as the hybrids from it.

mongolica *1m (3ft)   Blue   Summer*
D   W   C   H   S

Mongolia and Northern China. This is the other parent of *C. x clandonensis*, a very attractive shrub but difficult to retain except in very well-drained soils and sunny places. It appears to resent our dull summers and wet winters.

CASSIA, Leguminosae. Plants for warm and sunny places too tender to be reliable outdoors except in the mildest parts of the British Isles. They thrive in fertile, well-drained soils, can be grown from seed sown in warmth in spring or from late summer cuttings in a propagator and can be thinned or cut back in March.

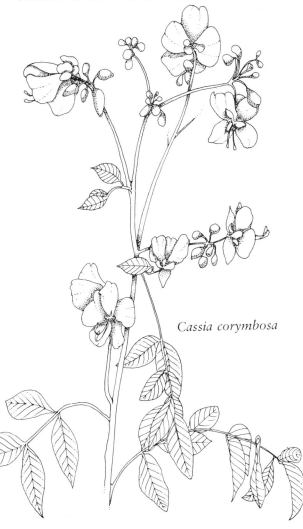

Cassia corymbosa

corymbosa *2–3m. (6–10ft)   Yellow*
L. Summer   E W T C S H

Northern Argentine. A handsome, sprawling plant that can be trained against a sunny wall or allowed to cover a bank. The saucer-shaped flowers are buttercup yellow carried in clusters and since they are freely produced they make a striking display for several weeks in late summer. It may be necessary to protect plants with plastic or polythene sheets in winter. This is a fine semi-climber for a sunny conservatory.

CASSINIA, Compositae. Shrubs with small sometimes coloured leaves and clusters of small daisy-type flowers. It is as foliage plants that they are chiefly valued and they are not difficult to grow in sunny places where frosts are not severe and the soil is well-drained. Growth damaged by frost should be removed in spring and other stems can be shortened then to preserve a well-balanced, neat plant. Increase is by summer cuttings in a propagator.

fulvida *1–2m. (3–6ft)   White   Summer*
E W T H

New Zealand. The leaves are tawny yellow, for which reason this small, densely branched shrub is sometimes called Golden Heather but it has no connection with true heathers. In warm gardens it is useful for its very distinctive foliage.

CASSIOPE, Ericaceae. These mainly Arctic and high mountain shrubs are so small that most gardeners would regard them as rock plants and it is in rock gardens and peat beds that they are of greatest value. The flowers are small and bell-shaped, the leaves tiny and overlapping. All require acid soil and ample moisture and are not easy to grow except in the north, since they do not become sufficiently dormant in winter in the south. Increase is by layering or by summer cuttings in moist peat.

fastigiata *15–30cm. (6–12in.)   White
Spring   E H L*

Himalaya. The tiny dark green leaves of this
species have a silvery margin and the flowers
are quite large for a cassiope. If one only is
required this could be it.

lycopodioides *4–7cm. (2–3in.)   White
L. Spring   E. Summer   E H L*

Japan. A tiny-tot for a peat bed and similar
places.

tetragona *10–25cm. (4–10in.)
White and red   Spring   E H L*

Arctic and sub-Arctic. Much like C. *fastigiata*
but the leaves are wholly green, the flowers
may be red-tinted and are a little smaller.

CEANOTHUS, Rhamnaceae. Californian
Lilac. Mountain Sweet. From a garden
standpoint this is a large and important genus
of shrubs, many evergreen, a few deciduous,
all beautiful but also all to a greater or less
degree tender. The flowers are individually
small but borne in clusters, close and
thimble-shaped in many of the evergreen
kinds, rather looser and more plume-like in
the deciduous kinds. The flowers of many are
honey-scented and much visited by bees.

In the mildest parts of the British Isles,
and particularly near the coast most can be
grown fully in the open but elsewhere many
may need the protection of a wall, preferably
one facing south or west. They are not fussy
about soil provided both fertility and
drainage are reasonable and most can be
readily increased by late summer or early
autumn cuttings in a propagator. Root
cuttings can also be taken in winter. Seed,
when available, also germinates readily in
spring under glass and in favourable places
self-sown seedlings sometimes appear
outdoors. Seedlings of species are likely to
resemble their parents but those of hybrids
and selected garden forms may show
variation. Pruning is not essential but can be
used to restrict growth of plants and can be
very useful when these are trained against
walls. Evergreen kinds should be spur-pruned
immediately after flowering, side-growths
being shortened to 5 or 6cm./2–3in.
Deciduous kinds can be cut back quite
severely in March and this can improve the
size and quality of the flower clusters.

americanus *1m. (3ft)   White   Summer
D W C   S H*

Eastern and Central USA. One of the least
attractive species but also one of the hardiest
and of interest as a parent of good garden
hybrids.

arboreus *3–6m. (10–20ft)   Blue   Spring
E W P S H*

California. This is one of the largest species
and in its selected garden form, 'Trewithen
Blue', has bright lavender-blue flowers deeper
coloured than those of the wild form, it is also
one of the most beautiful. Regrettably it is
distinctly tender and so more suitable for
coastal gardens of the south and west than for
cold inland districts

x **'Burkwoodii'** *2m. (6ft)   Blue   Summer
E P H*

A hybrid of somewhat uncertain parentage
but clearly combining qualities of evergreen
and deciduous species and being the only
evergreen ceanothus to flower much of the
summer. Since it is compact in growth it
requires little pruning. It is also one of the
hardiest kinds and an excellent garden shrub.
'Autumnal Blue' is of similar origin but the
flowers are not quite such a deep blue. It is at
least equally hardy.

x **delilianus** *2m. (6ft)   Blue or Pink
L. Summer   E. Autumn   D C H*

A group of hybrids between *Ceanothus
americanus* and a much more decorative but
tender Mexican species named C. *coeruleus*.
All are beautiful plants, thriving on hard

spring pruning and some feeding, which produces a shuttlecock of sturdy stems terminated by graceful plumes of flowers. There are several named varieties including: 'Ceres', lilac-pink; 'Gloire de Plantières', deep blue; 'Gloire de Versailles', light blue; Henri Desfosse', violet-blue; 'Indigo', deep blue; 'Marie Simon', pink; 'Perle Rose', rose-pink; and 'Topaz', medium blue. Varieties listed as C. x *pallidus* cannot be readily distinguished from C. x *delilianus* and are included in the selection above.

dentatus *2m. (6ft)   Blue   L. Spring*
E   W   P   H   S

California. A delightful and popular species with neat rather narrow leaves and clusters of bright blue flowers.

griseus *3–4m. (10–13 ft)   Blue*
L. Spring   E. Summer   E   W   P   H   S

California. This ceanothus closely resembles C. *thyrsiflorus* and some authorities regard it as no more than a natural variety of that species. It is variable in shades of blue and is probably a little less hardy than C. *thyrsiflorus*.

impressus *1.5–2.1m. (5–7ft)   Blue*
Spring   E   P   H   S

California. An exceptionally beautiful and relatively hardy evergreen species with neat, dark green leaves, deep blue flowers and a densely bushy habit.

prostratus *15cm. (6in.)   Blue   Spring*
E   W   P   S   H   L

Western North America. Unusual in being completely prostrate and in having holly-like leaves. Flower colour in the wild appears to be variable, including white as well as shades of blue. Since it has an extensive distribution in the coastal area of western North America it is probable that some forms are hardier than others.

rigidus *1–4m. (3–13ft)   Blue*
Spring   E   W   P   S   H

California. A beautiful shrub with neat dark green wedge-shaped leaves, deep blue flowers and stiff branches. In the open it is low and spreading but trained against a wall it can reach a considerable height. Unfortunately it is distinctly tender.

thyrsiflorus *4–8m. (13–26ft)   Blue*
L. Spring   E. Summer   E   W   P   S   H

California. A tall, relatively late-flowering evergreen species specially valuable for its hardiness. Because of its height it can be used to cover quite a large wall. There is a variety, or maybe a hybrid, from it named 'Cascade', which has arching stems and light blue

Ceanothus thyrsiflorus

flowers, an attactive shrub but one that, like *C. thyrsiflorus*, can become quite large with age. Another variety, named 'Repens', is a wild form much more prostrate in habit and suitable for planting on sunny banks or large rock gardens.

x veitchianus   *2.5–3m. (8–10ft)   Blue L. Spring   E. Summer   E W P H*

A hybrid of uncertain origin but probably related to *C. thyrsiflorus* or *C. rigidus*. It is a beautiful shrub, with neat shining green leaves and bright blue flowers. It is often confused with *C. dentatus* but its leaves are broader and more wedge-shaped.

CELASTRUS, Celastraceae. Rampant deciduous twiners of which one kind is fairly common in British gardens, planted for its decorative seeds and seed vessels. It is hardy and fast growing, not in the least fussy about soil or even situation and useful where there is room for a rampant climber to scramble up into an unimportant tree, camouflage an unsightly building or something of that kind. Unwanted growth can be cut out in winter. Increase is by seed or layering in spring or summer.

orbiculatus   *9–12m. (30–40ft)   Green Summer   D T S L*

North-eastern Asia. This is the best species, the clusters of little green pea-size fruits splitting open when ripe to reveal scarlet seeds embedded on a deep yellow interior. Male and female flowers are frequently produced on separate plants and then only the females produce the showy fruits and only if fertilized with pollen from a nearby male. However, there are hermaphrodite forms, that is, plants that have flowers of both sexes, and these will fruit freely even in isolation. Since seedlings from such plants may not also be hermaphrodite, when one has such a plant it is best to increase it by layering, thus ensuring exact resemblance.

CEPHALOTAXUS, Cephalotaxaceae. Plum Yew. Some of these are trees but a few are handsome, if rather large, evergreen shrubs related to yew. They thrive in all reasonably fertile soils, in sun or shade, can be pruned, if necessary, in May and increased either by summer or autumn cuttings or by seed.

harringtonia   *3–4m. (10–13ft)   Yellowish Spring   E T S H A*

Probably Chinese but introduced from Japan. One of the most handsome species with wide-spreading branches and narrow leaves up to 6cm./2½in. long, dark green and shining above, marked with whitish stripes below. A variety named 'Drupacea' is similar but smaller and more compact. It is sometimes listed as a separate species. Another variety, named 'Fastigiata', has erect branches and forms a broadly columnar bush rather like an Irish yew but with larger leaves.

Ceratostigma willmottianum

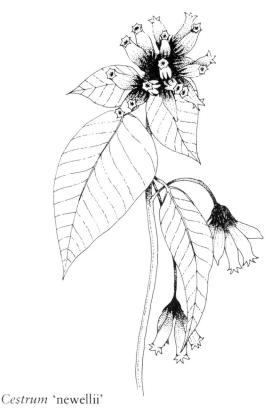

Cestrum 'newellii'

CESTRUM, Solanaceae. Those kinds grown outdoors in Britain are all shrubs of loose habit, easily trained against walls or fences, which can be the best place for them since they are not very hardy. The flowers are tubular, produced in clusters and in some kinds are very showy. All enjoy fertile, well-drained but not dry soils and warm sunny places. Unwanted stems can be cut out or shortened in spring, and growth killed or damaged in winter should be removed at the same time. Late summer cuttings root readily in a propagator and seed, if available, can be germinated in warmth.

elegans *2.5–3m. (8–10ft)   Red   Summer*
E   W   T   H   S

Mexico. The species most commonly seen, and a handsome plant with long flexible stems, softly downy leaves and dangling clusters of purplish-red flowers. Even better as

CERATOSTIGMA, Plumbaginaceae. Small shrubs or herbaceous plants related to plumbago and at one time known by that name. They like warm sunny places and reasonably well-drained soils including those overlying chalk or limestone. Stems damaged or killed in winter should be removed in March when, if preferred, all growth can be cut back to within a few centimetres of the ground. Increase is by seed under glass or summer cuttings in a propagator or pot placed inside a polythene bag.

willmottianum *0.6–1m. (2–3ft)   Blue*
L. Summer   Autumn   D   W   C   H   S

China. The best kind, a beautiful small shrub with slender stems and almost pure blue phlox-like flowers produced over a long period. Ideal for the front of a sunny border.

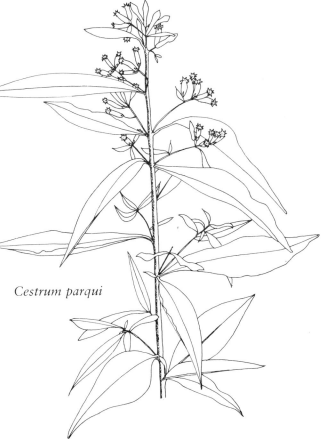

Cestrum parqui

a garden plant, because brighter in colour, is C. 'newellii', a plant of uncertain origin which might be derived from *C. elegans* or more probably from the very similar Mexican species *C. fasciculatum*.

parqui *2–3m. (6–10ft) Yellow*
L. Summer E. Autumn D W T H S

Chile. Though this is by no means so decorative a plant as *C. elegans*, because its flowers are small and a rather pale greenish-yellow, it is nevertheless attractive. It is probably a little hardier than the others, it can flower very freely and the flowers are scented at night.

CHAENOMELES, Rosaceae. Japanese Quince. Deciduous shrubs with apple-like flowers closely allied to and resembling the true quinces and at one time united with them in the same genus, *Cydonia*. Left to

Chaenomeles speciosa

themselves they make tangled bushes of tough, woody stems armed with spines and often spreading quite widely by suckers. However, in gardens they are more frequently trained like climbers against walls, fences etc. which means that they must be pruned annually and be given some support such as wires or trellis so that their stems can be trained where they are required. Much of this pruning can be done in May or June, after flowering, when young stems can be shortened to a few centimetres and unwanted stems removed, but further thinning can be carried out in autumn or winter if necessary. Japanese quinces succeed in all reasonably fertile soil and will grow in sun or shade provided this is not too dense. They can be increased by layering at any time, by summer cuttings in a frame or propagator or by digging up suckers with roots in autumn or winter. Seeds sown outdoors as soon as ripe or in spring will germinate, though maybe slowly, but seedlings of garden varieties are likely to differ from their parents.

japonica *0.6–1m. (2–3ft) Orange-red*
Spring E. Summer D T P H L V S

Japan. This is the species that used to be called *Cydonia maulei*, the shortest of the Japanese quinces but a wide-spreading bush excellent for planting on banks or at the front of a border. The fruits are pleasantly scented and, when ripe, can be used to make jelly.

speciosa *2–3m. (6–10ft) Red*
Winter Spring D T P H L V S

China. This species has suffered from a superfluity of names, including *Cydonia japonica* and *Chaenomeles lagenaria*. To many people it will always remain the much loved, early flowering 'Japonica'. In warm places it can be commencing to open its bright red flowers before Christmas and it should be at its peak by early March. There are numerous garden varieties including: 'Nivalis', white; 'Moerloosii', pink and white, for which reason it is sometimes called 'Apple

Blossom'; 'Phyllis Moore', pink and semi-double; 'Cardinalis', light crimson; 'Rubra Grandiflora', crimson, rather short but wide-spreading; and 'Simonii', blood-red and dwarf.

x **superba** *1.2–2.5m. (4–8ft)* *White to Crimson Spring E. Summer* *D T P H L V*

This is the group name given to hybrids between *Chaenomeles japonica* and *C. speciosa*. They exhibit characteristics of both parents and the group contains some excellent garden plants. One of the best known and most popular is 'Knap Hill Scarlet', dwarf and spreading in habit and with orange-scarlet flowers produced continuously for many weeks. Others are 'Crimson and Gold', crimson flowers revealing yellow anthers; 'Coral Sea', coral; 'Pink Lady', rose-pink and 'Rowallane', crimson.

CHIMONANTHUS, Calycanthaceae. Winter Sweet. Deciduous winter-flowering shrubs with very sweet-scented flowers. The kinds grown in gardens are hardy but need sunshine and warmth to ripen their growth and promote flowering and so are usually trained against sunny walls. They like fertile soil and good but not excessive drainage. Pruning, necessary for trained plants but not for those grown naturally, should be done immediately the flowers fade, and consists in cutting out weak or unproductive stems and shortening others if there is not room to train them in at full length. Wires, trellis or other support should be provided. Propagation is by seed sown under glass in spring or by layering in spring.

praecox *2.5–3m. (8–10ft)* *Yellow Winter D T L S*

China. The only species cultivated in the British Isles and formerly known as *Chimonanthus fragrans*. The lance-shaped leaves feel rough to the touch and the small flowers are semi-transparent, pale greenish-yellow flushed with purple towards the centre. They are quite unspectacular and might easily escape notice were it not for their exceedingly sweet perfume, which in favourable conditions can be carried a long way in the air. There is a variety named 'Grandiflora' with slightly larger, more strongly coloured flowers and another, named 'Luteus', in which the purple flush is missing.

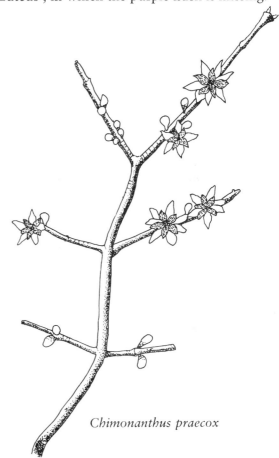

Chimonanthus praecox

CHIONANTHUS, Oleaceae. Fringe Tree. Deciduous shrubs with clusters of white flowers which have such narrow petals that they hang like fringes. They are hardy and easily grown in moderately rich, slightly moist but not waterlogged soil, and are highly decorative when they flower well but seem to require quite a lot of summer sun and warmth to ripen their growth and so ensure plentiful flower buds. Pruning is not essential but branches can be removed or stems shortened in March. Increase is by seed, when available, sown under glass in spring, or by layering in spring.

retusus *3–5m. (10–16ft)   White   Summer D T S L*

China. A well-branched and very beautiful shrub or small tree bearing loose, more or less erect, clusters of flowers with petals about 2cm./¾in. long.

virginicus *3–5m. (10–16ft)   White Summer   D T S L*

Eastern USA. Differs from the Chinese Fringe Tree in having dense hanging clusters of slightly scented flowers with petals up to 2.5cm./1in. long.

CHOISYA, Rutaceae. Mexican Orange Flower. Only one species is commonly cultivated in the British Isles and this is a slightly tender evergreen which succeeds best

Choisya ternata

in warm sunny places and reasonably fertile and well-drained soils. It does not require regular pruning but winter-damaged growth should be removed in spring, and if bushes get too large stems can be removed or shortened in June as soon as the first flowering is over. Summer cuttings root readily in a propagator or pot placed inside a polythene bag.

ternata   *1.5–2.1m. (5–7ft)   White Spring   E   W   O   H*

Mexico. A shrub that is handsome in leaf and beautiful in flower. Leaves are tripartite, light shining green and aromatic when bruised. The white flowers are borne in clusters, sweetly scented and somewhat resemble orange blossom. Though the main display is in April and May there are often a few more flowers later in summer.

CISTUS, Cistaceae. Rock Rose. A large genus of evergreen shrubs adapted by nature to thrive in hot, sunny and often dry places. They vary greatly in size and character but all have flat or saucer-shaped flowers rather like single roses. Many come from limestone areas and have no objection to alkaline soils though they will also thrive in moderately acid soils provided they are well drained. The smaller kinds are suitable for rock gardens, the larger ones for sunny banks and borders. All are to some degree tender, some more so than others. None requires regular pruning but growth damaged in winter should be removed in spring. All the species grow readily from seed sown under glass in spring, and in favourable places self-sown seedlings may appear. All can also be grown from summer cuttings in a propagator; this is the only way to increase the hybrids and garden varieties.

albidus   *1.2–1.5m. (4–5ft)   Rose E. Summer   E   W   T   H   S*

South-western Europe and North Africa. Despite its habitat this is one of the hardier kinds. The leaves are covered with grey down

and the flowers are a pale shade of magenta with a touch of yellow at the centre.

x corbariensis   *0.6–1m. (2–3ft)   White E. Summer   E   W   T   H*

A fine hybrid between C. *populifolius* and C. *salviifolius*, with more or less heart-shaped green leaves and medium-size white flowers, touched with yellow at the centre and very freely produced. This is a first-class garden shrub which can spread far wider than its height.

creticus   *0.6–1.2m. (2–4ft)   Rose E. Summer   E   W   T   H   S*

Eastern Mediterranean. A variable species much confused with others and often called C. *incanus* or C. *villosus* but as a garden plant inferior to C. *albidus* and C. *crispus*, which resemble it and are hardier.

crispus   *0.6m (2ft)   Magenta Spring   E. Summer   E   W   T   H   S*

South-western Europe and North Africa. A low-growing grey-leaved plant resembling C. *albidus* but with more strongly coloured flowers. It is apt to be confused with its hybrid C. x *pulverulentus* (q.v.)

x cyprius   *2–2.4m. (6–8ft) White and crimson   L. Spring   E. Summer E   W   T   H*

A natural hybrid between C. *ladanifer* and C. *laurifolius* with dark green gummy leaves and large white, crimson-blotched flowers carried in clusters. It is probably the hardiest of the so-called Gum Cistuses and a very handsome shrub.

ladanifer   *1–1.5m. (3–5ft) White and crimson   L. Spring   E. Summer E   W   T   H   S*

Southern Europe and northern Africa. The typical gum cistus with sticky, dark green leaves and large white flowers with central crimson blotch, carried singly. Habit is erect and relatively unbranched and growth is rather tender, which makes this species less satisfactory as a garden plant than some of its hybrids. See *C. palhinae*.

Cistus ladanifer

laurifolius   *2–2.5m (6–8ft)   White Summer   E W T H S*

South-western Europe and Mediterranean region. This is yet another species with gummy leaves, dark green and aromatic. The large white flowers are unblotched and carried in clusters. Many experts regard this as the hardiest species and though erect in growth it is more branched and makes a better bush than *C. ladanifer*.

libanotis   *30cm. (1ft)   White E. Summer   E W T H S*

Spain and Portugal. The small size and narrow leaves of this fairly hardy species make it look more like a helianthemum than a cistus. It is a good rock garden shrub. *C. clusii* closely resembles it.

x lusitanicus   *1.2m. (4ft)   White E. Summer   E W T H*

A variable hybrid between *C. ladanifer* and a downy-leaved white and yellow flowered Spanish and Portuguese species named *C. hirsutus*. It is not, however, very hardy and is most valuable as a garden plant in its variety 'Decumbens', which makes a wide-spreading bush, usually less than 1m./3ft high, with white, crimson-blotched petals.

palhinhae   *45–60cm. (1½–2ft)   White L. Spring   E. Summer   E W T H S*

Portugal. A handsome species with dark green, gummy leaves and large white flowers carried singly. It is fairly hardy and has been crossed with the more tender *C. ladanifer* to produce some excellent hybrids such as 'Blanche', white; 'Pat', white with crimson blotch; and 'Paladin', similar to the last. All these have a better, more widely branched habit than *C. ladanifer*. These hybrids should be increased by cuttings.

populifolius   *1.2m. (3–6ft)   White E. Summer   E W T H S*

South-west Europe. Very distinct in its broad, heart-shaped quite long-stalked leaves. This is an excellent garden plant, free-flowering, wide-spreading and moderately hardy.

x pulverulentus   *60cm. (2ft)   Magenta L. Spring   E. Summer   E W T H*

A natural hybrid between *C. albidus* and *C. crispus*, with grey-green leaves and magenta flowers. A specially good form of this has been named 'Sunset' and is an excellent short fairly hardy cistus to plant where such a strong colour is acceptable.

x **purpureus**   *1–1.2m. (3–4ft)*
Carmine and maroon   Summer
E W T H

A hybrid between *C. creticus* and *C. ladanifer*, with very large carmine maroon-spotted flowers. It makes a well-branched bush and is arguably the most spectacular of all the rock roses. Even though it is not very hardy it is well worth planting if a warm sunny position can be found for it. Cuttings root readily and a small annual stock, overwintered in a light frost-proof place will insure against winter losses.

'Silver Pink'   *60cm (2ft)*
L. Spring   E. Summer   E W T H

A beautiful hybrid of uncertain parentage, possibly *C. creticus* x *C. laurifolius*, with greyish leaves and soft pink flowers displaying yellow anthers. It is short but moderately spreading in habit and fairly hardy when sturdily grown.

x **skanbergii**   *30cm. (1ft)   Pink*
L. Spring   E. Summer   E W T H

A natural hybrid between two Mediterranean species, *C. monspeliensis*, with white flowers, and *C. parviflorus*, with rose-pink flowers. *C.* x *skanbergii* is dwarf and spreading, with grey-green leaves and small pink flowers very freely produced.

CLEMATIS, Ranunculaceae. In this great genus there are herbaceous as well as climbing species and in some instances hybrids between the two, so that it is hard to draw a sharp and convincing line between those that truly belong in this book and those that should be discussed elsewhere. Because of the extent of the genus and the necessity for brevity I have included only those that every gardener would recognize as climbers capable of making a more or less permanent framework of growth. Yet 'capable of making' is the operative phrase here, because with many of the summer flowering kinds, particularly the large-flowered hybrids, best results are often attained by removing much of the growth each year in late winter or early spring and so forcing the plants to make new growth, which is likely to be more vigorous and able to produce the finest quality flowers.

The stems of all clematises are slender when young though they may become fairly thick with age. Because of this they are easily broken and need to find adequate support readily. In the wild they scramble into bushes and trees, clinging to their stems with tendrils. In gardens they can be allowed to do just that, and they make excellent companions for climbing roses though this association may complicate pruning a little. Alternatively they can be grown up pillars or tripods, over trellis or perforated stone or concrete screens or on wires trained against walls.

All kinds of good rich soil not liable to dry out in summer but equally not likely to become waterlogged in winter. They enjoy sunshine and yet like cool soil so it often pays to plant them among small shrubs or herbaceous plants that will shade the soil but allow the clematis stems to grow up through them and get all the light that is going. It is also beneficial to give them an annual mulch of rotted manure, garden compost, old mushroom compost or something of the kind.

Some clematises actually prefer soils containing lime or chalk, and none object to these, but all are very soil tolerant and fertility is more important than pH. They do not like having their roots broken and so are best purchased in containers, but if the compost in the container is very different in texture from the soil in which they are to be planted it may be desirable to tease out very carefully some of the outer roots in the container ball and spread these out in the new soil to encourage them to grow out into it.

Pruning depends in part on time of flowering, in part on space available. Pruning of all spring flowering kinds should be delayed until the flowers have faded and should then be restricted to the minimum necessary to keep growth within bounds. Some old stems can be removed completely, others still vigorous and productive can be shortened. Those large-flowered kinds, such as 'Nelly Moser' and 'Henryi', that flower mainly in May–June can be pruned immediately this main crop is over, the object again being to keep growth within bounds by removing some of the oldest and shortening the younger growths. Large-flowered kinds, and they are numerous, that flower from about midsummer onwards can be cut back quite severely in February or March, even to within 30cm./12in. of the ground, since they flower on the young stems made after that time. Late-flowering species, such as *Clematis tangutica* and *C. flammula* usually require little pruning but if they grow too large they, too, can be thinned or cut down in February or March.

Species can be grown from seed sown under glass in spring. All kinds can be increased by layering at any time from spring to autumn. Summer cuttings can be rooted in mist or a propagator. Nurserymen usually graft the garden varieties onto seedlings of *C. vitalba*, our native Traveller's Joy or Old Man's Beard, or *C. viticella*.

The large-flowered hybrids in particular suffer from a disease known as clematis wilt, which causes stems, or on occasion whole plants, to die suddenly. Dead or dying stems should be cut out at once, wounds sealed with a tree wound dressing and plants sprayed several times between April and midsummer with a copper fungicide.

alpina   *2–2.5m. (6–9ft)*   *Blue and White Spring*   D O S L H

Europe and northern Asia. A lovely small climber with nodding flowers like little skirts of narrow blue sepals, and petals with a central tuft of white petal-like stamens. Colour is variable, 'Frances Rivis' being a specially bright and clear blue and 'Ruby' rose and creamy white.

armandii   *6–9m. (20–30ft)*   *White Spring*   E W O S L H

China. The hardiest evergreen clematis. The leaves are quite large, each composed of three lance-shaped leaflets, and shining green, the flowers white, fairly small, in fine clusters. This is a very handsome plant for a warm sunny position. It needs little pruning but weather-damaged stems should be removed quickly.

chrysocoma   *2–4m. (6–12ft)*   *Pink or White*   *L. Spring*   *Summer*   D O S L H

China. The true species seems to be rare in gardens and is a semi-woody shrub rather than a climber. What is usually distributed under this name is a variety named *sericea* (sometimes listed as *C. spooneri*) a climber rather like *C. montana* but less vigorous and with larger, pink-tinted, rather long-stalked flowers carried singly or in pairs.

x durandii   *2.5–3m. (8–10ft)*   *Violet blue Summer*   D C L H

A hybrid of *C. integrifolia* with *C. jackmanii* as its other presumed parent. A feature is the central cluster of yellow stamens livening the large deep violet-blue flowers.

flammula   *3–4m. (10–13ft)*   *White*   *L. Summer*   *Autumn*   D T S L H

Southern Europe. This charming species makes a dense tangle of slender stems producing loose sprays of small white sweetly-scented flowers in August and September. Just the plant to cover an old tree stump. The silken seed-heads that follow are as decorative as those of Old Man's Beard (*C. vitalba*).

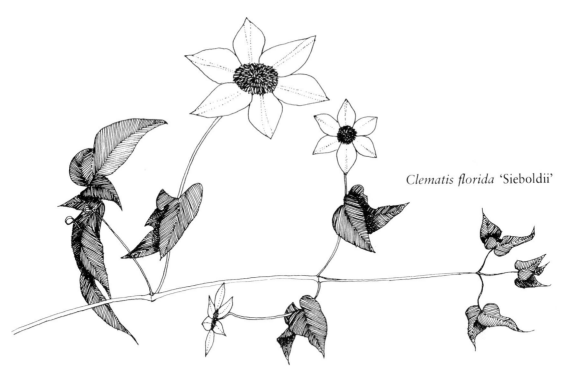

Clematis florida 'Sieboldii'

florida *2.5–3m. (8–10ft)   White   Summer*
D W O S L H

China. A characteristic of this species is that
the stamens are purple and in variety
'Sieboldii', which is the one usually planted in
gardens, these stamens are converted into a
circle of deep violet-blue segments in the
centre of the pure white flower. This is an
exceptionally beautiful clematis but not one
of the most vigorous or easiest to grow. It
should have specially good soil and a warm,
sunny place. A number of summer flowering
hybrids, including 'Belle of Woking', double
mauve flowers; and 'Duchess of Edinburgh',
white and green double; are usually referred
to as belonging to the Florida group but it is
difficult to trace any genuine connection with
this species and far better to treat them simply
as garden hybrids, to be pruned according to
time of flowering and space to be filled.

grata grandidenta *6–9m. (20–30ft)   White*
L. Spring   E. Summer   D O S L H

China. A very vigorous climber carrying its
small flowers in clusters.

x jackmanii *2.5–3m. (8–10ft)   Purple*
Summer   D C L H

This hybrid from C. *lanuginosa* with C.
viticella as the other presumed parent is one
of the most popular and easily grown of the
large-flowered kinds. The intense blue-purple
flowers are of medium size and very freely
produced on the current year's growth so
that, if desired, this clematis can be cut back
severely each February or March. 'Superba' is
a form of it with fuller flowers of a rather
more reddish-purple colour. A great many
other summer flowering, large-flowered
clematis varieties, such as sky blue 'Perle
d'Azur', and soft pink 'Comtesse de
Bouchard', are described as belonging to the
Jackmanii group and most probably do owe
some of their ancestry to this hybrid, but
almost certainly with other species or hybrids
brought in to increase the colour range.
However, all have the characteristic of
flowering on the strong young growth.

x jouiniana   *2.5–3m. (8–10ft)*
White and lilac   L. Summer   Autumn
D   C   L   H

A hybrid made by crossing C. *vitalba* with
one of the herbaceous kinds, C. *heracleifolia
davidiana*. The result is a moderately vigorous
climber bearing from August to October
masses of small flowers with narrow sepals,
which start yellowish-white but become
progressively flushed with lilac as they age.

lanuginosa   *2m. (6ft)   White, Lilac*
L. Spring to Autumn   D   O   L   H

China. This species does not seem to exist in
British gardens yet remains important as one
parent of some of the most popular
large-flowered hybrids. So complex was
clematis breeding in the early days and so
secretive the breeders that it is now impossible
to trace the precise parentage of these
varieties. However, hybrids described as
belonging to the Lanuginosa group generally
have large flowers and an extended flowering
season though some, such as the very popular
'Nelly Moser' with mauve and carmine
flowers, and 'Henryi', pure white, produce
most of their flowers in May–June with only a
few to follow later. If necessary these can be
pruned considerably in July, with loss of
further flowers that summer but no detriment
to the display the following year.

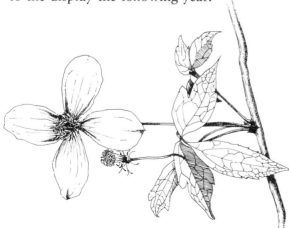

Clematis montana

macropetala   *2–2.5m. (6–8ft)   Blue, Pink*
L. Spring   E. Summer   D   O   S   L   H

China. One of the loveliest early flowering
species with pendant flowers composed of
narrow petals like those of C. *alpina*, but with
their 'skirts' filled by more narrow segments
of diminishing length like a ballet dancer's
tutu. The silky seed-heads that follow are also
attractive. The flowers are typically light blue
but there is a soft rose-coloured variety
named 'Markham's Pink'.

montana   *6–9m. (20–30ft)   White, Pink*
L. Spring   D   O   S   L   H

Himalaya. A very vigorous and beautiful
species, ideal for running up into trees or
covering walls and outbuildings. The flowers
are of medium size, solitary but very freely
produced so that the whole plant can
disappear beneath them for a week or so in
May. They can be sweetly scented but this
appears to be a genetic characteristic more
marked in some varieties than others. One,
with pale pink scented flowers, has been given
the name 'Elizabeth'. The best pink is
probably *rubens* though 'Tetrarose' has larger
flowers. C. *montana grandiflora* has extra
large white flowers and is recognized as a
botanical variety.

orientalis   *3–6m. (10–20ft)   Yellow*
L. Summer   E. Autumn   D   T   S   L   H

Caucasus, N. China, Manchuria, Himalaya.
The only species with which this is likely to be
confused is C. *tangutica*, but C. *orientalis* has
much thicker petals and smaller flowers. They
are bright yellow, nodding and bell-shaped
and are followed by silken seed-heads.

paniculata   *3–6m. (10–20ft)   White*
Spring   E   W   O   S   L   H

New Zealand. This evergreen species, often
called C. *indivisa*, is considerably more tender
than C *armandii*, which is a better garden
plant for that reason, but in the coastal
regions of the south and west it can be

successful and beautiful. It is usually offered as a variety named 'Lobata', with clusters of slightly larger white flowers.

patens *2.5–3m. (8–10ft) Blue, White
L. Spring E. Summer D O S L H*

Japan, China. The true species, which much resembles C. *florida*, is seldom planted in gardens but is important for the part it has played in producing large-flowered garden hybrids. Those referred to as belonging to the Patens group require little pruning but can be thinned or shortened after flowering. Examples are 'Barbara Dibley', violet-purple and carmine; 'Daniel Deronda', light blue, often double; 'Lasurstern', lavender; 'Madame Boisselot', white; 'The President', blue-purple with silvery reverse; and 'Vyvian Pennell', purple and carmine, double.

rehderana *4–7m. (13–23ft) Primrose
L. Summer Autumn D T S L H*

China. A highly distinctive species with clusters of small nodding, bell-shaped, primrose-yellow flowers that are sweetly scented. This is not a spectacular plant but it is a very pleasing one.

tangutica *3–4m. (10–13ft) Yellow
Autumn D T S L H*

Central Asia. The best yellow clematis, closely allied to C. *orientalis* but with slightly larger, deeper yellow flowers followed by similar masses of silken seed-vessels. The variety *obtusiuscula* differs mainly in botanical details.

texensis *1–3m. (3–10ft) Red
Summer E. Autumn D W C S L H*

Texas. A rather tender semi-herbaceous species which is chiefly important in the part it has played in producing garden hybrids such as 'Gravetye Beauty', red, and 'Duchess of Albany', pink. These have all inherited some of the distinctive C. *texensis* flower characteristics of nodding flowers, with petals

narrowing and reflexing towards the tip. They flower late on the current year's growth.

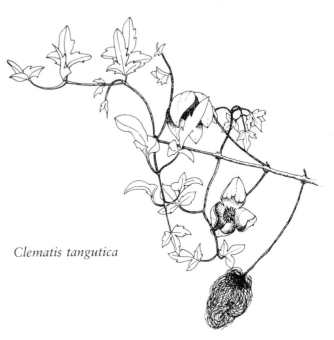

Clematis tangutica

vitalba *6–12m. (20–40ft) Whitish
Summer Autumn D T S L H*

Europe, including Britain. This is the familiar Old Man's Beard or Traveller's Joy, the native clematis that takes over hedgerows wherever the soil is markedly alkaline. Its flowers are too small and greenish-white to be very decorative but they are followed by clouds of conspicuous silken seed-vessels which remain for months, becoming progressively tatty with age. It is not a garden plant except in the wildest settings but it is invaluable as a stock on which nurserymen graft the fine garden hybrids.

viticella *2.5–3m. (8–10ft)
Blue to Purple Summer E. Autumn
D C S L H*

Southern Europe. This vigorous climber makes a great many slender stems which usually die back in winter, so it can with advantage be hard-pruned each February or March. The flowers come rather late, are of medium size in various shades of blue and purple. Some forms have been given distinguishing names and are increased vegetatively. 'Abundance' is pale purple, 'Kermesina', crimson and 'Royal Velours', deep purple. *C. viticella* has also been used in the breeding programme for large-flowered hybrids, and varieties referred to as belonging to the Viticella group include 'Ascotiensis', blue; 'Ernest Markham', red-purple; Lady Betty Balfour, deep blue purple; and 'Ville de Lyons', carmine. All these can also be hard-pruned in February–March.

CLERODENDRUM, Verbenaceae. The two kinds hardy enough to be planted outdoors in the British Isles differ considerably in character, since one *Clerodendrum bungei*, is usually killed to ground level each winter but shoots up again from the roots in spring, whereas the other, *C. trichotomum*, makes a large, well-branched bush or small tree. Both need warm and sunny places and fairly fertile well-drained soil. They can be grown from seed, root cuttings and also from suckers dug up with roots in spring or autumn.

bungei   *1–2m. (3–6ft)   Purple*
L. Summer   E. Autumn   D   W   C   S   H   V

China. A semi-herbaceous shrub with stout stems, large, heart-shaped leaves that emit a rather unpleasant odour when bruised, and dome-shaped heads of small, closely packed red-purple, pleasantly scented flowers in late summer or autumn. It spreads widely by suckers, which may need to be dug out to prevent the plant spreading too far.

trichotomum   *3–5m. (10–16ft)*
White and purple   L. Summer   E. Autumn
D   T   S   H   R

Japan, China. Unlike *C. bungei* this species usually retains a permanent framework of branches though these are rather soft and may be weather-damaged in winter. The broad downy leaves have a similar unpleasant odour when bruised but the flowers, carried in loose clusters, are sweetly scented. The narrow petals are white, the backing sepals are purplish-red and the small berries that may follow them, especially in a warm autumn, are turquoise blue. Variety *fargesii* has smooth leaves and is said to fruit more freely.

CLETHRA, Clethraceae. Deciduous trees and shrubs all of which require lime-free soil. They grow best in soil that contains plenty of peat or leaf-mould to retain moisture in summer and yet prevent waterlogging in winter. Pruning is not essential but stems can be removed or shortened in February. Increase is by seeds in peat and sand in spring, late summer cuttings in a propagator or layering in spring or summer.

alnifolia   *2–2.5m. (6–8ft)   White*
L. Summer   D   T   S   L   H

Eastern North America. The alder-leaved clethra is probably the best shrubby species for general planting. It is hardy and has slender spikes of small urn-shaped sweetly scented white flowers. The best variety is 'Paniculata', in which the flowers are in finer sprays. Another variety, 'Rosea', has red buds opening to pink flowers.

tomentosa   *2–2.5m. (6–8ft)   White*
Autumn   D   T   S   L   H

South-eastern USA. A species much like *C. alnifolia* but flowering a few weeks later and with even finer white flower spikes.

CLIANTHUS, Leguminoseae. Parrot's Bill, Lobster Claw, Glory Pea. The popular names describe the unusual shape and exceptional beauty of the flowers of this rather tender evergreen climber. It is most suitable for planting outdoors in the mild coastal regions of the south and west but does survive for long periods against sunny walls and in sheltered patios. It likes reasonably good well-drained soils, may need some protection from cold in winter and from slugs and snails in spring and summer. It is rarely very long-lived and may need to be renewed every few years. Increase is by seed in spring, in a warm greenhouse or by summer cuttings in a propagator. Little pruning is required but winter-damaged growth should be removed in spring.

puniceus *3–4m. (10–13ft) Red or White E. Summer E W T S H*

New Zealand. A sprawling plant which needs to be tied to wires, trellis or other support. The scarlet flowers, like long claws, hang in clusters. There is a pure white variety named 'Albus' and the two look well planted together.

COLLETIA, Rhamnaceae. Extraordinary South American shrubs in which the work of leaves is done by green spines to which the tiny bell-shaped flowers are attached. They

Colletia cruciata

are curious rather than beautiful, but being intensely spiny they do make quite good living fences. All thrive in sunny places and well-drained soils. Any pruning necessary to keep plants shapely or within the space available may be done in spring or summer. Increase is by summer cuttings in a propagator.

armata *2.5–3m. (8–10ft) White Autumn Winter D K H*

Southern Chile. In this species the grey-green downy spines are awl-shaped and the flowers are pleasantly scented. Leaves, when present, are tiny.

cruciata *2.5–3m. (8–10ft) Whitish Autumn D K H*

Uruguay. This species has both awl-shaped and flat, triangular spines, the former mainly on young plants the latter on old plants. The tiny flowers are yellowish-white.

infausta *2.5–3m. (8–10ft) Brownish Spring E. Summer D K H*

Chile. A species with awl-like spines much like *C. armata* but without down.

COLUTEA, Leguminoseae. Bladder Senna. Deciduous shrubs with small pea-type flowers followed by remarkable inflated seed-pods like little bladders. Most come from hot, dry regions and in gardens they like sunny places and well-drained soils. Most can be grown from seed sown under glass in spring or from summer cuttings in a propagator. Pruning is not essential but surplus stems can be removed or shortened in spring.

arborescens *2.5–3m. (8–10ft) Yellow Summer D T S H*

South-Eastern Europe and Mediterranean region. A bushy shrub with compound leaves composed of small, rounded leaflets, small but abundant yellow flowers and parchment-coloured seed-pods which can be

8cm./3½in. long. A bush covered with them is distinctly decorative.

x media   *2.5–3m. (8–10ft)   Copper Summer   D T H*

A hybrid between *C. arborescens* and *C. orientalis* much like the former but with copper-coloured flowers.

orientalis   *1.5–2m. (5–6ft) Copper or Reddish   Summer   D T S H*

Caucasus. Not such a good plant as the other two but interesting for its grey foliage and coppery or bronzy-red flowers.

Convolvulus cneorum

CONVOLVULUS, Convolvulaceae. Most kinds are herbaceous plants, some of them pernicious weeds, but the species described below is a neat evergreen shrub of great beauty, well worth planting wherever there is a warm sunny position suitable for it. It is not fully hardy and is most likely to survive for years in well-drained places such as rock gardens and dry walls. As a rule it needs no pruning but it can be reduced in May. Increase is easy, by summer cuttings in a propagator.

cneorum   *0.6–1m. (2–3ft)   White and pink L. Spring   Summer   E W K H*

Southern Europe. This species makes a dense bush of narrow silvery leaves and has the typical widely funnel-shaped convolvulus flowers, pure white more or less tinged with pink. Though it always remains dwarf it can spread quite widely.

CORNUS, Cornaceae. Dogwood. A big genus of deciduous shrubs and trees many of which are easy to grow though a few are rather tender. Some are cultivated primarily for the bark colour on young stems, some for their coloured leaves and some for flowers, which though small are in certain kinds surrounded by large bracts that look like petals. With such a variety of species it is difficult to generalize about cultivation. Most succeed in all fertile soils and in reasonably light places. A few tender kinds need sun, warmth and good drainage but others will thrive in moist soil. One or two object to chalk or lime. Those grown for bark or foliage colour can be hard-pruned in March. Those grown for flower require little pruning but some stems can be removed or shortened after flowering. Many can be grown from summer or autumn cuttings, or from layers. A few can be grown from seed, if available, sown under glass in spring.

alba *2–3m. (6–10ft) Yellowish*
E. Summer D C H A L

Siberia. A thicket-forming shrub with red stems valuable for its garden varieties, of which the following are the best:

'Elegantissima'. Leaves greyish-green and white.
'Sibirica'. Young stems an extra bright red. This is sometimes called 'Westonbirt' or 'Atrosanguinea'.
'Spaethii'. Leaves almost entirely yellow.

alternifolia *3–6m. (10–20ft) Yellowish*
E. Summer D T H L

Eastern North America. Again it is a variety with variegated foliage that is worthy of garden space; 'Argentea' with oval leaves heavily margined with creamy-white. The branches are held horizontally giving this large shrub a distinctive shape. *Cornus controversa* 'Variegata' repeats this leaf colour and branch pattern but is a small tree.

florida *3–6m. (10–20ft) White or Pink*
L. Spring D O H S

Eastern USA. This lovely plant can be a large shrub or a small tree on a distinct trunk. It is open-branched and the beauty lies in the broad bracts that surround the tight clusters of tiny green flowers. These are either white or some shade of pink. Superior varieties have been selected and named, e.g. 'Apple Blossom', soft pink; 'Cherokee Chief', deep rose; 'Rubra', medium pink; and 'White Cloud', white.

kousa *3–6m. (10–20ft) White*
L. Spring E. Summer D O H S

Japan, China, Korea. A large rather horizontally-branched shrub, its stems wreathed in May–June with the large white 'flowers' that are really bracts. These become stained with red as they fade. A superior form, especially free-flowering, is named *chinensis*.

mas *3–6m (10–20ft) Yellow L. Winter*
E. Spring D T S L V H

Europe. This is the Cornelian Cherry so called because of its small red fruits which can be used to make syrup or preserve. It is a large, loosely-branched shrub or even a small tree under favourable conditions, producing clusters of small yellow flowers as early as February if the weather is mild. At that season its colour, though scarcely spectacular, is very welcome. There are also several varieties with coloured leaves though the naming of these is somewhat confused. 'Elegantissima', also called 'Tricolor', has leaves that may be entirely yellow, bordered with yellow or flushed with pink. 'Variegata' has leaves bordered with creamy white and some catalogues also list 'Aurea' as entirely yellow.

stolonifera *2–2.5m. (6–8ft) Whitish*
L. Spring E. Summer D C A L V

North America. Often known as the Red Osier Dogwood because its whippy, willow-like stems have dark red bark. It suckers freely, making an ever-widening thicket of growth which may need to be chopped back with a spade from time to time to keep it in bounds. Bark colour is most developed on young stems so this is a shrub that is improved by hard pruning each March. 'Flaviramea' is a good variety, with greenish-yellow stems.

COROKIA, Cornaceae. Evergreen New Zealand shrubs which are all a little tender, excellent for coastal gardens, especially of the south and west, and for warm, sheltered places inland but unreliable elsewhere. They thrive in all reasonably fertile and well-drained soils and are best left unpruned since it is easy to spoil their distinctive habit. Any thinning or reduction that is essential is best done immediately after flowering.

cotoneaster   *2–2.5m (6–8ft)   Yellow*
L. Spring   E   W   O   H   L

New Zealand. A very distinctive shrub
making quite a dense bush of thin but rigid
stems many of which are twisted like a
corkscrew. The star-shaped yellow flowers,
carried singly close to these stems, are too
small to make much display but they are
attractive. The little rounded leaves are dark
green and smooth above but covered with
grey down beneath.

CORONILLA, Leguminosae. Deciduous and
evergreen shrubs with small yellow pea-type
flowers produced in clusters over a long
season. The deciduous kinds are hardy, but
evergreen. *Coronilla glauca* is a little tender
and needs a warm sheltered place, or it may
be trained against a sunny wall. All like
well-drained soils. Little pruning is required.
Propagation is usually by late summer
cuttings in a propagator.

emeroides   *1.2–1.5m (4–5ft)   Yellow*
L. Spring   Summer   D   T   H   S

South-eastern Europe, Crete, Syria. The
feather-pattern leaves, each composed of
seven rounded leaflets, are attractive and the
flowers make a bright display for months.
Excellent for hot sunny banks and borders.

emerus   *2–2.5m. (6–8ft)   Yellow*
L. Spring   Summer   D   T   H   S

Central and Southern Europe. Much like *C.
emeroides* but a little taller and often with
nine leaflets per leaf. It is called the Scorpion
Senna because the slender seed pods curl up at
the tip like a scorpion's tail.

glauca   *2–3m. (6–10ft)   Yellow*
L. Spring   Summer   E   W   T   H   S

Southern Europe. The most attractive species
but also the least hardy. The little rounded
leaflets are grey-green, the yellow flowers very
bright and at their peak in spring, though in
favourable places more may be produced in

Coronilla glauca

autumn and winter. There is a variety with
heavily cream-variegated leaves named
'Variegata'.

CORREA, Rutaceae. Very attractive but
distinctly tender Australasian evergreens with
small narrowly bell-shaped flowers in late
winter and spring. They are for the mildest
gardens only as they will not survive much
frost but can be grown successfully in coastal
areas of the south-west and west. They like
warm sunny places and well-drained soils,
need little pruning and can be grown from
seed, if available, but are usually increased by
summer cuttings in a propagator. The naming
of this genus is rather confused.

backhousiana *2–2.5m (6–8ft)   Yellow*
L. Winter   Spring   E   W   O   H   S

Tasmania. One of the hardiest species. The
dangling funnel-shaped flowers are pale
greenish-yellow and the rounded leaves are
smooth and dark green above, but covered
with brown down beneath. It makes a
well-branched plant.

x harrisii *1–1.2m. (3–4ft)   Scarlet*
L. Winter   Spring   E   W   O   H

A hybrid between *Correa pulchella* and *C.
reflexa* with very attractive pendant light
scarlet flowers. The leaves are neat and
rounded. A really choice and unique shrub for
a specially sheltered corner.

pulchella *1m. (3ft)   Pink   Winter*
E   W   O   H   S

Australia. A charming little shrub with neat
green leaves and dangling pink flowers.

CORYLOPSIS, Hamamelidaceae. Though
these deciduous shrubs and small trees belong
to the witch hazel family one would scarcely
guess this from a superficial observation. The
small flowers are very pretty cup-shaped,
carried in clusters or catkin-like trails in early
spring on the bare branches before the leaves
unfold. They thrive in most reasonably fertile
soils though one species, *Corylopsis
pauciflora*, is said to dislike chalk or
limestone. Little pruning is required but stems
can be thinned or shortened after flowering.
Plants can be grown from seed if available but
layering and summer cuttings are more usual
methods of increase.

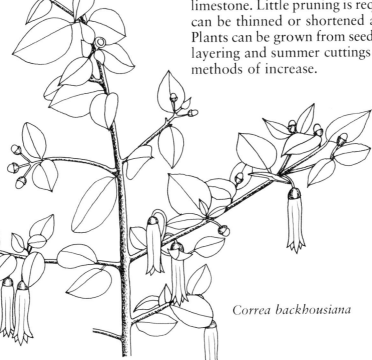

Correa backhousiana

pauciflora *1.2–4m. (4–5ft)   Primrose*
E. Spring   D O H L

Japan. A well-branched shrub with primrose yellow flowers in small clusters. Individually the flowers can be 2cm./1in across, quite large for a corylopsis. Young growth is apt to be damaged by spring frost.

sinensis *3–4m. (10–13ft)   Primrose*
E. Spring   D O H S

China. An open-branched shrub carrying its pale primrose, sweetly-scented flowers in trails up to 5cm./2in. long.

spicata *1.2–2m. (4–6ft)   Yellow*
E. Spring   D O H S

Japan. One of the most attractive species, with hazel-like stems bearing trails of up to a dozen small yellow, sweetly-scented flowers.

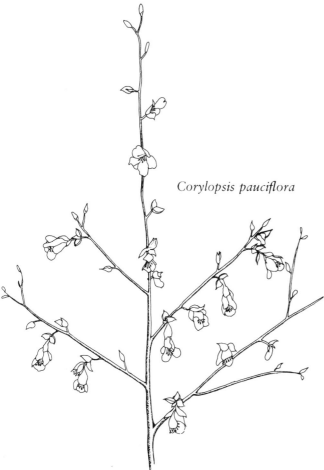

Corylopsis pauciflora

willmottiae *2–4m. (6–13ft)   Yellow*
E. Spring   D O H S

China. A species much like C. *spicata* but with larger trails of soft yellow, scented flowers. So free-flowering is it that it was once mistakenly named C. *multiflora*.

CORYLUS, Corylaceae. Hazel, Filbert. Though the hazels are mainly grown for their edible nuts several kinds have decorative foliage and most can be used for shelter and various ornamental purposes. Nut groves under-planted with bulbs or small perennials have been admired features of many gardens. All enjoy good soil not liable to dry out severely in summer. All can be thinned or cut back in winter or spring, the best time when nuts are required being immediately the female flowers can be seen. These are small and held close to the stems in contrast to the male flowers, which hang in conspicuous catkins. When pruning for nuts, as many female flowers as possible should be retained since these are the ones that produce nuts when fertilized with pollen from the male catkins. In winter whole branches can be removed if necessary to keep the bushes open and well-balanced. Increase is by layering at any time or digging up rooted suckers in autumn or winter.

avellana *3–5m. (10–16ft)   Yellowish*
L. Winter   E. Spring   D T L V

Europe (including Britain). This is common hazel or cobnut. Numerous varieties have been selected for their nut-producing qualities. Ornamental varieties are: 'Contorta', with extraordinary spiralling stems; 'Aurea', with yellowish leaves; 'Fusco-rubra', with purple leaves (it may appear in lists as 'Purpurea'); and 'Pendula', with pendulous branches. If a main stem of 'Pendula' is first trained up straight and then permitted to branch it will form a small weeping tree.

maximia *3–6m. (10–20ft)* *Yellowish L. Winter E. Spring D T L V*

Southern Europe. This is the filbert, the nuts of which are enveloped in a much larger husk than that surrounding the cobnuts. It is also more vigorous and has slightly larger leaves. It has a valuable ornamental variety named 'Purpurea' with very dark purple leaves and purple catkins.

COTINUS, Anacardiaceae. Deciduous shrubs with the peculiarity that their insignificant flowers are borne among silken filaments which in one species are so numerous that they constitute one of its most decorative features. All kinds succeed in sunny open places and not over-rich but well-drained soils. Pruning is not essential but stems can be removed or shortened in late winter or early spring. Plants can be raised from seed but garden varieties are increased by layering at any time or by late summer or autumn cuttings in a propagator.

coggygria *2–4m. (6–12 ft)* *Yellowish Summer D T S L A H*

Central and southern Europe. This is the fine shrub that for generations was known as *Rhus cotinus* and has acquired the popular names Venetian Sumach, Smoke Tree and Wig Tree. The last two refer to the extraordinary inflorescences and seeding bodies enveloped in billowy masses of filaments, which may be grey, pink or purple. For many weeks in summer and autumn they are highly decorative. Bushes branch widely, often rooting as they spread, and the rounded leaves colour brilliantly before they fall in autumn. There are several garden varieties; including 'Notcutt's Variety' and 'Royal Purple', both with dark red-purple leaves but not so effective in flower and seed; 'Flame', specially good for autumn leaf colour; 'Foliis Purpureis', with young leaves purple and inflorescences pink; and *purpureus*, with green leaves and pink or purplish filaments.

obovatus *3–4m. (10–13ft)* *Yellowish E. Summer D T S L A H*

Southern USA. Far inferior to *C. coggygria* in inflorescences but even more brilliant in autumn leaf colour of copper, scarlet and crimson. It has been known as *C. americanus* and also as *Rhus cotinoides*, names still sometimes used.

COTONEASTER, Rosaceae. This great genus has contributed marvellously to the beauty of gardens. It is widely spread in Europe and Asia, where it has produced a great diversity of species, both deciduous and evergreen, and to these must be added hybrids both natural and man-made. In stature the range is from ground-hugging plants to small trees, leaves vary from tiny to quite large, most produce fine crops of berries and many are also highly attractive in flower. All are easy to grow in a wide variety of soils from moderately acid to alkaline, heavy medium or light. They are happiest in good light but will grow in shade. Pruning is unnecessary but if plants grow too large they can be reduced, the evergreens preferably in May, the deciduous kinds in March. A few can even be grown as hedges and clipped in summer. Species can be grown from seed sown as soon as ripe or in spring outdoors or in pots. Germination of some kinds may be improved if seeds are kept moist for three or four months at a temperature of 20–25°C/68–75°F, then for three months at 4°C/39°F. Some kinds produce self-sown seedlings freely, sometimes in places in which it would be difficult to plant but the seedlings are nevertheless welcome. All can be grown from late summer cuttings in a propagator and this is the best way to increase garden varieties and hybrids. The one snag is the bacterial disease, fireblight, which causes stems and sometimes whole plants to wither and die quite suddenly. Because this disease also attacks fruit trees and could constitute a considerable hazard to commercial fruit production it is notifiable to the local Plant Health Inspector. Affected plants should be grubbed out and burnt.

adpressus   *30cm. (1ft)   White and Pink
E. Summer   D T S H*

China. A prostrate shrub with small oval leaves, solitary, stem-hugging flowers followed by bright red berries. First class for rock gardens and ground cover.

buxifolius   *60cm. (2ft)   White   E. Summer
E O S H*

India. A densely branched small-leaved evergreen with red berries. It is small enough for rock gardens.

congestus   *45–60cm. (1½–2ft)   Pink
E. Summer   E O S H*

Himalaya. This species forms dense mounds of short stiff decurving stems. The flowers are palest pink the berries bright red. Excellent for rock gardens.

conspicuus   *1–2.5m. (3–8ft)   White
L. Spring   E O S H*

Tibet. A splendid shrub, making a dome-shaped bush with small leaves and bright red berries, which appear to be distasteful to birds so usually remain throughout the winter. It is variable in size, one of the most compact forms, about 1m./3ft high but up to 2m./6ft in diameter, having received a First Class Certificate and an Award of Merit from the Royal Horticultural Society under the name 'Decorus'.

dammeri   *Prostrate   White
L. Spring   E. Summer   E O S H L*

China. A ground-hugging evergreen with leaves up to 4cm./2in. long, white flowers and bright red berries. An ideal shrub for banks or for use as ground cover in sunny or partially shady places.

dielsianus   *2m. (6ft)   Pink   E. Summer
D T S H*

China. An elegant shrub with long slender stems, medium size oval leaves and small clusters of palest pink flowers followed by bright red berries. From a decorative standpoint it may be compared with *C. franchetii* and *C. pannosus*, but these are evergreen, not deciduous. A variety named 'Elegans' has slightly smaller leaves, some of which may be retained in mild winters.

franchetii   *2.5m.–3m. (8–10ft)   White
L. Spring   E O S H*

Tibet, China. Another very elegant shrub with oval, pointed leaves, dark green above but with white or brown felt beneath. The flowers and scarlet berries are carried in good clusters on stems that arch outwards. A variety named 'Sternianus' differs in having more globular

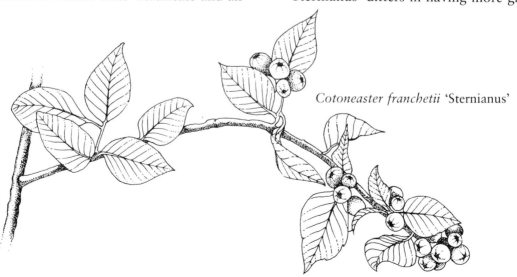

Cotoneaster franchetii 'Sternianus'

berries and thinner leaves, which often colour brilliantly in the autumn, making it one of the most handsome cotoneasters at that season. This form is often listed as C. *wardii* but that name belongs to another species not ordinarily seen in gardens.

frigidus   *4–6m. (13–20ft)   White E. Summer.   D T S H*

Himalaya. This is not only one of the largest and most handsome species but it is also a prolific parent of hybrids, often spontaneous, with other species such as C. *henryanus* and *salicifolius* so that, if grown from seed, it is sometimes difficult to decide whether the seedlings are pure or hybrid. Typical C. *frigidus* has stout, erect but well-branched stems, rather long oval leaves, white flowers carried in flat trusses and quite large red berries. It can be pruned as a tree with a single trunk and a head of branches or it can be allowed to grow naturally, in which case it will require a lot of room. There is a variety named *fructu-luteo*, with pale yellow fruits. Among the many hybrids related to C. *frigidus* the following are specially good:

'Cornubia'. Presumed to be a hybrid between C. *frigidus* and C. *salicifolius* since it exhibits characteristics of both. The stems are more slender and arching than those of C. *frigidus*. It makes a very large bush, is semi-evergreen and berries prodigiously.
'Exburiensis' and **'Rothschildianus'.** Two very similar shrubs with long arching stems and yellow berries. Both are evergreen.
'John Waterer'. A selected form of a group of hybrids collectively known as *Cotoneaster* x *watereri*. It is more or less evergreen and has clusters of scarlet berries.

henryanus   *3–3.5m. (10–12ft)   White E. Summer   E O S H*

China. An attractive shrub of open habit with broadly lance-shaped leaves, green above but grey, becoming tawny with age, below. The flowers are produced in good clusters and are

Cotoneaster frigidus

followed by deep crimson berries. It is easily confused with C. *salicifolius* but has larger leaves. From a decorative standpoint there is little to choose between them.

horizontalis   *0.6–1m. (2–3ft) White and pink   L. Spring   D T S H*

China. This is the species known as the Fishbone or Herringbone Cotoneaster because of the highly distinctive horizontal branch pattern. Grown in the open it makes a very wide but low bush but planted against a wall or fence it grows upwards for at least 2m./6ft spreading itself almost flat and requiring little or no support. The leaves are small and rounded, green in summer but turning yellow, copper, scarlet and crimson before they fall in autumn. The white, pink-flushed flowers, produced singly close to the branches, are always favourites with bees and are followed by good crops of bright red berries. There is a very attractive variety with white-edged leaves named 'Variegatus'.

lacteus   *2.5–3m. (8–10ft)   White Summer   E O S H*

China. Another species much like *C. henryanus* and *C. salicifolius* but with broader leaves than either and berries that ripen late, and so are likely to be left alone by birds until the others have been stripped.

microphyllus   *0.6–1m. (2–3ft)   White E. Summer   E O S H*

Himalaya and China. A shrub with rigid branches which are nevertheless able to mould themselves to boulders, walls etc. The small narrow leaves are very dark green and glossy, the flowers are held close to the stems and the berries are deep red. It is an ideal plant for banks, low walls, terraces and large rock gardens but it needs room since it can spread widely. There are several varieties including *cochleatus* and *thymifolius*, both of which are smaller and more prostrate.

pannosus   *2.5–3m. (8–10ft)   White E. Summer   E O S H*

China. Much like *C. franchetii* but the leaves are shorter, the flower clusters larger and the berries crimson.

prostratus   *1–1.5m. (3–5ft)   White E. Summer   E O S H*

Himalaya. Close to *C. microphyllus* but usually taller and with broader leaves. It is also listed as *C. rotundifolius*.

salicifolius   *3–4m. (10–13ft)   White E. Summer   ED O S H*

China. A loosely branched and elegant semi-evergreen shrub with rather narrow leaves up to 8cm./3in. long, flowers carried in downy clusters and bright red berries. Botanists recognize two distinct natural varieties; *floccosus*, with smaller, more glossy leaves and wand-like branches, and *rugosus*, a robust form with larger leaves and berries. In addition numerous varieties have been selected in gardens, several of them, such as 'Herbstfeur' ('Autumn Fire'), 'Parkteppich' and 'Repens' either prostrate or pendulous and one, named 'Fructuluteo' with yellow berries.

simonsii   *2.5–4m. (8–13ft)   White E. Summer   ED T K S H*

Assam. This species has a fairly stiff erect habit and makes quite a good hedge, especially in combination with something else. In mild winters it may retain many of its fairly small rounded leaves. The berries are scarlet.

CRINODENDRON, Elaeocarpaceae.

Evergreen shrubs from Chile notable for their highly distinctive crimson or white flowers, urn-shaped and carried in hanging clusters. They make rather narrowly erect shrubs or even small trees under the favourable mild and moist conditions of coastal gardens in the west and south west but are not sufficiently hardy for the coldest gardens. All require lime-free soil. Little pruning is necessary but dead or damaged stems should be removed in spring, and a little further thinning can be carried out then if necessary. Increase is by summer cuttings in a propagator.

hookerianum   *3–6m. (10–20ft)   Crimson L. Spring   E W T H*

Chile. The most popular species, and one which grows so freely in west coast gardens that it is sometimes planted as a windbreak.

Inland it may require the protection of a wall, preferably one that is warm without being too sunny and dry. A westerly aspect is ideal.

patagua *3–6m. (10–20ft) White L. Summer E W T H*

Chile. Faster growing than C. *hookerianum* but not so spectacular because its flowers are white. Nevertheless this is a useful and unusual addition to late summer flowering shrubs. Should be trained against a wall except in the mildest places.

Crinodendrum hookerianum

CYTISUS, Leguminosae. Broom. This large genus of pea-flowered shrubs covers a wide range of forms and colours. All enjoy warm sunny positions and well-drained slightly acid or neutral soils. Pruning differs according to species. All brooms can be grown from seed sown in spring outdoors or under glass, but hybrid varieties may vary when grown in this way and so are usually increased by late summer cuttings, taken with a heel of older wood and inserted in sandy soil in a frame or propagator. Nurserymen usually graft on to seedlings in spring.

ardoinii *12–15cm. (5–6in.) Yellow Spring D F S H*

Maritime Alps. A delightful almost prostrate shrub suitable for rock garden planting, the front of a border or a sunny bank or terrace wall. Though the small, three-parted leaves fall in autumn the green stems give an evergreen effect.

battandieri *4–6m. (13–20ft) Yellow E. Summer D F S H*

Morocco. Despite its African habitat this beautiful shrub has proved completely hardy in the British Isles. It makes long, flexible but sturdy stems with quite large, three-parted leaves and yellow flowers closely packed in short spikes. They are quite strongly pineapple-scented. This highly distinctive broom can be grown as a large loosely-branched bush in the open or it can be trained against a sunny wall. Surplus growth can be removed in spring or immediately after flowering.

x beanii *15–45cm. (6–18in.) Yellow L. Spring D F H*

A hybrid which appeared by chance in the Royal Botanic Gardens, Kew and is believed to be the offspring of *Cytisus ardoinii* and C. *purgans*. It makes a neat bush suitable for a rock garden or terrace wall and as a rule requires little or no pruning.

x **burkwoodii** *2.5–3m. (8–10ft)*
Cerise and Crimson
L. Spring E. Summer D F H

This fine hybrid of uncertain parentage is
unusual in colour and vigorous in habit.
When pruning after flowering be careful not
to cut back into old wood.

x **dallimorei** *2.5–3m. (8–10ft)*
Pink and Crimson L. Spring E. Summer
D F H

A hybrid between *Cytisus* 'Andreanus' and *C.
multiflorus* with numerous small flowers in
various shades of pink. It is exceptionally
beautiful and has numerous forms or
sub-hybrids, such as 'Burkwoodii', cerise and
maroon; 'Donard Seedling', mauve-pink and
red; 'Dorothy Walpole', cerise and crimson;
and 'Johnson's Crimson', crimson.

x **kewensis** *20–30cm. (8–12in)*
Pale yellow
L. Spring D F H

Another of the fine hybrids raised at Kew
between *Cytisus ardoinii* and *C. multiflorus*.
It makes a wide but low shuttlecock of
growth and is a first-class rock garden or
terrace shrub.

monspessulanus *2–2.5m. (6–8ft) Yellow*
Spring ED W F S H

Southern Europe. This highly decorative
shrub, popularly known as the Montpelier
Broom, resembles the 'Florists' Genista',
C x spachianus. The flowers are produced
in small but highly decorative clusters. It is
not fully hardy nor as a rule very long-lived
but it usually produces seed freely so it is
a good idea to save some as soon as it is ripe.
The best time for sowing is in early spring,
preferably in a greenhouse.

multiflorus *2.5–3m. (8–10ft) White*
L. Spring D F S H

Spain and Portugal. A tall shrub with slender,
whippy stems bending in May beneath the
load of small but very numerous white
flowers. It is often called the White Spanish
Broom and was formerly known as *C. albus*.

Cytisus battandieri

nigricans   *1–1.5m. (3–5ft)   Yellow Summer   D T S H*

Europe. This species starts into growth late, does not commence to flower until July and can continue well into August. The small bright yellow flowers are carried in short slender spikes. This species is unusual in flowering on the current year's growth so that most pruning is best done in spring, when stems can be thinned or shortened but not cut back into hard old wood. It is wise to remove faded flowers unless seeds are required for propagation.

x 'Porlock'   *2.5–3m. (8–10ft)   Yellow Spring   ED W F H*

This fine hybrid betwwen *Cytisus monspessulanus* and *C.* x *spachianus* combines the good qualities of both including much of the sweet scent of *C.* x *spachianus*. It needs a warm sunny sheltered spot and should be pruned like *C. monspessulanus*.

x praecox   *1.2–2.5m. (4–8ft)   Sulphur Spring   D F H S*

This name is given to a group of hybrids between *Cytisus purgans* and *C. multiflorus* which differ quite a lot in habit, some being quite small and compact others much taller, though usually dense in growth. The sulphur yellow flowers have a heavy odour which is unpleasant indoors but not unacceptable in the garden. Plants can be raised from seed but the seedlings are likely to vary both from their parents and from one another. Some good forms have been given distinguishing names and are propagated vegetatively. 'Allgold' has yellow flowers; 'Gold Spear' is compact in habit and 'Albus' is white. Collectively these hybrids are known as the 'Warminster Broom', the original cross having been made in the nineteenth century by a nurseryman in Warminster.

purgans   *1m. (3ft)   Yellow   Spring D F S H*

France and Spain. A good short-stemmed broom with deep yellow flowers. It needs warmth and sun and is not very common in gardens. It deserves to be more widely planted.

purpureus   *30–45cm. (1–1½ft)   Purple L. Spring   D F S V*

Central and south-eastern Europe. A sprawling plant spreading at least in part by underground stems and so making dense ground cover. The flowers vary in colour from a rather ineffective purplish-lilac or pink to quite rich purple, so it is wise to select plants when in bloom.

scoparius   *2–3m. (6–10ft)   Yellow L. Spring   D F S H*

Western Europe (including the British Isles). This very showy shrub is the 'Common Broom' found mainly on sandy, lime-free soils. However, in gardens it has a much wider soil tolerance and is usually easy to grow, often spreading rapidly by self-sown seeds. It is also variable in gardens and hybridizes with some other brooms, so that there are a great many named garden forms connected with it. These include 'Andreanus' and 'Firefly', both yellow stained with crimson; 'Cornish Cream', cream; 'Pendulus', which makes a weeping standard if grafted onto a straight stem of the common type; *prostratus*, found wild in Cornwall and the Channel Islands, and almost completely prostrate and rock-hugging; and 'Golden Sunlight', deep yellow.

sessilifolius   *2m. (6ft)   Yellow   E. Summer D F S H*

Europe and North Africa. This is a fine yellow-flowered species to continue the display after *Cytisus scoparius* and its allies have finished. The flowers are carried in short spikes.

x **spachianus**   *3–6m. (10–20ft)   Yellow Spring   E W F S H*

This appears to be the latest name given by botanists to the lovely sweet-scented evergreen which gardeners know as the 'Florists' Genista' and which has at various times been called *Genista fragrans* and *Cytisus racemosus*. It is now said to be a hybrid between *C. stenopetalus* and *C. canariensis*. Whatever the truth of these botanical opinions this is one of the truly great evergreen shrubs for mild gardens, particularly near the coast in the south and south west where light is good, there is plenty of warmth and not a great deal of frost. Under such conditions *C.* x *spachianus* becomes a welcome weed, spreading rapidly by self-sown seedlings which, despite their supposedly hybrid origin, differ little from one another, except occasionally in the precise shade of their yellow, very sweetly scented flowers.

supranubius   *2–2.5m. (6–8ft)   Rose and white   L. Spring   D W F S H*

Canary Isles. A slightly gaunt shrub with stiff stems, small three-parted leaves and little clusters of small but attractive rose and white pea-type flowers. It is often known as *Spartocytisus nubigenus*.

DABOECIA, Ericaceae. St Dabeoc's Heath. This small genus of two species has close affinity with the bell heathers and has much the same decorative merit in gardens, but the urn-shaped, nodding flowers are carried in rather loose one-sided spikes so that the effect is less solid than that of some other heathers. Cultivation is identical with that of the hardy species of *Erica*.

cantabrica   *40–60cm. (16–24in.)   Purple Summer   Autumn   E K H S L*

Western Europe including Ireland. This is the more popular of the two species, the other being the shorter less hardy *D. azorica* from

Cytisus x *spachianus*

the Azores. The flowers of *D. cantabrica* are magenta purple but there are hybrids between it and *D. azorica* which have retained some of the purer red of that species. In gardens *D. cantabrica* is frequently known as *D. polifolia*.

DANAE, Liliaceae. Alexandrian Laurel. There is only one species, an elegant small foliage shrub useful for its ability to thrive in shady places. The flowers are small, yellowish-green and of no beauty but they are followed by currant-red berries. A botanical peculiarity is that there are no true leaves, their function being performed by flattened, leaf-like branches technically known as phylloclades.

racemosa *0.6–1m. (2–3ft) Green*
Summer E C S V

Asia Minor. The 'leaves' are narrow and pointed and the numerous stems come straight from the roots, then branching into two. This suckering habit enables a plant to spread indefinitely and makes it easy to lift and divide in autumn and spring. *D. racemosa* prefers not to be exposed to strong sunshine and grows best in rather fertile soils that do not dry out badly in summer.

DAPHNE, Thymeliaceae. These are mostly small evergreen or deciduous shrubs usually with richly scented flowers. Some are easy to grow but many are a little difficult, fussy about soil and requiring good drainage which nevertheless does not deprive them of moisture in the summer. Plenty of humus, as leaf-mould or peat, mixed with the soil can provide at least part of the solution. Most seem to thrive best in neutral or slightly acid soil but *D. mezereum* grows well on chalk or limestone. All transplant badly and should be planted young or from containers. They are best left unpruned. Most can be increased by summer cuttings and some by layering in spring or early autumn.

bholua *1–2m. (3–6ft) Purple Winter*
D E H S

Himalaya. This very beautiful and richly scented winter flowering shrub exists in two forms, one deciduous the other semi-evergreen. It may well be that the deciduous form, especially if from plants collected at high altitude, is the more suitable for British gardens. Colour varies greatly from a rather wishy-washy purple to quite a rich shade.

blagayana *15–30cm. (6–12in.) Ivory*
Spring E H L S

South-eastern Europe. This lovely sprawling shrub is ideal for the rock garden. The clusters of creamy-white flowers are very sweetly scented. Reginald Farrer's advice was that it should be grown in 'a rough soil of stones and peat and loam', and added, 'and then . . . stoned with stones until (it) – does not die – but lives the more gloriously'.

x burkwoodii *1–1.2m. (3–4ft) Pink*
L. Spring ED H

A fine hybrid between *Daphne caucasica* and *D. cneorum*, which makes a neat well-branched bush smothered in clusters of small pink, sweetly scented flowers. There is a variety named 'Somerset' which does not differ significantly in garden merit.

caucasica *1–2m. (3–6ft) White*
L. Spring E. Summer D H S

Caucasus. Not one of the best species for garden planting but interesting as one of the parents of *D x burkwoodii*.

cneorum *20–30cm. (8–12in.) Rose pink*
L. Spring E H L S

Europe. One of the most beautiful species, a dwarf spreading shrub smothered in rose-pink sweetly-scented flowers in May. In some gardens it grows freely, in others it proves temperamental and short-lived. It is one of the few daphnes which actually seems to prefer chalk or limestone soils, but with plenty of humus added to hold moisture in summer without impairing drainage in winter. It is sometimes called the 'Garland Flower'.

collina *60–90cm. (2–3ft) Purple*
L. Spring E H S

Mediterranean region. A delightful compact bush with neat evergreen leaves and richly scented purple flowers. There is a dwarfer form named 'Neapolitana' which also has a more extended flowering season. Some authorities believe that this is a hybrid between *Daphne collina* and *D. cneorum* in which case its name should be *D. x neapolitana*.

genkwa   *1m. (3ft)   Lilac   Spring   D H S*

China. A lovely shrub with flowers produced on the bare stems before the leaves appear in spring. In gardens it is often temperamental and short-lived and is probably best in moderately acid soil.

laureola   *0.6–1m. (2–3ft)   Green L. Winter   Spring   E S H*

Europe (including Britain) North Africa. This is our native Spurge Laurel, a leafy plant with yellowish-green flowers which commence to open in late winter. It is by no means spectacular but useful as ground cover in woodlands especially on soils overlying chalk or limestone.

mezereum   *1–1.5m. (3–5ft)   Purple L. Winter   E. Spring   D S H*

Europe, including Britain and Siberia. This is the Mezereon, which makes a number of erect stems bearing almost stemless, purple richly-scented flowers before the leaves appear. There is also a white flowered variety named *alba*. In both the flowers are followed by red berries and when these ripen and fall off in autumn self-sown seedlings often appear in succeeding years. It is wise to keep some of these since *D. mezereum* is rarely long-lived and has a disconcerting habit of dying suddenly and unexpectedly for no obvious cause.

odora   *1–2m. (3–6ft)   Purple Winter   Spring   E W H L*

China. Though this fine shrub never makes a spectacular display it is nevertheless one of the most desirable of small evergreens both for its shining green lance-shaped leaves and its richly-scented flowers, which start to open in mid-winter. It is not fully hardy but succeeds in all reasonably sheltered places. There is a variety named 'Aureo-marginata', with yellow-edged leaves, which is distinctly hardier than the green-leaved type and which

I have never seen damaged by frost. There is also a variety named 'Alba' with white flowers.

pontica   *1–2m. (3–6ft)   Yellowish   Green Spring   E H S*

Asia Minor. Like *Daphne laureola* this evergreen species is unspectacular, but will grow in semi-shade and is useful in wild or woodland gardens.

retusa   *60cm. (2ft)   White and   purple L. Spring   E. Summer   E H S*

China and Himalaya. A compact densely-branched shrub with scented flowers that are purple outside and white within. It is fully hardy and not difficult.

Daphne odora 'Aureo-marginata'

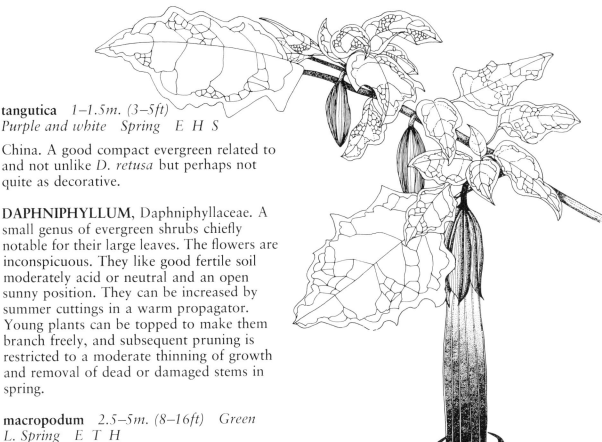

tangutica *1–1.5m. (3–5ft)*
Purple and white   Spring   E H S

China. A good compact evergreen related to
and not unlike *D. retusa* but perhaps not
quite as decorative.

DAPHNIPHYLLUM, Daphniphyllaceae. A
small genus of evergreen shrubs chiefly
notable for their large leaves. The flowers are
inconspicuous. They like good fertile soil
moderately acid or neutral and an open
sunny position. They can be increased by
summer cuttings in a warm propagator.
Young plants can be topped to make them
branch freely, and subsequent pruning is
restricted to a moderate thinning of growth
and removal of dead or damaged stems in
spring.

macropodum   *2.5–5m. (8–16ft)   Green
L. Spring   E T H*

Japan. The most popular species and a really
good foliage plant but the flowers have a
rather unpleasant smell.

DATURA, Solanaceae. Soft-stemmed shrubs
mostly far too tender to be grown outdoors in
the British Isles but one species will survive in
some coastal areas of the south-west and west.
It likes fertile well-drained soil and a warm
sunny position. It can be pruned in early
spring, when dead and damaged growth
should be removed and other stems shortened
according to the space available. Increase is
by summer cuttings in a propagator.

sanguinea   *2–3m. (6–10ft)*
Orange-red, buff and green   Summer
D W T H

Peru. A fast-growing, open-branched shrub
that in favourable circumstances can attain

Datura sanguinea

the proportions of a small tree. The pendant
flowers are long and tubular, greenish or
parchment-coloured in the upper part but
becoming orange-red towards the mouth. It
will withstand a few degrees of frost but even
when killed almost to ground level may shoot
up strongly from the base.

DECAISNEA, Lardizabalaceae. Deciduous
shrubs the most popular of which, *D. fargesii*,
is grown primarily for its extraordinary
sausage-shaped, slatey-blue fruits, which
hang in clusters. It is also quite a handsome
foliage shrub. It needs good fertile soil, not

liable to dry out badly in winter, and will grow in full sun or semi-shade. Regular pruning is unnecessary but old or unwanted stems can be removed in spring. Increase is by seed sown in a greenhouse in spring.

fargesii   *2.5–3m. (8–10ft)*
Yellowish-green   E. Summer   D T S

China. The leaves are compound, up to 1m./3ft long, with as many as a dozen quite large leaflets, the small flowers yellowish-green and the fruits as described above. It makes a loosely branched shrub.

DENDROMECON, Papaveraceae. Tree Poppy. This is one of the few shrubby members of the poppy family. There are two species, both Californian and rather tender but suitable for mild maritime gardens and for training against sunny walls in some not too cold inland gardens. Soil needs to be reasonably well-drained. The only pruning necessary is to cut out dead, damaged, old or weak growth in spring. Propagation is by firm shoots in late summer in a propagator.

rigida   *2–3m. (6–10ft)   Yellow*
Summer   E W T H

California. This is the most frequently planted species, an attractive plant with erect semi-woody stems, milky green leaves and golden scented poppy-like flowers.

DESFONTAINIA, Potaliaceae. Evergreen South American shrub suitable for the mild, rather humid gardens of the west and south-west coastal regions of the British Isles. It is not very fussy about soil but succeeds best where it is moderately acid and contains plenty of humus. Dead or damaged growth should be removed in spring and at the same time stems can be shortened a little if desired. Increase is by summer cuttings in a propagator.

spinosa   *2–3m. (6–10ft)*
Red and yellow   L. Summer   Autumn
E   W   K   H

Andes. The leaves of this well-branched shrub so closely resemble those of a holly that even experts can be fooled until the bush produces its narrowly funnel-shaped yellow and scarlet flowers.

DESMODIUM, Leguminosae. Tick-trefoil. A fairly large genus of shrubs and herbaceous plants of which only a few have much garden value. Like so many members of the pea family they like warm sunny places and well-drained soil. Stems can be cut almost to soil level each spring.

tiliifolium   *1m. (3ft)   Pink or Lilac*
L. Summer   Autumn   D W C S V

Himalaya. The stems are only half woody and usually die back a lot in winter. The small flowers, which may be any shade from pale lilac to quite a deep rose-pink, are carried in large sprays which are followed by pods of seeds. These provide the best means of increase if sown in spring in a frame or greenhouse.

DEUTZIA, Philadelphaceae. This is a big genus of Asiatic shrubs all of which are deciduous and many highly decorative. All will grow in any reasonably fertile soil and an open preferably sunny place. Plants make a lot of growth direct from the base and benefit from fairly severe thinning and shortening as soon as the flowers fade. Increase is by summer cuttings in a propagator or autumn cuttings in a frame.

discolor   *2m. (6ft)   White or Pink*
E. Summer   D   F   H   A

China. A good shrub with clusters of white or pink-tinted flowers.

x elegantissima   *1.2–1.5m. (4–5ft)*
Pink   E. Summer   D F H A

A hybrid, probably between *Deutzia purpurascens* and *D. sieboldiana*. It is variable in character and some forms have been selected and named. Specially recommended are 'Fasciculata' and 'Rosalind', both with rose-pink flowers.

gracilis   *1.5–2m. (5–6ft)   White*
L. Spring   E. Summer   D F H A

Japan. Commercial pot-plant growers use this species for forcing into early flower. It is quite satisfactory out of doors and the flowers, borne in erect sprays, make a fine display.

x hybrida   *1.2–2m. (4–6ft)*
White to Purple   E. Summer   D F H A

The name given to a group of hybrids of uncertain origin but probably between *Deutzia longifolia* and either *D. purpurascens* or *D.* x *elegantissima*. All have fair size flowers in good clusters. Typical named varieties belonging here are 'Contraste', lilac and purple, petals rather narrow; 'Jaconde', white and purple; 'Magician', pink, purple and white; 'Mount Rose', rose-pink, and 'Perle Rose', pink, rather smaller-flowered than the others but very prolific.

x lemoinei   *2–2.5m. (6–8ft)   White*
L. Spring   E. Summer   D F H A

A group of hybrids between *Deutzia gracilis* and *D. parviflora*, with good sprays of white flowers. Named varieties are 'Avalanche', white and scented, and 'Boule de Niege', shorter and more compact in growth.

longifolia   *1.2–2m. (4–6ft)*
Purplish rose or White   E. Summer
D F H A

China. One of the finest species in flower. The leaves are rather narrowly lance-shaped, the flowers of good size freely produced, varying in colour from white to quite a deep purplish-rose. The best form, named 'Veitchii' received the Award of Garden Merit in 1969.

x magnifica   *2m. (6ft)   White   Summer*
D F H A

Another group of hybrids, this time between *Deutzia scabra* and *D. vilmoriniae*. The flowers may be single or double but are always produced in dense clusters. Good named varieties are 'Eburnea', single white; 'Latiflora' single, white, extra large flowers; 'Longipetala', single, white, with long petals, and 'Magnifica' itself, double, white.

Deutzia purpurascens

x **maliflora**   *1.2–2m. (4–6ft)   Pink to White*
E. Summer   D F H A

Hybrids between *D* x *lemoinei* and *D. purpurascens*, of which the best form is 'Fleur de Pommier'. It has large clusters of frilled flowers which open pink but fade to white.

purpurascens   *2m. (6ft)   White and purple*
E. Summer   D F H A

China. From a garden standpoint this is very close to *Deutzia discolor* and has similar clusters of white flowers flushed with purple outside.

scabra   *2–3m. (6–10ft)   White or Pink*
E. Summer   D F H A

Japan and China. One of the most frequently planted species and a very handsome and vigorous shrub. It has numerous named forms such as 'Candidissima', white, double flowers; 'Flore Pleno' (sometimes written 'Plena'), double, white flushed with purple; 'Pride of Rochester', double, white flushed with pale purple; and 'Watereri', single, white flushed with pink, extra large flowers.

setchuenensis   *1.2–2m. (4–6ft)   White*
Summer   D F H A

China. A very distinctive species with slender but wiry stems bearing flat clusters of white flowers for many weeks in summer. This description is really of the variety of the species named 'Corymbiflora' which is superior to the type and appears to be the kind principally cultivated in Britain.

DIPELTA, Caprifoliaceae. Shrubs so closely allied to *Weigela* that most gardeners would probably mistake them for members of that genus. Cultural requirements are identical.

floribunda   *3–4m. (10–13ft)   Pale pink*
L. Spring   E. Summer   D F H A

China. The species most commonly grown. The flowers are bell-shaped, pale pink with

some yellow inside and scented. Stems are long and flexible and rather loosely branched.

DISANTHUS, Hamamelidaceae. There is only one species and this requires moderately acid, lime-free soil, plenty of humus and the shelter of thin woodland or something else that will give broken light – in fact very much the conditions that suit many rhododendrons. It requires little pruning but stems can be thinned or shortened in spring. Increase is by seed or by layering in spring.

cercidifolius   *2.5–3m. (8–10ft)   Purple*
Autumn   D T S L

Japan. The name refers to the heart-shaped leaves similar to those of the Judas Tree (*cercis*). It is for these, and in particular for their vivid autumn colour, that this shrub is mainly grown, for the narrow-petalled flowers are not very conspicuous.

DRIMYS, Winteraceae. Only two species are commonly grown in British gardens and one of these, *Drimys winteri*, is usually a tree, though some slow-growing and relatively dwarf bushy varieties are available. The truly shrubby species, *D. lanceolata*, generally appears to be hardier, though here again there are differences according to the locality from which the original stock was collected. It will grow in all reasonably well-drained and fertile soils in warm and sunny places. Little pruning is required but plants can be shaped and thinned in early summer after flowering. Increase is by summer cuttings in a warm propagator, by layering in spring or by seed.

lanceolata   *2.5–4m. (8–13ft)*
White and Buff   L. Spring   E K H L S

Tasmania. The beauty of this densely branched shrub is largely in the contrast between the red colouring of stems, buds and leaf-stalks and the dark green of the narrow leaves. The small spidery flowers, which are of two sexes, may be followed by clusters of small blackberry-like fruits. The leaves are aromatic, hence the name *D. aromatica* by which this shrub is commonly known in gardens.

ECCREMOCARPUS, Bignoniaceae. Glory Flower.

Soft-stemmed climbers supporting themselves by tendrils. They are not very hardy, and *Eccremocarpus scaber*, the kind commonly grown, usually dies back to ground level in winter, but if growing in well-drained soil, in a warm sunny position, it usually shoots up again in spring from the rather fleshy roots, and is so fast-growing that it can cover a considerable area in a single year. It is very easily raised from seed sown in a greenhouse or propagator and requires no pruning other than the removal of dead or damaged growth in spring.

scaber *2.5–3m. (8–10ft) Yellow, Orange or Red   Summer   D W T S*

Chile. A charming climber with slender stems, small divided leaves and clusters of pendant tubular flowers which are normally orange red, but there are also two varieties, one with yellow the other with crimson flowers.

EDGEWORTHIA, Thymeliaceae.

Only one species is at all commonly grown in British gardens and this is not very hardy. It is most suitable for maritime gardens and the milder counties but could be tried in any place where frosts are neither severe nor prolonged. It will grow in all reasonably fertile and well-drained soils. Weak or old stems should be cut out in spring. Increase is by summer cuttings in a propagator.

papyrifera *2–2.5m. (6–8ft)   Yellow L. Winter   E. Spring   D W T H*

China. A shrub with slender flexible olive-green stems and tiny pale-yellow tubular flowers packed in clusters of up to fifty. It is not showy but is highly distinctive.

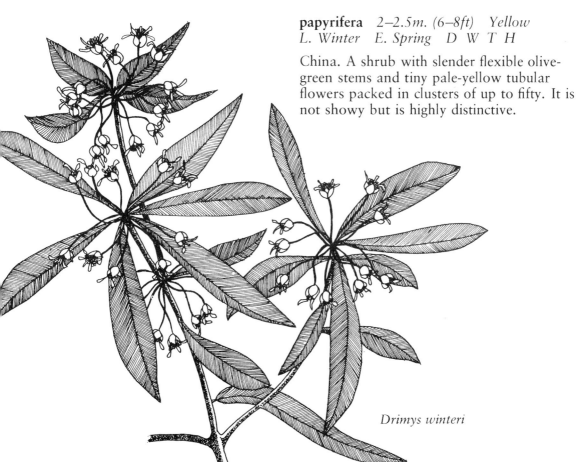

Drimys winteri

ELAEAGNUS, Elaeagnacae. Oleaster.
Evergreen and deciduous shrubs distinguished
by the fact that the young shoots and leaves
are covered with tiny scales which give them
an almost metallic sheen. They are therefore
handsome foliage plants. The flowers are
usually insignificant but in some kinds are
sweetly-scented, the scent often being
air-borne for quite a distance. All produce the
best foliage effects in moderately fertile soil.
They are easy and mostly fast-growing. If
they grow too large they can be pruned any
time between May and August. Increase is by
autumn cuttings in a propagator or by
layering.

angustifolia   *3–6m. (10–20ft)   Silvery
L. Spring   D K A L*

Western Asia. Perhaps more of a tree than a
true shrub, this species is grown for its narrow
leaves, which are silvery beneath. The
branches are also silvery and spiny and the
small flowers are sweetly scented.

x ebbingei   *3–4m. (10–13ft)   Silvery
Autumn   E K A L*

A group of hybrids from *Elaeagnus
macrophylla* with *E. pungens* as the probable
other parent. All are fast-growing and
handsome, with leaves silvery beneath and
small silvery fragrant flowers. 'Gilt Edge' is a
variety with a narrow band of yellow around
each leaf.

macrophylla   *2.5–3m. (8–10ft)   Silvery
Autumn   E K A L*

Korea, Japan. The leaves are silvered on both
surfaces when young but as they age the
upper surface becomes dark lustrous green.
The insignificant flowers are very sweetly
scented.

pungens   *2.5–4.5m. (8–15ft)   Silvery
Autumn   E K A L*

Japan. The most popular elaeagnus though
not in its normal green-leaved form. It is the
variegated forms that gardeners admire, such

Eccremocarpus scaber

as 'Aurea' (also known as 'Dicksonii'), with a wide band of yellow around each leaf; and 'Maculata', with an irregular yellow patch in the centre of each green leaf. The small flowers are fragrant.

umbellata *3.5–5m. (12–16ft) Silvery L. Spring E. Summer D K H L S*

Himalaya, China, Japan. A big well-branched shrub with leaves green above and silvery beneath, young shoots with brown scales, silvery sweetly scented flowers followed by berries which change from silver to red.

ELSHOLTZIA, Labiatae. Only one species is likely to be seen in British gardens and this is only semi-woody, most of the rather soft stems dying back close to the base each winter. In March all stems should be cut back to live growth buds near the base. It likes sun, warmth and reasonably fertile soil and can be increased by early summer cuttings in a propagator.

stauntonii *1.5m. (5ft) Pale purple Autumn D C H*

China. The lance-shaped leaves smell of mint when bruised, the small pinkish-purple flowers are carried in slender spikes. Unusual but not particularly exciting.

EMBOTHRIUM, Proteaceae. Fire Bush. Evergreen or occasionally partly deciduous shrubs which in some favourable places can attain tree-like proportions. They require lime-free soil containing plenty of humus and thrive best where the air is moist and fairly warm. Nevertheless some forms are much hardier than is generally supposed and can be grown successfully in many parts of the British Isles. As a rule no pruning is necessary but dead or damaged stems should be removed in spring. Propagation is by summer cuttings in a propagator or by root cuttings in a greenhouse in winter.

Elaeagnus x *ebbingei*

coccineum *4–6m. (13–20ft) Scarlet L. Spring E. Summer E W T H R*

Chile, Argentine. The inflorescences are highly distinctive, clusters of curling, narrowly-tubular flowers in some shade of red from near crimson to scarlet. There are several forms differing in leaf, habit and hardiness. The best for general planting is 'Lanceolatum' and the even hardier Andean variation called the 'Norquinco Valley' form. Both are more erect and less widely branched than typical *E. coccineum*, with narrower leaves and bearing orange-scarlet flowers all along the stems, particularly close packed in the 'Norquinco Valley' form. There is a good deal of confusion in the naming and description of these varieties since they are closely alike.

ENKIANTHUS, Ericaceae. Deciduous shrubs or small trees of which one is of particular value as a hardy and decorative garden plant. It requires exactly the same conditions as rhododendrons, namely an acid soil rich in humus, cool and moist in summer but not waterlogged in winter. Like rhododendrons it also thrives best in dappled shade or intermittent sunshine. Pruning is usually unnecessary but stems can be cut hard back in March with loss of one season's flower. Increase by seed or summer cuttings in peat or sand or by layering in spring or summer.

campanulatus *2–3.5m. (6–12ft)* *Cream and red* L. *Spring* D T S H L

Japan. The most popular species, much-branched, with slender but stiff stems carrying clusters of nodding bell-shaped flowers which are typically cream-coloured with reddish veining. There are also bronzy-red varieties, the best of which is named *palabinii* and one with white flowers called *albiflorus*.

EPHEDRA, Ephedraceae. Shrubby Horsetail. A very curious genus of extremely ancient origin, dating back to those far distant ages when horse-tail (*Equisetum*) was a major element of vegetation. Ephedras have a similar primitive appearance, with cylindrical, jointed, virtually leafless stems and small unisexual flowers. They are planted usually for curiosity but could have decorative merit in some foliage associations. They require well-drained soil but do not appear to be otherwise fussy. Increase is by seed, layering or division, and pruning is unnecessary, though surplus growth can be removed safely in spring.

distachya *1m. (3ft)* *Yellow. E. Summer* E T S L V

Europe and Asia Minor. The rush-like stems are bright green and the small flowers may be followed by red berries.

ERCILLA, Phytolaccaceae. A small genus of which only one species is seen occasionally in British gardens. This is a climber requiring a warm, sunny wall or fence. It will grow in any reasonably fertile and well-drained soil. The tangle of growth can be thinned in spring after flowering and the plant can be increased by summer cuttings in a propagator or by layering in spring or autumn.

volubilis *4–5m. (13–16ft)* *White Spring* E W O H L

Chile. A climber which makes a tangle of slender stems equipped with aerial roots like ivy but not, as a rule, sufficient of them to support the quite heavy mass of growth. It is therefore wise to provide wires or trellis and some ties for additional support. The flowers are small, white and more or less stained with pink, tubular and carried in small but dense spikes.

ERICA, Ericaceae. Heath, Heather. This is the largest of the three genera that gives gardens their heathers or heaths, the other two being *Calluna* and *Daboecia*. In calluna it is the calyx that is coloured, in erica and daboecia the inner circle of petals, usually bell or urn-shaped, that is coloured and the flowers are usually individually larger though there may not be so many of them. All are alike in their preference for acid soils containing plenty of peat or leaf-mould, open-textured and yet retaining plenty of moisture even in summer, but a few will grow in soil containing lime. It is a popular illusion that heathers will thrive in dry places. They will not and an examination of the soil in the bogs and moorlands on which most grow will show why. All flower most freely in light and open places and tend to get straggly in shade. The shorter kinds make excellent ground cover, the taller 'tree heathers' look well planted as individual specimens or in small groups. The habit of most is improved by light clipping in spring or, if they are in flower then, as soon as the flowers fade. All can be increased by short cuttings of firm young growth in peat and sand in a frame or propagator and the shorter kinds by layering or even by division in spring. Seed also germinates readily but seedlings are likely to vary from their parents and may be inferior to them, reverting more or less to the wild type.

arborea   *3–6m. (10–20ft)   White   Spring*
E W F H S L

Southern Europe, Northern Africa, Asia Minor and the Caucasus. This is the Tree Heath, a densely branched shrub that, in very favourable conditions, can become a small tree. It is a little tender and most suitable for maritime gardens in most parts of the British Isles but a variety named *alpina* is fully hardy, stiffer in growth and not so tall. It is the best kind for general planting. The flowers of both are honey-scented.

australis   *1–1.2m. (3–4ft)   Heather purple*
Spring   E. Summer   E W F H S L

Spain and Portugal. A rather straggly shrub improved by regular light pruning in June. It is a little tender and so is unsuitable for the coldest parts of the British Isles. There is a beautiful white-flowered variety named 'Mr Robert'.

canaliculata   *3–5m. (10–16ft)   Pink*
Winter   E. Spring   E W F H S L

South Africa. One of the few South African species that can be grown outdoors in the milder parts of Britain especially in the coastal gardens of the west and south west. It is a Tree Heath making a large bush and can be one of the most spectacular winter flowering shrubs.

carnea   *15–25cm. (6–10in.)   Rosy red*
Winter   Spring   E F H L S V

Alps, Apennines and mountains of Eastern Europe. Botanists are now calling this species *Erica herbacea* but it seems unlikely that this will be adopted by nurserymen and gardeners. It is in many ways the most useful of all heathers since it is dwarf and compact, has produced a great many good varieties and is one of the few heathers that will tolerate lime in the soil. Among the best varieties are 'Alan Coates' short, pink, mid-season; 'King George', also called 'Winter Beauty', rosy-crimson, early; 'Springwood Pink', pink, rather long stems, mid-season; 'Springwood White', similar to the last but white; and 'Vivellii', carmine-red, mid-season.

ciliaris   *15–30cm. (6–12in.)   Heather pink*
Summer   E. Autumn   E F H L S V

South-western Europe, south-western England, west Ireland and Morocco. This is known as the 'Dorset Heath' since some of the best forms have been collected in that county. It is a rather sprawling plant with pitcher-shaped flowers arranged in whorls and is a valuable garden plant because of its late flowering. Good varieties are 'Maweana', with stiffer stems and large flowers; 'Mrs C.H. Gill', with deeper coloured flowers and a more compact habit; and 'Stoborough', rather tall with white flowers.

cinerea   *15–60cm. (6–24in.)   Purple*
L. Summer   E. Autumn   E F H L S V

Western Europe (including Britain). This is the Bell-Heather, a common moorland species in Britain found wild in drier places than many other heathers. It forms wide mats of growth, makes excellent ground cover and has produced a number of good varieties. Typical of these are 'Alba Major', white, fairly large; 'Alba Minor', white, smaller and more compact; 'Atrorubens', ruby-red; 'C.D. Eason', rose-red; 'Eden Valley', lilac-pink; 'Golden Drop', heather-purple flowers, coppery-yellow foliage becoming bronze-red in winter; 'P.S. Patrick', long spikes of purple flowers; and 'Rosea', bright pink, starts to flower early.

x darleyensis   *45–60cm. (18–24in.)*
Rosy-red   Autumn to Spring
E F H L S V

A fine hybrid between *Erica carnea* and *E. mediterranea*, much like the former in flower but rather taller and more bushy, and with a very extended flowering season from November to May. It is fully hardy, is one of the few heathers that will tolerate some chalk or lime and is certainly one of the most valuable garden kinds.

lusitanica   *2.5–3m. (8–10ft)   White*
Winter   Spring   E W F H S L

South-western Europe. This Tree Heath closely resembles *Erica arborea* but is more erect in growth and even less hardy; a fine shrub for the milder counties and for specially sheltered gardens.

Erica mediterranea

mediterranea   *2–3m. (6–10ft) Rosy-red*
Spring   E F H S L

South-western Europe and Ireland. Yet another of the quite tall heathers, though nothing like as large as *Erica arborea*. This is a decorative and fully hardy shrub with some tolerance of lime or chalk. Some botanists consider that it should be called *Erica erigena* but the name *E. mediterranea* is so well established in gardens that it seems unlikely to be abandoned for horticultural purposes. It is sometimes called the Irish Heath.

terminalis   *2–2.5m. (6–8ft)   Pink*
Summer   E. Autumn   E F H S L

Southern Spain, Italy, Corsica and Sardinia. Despite its mediterranean habitat this tall heather appears to be hardy enough to plant in most parts of the British Isles where there is sufficient sunshine for its requirements. It has a good well-branched habit and is one of the most tolerant of all heaths to lime or chalk.

tetralix   *20–60cm. (8–24in.)   Rose-pink*
Summer   E. Autumn   E F H S L V

North and Western Europe (including the British Isles). This is known as the Cross-leaved Heath because the narrow leaves are arranged in whorls of four each forming a cross. It is a sprawling plant which has produced several good garden varieties, such as 'Alba Mollis' with white flowers and leaves grey with down; 'Con Underwood' with silvery leaves and crimson flowers', and 'L.E. Underwood', grey leaves and pink flowers.

vagans   *30–75cm (1–2½ft)   Lilac*
Summer   E F H S L V

South-western Europe and Cornwall. A sprawling shrub with flowers packed in dense spikes. It has produced several fine garden varieties including 'Lyonesse', white; 'Mrs D.F. Maxwell', cerise; and 'St Kevern', rose-pink.

x veitchii   *2–2.5m. (6–8ft)   White*
Spring   E W F H L

A fine hybrid between *Erica arborea* and *E. lusitanica*, intermediate in height between them and one of the best of the medium size Tree Heaths. The white sweetly-scented flowers are borne in broadly conical sprays. The form of this hybrid commonly sold is named 'Exeter'.

x watsonii   *20–30cm. (8–12in)   Pink*
Summer   Autumn   E F H L V

Hybrids between *Erica ciliaris* and *E. tetralix*, some of which occur spontaneously in the wild. The flowers resemble those of *E. ciliaris*, the leaves those of *E. tetralix*. There are several named varieties, including 'Dawn', rose-pink and late; 'H. Maxwell', light pink and rather taller than 'Dawn'; and 'Truro', rose-pink.

ERINACEA, Leguminosae. Hedgehog Broom. At a short distance this plant appears harmless enough, a low mound of grey growth covered in spring with lavender-blue, pea-type flowers, but lay a hand on it and it will be found to be well-armed with sharp spines. It is an unusual and attractive shrub for a warm sunny place in rock garden or scree in well-drained not too rich soil. Pruning is unnecessary. Increase is by seed, if available, by summer cuttings or by layering in spring.

anthyllis   *20–25cm. (9–10in)*
Lavender blue   Spring   D S H L

Spain, North Africa. Short but can spread quite widely. Flowers are produced freely if there is plenty of warmth and sunshine.

ESCALLONIA, Escalloniaceae. Quite a large genus of mainly evergreen but occasionally deciduous shrubs, some on the borderline of hardiness but otherwise easy to grow in all reasonably fertile soils. Most grow well by the sea and are often used as windbreaks. The stems are usually long and arching, the leaves small, the flowers appearing tubular but the separate petals rolled back at the mouth, produced freely in clusters. Escallonias will usually break out into new growth even if cut hard back into old wood in May, but this prevents flowering that year and plants can usually be kept within bounds by moderate thinning and shortening after flowering. All kinds grow readily from summer cuttings.

bifida   *2.5–3m. (8–10ft)   White*
E. Autumn   E W O H S

Eastern South America. The best white-flowered species but more tender than its hybrid, *Escallonia* 'Iveyi', and so only suitable for training against a sunny wall except in the mildest parts of the British Isles.

x exoniensis   *3–4m. (10–13ft)   White or*
Pink   Summer   E. Autumn   E W O H

A hybrid between *Escallonia rosea* and *E. rubra*, with a long flowering season. It is moderately hardy but will be damaged or killed by severe or prolonged frosts.

'Iveyi'   *3–4m. (10–13ft)   White*
Summer   E O H

A hybrid between *Escallonia bifida* and another hybrid, *E. x exoniensis*. It is one of the best white-flowered escallonias, is hardy enough to be grown in all but the coldest parts of Britain and is a first-class garden shrub.

x langleyensis   *2.5–3m. (8–10ft)   Rose*
Summer   E O H

One of a number of hybrids raised by crossing *Escallonia virgata* with *E. rubra*. All are fine garden shrubs, varying in habit and flower colour:

'Apple Blossom'. Stiffly branched, with pink and white flowers.
'Crimson Spire'. Erect in growth with crimson flowers.

Escallonia 'Apple Blossom'

macrantha   *2–3m. (6–10ft)   Carmine Summer   E W O H S*

Island of Chiloe. Some botanists regard this fine escallonia as a variety of *E. rubra*. The leaves are quite large, up to 8cm./13in. long and half as wide. It is rather tender but first-class in maritime gardens, where it is often used as a hedge. 'C.F. Ball', with large bright red flowers, is probably a variety of this species.

rosea   *1.2–2.5m. (4–8ft)   White   Summer E W O H S*

Chile. Despite its name, the flowers of this species are white. They are also scented and borne in spikes up to 7cm/3in. long. It is not one of the hardiest but grows well against a sunny wall.

rubra   *3–4m. (10–13ft)   Pink to Crimson Summer   E O K H S*

Chile and Argentina. A very variable species in habit, hardiness and flower colour. It has been known as *Escallonia punctata* and *E. sanguinea*. In mild maritime regions it is frequently used as a hedge plant. 'Woodside' is a dwarf variety no more than 60cm./2ft high, but it has the habit of producing some strong shoots which should be removed immediately.

virgata   *2–2.5m. (6–8ft)   White Summer   D O H S*

Chile. The hardiest species and one of the few that drops its leaves in winter. The flowers are flatter and more open than in most escallonias and in habit it is variable, from very low and spreading to quite narrowly erect. It deserves to be more widely planted.

EUONYMUS, Celastraceae. Spindle-tree. Evergreen and deciduous shrubs, and occasionally trees, which have great utilitarian and decorative value in the garden. *Euonymus japonicus* makes an excellent hedge, especially in maritime localities. Many

'**Donard Beauty**'. Arching stems, rose-red flowers.
'**Donard Brilliance**'. Arching stems, deep rose-red flowers.
'**Donard Radiance**'. Stiffer in habit, with shorter stems and soft rose flowers.
'**Edinensis**'. Bushy in habit, pale pink flowers.
'**Gwendolyn Anley**'. Relatively short and bushy, with pale pink flowers, and is notably hardy.
'**Langleyensis**'. Muted rose-pink, with arching stems.
'**Peach Blossom**'. Soft pink flowers and a bushy, well-branched habit.
'**Slieve Donard**'. Combines pale and deep rose and has arching stems.
'**William Watson**'. Relatively short and bushy and has red flowers.

of its varieties, and also those of other evergreen species, are handsome foliage plants and most of the deciduous species produce good crops of highly distinctive fruits. All are easy to grow in almost any reasonably fertile soil. The evergreen kinds will grow in sun or partial shade but the deciduous kinds fruit best in a light and preferably sunny place. Evergreens can be thinned at any time from May to September, and if necessary can be cut back quite severely in May. Deciduous kinds need little pruning but can be thinned or reduced in size in spring. Evergreens are readily increased by summer cuttings in a propagator, autumn cuttings in a frame or layering at almost any time except mid-winter. Deciduous kinds are best increased by seed sown outdoors or in a greenhouse in spring, but seedlings may vary a little so selected forms are increased, like evergreen kinds, by cuttings or layers.

alatus *2–2.5m. (6–8ft)* *Green* *L. Spring* *D T S H A L*

China and Japan. The 'Winged Spindle-tree', so known from the thin cork 'wings' that develop along the branches. This species is grown almost exclusively for the rich scarlet to crimson colour of its ripening leaves in autumn.

europaeus *3–6m. (10–20ft)* *Greenish* *L. Spring* *D T S H A L*

Europe (including the British Isles). The common Spindle Tree has an open, rather angularly branched habit, inconspicuous flowers followed by four-lobed red fruits, which split open to reveal orange seeds. The oval leaves colour well before they fall. There are several varieties including *intermedius*, which occurs in the wild, has larger broader leaves and is notably free-fruiting, and 'Red Cascade', which has larger, more deeply coloured fruits than the type.

fortunei *15–60cm. (6–24in.)* *Greenish* *E. Summer* *E K H A L*

Japan. This is a very variable plant, sometimes completely prostrate or climbing, sometimes bushy. Probably the prostrate form represents a juvenile development and, like ivy, when it attains sufficient maturity it fans its branches out and becomes bushy. *Radicans* is one of the prostrate or climbing forms, rooting into the soil as it grows or using aerial roots to cling like an ivy if it climbs. It will grow in sunshine or in quite dense shade. It has numerous forms, including *carrierii* which is bushy, green-leaved and produces greenish-white flowers followed by orange fruits; 'Odorata', leaves turning purplish-red in winter; 'Kewensis', leaves very small; 'Silver Queen', bushy or sometimes climbing with quite large leaves heavily variegated with white; 'Variegatus', creeping or climbing, leaves greyish-green edged with white; and *vegetus*, bushy or climbing with broad green leaves and pink, red-seeded fruits.

japonicus *3–5m. (10–16ft)* *Greenish* *Summer* *E K H A L*

Japan. This fine evergreen is just a little tender but in coastal areas it is much planted as a hedge or windbreak. The leaves are dark green yet shining. There are numerous varieties including 'Albomarginata', with a narrow border of yellow to each leaf; 'Aureus', often almost entirely yellow with only a thin margin of green; 'Duc d'Anjou', leaves yellow or grey-green with a central splash of green; 'Macrophyllus', extra large green leaves; 'Microphyllus', leaves very small; and 'Ovatus Aureus' leaves rather large, broadly edged with yellow, growth slow.

latifolius *3–5m. (10–16ft)* *Greenish* *L. Spring* *D T S H A*

Europe. This fine shrub closely resembles *E. europaeus* but it has larger leaves and fruits and better autumn foliage colour.

planipes   *3–5m. (10–16ft)   Greenish
E. Summer   D T S H A*

Japan, Korea, China and eastern Russia.
There is some confusion about the correct
name of this shrub, some authorities calling it
Euonymus sachalinensis. It closely resembes
E. latifolius and is an equally good garden
shrub.

yedoensis   *3–4m. (10–13ft)   Greenish
E. Summer   D T H A S*

Japan. There is confusion about the correct
name of this plant, some authorities believing
that it is not a true species but a variety of
another species which should be known as
Euonymus hamiltoniensis sieboldianus.
Whatever the name it is a handsome shrub,
thinner-stemmed and more elegant than *E.
latifolius*, with pink fruits and orange seeds.

EUPATORIUM, Compositae. Only one
shrubby species of this very large genus is at
all commonly grown in British gardens. It is
not very hardy, requires a warm, sheltered
and sunny place and reasonably well-drained
soil. Stems can be pruned hard each spring to
within 5 or 10cm./2–4in. of the base, and it
can be increased either by summer cuttings in
a propagator or by seed sown in a warm
greenhouse in spring.

ligustrinum   *2–2.5m. (6–8ft)
Creamy-white   Autumn   E W C S H*

Mexico. This can make a large bush of
slender but erect stems, bearing in autumn
clusters of small creamy-white or pink-flushed
daisy flowers which are sweetly scented. At its
late season it is very welcome but it will not
survive much frost and so is most suitable for
maritime or particularly sheltered gardens. In
many gardens this plant is still known by its
old name *Eupatorium micranthum*.

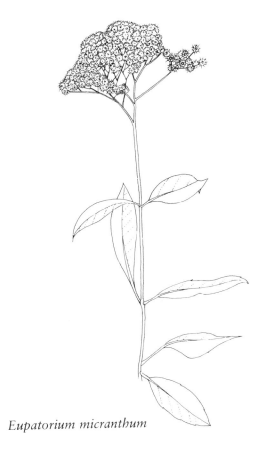

Eupatorium micranthum

EURYOPS, Compositae. This is a big genus
of African plants but few are sufficiently
hardy to be grown outdoors in the British
Isles. However, the species described below is
hardy if planted in well-drained soil in a
sunny position and is easily increased by
summer cuttings in a propagator. It is too
small and neat to require pruning.

acraeus   *30–90cm. (1–3ft)   Yellow
L. Spring   E W H*

South Africa. A neat evergreen with narrow,
silvery leaves, a compact habit and clusters of
small light yellow daisy-type flowers in late
spring. It is just right for a sunny terrace or
rock garden or a sunny wall. It has been much
confused with *E. evansii*, a different, and
probably less hardy species.

EXOCHORDA, Rosaceae. A small genus of deciduous shrubs all with white flowers borne in short spikes. They enjoy fertile soil and prefer a sunny position. All can be grown from seed sown in a greenhouse in spring or by cuttings of firm young growth rooted in a warm propagator in early summer. Rooted suckers can often be dug up in autumn with sufficient roots to be replanted elsewhere. The old flowering stems can be removed or shortened when the flowers fade.

giraldii *3–4m. (10–13ft)   White L. Spring   E. Summer   D F S H V*

China. A well-branched rather wide-spreading shrub which should be given plenty of room if it is to display its full decorative quality.

korolkowii *3–4m. (10–13ft)   White L. Spring   D F S H V*

Turkestan. A very handsome species, fully hardy with quite large flowers for the genus. It thrives on soils overlying chalk or limestone but will also succeed in moderately acid soils.

x macrantha *2.5–3m. (8–10ft)   White Spring   D F H V*

A hardy and free-flowering hybrid between *Exochorda korolkowii* and *E. racemosa* which combines the best qualities of both.

racemosa *2.5–3m. (8–10ft)   White L. Spring   D F S H V*

China. Possibly the largest-flowered species though there is really little to choose between this and *E. korolkowii* and it is far less satisfactory than that species on alkaline soil.

FABIANA, Solanaceae. In habit and leaf these shrubs look rather like tree heaths but in fact they belong to the potato family. So far only one species has made much impact in British gardens and even this is not common, probably because it is not reliably hardy in all parts of the country. In most maritime gardens and in warm, sheltered places inland it succeeds and it is then not difficult to please in any reasonably fertile and well-drained soil. If necessary it can be trimmed, or even cut back quite severely in July after flowering. It is easily increased by summer cuttings in a propagator.

imbricata *2–2.5m. (6–8ft)   White E. Summer   E W F H*

Andes of Bolivia, Argentina and Chile. With such a wide mountain distribution one would expect this to be a variable species, and it is. Typically it is an erect shrub, taller than broad, with very small leaves and white tubular flowers. A wild variety named *violacea* has lilac-blue or mauve flowers and is also distinctly variable. A garden clone, named 'Prostrata', appears to be derived from *violacea* and is distinct in its much more horizontally branched habit, which produces a mature bush considerably wider than it is tall. The flowers are a rather wishy-washy mauve.

Exochorda x *macrantha*

FATSHEDERA, Araliaceae. A fascinating bi-generic hybrid much used as a house plant but fully hardy and therefore quite suitable for planting in the garden. It grows fastest and produces the best foliage in fairly rich soil and will thrive in either sun or shade even when quite dense. It can be trimmed or cut back at any time from May to August, and is readily increased by summer cuttings in a propagator or by layering at any time except winter.

lizei *2–3m. (6–10ft)* *Pale green Autumn* E K H L

The parentage of this handsome foliage plant is *Fatsia japonica* fertilized by *Hedera helix* 'Hibernica', the Irish Ivy. It is a sprawling shrub with large leaves more like those of *Fatsia* than of ivy. It can be readily trained to stakes, wires or trellis but it requires tying as, unlike ivy, its stems have no means of support.

FATSIA, Araliaceae. Japanese Aralia. Figleaf Palm. There is only one species in this genus and it is a remarkably handsome foliage plant, very popular for house and office decoration but sufficiently hardy to be planted outdoors in many parts of the British Isles. It succeeds particularly well in maritime and sheltered town gardens in semi-shade. For the best foliage the soil should be fertile but this is not a fussy plant and it will grow in most soils. Pruning is necessary only if plants get too large and then stems can be shortened or cut down in April-May. Increase is by stem cuttings in summer, or root cuttings in spring, in a propagator.

japonica *2–4m. (6–13ft)* *Ivory Autumn* E W K H R

Japan. The stems are stout, many of them coming direct from the roots. The large, shining, dark green leaves are not unlike those

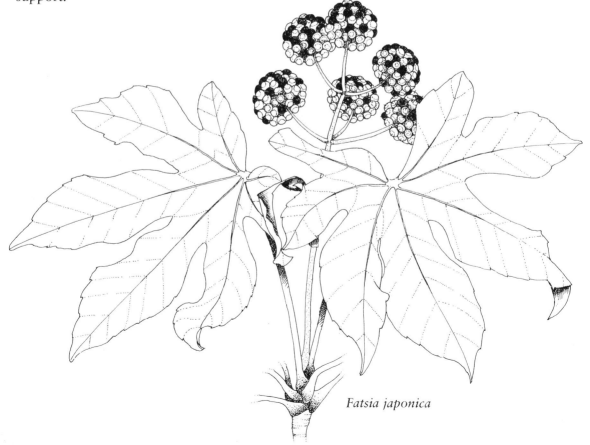

Fatsia japonica

Itea ilicifolia

above: *Daphne odora* 'Aureo-marginata' below: *Acer palmatum* 'Dissectum'

above: *Cistus* x *corbariensis*   below: Woodland with azaleas

Clematis armandii

of the fig but the lobes are pointed. The small milky-white flowers are carried in globose clusters themselves disposed in candelabra-like sprays and are followed by round black fruits.

FEIJOA, Myrtaceae. Only one species is occasionally grown outdoors in Britain and even this is not fully hardy. However, it succeeds in many maritime gardens and also inland if it can be given a suitably sheltered and sunny place. It can be trained against a sunny wall. It likes reasonably good and well-drained soil. Pruning is not essential except to restrict growth and is then best done by a little shortening or thinning of stems in summer immediately after flowering. Increase is by seed in a greenhouse in spring or by summer cuttings in a propagator.

sellowiana   *3–5m. (10–16ft)   Red Summer   E W F S H*

Southern Brazil and Uruguay. This species makes a dome-shaped, densely branched shrub with rounded leaves and flowers of four red petals paling towards their tips and with a central 'brush' of crimson stamens. They may be followed by egg-shaped edible fruits which have a distinctive and pleasant flavour, but if these are to be produced at all freely the bushes must not only be in a warm sunny place but also there must be at least two of them, genetically unrelated, that is, seed raised and not increased by cuttings from a common parent. This is necessary for pollination.

FICUS, Moraceae. Fig. Though figs are thought of mainly as fruit trees there are purely ornamental kinds and even the common fig is a handsome foliage shrub or small tree. It needs warmth and sunshine to be successful and a restricted root run if it is to prove fruitful as well as ornamental. It can be trained against a wall, or be grown as a well-branched and large bush. If it gets too large it can be cut back as much as necessary

Feijoa sellowiana

in February or March or whole branches can be removed. Figs are likely to grow again even if cut down to within 50cm./20in. of ground level. Increase is by summer cuttings in a propagator, by layering in spring or summer or by digging up rooted suckers in autumn. Very different in appearance and requirements is the climbing fig, *Ficus pumila*, an ivy-like climber which clings to walls, tree trunks etc. with aerial roots, has small dark green leaves and needs an even warmer and more sheltered place than the common fig. In most parts of Britain it is grown in conservatories, but near the sea and in very favourable situations it succeeds outdoors. It can also be increased by summer cuttings in a propagator or by layering.

carica *3–6m. (10–20ft)*
Flowers inside, all-year fruits
D W T H L V

Western Asia and Eastern Mediterranean.
The well-known fruiting fig with large shining
green deeply-lobed leaves. A peculiarity is
that the flowers are formed inside the
receptacles, which if fertilization takes place,
swell to form the edible fruits.

pumila *2–3m. (6–10ft) E W K H L*

China, Japan, Formosa. The Small or
Climbing Fig produces fruit only when it
reaches the adult state which is unlikely to be
attained outdoors in Britain. It is cultivated
solely as a decorative self-clinging evergreen
climber.

FORSYTHIA, Oleaceae. Golden Bells. These
are among the most popular and spectacular
of early-flowering shrubs, capable of making
great mounds of golden colour in March if the
weather is favourable and certainly by early
April. Forsythias like good fertile soil and
open sunny places. They often flower better
in town and suburban gardens than the
country where birds, undeterred by traffic and
passers-by, are liable to strip off all the flower
buds before they have a chance to open.
Bushes can be allowed to grow unrestricted
but the finest flowers are produced if the old
flowering stems are cut out directly the
flowers have faded, leaving all the young
stems to flower the following year.
Propagation is by summer cuttings in a
propagator, autumn cuttings in a frame or
outdoors, or layering at any time.

x intermedia *2–2.5m. (6–8ft)   Yellow*
Spring   D F H A L

The collective name given to numerous
hybrids between *Forsythia suspensa* and *F.*
viridissima. Some of the best garden varieties
are to be found here, with large flowers, freely
produced and richly coloured. Among the
most popular are 'Lynwood' and 'Spectabilis',

Forsythia x *intermedia*

both rich daffodil-yellow, and 'Spring Glory',
sulphur-yellow. All these have the normal
number of chromosomes but there are also
polyploid sports (varieties with more than the
normal number of chromosomes) some of
which are larger in all their parts than normal
forsythias but are usually less free-flowering.
The two best known are 'Arnold Giant' and
'Beatrix Farrand' but there is some confusion
about the latter name since it appears to have
been used for more than one variety.

ovata *1.2–1.5m. (4–5ft) Yellow*
E. Spring D F H A L

Korea. A relatively small species chiefly notable for its early flowering. It is closely allied to (some authorities would say identical with) *F. japonica*.

suspensa *2.5–3m. (8–10ft) Yellow*
Spring D F H A L

China. The stems of this species are long and lax. If allowed to grow naturally they sprawl outward, forming a wide loosely-branched bush, but they are readily trained against a wall and may then reach a length of up to 9m./30ft. There are numerous varieties, of which the following are typical: 'Sieboldii' is the oldest garden variety and it has golden-yellow flowers; 'Fortunei' has shorter and stiffer stems; 'Nymans Variety' has paler yellow flowers and *atrocaulis* has stems that are light purple when young but become nearly black as they age. The contrast with the yellow flower is striking.

viridissima *1.5–2.5m. (5–9ft) Yellow*
Spring D F H A L

China. Though not quite such a decorative shrub as *Forsythia suspensa* this species has stiffer and shorter stems and it is this characteristic which it has passed on to the best of its offspring in the hybrid *F. x intermedia*. It has also produced the best truly dwarf forsythia, named 'Bronxensis', seldom over 30cm./12in. high and not much more in width. It flowers freely in some gardens, more shyly in others but is seldom wholly without flowers as is common with the wide-spreading 'Arnold Dwarf', said to be a hybrid between *F. ovata* and *F. x intermedia*.

FOTHERGILLA, Hamamelidaceae. American Witch Hazel. Though the fothergillas are related to the witch hazels (*hamamelis*) the flowers are very different, without petals and formed mainly of little clusters of stamens like short paint brushes.

They are attractive but not conspicuous and these shrubs are grown mainly for their magnificent autumn leaf colour. They thrive in most reasonably fertile soils that are not alkaline, but are generally unsuitable for soils overlying chalk or limestone. Little pruning is necessary but old, thin or weak stems can be cut out in winter. Increase is by summer cuttings in a propagator or by layering in spring or autumn.

major *2–3m. (6–10ft) Yellowish*
L. Spring D T H L

Allegheny Mountains, USA. This is the species commonly grown in gardens, and plants listed as *Fothergilla monticola* are regarded by botanists as no more than natural variations, usually shorter in growth, of this species. The leaves become yellow, orange and deep crimson before they fall.

Fothergilla major

FREMONTODENDRON, Sterculiaceae.
This is the name now given to the American
Shrubs commonly known in gardens as
Fremontia. They are rather tender and
suitable only for the milder parts of the British
Isles, particularly coastal districts or for
training against sheltered and sunny walls.
They are not fussy about soil provided
drainage is good, and they grow well over
chalk or limestone subsoils. Little pruning is
required but stems can be shortened or
thinned in May if necessary. Increase is by
seeds in warmth in spring or by summer
cuttings in a propagator.

californicum   2–4m. (6–13ft)   *Yellow*
Summer   E   W   T   S   H

California. A loosely-branched shrub with
variably lobed leaves covered in brown felt
beneath. The flowers are saucer-shaped,
bright yellow, carried singly on short stalks
and often followed by well-filled seed pods.
When bruised the wood is aromatic.

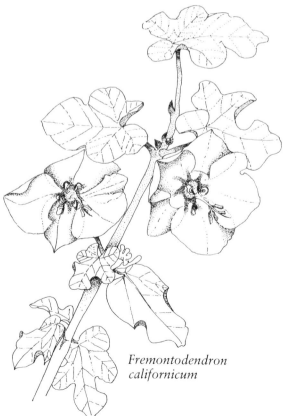

*Fremontodendron
californicum*

mexicanum   3–4m. (9–13ft)   *Yellow*
Summer   E   W   T   S   H

Lower California and Mexico. The more
southerly distribution of this species makes it
even less hardy than *F. californicum* but the
flowers are an even richer yellow and, in a
warm climate, may be more freely produced.
There is a hybrid between *F. californicum* and
F. mexicanum named 'California Glory',
which is probably better than either as a
decorative plant but has been insufficiently
tested in Britain for a full assessment of its
merits here to be made.

FUCHSIA, Onagraceae. This is one of the big
genera of highly ornamental shrubs and one
which has been so much hybridized that the
precise parentage of many garden varieties
cannot be traced. In the wild the hundred or
so species have a wide distribution in Central
and Southern America and New Zealand and
they differ greatly in hardiness, most being
only suitable for greenhouse cultivation in the
British Isles. However, a few species are
reasonably hardy and there are numerous
fairly hardy hybrids which will grow well in
maritime gardens and in sheltered places
inland. Even when cut to ground level by
winter frost many will sprout up again direct
from the roots the following spring. It helps
to plant rather deeply, covering the roots with
4 or 5cm./2–3in. of soil and then, in late
autumn, adding a further 4 or 5cm. of peat or
leaf-mould as an additional winter protection
for the roots and basal buds. In mild places
fuchsias can be allowed to grow with little or
no pruning, or they can be thinned and
shortened in late winter before the sap is
flowing freely. In cold places it is better to cut
back all stems to within a few centimetres of
soil level in February or March. Fuchsias are
very easily grown from summer cuttings
rooted in a frame, propagator or pot of sand
placed inside a polythene bag. Seed also
germinates freely in spring in a warm
greenhouse but seedlings of hybrid fuchsias
are likely to differ from their parents.

Fuchsia magellanica 'Riccartonii'

coccinea   *2–3m. (6–10ft)   Red and purple*
Summer   D   W   C   H   S

Brazil. A fairly hardy species with long lax stems that can be trained against a wall or fence if desired. It played a prominent part in the nineteenth century in the production of garden hybrids but has since become a very scarce plant and is only occasionally seen. Its flowers are small and much like those of *F. magellanica*.

magellanica   *2–3m. (6–10ft)*
Red and purple   D   W   C   H   S

Chile. By far the most important species for outdoor cultivation in Britain for the most southern forms, from Tierra del Fuego, are among the hardiest of all fuchsias. Varieties of *F. magellanica* have also been widely used in breeding programmes and have contributed their vigour and hardiness to many good garden varieties. It is difficult to disentangle the natural varieties of this species from some of the hybrids which closely resemble them, but for purposes of garden decoration the following may all be regarded as related to *F. magellanica*:

'**Globosa**'. Dwarf and spreading with globular flower buds opening to rather broad crimson and violet flowers.

'**Gracilis**'. Very different from the last, with long slender flowers notable for their narrow pointed scarlet sepals hanging like skirts around the much shorter violet petals. This is a very beautiful and hardy fuchsia.

'**Pumila**'. Only 15–20cm./6–8in. high, with small bright red and violet-blue flowers.

'**Riccartonii**'. A vigorous and hardy fuchsia, stiffly and rather angularly branched with small scarlet and violet flowers very freely produced. It is one of the hardiest kinds and is frequently used in maritime areas as a hedge or shelter belt.

'**Thompsonii**'. Much like 'Gracilis' but bushier and shorter.

'**Variegata**'. A variegated form of 'Gracilis' identical in habit and flower but with a cream border to each green leaf.

'**Versicolor.**' Another variegated form of 'Gracilis' but this time with grey-green leaves flushed and splashed with cream and pink. It is liable to revert to the green-leaved type and any stems bearing green leaves should be removed completely as soon as seen.

microphylla   *2m. (6ft)   Red and Carmine*
Summer   D   W   C   H   S

Central America. Despite its origin in a tropical region this interesting species grows outdoors in the milder parts of the British Isles, particularly in coastal areas of the south and west. It makes a densely branched bush with small leaves and flowers. It is by no means spectacular but it is unique and always attracts a lot of attention.

Fuchsia Hybrids

There are a great many of these and additions are constantly being made to the list. These hybrids cover a wide range of habits as well as flower types, sizes and colours. Some are dwarf plants barely 30cm./12in high, some spread widely or have arching stems and some grow erect to as much as 2m./6ft. Flowers range from small to large and colours from white to crimson and deep purple, most varieties showing contrast between the colour of the sepals (the outer coloured ring) and the petals which form the central often skirt-like or bell-shaped part of the flower. Nor is there any standard of hardiness. Some varieties will withstand quite a lot of frost and can be planted in many parts of the British Isles, even the far north. Other kinds will survive a little frost and are quite safe in mild and sheltered places but unreliable where it is very cold, particularly if the soil is poorly drained as well. The following are typical and have proved reliable:

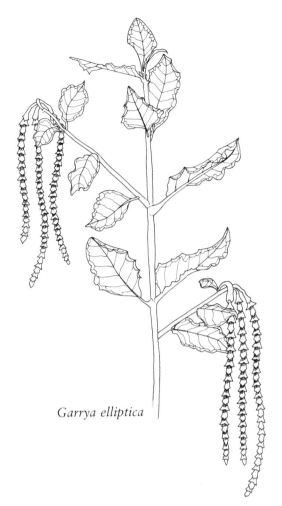

Garrya elliptica

'**Alice Hoffman**'. Rather small plant with small red and white flowers.
'**Brilliant**'. Medium size plant with large scarlet and purple flowers.
'**Brutus**'. Medium size, well-branched plant with cerise and violet-purple flowers.
'**Chillerton Beauty**'. Medium size rather spreading plant with pink and violet purple flowers.
'**Corallina**'. Wide-spreading plant with scarlet and purple flowers.
'**Dunrobin Bedder**'. Small but rather spreading plant with small red and purple flowers.
'**Enfante Prodique**'. Medium size plant with double scarlet and purple flowers.
'**Howlett's Hardy**'. Rather short plant with quite large scarlet and violet-blue flowers.
'**Lady Thumb**'. A counterpart of 'Tom Thumb' with rose-pink and white flowers.
'**Lena**'. Rather weak stems bending beneath the weight of large, semi-double white, pink and mauve flowers.

'**Madame Cornelissen**'. Erect, rather stiff growth with scarlet and white flowers.
'**Margaret**'. Very vigorous erect plant with semi-double scarlet and blue-violet flowers.
'**Mrs Popple**'. Vigorous well-branched plant with quite large light crimson and blue-violet flowers.
'**Mrs W.P. Wood**'. A vigorous well-branched bush with small, almost white, pink-tinted flowers.
'**Phyllis**'. A medium size plant with quite large semi-double flowers in two shades of rose-pink.
'**Rufus**'. Medium size plant with red flowers. Often called 'Rufus the Red'.
'**Tennessee Waltz**'. Medium size plant with large rose and mauve flowers.
'**Tom Thumb**'. Dwarf bushy plant with small rose-pink and violet-purple flowers.

GARRYA, Garryaceae. Evergreen shrubs of which one species is frequently planted both for its foliage and unique winter flowers. It is fairly hardy but likes a warm sheltered sunny position in well-drained soil. It can be grown naturally as a big bush, in which case it requires little pruning, or it can be trained against a wall, when it will probably be necessary to thin or shorten some stems in spring when the flowers fade. Summer cuttings can be rooted in a propagator.

elliptica   *2–4m. (6–13ft)   Grey-green Winter   E   W   O   H   S*

California and Oregon. The leaves are rounded and dark green and the small greyish-green flowers are clustered in trailing catkins which are much longer, more slender and more decorative in male plants. Females, which will produce small egg-shaped purplish-brown fruits if a male grows near enough for pollination, carry their flowers in shorter broader catkins.

GAULTHERIA, Ericaceae. This is a very large genus of evergreen shrubs many of which make dense thickets of growth and are useful as ground cover or as shelter for birds. Not many are highly decorative. All require acid soil containing plenty of humus and not liable to dry out badly in summer. Pruning is required only to prevent plants spreading too far and is usually best done with a sharp spade in spring or autumn, the outlying parts of the thicket being chopped or dug out, roots and all. This also provides a means of increasing many kinds, but gaultherias can also be raised from seed sown in moist peaty soil in spring and by summer cuttings in a shady frame or propagator.

forrestii   *0.5–1.5m. (1½–5ft)   White Spring   E   T   S   H   V*

China. One of the most handsome species. The flowers are small and urn-shaped, crowded in slender spikes, and they are also scented.

miqueliana   *20–30cm. (8–12in)   White E. Summer   E   T   S   H   L*

Japan. A small evergreen very suitable for a peat garden. The little flowers are almost globe-shaped and are followed by small white or pink edible fruits.

oppositifolia   *1m. (3ft)   White L. Spring   E. Summer   E   W   T   S   H   L*

New Zealand. One of the less hardy species but an attractive evergreen for a sheltered situation. The small bell-shaped flowers are carried in clusters well above the leaves.

procumbens   *Prostrate   Palest pink Summer   E   T   S   H   V*

Eastern North America. This creeping evergreen shrub has a number of popular names including Partridge Berry, Box Berry and Creeping Wintergreen. It makes good ground cover even in the most shady places and its small pale pink flowers are followed by showy, holly-red fruits which are just about edible.

shallon   *1–2m. (3–6ft)   Pale pink L. Spring   E. Summer   E   T   S   H   V*

Western North America. The best thicket-forming species and a plant that can take complete command of quite large areas of ground if it is sufficiently acid and moist. The flowers are small, urn-shaped and rather hidden by the abundant, quite large leaves.

GENISTA, Leguminosae. Broom. This is the second of the two big genera to provide the shrubs popularly known as brooms, the other being *Cytisus*. The distinctions between the two are botanical rather than horticultural and even the botanists have not always been too sure of their ground, switching species from one genus to the other or occasionally fashioning new genera to contain them. It is not surprising, therefore, that in gardens the general requirements of *Genista* and *Cytisus* are identical. They may be summed up as sun, warmth and good drainage, with a minimum of pruning and no cutting back into old wood, which rarely produces new growth. When plants need to be restricted, they are either thinned back lightly, usually immediately after flowering, or whole branches are removed, leaving no stumps to die and decay. Summer or early autumn cuttings can usually be rooted in a propagator, but with some difficulty, and seed remains the best method of propagation except for hybrids and selected garden varieties.

aethnensis   *4–6m. (13–20ft)   Yellow Summer   D   O   S   H*

Sardinia, Sicily. Despite its mediterranean origin the Mount Etna Broom is quite hardy. It is also highly distinctive in habit, a rather tall shrub with thin hanging whip-like branches wreathed in small yellow flowers during July and August. It is easily blown about by wind and needs very secure staking, especially when young and before its roots have anchored it firmly.

cinerea   *2.5–3m. (8–10ft)   Yellow Summer   D   O   S   H*

South-western Europe. Another beautiful and highly distinctive shrub, with slender but fairly stiff branches covered with silken hairs while young, and small clusters of bright yellow flowers which are sweetly scented. In gardens it is much confused with G. *tenera*, which it resembles closely, but its flowers are produced in smaller clusters held closer to the main stems.

hispanica   *30–50cm. (12–20 in.)   Yellow L. Spring   E. Summer   D   O   S   H*

South-western Europe. A very distinctive shrub, dwarf but wide-spreading and very spiny like gorse, for which reason it is called the Spanish Gorse. It is an excellent ground-covering shrub, deciduous but

seeming to be evergreen because of its dense habit and green stems and spines. The flowers, though smaller than those of gorse, have a similar bright colour and are very freely produced.

lydia   *40–60cm. (16–24in)   Yellow L. Spring   E. Summer   D   O   S   H*

South-eastern Europe and western Asia Minor. An elegant small shrub, dwarf but spreading, with slender arching stems and bright yellow flowers. Ideal for sunny rock gardens, raised rock beds and terrace walls.

sagittalis   *Prostrate   Yellow E. Summer   D   O   S   H*

Europe. Immediately recognizable by its ground-hugging habit and conspicuously winged stems. As the wings are green and almost leaf-like they convey the impression of an evergreen plant. Ideal for rock gardens, walls and sunny banks.

tenera   *2.5–3m. (8–10ft)   Yellow Summer   D   O   S   H*

Madeira. In gardens and nurseries this fine summer flowering broom is often grown as *Genista virgata*. It makes a big open shuttlecock bush of slender stems with small yellow flowers in quite large clusters. It is closely allied to G. *cinerea* and some botanists believe that the two are merely varieties of one species.

tinctoria   *20–60cm. (8–24in.)   Yellow Summer   E. Autumn   D   O   S   H*

Europe (including Britain), northern Asia. This is the Dyer's Greenweed from which a yellow dye can be obtained. It is a sprawling plant making a tangle of wiry stems and producing small yellow flowers over a long season. It has a fine double-flowered variety named 'Plena', but this never produces seed and so must be increased by cuttings.

GEVUINA, Proteaceae. Chilean Hazel. Only one species of this small genus of evergreen shrubs from the Southern Hemisphere is likely to be seen in British gardens and that rarely for it is not very hardy. It is most suitable for planting in the mild maritime gardens of the south-west and west. It is not fussy about soil so long as fertility and drainage are reasonable but is all the better for some shade, the dappled light provided by thin woodland. Pruning is normally unnecessary but if it grows too large it can be thinned or cut back in May. Increase is by summer cuttings in a propagator or by seeds in a warm greenhouse in spring.

avellana   *3–8m. (10–26ft)   White*
L. Summer   E   W   T   S   H

Chile. A handsome evergreen shrub or small tree with long compound shining green leaves and a rather loosely branched habit. The small ivory-white spidery flowers are carried in a slender spike and may be followed by dark brown or black edible nuts.

GREVILLEA, Proteaceae. The two species at all commonly seen in British gardens are both rather tender and more suitable for maritime districts and sheltered gardens inland than for general planting, though in well-drained soil they will survive some frost. They like moderately acid soils with plenty of humus, which can be added as peat or leaf-mould, and prefer sunny places. They are often planted close to walls or fences for protection but are not suitable for training. They should be allowed to retain their natural bushy habit

the only pruning being to remove weak or damaged stems in May. Propagation is by summer cuttings in a propagator.

rosmarinifolia   *1.5–2m. (5–6ft)   Red*
L. Winter to E. Summer   E   W   T   H

New South Wales. A wide-spreading shrub with narrow leaves like those of rosemary, which it superficially resembles. However, the flowers are very different, with narrow curling segments (botanically they are neither sepals nor petals since this is a very ancient family which pre-dates such differentiation) and long red stamens. This is a beautiful and distinctive shrub with a long flowering season.

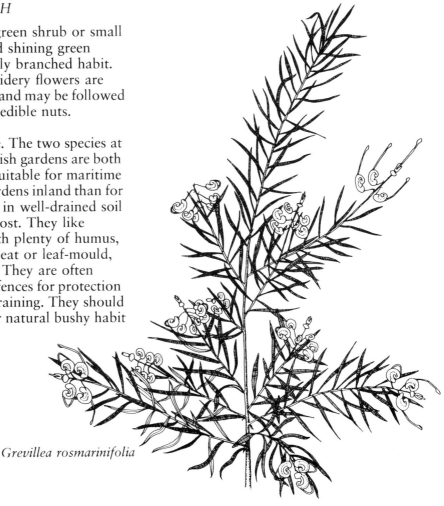

Grevillea rosmarinifolia

sulphurea *1–2m. (3–6ft) Pale yellow
L. Spring E. Summer E W T H*

New South Wales. In leaf and habit this
closely resembles *Grevillea rosmarinifolia* but
the sulphur-yellow flowers do not start to
open until May.

GRISELINIA, Cornaceae. Only one species is
at all commonly planted in British gardens
and this mainly in maritime areas, where it is
popular as a hedge plant and windbreak. For
these purposes it is excellent but it is also a
handsome and distinctive evergreen which is a
good deal hardier than it is usually supposed
to be. It could almost certainly be grown in all
but the coldest parts of the British Isles. It will
thrive in most soils that are reasonably fertile,
can be pruned in May as necessary to keep it
within bounds, and is easily increased by
summer or early autumn cuttings in a
propagator or pot placed inside a polythene
bag.

littoralis *3–6m. (10–20ft) Yellowish
L. Spring E W K H*

New Zealand. A well-branched shrub with
sturdy stems and rounded leathery shining
leaves of a distinctive yellowish-green. The
small flowers are of no beauty and this is
solely a foliage shrub. There is a handsome
variegated variety named 'Variegata', with
broad leaves bordered with yellow which
becomes paler with age. A sport from this
reverses the colouring, with yellow in the
centre of the leaf and light green around the
outside.

HAKEA, Proteaceae. Another attractive
genus belonging to the very primitive Protea
family. These are Australasian plants closely
allied to *Grevillea* and with similar
requirements in the garden. None is fully
hardy but several species will grow in mild
places particularly near the coast. None likes
lime or chalk. Little pruning is required.
Increase is by seed in spring or by summer
cuttings in a propagator.

lissosperma *2.5–3m. (8–10ft)
White or Ivory L. Spring E W T H S*

Tasmania. A shrub with spine-like leaves and
clusters of tubular flowers which are
interesting rather than beautiful. *H.
microcarpa*, from eastern Australia and
Tasmania and *H. sericea*, from Tasmania,
New South Wales and Victoria are similar,
and because of their wide distribution there
may be differences in hardiness according to
their place of origin.

X HALIMIOCISTUS, Cistaceae. This is the
name given to hybrids between two closely
allied genera, *Halimium* and *Cistus*. They are
therefore from a garden standpoint Rock
Roses requiring treatment in every way
identical to that recommended for *Cistus*.

'Ingwersenii' *30–45cm. (12–18in.) White
L. Spring Summer E T H*

A natural hybrid, presumed to be between
Halimium umbellatum and *Cistus
psilosepalus* (syn. *hirsutus*) found by Mr Will
Ingwersen in Portugal. It is an attractive small
shrub suitable for sunny rock gardens and is
quite hardy.

sahucii *30–45cm. (12–18in.) White
E. Summer E T H*

A natural hybrid between *Halimium
umbellatum* and *Cistus salviifolius* which
grows wild in France. It has the same garden
use as *H.* x 'Ingwersenii' but a shorter
flowering season.

HALIMIUM, Cistaceae. A small genus of
evergreens closely allied to *Helianthemum*
and having an identical decorative use in
gardens. Cultivation is as described for
Helianthemum.

alyssoides *60cm (2ft) Yellow L. Spring
E O S H*

South-western Europe. A very attractive small
shrub very suitable for a warm sunny position

on a bank or in the rock garden. The bright yellow flowers are produced freely.

halimifolium *1m. (3ft) Yellow*
L. Spring E. Summer E W O S H

Mediterranean region. A rather variable shrub sometimes with wholly yellow flowers but more often, in the forms favoured in gardens, with a maroon spot at the base of each petal. It has a reputation for being rather tender but this probably depends upon the place of its origin since it is likely that some wild forms are hardier than others.

libanotis *30–45cm. (12–18in.) Yellow*
E. Summer E W O S H

Portugal, Spain, Morocco. There is confusion about this name, some botanists preferring *H. commutatum*, but this is seldom used in gardens. It is an attractive small shrub with yellow flowers freely produced but it needs a specially warm and sunny place and well-drained soil.

ocymoides *60–90cm. (2–3ft)*
Yellow and maroon L. Spring E. Summer
E O S H

Portugal and Spain. One of the hardiest of the halimiums and a very attractive small shrub for sunny places. The bright yellow flowers have a nearly black blotch at the base of each petal. Habit is variable, in some forms erect, in others sprawling.

umbellatum *30–45cm. (12–18in.)*
White and yellow E. Summer
E O S H

Mediterranean region. A most attractive shrub with white flowers bearing a small yellow flush at the base of each petal. Because of its wide distribution in the wild it is somewhat variable in character, some forms being better than others.

HAMAMELIS, Hamamelidaceae. Witch Hazel. These are among the most attractive of winter flowering shrubs but most are large and so require, eventually, a good deal of room. All prefer fertile soils, neutral or moderately acid and not liable to dry out severely in summer. Pruning is liable to spoil the distinctive, open horizontal-branched habit but some thinning or reduction can be done in spring after flowering. Cuttings are difficult to root and nurserymen usually graft garden varieties under glass in spring using seedling witch hazels, usually *Hamamelis virginiana*, as root stocks. Private gardeners will probably prefer to layer young stems in spring or summer. Seed takes a long time to germinate unless prepared by being kept moist at a temperature of about 20°C/68°F. for five months, then at 3–4°C./37–39°F. for at least three months.

x intermedia *3–4m. (10–13ft)*
Yellow or Red Winter D T G L

The collective name given to numerous hybrids between *Hamamelis japonica* and *H. mollis*. They are so variable in character that it is necessary to describe them under their varietal names. All have strongly-scented flowers:

'Allgold'. Favours *H. mollis* and has yellow flowers.
'Carmine Red'. Leans towards some highly coloured forms of *H. japonica*, and has bronzy flowers which in some situations appear to be more red than they really are.
'Feuerzauber'. German variety translated for the English-speaking market to either 'Fire Charm' or 'Magic Fire'. The flowers are coppery-red.
'Jelena'. Also looks red at a distance but its flowers are actually a mixture of red and dull yellow.
'Moonlight'. Appears to have had *H. mollis* 'Pallida' as one of its parents since its sulphur-yellow flowers resemble those of that fine shrub.

'Orange Beauty'. Considered by some authorities to be identical with 'Jelena' and by others to be distinct – more orange-yellow without red.

japonica   *3–4m. (10–13ft)   Yellow and red Winter   D T G L S*

Japan. The Japanese Witch Hazel is a large spreading shrub or even a small tree under particularly favourable conditions. It flowers a little later than some and is variable. Typically, the petals are yellow and the sepals are reddish but several selected forms are available. One, named *arborea*, is tall and spreading and usually has yellow petals and bronze-red calyces, but it is variable. The flowers are not strongly scented. Another, named *flavo-purpurascens*, has yellow petals suffused with bronzy red and a dark purple calyx. 'Sulphurea' has sulphur-yellow flowers and a red calyx and 'Zuccariniana' is

Hamamelis mollis

late-flowering, rather upright in habit with pale sulphur-yellow petals and a cool greenish calyx.

mollis   *3–4m. (10–13ft)   Yellow   Winter D T G L S*

China. The Chinese Witch Hazel is in many ways the best for general garden planting since it flowers early. Its flowers are relatively large and very sweetly scented and it has an attractive horizontally branched habit. Typically the petals are golden yellow and the calyx is reddish-brown but a variety named 'Pallida' has extra large sulphur-yellow flowers. Another variety, named 'Brevipetala', has short butter-yellow petals, and there are other selected forms such as 'Coombe Wood', said to have larger yellow flowers than the type, and 'Goldcrest', in which yellow petals are suffused with red towards the base.

vernalis   *2.5–3m. (8–10ft)   Yellow or Red Winter   D T G L S*

Central USA. The flowers are small but very abundant and colour varies from yellow to red. Several varieties are available such as 'Imp', with coppery petals deepening to claret at the base, and 'Sandra', with yellow flowers and leaves that are purple when young, become green, but then change to orange and scarlet before they fall in autumn.

virginiana   *4–6m. (13–20ft)   Yellow Autumn   Winter   D T G L S*

Eastern North America. The flowers are small and open so early that for a time they are partly hidden by the leaves which turn bright yellow before they fall. This is the witch hazel most commonly used as root stock on which to graft other kinds.

HEBE, Scrophulariaceae. Shrubby Veronica. This very large genus of evergreen shrubs, comprising something like a hundred species as well as innumerable hybrids and garden varieties, is of great garden importance since many kinds are very decorative in foliage, flower, or both and some continue to flower for a considerable time. However, most of the species come from New Zealand and few are reliably hardy throughout the British Isles. It would be roughly, though not entirely, true to say that there is some correlation between size of leaf and hardiness. Certainly it is true that most of the species with tiny leaves held close to the slender stems, the 'whipcords' in garden parlance, are far hardier than the large and rather thick-leaved *Hebe speciosa* and its numerous progeny.

In general hebes like warm sunny places and reasonably well-drained soils but few are fussy. They grow well by the sea and survive salt-laden wind better than most. They submit well to pruning or even to clipping and will usually make new growth even when cut back into quite old wood. May is the best month for any hard pruning but light pruning can be done at any time from then until late August. Summer cuttings root readily in frame, propagator or polythene bag and seed also germinates freely in spring, sometimes spontaneously around growing plants. However, some species cross-fertilize so readily that seedlings are often hybrids, differing in important features from their parents. It is this readiness to hybridize that accounts for the proliferation of garden varieties.

albicans *30–60cm. (1–2ft) White Summer E T H S*

New Zealand (South Island). This attractive species makes a low, broadly dome-shaped bush with oval grey-green leaves and short spikes of white flowers. It is well worth growing for its foliage alone.

anomala *1m. (3ft) White or Pink Summer E T H S*

New Zealand. A compact bushy plant with neat oval or lance-shaped leaves and clusters of short flower spikes which may be white or pale pink. It is closely allied to *H. odora*.

x **'Autumn Glory'** *60–80cm. (24–30in.) Blue Summer Autumn E W T H*

A hybrid of uncertain origin, possibly between *H. pimeloides* and *H.* x *franciscana*. It has neat shining green leaves and short spikes of deep violet-blue flowers produced continuously from midsummer until autumn.

x **'balfouriana'** *1m. (3ft) Blue Summer E T H*

Another hybrid of uncertain parentage, possible the offspring of *H. pimeloides* and *H. vernicosa*. It has small leaves, purple stems and purplish-blue flowers in short spikes.

brachysiphon *1.2–2m. (4–6ft) White Summer E T H S*

New Zealand. One of the hardiest of the larger species. It makes a densely branched, dome-shaped bush with small oval leaves and short spikes of white flowers very freely produced. For years it was known in gardens as *Veronica traversii*

buxifolia *0.6–1.5m. (2–5ft) White E. Summer E T H S*

New Zealand (both North and South Islands). Another of the hebes with neat box-like foliage. It is closely allied to *H. anomala* and *H. odora* and by some authorities is regarded as no more than a variety of the latter.

x **'Carl Teschner'** *20cm. (8in.) Violet to White Summer E T H*

A sprawling hybrid with dark purple stems, small dark green, purple-edged leaves and short spikes of deep violet-blue flowers. Numerous seedlings have been raised from it, some much like it. The original parentage is believed to be *H. elliptica* x *H. pimeloides*.

carnosula *30–60cm. (1–2ft)   White*
Summer   E T H S

New Zealand (South Island). This species is much confused with *H. pinguifolia* which it closely resembles. The small shell-like leaves are less grey-green than those of *H. pinguifolia* and this may make the latter a better decorative plant, but there are clearly many variations of both species and so this general observation may not apply to all.

cupressoides *60–120cm. (2–4ft)   Mauve*
Summer   E T H S

New Zealand (South Island). One of the most popular of the 'whipcord' hebes, with scale-like leaves held close to the stems so that the plant resembles a dwarf conifer. The small mauve flowers are freely produced.

elliptica *1–3m. (3–10ft)   White or Mauve*
Summer   E W T H S

New Zealand, Chile, Tierra del Fuego, Falkland Islands. In view of its very wide distribution in the world it is not surprising that this is a variable plant. What is surprising is that it is scarce in gardens, its name usually being attached to one of its hybrids, such as *H. x franciscana*. Most garden forms of *H. elliptica* are fairly low-growing, bushy, with pale green elliptic leaves and rather large white scented flowers.

x 'Fairfieldii' *45–60cm. (1½–2ft) Lilac*
Spring   E W T H

An attractive hybrid, probably between *Hebe hulkeana* and *H. lavaudiana*, much like the former but with larger flowers, stiffer stems and less shining green leaves. It is not very hardy.

x franciscana *60–80cm. (2–2½ft)*
Blue, Purple or White   Summer Autumn
E W T H

A popular garden plant, a hybrid between *Hebe elliptica* and *H. speciosa*. There are numerous forms differing in the colour of their flowers, which may be anything from pale blue to deep purple (occasionally white) and are always individually rather large and crowded into short thick highly decorative spikes. However, it is usually distinctly tender though very salt-resistant, and so more suitable for coastal than for inland gardens except in warm sheltered places. There is a handsome variety named 'Variegata' with leaves broadly edged with cream.

hectori *15–45cm. (6–18in.)*
White or Pinkish   Summer   E T H S

New Zealand (South Island). One of the small 'whipcord' varieties, often rather sprawling in habit, with tiny leaves closely packed to the yellowish-green, often rather sprawling stems. It is hardy and distinctive, suitable for a sunny rock garden or raised bed but seldom free-flowering.

hulkeana *0.6–2m. (2–6ft)*
Lavender or Lilac   L. Spring   E. Summer
E W T H S

New Zealand (South Island). This very beautiful species is distinct in its slender, more or less erect stems bearing sprays of quite large lavender or lilac flowers. It has a reputation for tenderness yet has survived outdoors even in some Scottish gardens. Good drainage or variety may be the explanation.

lycopodioides *30–45cm. (12–18in.)*
White   Spring   E T H S

New Zealand (South Island). Another of the 'whipcord' varieties with tiny scale-like leaves. The four-sided stems are stiff and erect but more loosely branched than those of *Hebe cupressoides*. The flowers when they appear, which is not very often, are white with blue anthers carried in small clusters.

macrantha   *30–60cm. (1–2ft)*   *White*
E. Summer   *E   W   T   H   S*

New Zealand (Southern Alps). This species
has remarkably large flowers, each about
18mm./³⁄₄in. across, pure white and in a
cluster at the end of each stem. Unfortunately,
the habit of the plant is unattractive, the stems
usually becoming bare for most of their
length, with all the leaves confined to the top.

ochracea   *60cm. (2ft)*   *White*
L. Spring   E. Summer   *E   T H S*

New Zealand (South Island). This fine shrub
has been much confused with *Hebe
armstrongii*, which is similar in habit but has
yellowish-green leaves. Those of *H. ochracea*
are a unique shade of yellowish-copper. It is
one of the 'whipcord' species with tiny leaves,
but it is densely branched and all the
subsidiary branches grow semi-horizontally
in one direction as if they had been combed.
The flowers are small and add little to the
attractiveness of this plant. There are several
varieties including a low-growing one named
'James Stirling'.

odora   *1m. (3ft)*   *White   Summer*
E T H S

Auckland Islands. This small-leaved species is
very closely allied to *Hebe buxifolia*, and
botanists seem to think that they are one and
the same species in which case *odora*, being
the earlier name, should take precedence.
However, from a garden standpoint it is
distinct in having sweetly scented flowers.

pimeloides   *15–45cm. (6–18in.)*   *Purple*
Summer   *E   H   S*

New Zealand (South Island). An attractive
but variable species characterized by its small
grey-green leaves set along the slender stems
in four rows. Garden varieties differ in habit,
some being quite prostrate, and in the degree
of greyness in the foliage. One named
'Quicksilver' has been selected for its
blue-grey leaf colour.

pinguifolia   *15–30cm. (6–12in.)*   *White*
Summer   *E   T   H   S*

New Zealand (South Island). This species
with small grey-green, shell-shaped leaves is
closely allied to *H. carnosula* and by some
experts is considered identical with it. From a
garden standpoint it is chiefly valuable for its
variety 'Pagei', one of the most popular
dwarf, dome-forming hebes with grey leaves.
It is much planted as ground cover in sunny
places and well-drained soil.

propinqua   *30–60cm. (1–2ft)*   *White*
Summer   *E   T   H   S*

New Zealand (South Island). Closely allied
to, and much resembling, *Hebe cupressoides*
though the small flowers, seldom seen, are
white not mauve. It has a variety named
'Aurea' with yellowish-green leaves which is
often wrongly listed as either *Hebe
salicornoides* 'Aurea' or *H. armstrongii*
'Compacta'.

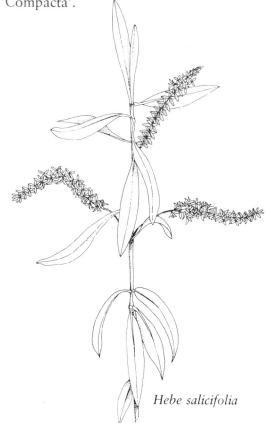

Hebe salicifolia

salicifolia *3–4m. (10–13ft)*
White or Mauve   Summer   E T H S

New Zealand (South Island). A big
well-branched shrub with long narrow leaves
and narrow trails of white or mauve-tinted
flowers. It is both variable in itself and also
crosses freely with other hebes, including *H.
speciosa* and its hybrids. One of the best of
these is 'Midsummer Beauty' with broader
leaves than *H. salicifolia* but similar long
trails of purplish-lavender flowers. It can
continue to flower intermittently from
midsummer until late autumn but is not as
hardy as *H. salicifolia*.

speciosa *1–1.5m. (3–5ft)   Reddish-purple*
L. Summer   Autumn   E W T H S

New Zealand (North Island). It is probable
that the true species does not exist in Britain
outside botanic gardens, but in all maritime
gardens and many warm and sunny inland
gardens its place is taken by its numerous

Hebe speciosa
'Andersonii Variegata'

hybrids. These are all characterized by quite
large, broadly lance-shaped leaves and fine
upstanding spikes of flowers often richly
coloured. All are among the more tender
hebes and will only survive a few degrees of
frost but they do not mind wind even when it
is salt-laden.

Typical *H. speciosa* hybrids are 'Alicia
Amherst', often wrongly known as 'Veitchii',
which is a different variety, deep
violet-purple; 'Andersonii Variegata', soft
lavender flowers, leaves heavily variegated
with cream; 'Gauntlettii', salmon-pink; 'La
Seduisante', crimson; 'Purple Queen',
blue-purple', and 'Simon Delaux', deep
crimson.

Hebe Hybrids

In addition to the hybrids described
separately or under the species which they
most resemble, there are a great many others
some of which have been given names and
many of which are excellent garden plants. In
most cases little or nothing is known about
their parentage and in some instances this
could be quite complex since hybrids
cross-fertilize with other hybrids. The
following are all worth planting:

'Bowles' Hybrid'. A low-growing bushy plant
with rather thin spikes of lilac flowers
produced from midsummer until Christmas.
It is only moderately hardy.
'Carnea'. A bushy plant about 1m./3ft. high
with slender spikes of pink flowers which fade
to white. Only moderately hardy.
'Edinensis'. A dwarf plant, usually less than
30cm./1ft high with small leaves (but not
quite the 'whipcord' habit) and rather sparse
white or mauve flowers. It is hardy.
'Great Orme'. Close to 'Carnea' but with
deeper pink flowers. Only moderately hardy.
'Margery Fish'. A compact shrub up to
1m./3ft high with good spikes of violet-blue
flowers produced in summer and autumn.
One of the hardier kinds.

'**Marjorie**'. A fairly short but wide plant with short spikes of light blue flowers produced in summer and autumn. Hardy.

'**Mrs Winder**'. A small densely branched bush with purple stems and leaves, and may be identical with 'E.A. Bowles' (not 'Bowles' Hybrid') and 'Warleyensis' but 'Waikiki', which is also confused with it, is said to be shorter and more spreading. All are fairly hardy.

'**Spender's Seedling**'. A fairly short (1m./3ft) plant with narrow leaves and long slender spikes of white flowers. It is fairly hardy.

HEDERA, Araliaceae. Ivy. The ivies arouse a good deal of contention among gardeners, some admiring their great variety of leaf size, form and colour and others regarding them as dangerous intruders liable to kill trees and damage buildings. In fact no harm need be done if the right ivies are chosen for the right positions and are kept under proper control. Ivies can be clipped or more drastically cut back during May or June and it is essential to keep them out of house gutters and from growing onto or, worse still, under roofs. If they cling to trees they must not be allowed to grow out over the top nor to hang so heavily on branches that they drag them off. There are a great many varieties of ivy, some much faster-growing than others. A lot depends on selecting varieties which will not prove too vigorous for the situation they are to occupy.

Ivies grow in all soils from light to heavy, acid to alkaline, and they positively like chalk and limestone. They can be grown in sun or shade, even quite dense shade but yellow 'variegation' is best produced in sun. Not all kinds are fully hardy and here again choice must be made to suit the site. Most ivies are self-supporting by aerial roots which will cling to almost any surface, but when ivies start to flower and fruit their growth changes, becoming bushy instead of climbing and failing to produce aerial roots. Cuttings taken from these bushy growths will produce bushy plants. Ivies can be grown from summer cuttings in a propagator, frame or polythene bag but without warmth they sometimes take quite a time to form roots. Stems can also be trained out over the soil, allowed to root and then be lifted and cut into convenient pieces.

canariensis *Vigorous Greenish-yellow L. Summer Autumn E T H L*

Portugal, Canary Islands, Madeira, The Azores, north-western Africa. Because of its distribution in the wild this ivy is less hardy than *Hedera helix* but it can be grown outdoors in most parts of the British Isles provided it is given a sheltered position. The two most popular varieties are 'Azorica', with bright green leaves up to 15cm./6in. across and 'Gloire de Marengo', also known as 'Variegata', with the green colour confined to the areas around the veins the rest of the leaf being greyish with a broad irregular margin of cream.

colchica *Vigorous Greenish-yellow L. Summer Autumn E T H L*

Caucasus, Asiatic Turkey. This handsome ivy is notable for its very large leaves often, but not always, more or less heart-shaped and seldom deeply lobed. In gardens the species with dark green leaves is not so often seen as the fine variegated variety named 'Dentata Variegata', in which the leaves are broadly edged with pale butter-yellow with a zone of greyish-green inside and full green confined to the central portion. Some leaves may be almost wholly pale yellow. This is particularly marked in some of the named variants such as 'Paddy's Pride'. There are bushy, non-climbing forms of both green-leaved and variegated *Hedera colchica*.

helix *Very vigorous Greenish-yellow L. Summer Autumn E T H L*

Europe (including Britain). The common ivy is an extraordinarily variable plant which has produced hundreds of variants, from quite small relatively slow-growing plants with small leaves to extra vigorous large-leaved varieties. Some have deeply or narrowly lobed

Hedera colchica
'Dentata Variegata'

leaves, others have unlobed leaves or leaves that are wrinkled, curled or raggedly slashed. There are also many variegated forms with white, grey, pink, cream or yellow colourings variously disposed on the leaves. Almost all are as easily grown in sun or shade as ordinary ivy but just a few of the small-leaved variegated varieties specially developed for house cultivation are not quite so reliable outdoors. The following are popular varieties but there are many more:

'**Adam**'. A small-leaved variety with white, grey and grey-green variegations. Like many varieties selected in the first place for indoor cultivation it has the habit of branching frequently and so making a bushy, rather than climbing plant but it is not a true arborescent (adult) form.

'**Arborescens**'. The adult or bushy form of the common ivy. It makes a big densely branched bush producing in autumn plenty of its globular clusters of greenish-yellow flowers followed by black fruits.

'**Buttercup**'. The young leaves are wholly yellow and even with age they only develop sufficient chlorophyll to become yellowish-green. The best 'all-yellow' ivy.

'**Caenwoodiana**'. Leaves are small and divided into narrow lobes.

'**Cavendishii**'. Leaves broadly edged with cream and sometimes flushed with pink, especially in winter.

'**Chicago**'. Leaves small, dark green or more or less flushed with bronze.

'**Conglomerata**'. Very dwarf and slow-growing, with small crowded wavy-edged leaves. A variant of this, named 'Conglomerata Erecta', is stronger-growing and more stiffly erect, with the leaves on the young stems very regularly arranged and held horizontally so that the whole plant has a curiously formal appearance.

'**Cristata**'. A vigorous ivy with rounded light green leaves that are crimped around the edges.

'**Deltoidea**'. Rather stiff in growth with lobes confined to the base of the leaf, the rest of which is almost triangular.

'**Digitata**'. Leaves with five narrow, finger-like lobes.

'**Glacier**'. Leaves mainly grey-green with a border of white.

'**Goldheart**'. This fine variety is also known as 'Golden Jubilee'. The rather small dark green leaves have a central blotch of yellow. This colour is produced in sun and shade.

'**Green Fern**'. Leaves broad-ended but raggedly slashed.

'**Green Ripple**'. Green leaves with jagged lobes, the central lobe long and narrow.

'**Hibernica**'. The 'Irish Ivy' is characterized by its large, very dark green leaves. There is a yellow variegated form of this named 'Hibernica aurea'.

'**Marginata elegantissima**'. This appears to be the original (and, therefore, valid) name for an attractive small-leaved ivy which is often grown as either 'Elegantissima' or 'Tricolor'. The leaves are greyish-green edged with white and often flushed with pink, especially in winter.

'Poetica'. The Poet's Ivy is recognized as a variety occurring in the wild in south-eastern Europe, Asia Minor and the Caucasus. The leaves have shallow lobes and are bright green but often become coppery in winter.

'Sagittifolia'. A fairly vigorous ivy with very narrow lobes, the lower ones swept backwards like the barbs of an arrow-head.

HEDYSARUM, Leguminosae. Though this is a very large genus only one species has been taken up by British gardeners and even this is by no means common. It is a good shrub for warm sunny places and well-drained even rather sandy and dry soils. Long stems can be cut back quite severely in spring to keep the base of the shrub well furnished with young growth. Seed sown under glass in spring provides the best method of increase.

multijugum   *1–1.5m. (3–5ft)   Magenta Summer   D   C   S*

Mongolia. This is a shrub that does not branch much unless encouraged to do so by pruning. The leaves are composed of a number of small leaflets producing a light, rather ferny effect, and the small pea-type flowers are carried in slender erect spikes.

HELIANTHEMUM, Cistaceae. Sun Rose. These are the small relatives of *Cistus*, similar in their preference for warm sunny places and well-drained soils, and because of their short but often sprawling growth are suitable for rock gardens, terrace walls and banks. Most are improved in habit by light thinning immediately after flowering. All can be raised from seed sown in spring but seedlings of the garden varieties are likely to differ from their parents so these are increased by summer cuttings in a frame or propagator.

lunulatum   *10–20cm. (4–8in.) Yellow and orange   Summer   E O S H*

Italian Maritime Alps. A very neat little shrub with small leaves and abundant yellow flowers with an orange zone at the centre.

nummularium   *20–40cm. (8–16in.) Various   L. Spring   E. Summer E O S H*

Europe (including Britain), Asian Minor and the Caucasus. This is the common Sun Rose, a favourite with British gardeners and a plant that has been greatly developed by selection rather than by hybridization. Typically it has wiry sprawling stems, small leaves, green above and grey beneath, and plain yellow flowers, but in gardens many desirable variations have been selected, named and kept true by vegetative propagation. The following are typical of the race:

'Amy Baring'. Bronzy-orange with deeper centre.

'Ben Fhada'. Yellow with orange centre, leaves grey.

'Ben Hope'. Carmine with orange centre, greyish-green leaves.

'Ben Nevis'. Yellow with mahogany-crimson centre.

'Jubilee'. Fully-double yellow flowers, leaves grey.

'Mrs C.W. Earle'. Fully-double scarlet flowers.

'Rhodanthe Carneum'. Rose-pink flowers, grey leaves.

'The Bride'. White with yellow centre, grey leaves.

'Wisley Pink'. Soft pink.

'Wisley Primrose'. Primrose with grey leaves.

HELICHRYSUM, Compositae. Most of the hardy shrubs grown in gardens under this name have been transferred by botanists to another genus, *Ozothamnus*, where they are described in this book. However, one popular species remains, a grey-leaved shrub for warm sunny places. It can be trimmed in spring or early summer to improve its habit. Increase is by summer cuttings in a propagator.

splendidum *1–2m. (3–6ft)   Yellow*
Summer   E   W   K   H

Mountains of Africa. A bushy shrub with small narrowly oblong leaves, silvery with dense down which also covers the rather soft stems. The flowers have little beauty and it does not matter if they are removed by clipping or pruning.

Hibiscus syriacus 'Violet Claire Double'

HIBISCUS, Malvaceae. Most species of this large genus are too tender to be grown outdoors in the British Isles but two rather similar species are much planted in the milder and sunnier parts for their late flowering. They like good well-drained fertile soil and a sheltered, sunny position. The only pruning necessary is to remove dead, damaged or weak growth in the spring but, if desired, branches can be shortened and plants shaped at the same time. Propagation of the garden varieties must be vegetative, and nurserymen frequently graft some varieties on to seedlings or cuttings of common kinds. Amateurs usually increase by late summer cuttings or by layering in spring or summer.

sinosyriacus   *2.5–3m. (8–10ft)   Various*
Autumn   D   T   H   L

China. A vigorous shrub much like the better known *Hibiscus syriacus* but with larger leaves and flowers. There are several garden varieties differing in the colour of their flowers. 'Autumn Surprise' is white and cerise; 'Lilac Queen', white flushed with lilac and with a crimson zone at the centre; and 'Ruby Glow' is white with a cerise centre.

syriacus   *2.5–3m. (8–10ft)   Various*
L. Summer   Autumn   D   T   H   L

China, India. This is the popular species, a shrub with erect, rather stiff stems, deeply toothed leaves and mallow-type flowers produced in succession from July until October. There are double-flowered as well as single-flowered varieties and considerable choice in colours. The following are typical:

'Blue Bird'. Violet-blue with a deeper-coloured centre. Single.
'Coelestis'. Similar to 'Blue Bird' but flowers not quite so large.
'Duc de Brabant'. Fully double magenta flowers.
'Hamabo'. Single white with crimson centre.

'**Lady Stanley**'. Semi-double, white flushed with pink and with crimson centre. Considered to be synonymous with 'Elegantissima'.
'**Monstrosus**'. Single, white with maroon centre. Two newer varieties. 'Dorothy Crane' and 'Red Heart' are similar but even better.
'**Monstrosus Plenus**'. Like 'Monstrosus' but double.
'**Violet Claire Double**'. Purple semi-double deeper at the base. This variety is also known as 'Puniceus Plenus', 'Roseus Plenus' and 'Violaceus Plenus'.
'**Woodbridge**'. Large single magenta flowers with a deeper coloured zone at the centre.

HIPPOPHAE, Elaeagnaceae. Sea Buckthorn. Though, as the popular name suggests, these are shrubs that thrive near the sea and are relatively unaffected by salt-laden wind, they also grow well inland and are not at all difficult to please provided the soil is reasonably well-drained and the situation is open, preferably sunny. The flowers are of two sexes and these are borne on separate bushes. Only the females can produce berries and then only if there is a male bush sufficiently near to ensure pollination so these are not shrubs to plant in isolation. Little pruning is desirable but stems can be shortened or removed in spring and suckers can be chopped back with a spade or mattock in autumn or winter. Seeds germinate readily in spring but seedlings may be of either sex so there is advantage in increasing by layers or suckers which will have the same sex as the plant from which they are taken.

rhamnoides   *3–6m. (10–20ft)   Greenish Spring   D T S L V*

Europe (including Britain) and Asia. The most decorative species, with narrow silvery leaves and small shining orange berries that have a very staining juice. The habit is densely branched and thicket-forming so that one bush can gradually spread over a considerable area.

HOHERIA, Malvaceae. New Zealand trees and shrubs. The evergreen species are rather tender but the two deciduous kinds described here are fairly hardy though they are not usually very long-lived. They are suitable for planting in all the milder parts of the British Isles and will withstand quite a lot of frost if they are in good condition. They like sunny warm places and well-drained soil, and are readily raised from seed sown in spring under glass or in a sheltered place outdoors. Self-sown seedlings often appear around established bushes. Late summer cuttings can also be rooted in a propagator. Pruning consists in cutting out weak, old or damaged growth in spring.

glabrata   *3–6m. (10–20ft)   White Summer   D T S*

New Zealand (South Island). An open-branched shrub with smooth green leaves and clusters of slender-stalked white scented flowers produced with great profusion about midsummer. They do not last long but make a marvellous display while at their peak.

lyallii   *3–6m. (10–20ft)   White Summer   D T S*

New Zealand (South Island) Much like the foregoing but the leaves are greyish with a covering of soft down, and it is more likely to grow into a small tree rather than a big shrub. Of the two it is also probably the hardier though this may depend upon the original provenance of the plants from which the garden stock is descended, since hoherias have a wide natural distribution in New Zealand and it is probable that some plants are more accustomed to frost than others.

HOLBOELLIA, Lardizabalaceae. At least one species of these vigorous evergreen twining plants is hardy throughout the British Isles and a second is sufficiently hardy to be grown in all the milder parts of the south and west as well as in many town gardens. Neither of these species is difficult to grow in soil that is reasonably fertile and well drained and in a light, preferably sunny, position. The only pruning necessary is to thin out the older or weaker stems in spring to relieve the very considerable weight of growth that can build up after a few years. Increase is by summer cuttings in a propagator, layering in spring or seed in a frame or greenhouse in spring.

coriacea *4–8m. (13–26ft)*
White and Purple Spring E T H L S

China. This is the hardiest species. Each leaf is composed of three separate leaflets. The flowers, produced in pendant clusters, are of two sexes but both are produced on the same plant. The males are white with purple stamens, the females have thicker sepals, greenish-white flushed with purple. Though this is not a spectacular plant it is attractive and interesting.

latifolia *5–10m. (16–32ft)*
White and Purple E. Spring
E W T H L S

Himalaya. This handsome climber is even more vigorous but less hardy than *Holboellia coriacea*. The male and female flowers resemble those of *H. coriacea* and are sweetly scented.

HYDRANGEA, Hydrangeaceae. Although botanically this is not a very big genus, it has provided gardens with a great many varieties. Most hydrangeas flower late and in some the flowers change colour as they fade, remaining decorative for many weeks. Few hydrangeas are completely hardy throughout the British Isles but most thrive in the milder and more sheltered parts and all succeed well by the sea. They like good fertile soil with plenty of moisture while they are in growth, and will grow in sun or partial shade but usually flower most freely when they have plenty of light. A peculiarity of hydrangeas, particularly marked in the *H. macrophylla* varieties, is that coloured flowers tend towards blue and blue-purple in acid soils and red or red-purple in alkaline soils. Pruning differs according to species. *Hydrangea paniculata* and *H. arborescens* flower on the current year's growth and can be cut hard back each February or March, leaving each stem with about two growth buds. *H. macrophylla*, *H. serrata* and the numerous garden varieties derived from them flower on young shoots produced from the previous year's stems and, in some varieties, this is restricted to shoots produced from the uppermost buds. These are the most difficult to manage in cold places because, if the terminal buds are damaged or destroyed in winter, there may be a lot of new growth but no flowers. They cannot be hard-pruned like *H. paniculata* but weak or old branches can be cut right out in spring and the old, faded flower-heads removed. This kind of thinning also suits those hydrangeas such as *H. aspera*, *H. sargentiana* and *H. quercifolia*, which make very large bushes. All kinds can be increased by spring or summer cuttings in a frame, propagator or pot of sandy soil inside a polythene bag and *Hydrangea petiolaris* also by layering in spring or summer.

arborescens *1.2–3m. (4–10ft) White*
L. Summer D C H

Eastern USA. It is not the species itself that is much cultivated in gardens but a variety of it named 'Grandiflora', which has the 'snowball' type of flower-head in which all the flowers are sterile and so have the large bracts which are characteristic of sterility in this genus. It is a very handsome shrub capable of making a really substantial display and it is also one of the hardiest hydrangeas.

aspera *2.5–3m. (8–10ft) Pink to Purple*
Summer D W T H

Nepal, China, Formosa. This is the hydrangea which usually appears in gardens as *H. villosa*. It makes a big bush, becoming very broad in time, has downy leaves and flat heads of flowers, the central fertile ones small and bead-like, the outer sterile ones surrounded by large bracts, occasionally white but usually mauve or pinkish-purple. It is a very handsome free-flowering species but not very hardy, though with such a wide natural distribution it is probable that some forms are hardier than others.

involucrata   *45–60cm. (18–24in.)*
White or Bluish   L. Summer   E. Autumn
D W T H

Japan and Formosa. A dwarf shrub with flowers produced in flat heads, the central ones small and blue the outer ones sterile and surrounded by quite large bracts which may be white but are more usually bluish-mauve or pink. It is not very hardy.

macrophylla   *1–3m. (3–10ft)   Various*
L. Summer   E. Autumn   D W T H

Japan. This is the species that has been most lavish in producing garden varieties. Broadly these can be divided into two groups; one which botanists call *normalis* and gardeners call 'lace caps' in which the flowers are in flat heads the central part of each cluster composed of small fertile flowers, the outer ring of sterile flowers with showy bracts; the other group, known as 'Hortensia', in which all the flowers are sterile and have bracts and so the head becomes ball-shaped. It is possible to make a second, purely horticultural division between those which flower mainly from terminal buds and those that will flower from lateral buds even when the terminals have been cut off or destroyed by frost. The 'Hortensia' or mop-headed varieties make the most solid display but the 'lace caps' are more graceful and look better in wild or semi-wild settings. There are a great many garden varieties of which the following are typical:

'**Altona**'. A Hortensia variety, rose-pink or blue according to soil, but becoming green and red as flowers age.
'**Ayesha**'. Small double flowers like those of lilac, mauve-pink in colour.
'**Baardse's Favourite**'. Deep pink hortensia flowers on a dwarf plant.

'**Blue Prince**'. Hortensia type, blue in acid soil but deep rose in alkaline soil.
'**Blue Wave**'. A popular lace-cap type but only blue in acid soil; otherwise mauve or pink.
'**Europa**'. Large-flowered Hortensia with deep pink flowers in alkaline soil, blue if it is acid.
'**Générale Vicomtesse de Vibraye**'. One of the easiest Hortensias from which to get blue flowers even in neutral soils and also one that flowers well even when the winter terminal buds are lost.
'**Goliath**'. A large-flowered Hortensia with deep pink flowers.
'**Hamburg**'. A large-flowered Hortensia starting a deep rose but ageing to intense crimson.
'**Lanarth White**'. Lace cap variety with white sterile flowers and blue or pink fertile flowers.
'**Madame E. Moullière**'. White Hortensia unchanged by the soil.
'**Maréchal Foch**'. Hortensia, rose or deep blue according to soil.
'**Mariesii**'. Lace cap with pink or mauve sterile flowers.
'**Parsifal**'. Hortensia with deep rose or deep blue flowers but mixtures of these can occur in the same bush since it does not take much soil change to alter the colour.
'**Sir Joseph Banks**'. Strong-growing and with immense ball-like clusters of bloom, which are usually rather washy pink or blue according to soil. It is not very hardy but grows well by the sea.
'**Veitchii**'. A lace cap with white sterile flowers and blue fertile flowers.
'**Westfalen**'. Hortensia with crimson or blue-purple flowers.
'**White Wave**'. A white lace cap much like 'Veitchii' but possibly a better garden plant.

paniculata   *1.5–3m. (5–10ft)   White*
Summer   E. Autumn.   D C H

Japan, Sakhalin, China. One of the hardiest species and a very handsome garden plant. The flowers are carried in conical clusters and are ivory-white at first but become progressively stained with pink or red as they fade. Left to its own devices this species will eventually make a large bush, but the size of the flower clusters will tend to diminish as that of the plant increases. The finest flowers are produced on bushes that are hard-pruned annually in late winter or early spring. There are several distinct varieties. 'Grandiflora' is the most popular because of the great size of the flower clusters and the number of sterile flowers with showy bracts. 'Praecox' flowers earlier but has smaller clusters with fewer sterile flowrs in proportion to small fertile flowers. 'Floribunda' and 'Tardiva' are intermediate in flower character and are later flowering, 'Tardiva' very much so and sometimes still in flower in October.

petiolaris   *8–16m. (25–50ft)   White   E. Summer   D T H L*

Japan, Sakhalin, Formosa. This is a vigorous climber, clinging to walls, tree trunks etc. by aerial roots like an ivy. The flowers are of the 'lace cap' type, that is flat clusters of small, whitish fertile flowers surrounded by a usually broken ring or sterile flowers with large white bracts.

quercifolia   *1.2–2m. (4–6ft)   White   Summer   D W T H L V*

South-eastern USA. The leaves of this handsome species resemble those of one of the large-leaved, American red or scarlet oaks and, like them, they colour well in the autumn. The flowers are mainly small and fertile but surrounded by a few sterile flowers with large white bracts which become purple with age.

sargentiana   *2.5–3m. (8–10ft)   Pale pink and Lilac   L. Summer   D W T H L*

China. In many respects this resembles *Hydrangea aspera* but the leaves are larger and less softly downy and the flower clusters are also larger but as a rule less numerous. In shade it can become gaunt and ungainly and it is best planted in a sunny but fairly sheltered place.

Hydrangea serrata 'Acuminata'

serrata   *1m. (3ft)   Various   Summer   D T H*

Japan, Korea. This is closely allied to *Hydrangea macrophylla* and, from a garden standpoint, might be regarded as a smaller, more wiry-stemmed, hardier version of it. There are a number of natural and garden varieties of which the following are typical:

'Acuminata'. Leaves rather long and pointed. Bracts of sterile flowers blue in acid or neutral soils.
'Bluebird'. Despite the name the bracts of the sterile flowers are usually pink and become pale blue only in markedly acid soil.
'Grayswood'. The small fertile flowers make a blue 'pad' to a broken ring of sterile flowers with bracts that start white but age to pink and finally crimson.
'Preziosa'. One of the few *H. serrata* varieties with the ball-like type of flower cluster in which all, or nearly all, the flowers are sterile. The bracts start pink but later deepen to red and become speckled and blotched with crimson.
'Rosalba'. A rather vigorous form with saw-edged white bracts which become progressively blotched with crimson as they age.

HYPERICUM, Hypericaceae. St John's Wort. This is a very big genus including many herbaceous species as well as tiny semi-woody plants whose main place is the rock garden and so fall outside the scope of this book. Yet this still leaves an impressive number of genuinely shrubby species most of which are hardy and easily grown in any reasonably fertile soil. Hypericums will grow in shade but are happier and flower most freely in good light, preferably with some direct sunshine. A few kinds, most notably *Hypericum calycinum*, can be pruned quite severely each spring but for most a moderate thinning of old and weak stems, coupled with a little shortening where this will improve habit and keep plants within bounds, is all that is required. It is best done in April or May when it can be seen if there is any winter damage. Plants can be raised from seed sown in spring but the usual method of increase is by summer cuttings in frame, propagator or polythene bag. *Hypericum calycinum* can also be increased by division in spring or early autumn.

androsaemum   *60–90cm. (2–3ft)   Yellow Summer   D C S H*

Europe (including Britain) and North Africa. This is a semi-woody plant known in Britain as Tutsan and chiefly valued in gardens for its seed capsules, shining and at first red-purple but gradually becoming dark crimson. The flowers are small, carried in clusters.

augustinii   *1–2m. (3–6ft)   Yellow Summer   E. Autumn   D T S H*

China. A handsome species making a rounded bush and bearing quite large, saucer-shaped, daffodil-yellow flowers very freely.

calycinum   *Prostrate   Yellow Summer   E. Autumn   ED C H V*

South-eastern Europe. This is the 'Rose of Sharon', a rampant prostrate shrub retaining its leaves except in the coldest weather and with large bright yellow flowers each bearing

a central 'brush' of long golden stamens. It is a very handsome plant which will grow in sun or shade in all manner of soils, including chalk and limestone. It will withstand draught and is excellent for binding the soil on steep banks. Its one fault is that it is very invasive, spreading inexorably by tough stolons which take quite a lot of chopping through when the plant has to be curbed.

forrestii   *2m. (6ft)   Yellow   Summer D T S H*

China, Assam, Burma. An attractive, bushy species with saucer-shaped golden yellow flowers produced very freely and usually followed by shining reddish-bronze

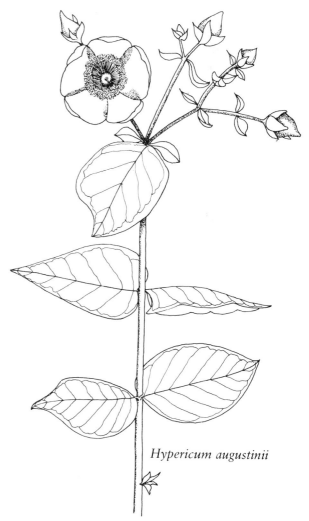

Hypericum augustinii

seed-capsules. The leaves often colour well in autumn and some may be retained for most or all the winter especially if the weather is mild.

'Hidcote'   *1.5m. (5ft)   Yellow Summer   E. Autumn   ED T H*

A shrub of uncertain origin, maybe an accidental hybrid between *Hypericum forrestii* and *H. calycinum*, but if so, much more favouring the former parent in habit and flower. It is, however, evergreen, except in very cold winters, the flowers are not quite so regularly saucer-shaped as those of *H. forestii* and they are produced over a longer season. It has established itself as the most popular hypericum for garden decoration.

hookeranum   *0.6–2m. (2–6ft)   Yellow Summer   E T S H*

Himalaya, India, Burma, Thailand. A variable species similar in many respects to *H. forrestii*, with which it has been confused. There is a fine hybrid named 'Rowallane' raised from a form of this species named 'Rogersii', crossed with *H. leschenaultii*. This has very full, shallow cup-shaped, golden yellow flowers and is rather tall but distinctly tender and may need to be trained against a sunny wall in cold gardens.

x inodorum   *1–1.5m. (3–5ft)   Yellow Summer   E T C H*

A hybrid between *Hypericum androsaemum* and a small European species named *H. hircinum*, the leaves of which have an unpleasant odour when crushed. The name 'inodorum' records that the leaves of the hybrid have no such smell. The hybrid is usually represented in gardens by a selected form, named 'Elstead', which has small yellow flowers followed by abundant crops of shining reddish-bronze seed-capsules. It is frequently attacked by a rust disease which turns the leaves brown. This should be combated by spraying in summer with a systemic fungicide.

leschenaultii   *1.2–2.5m. (4–8ft)   Yellow Summer   ED W T S H*

Malaysia. A beautiful but distinctly tender species with very regularly formed, shallow cup-shaped yellow flowers. In many British gardens it needs the protection of a sunny wall.

x moserianum   *30–45cm. (12–18in.) Yellow Summer   D W T H*

A hybrid between *Hypericum patulum* and *H. calycinum*, which makes a low rather spreading plant. It is rather tender and is often damaged by frost in cold gardens. It has a beautiful variety named 'Tricolor', in which the leaves are splashed with pink and white.

patulum   *1m. (3ft)   Yellow   Summer ED W T S H*

China. Plants grown in gardens under this name are usually *Hypericum forrestii*. True *H. patulum* has yellow saucer-shaped flowers, retains its leaves except in very cold weather and is not reliably hardy in all parts of the British Isles.

ILEX, Aquifoliaceae. Holly. Many hollies will grow into trees of considerable size if permitted to do so but all are so amenable to pruning that they can, if desired, be kept to shrub-like proportions and may also be trimmed as hedges, screens and windbreaks. All are easily grown in most soils but their preference is for those that are fertile and not liable to dry out badly in summer. They will grow in sun or shade. Flowers of different sexes are produced on separate plants. Only the females will produce berries and then only if there is a male sufficiently near for pollination. Species can be increased from seed sown outdoors as soon as ripe but garden varieties and hybrids do not come true to type from seed and must be increased by summer or autumn cuttings in a propagator or by grafting in spring onto seedlings.

x **altaclarensis** *3–20m. (10–65ft)* *Whitish*
L. Spring E K A H G

The name given to a large group of hybrids
between *Ilex aquifolium* and *I. perado*. All are
very vigorous and most have leaves larger
than those of the common holly. The
following are typical of the many named
varieties:

'**Camellifolia**'. A female with large leaves
many of which have no spines.
'**Golden King**'. A female with leaves broadly
edged with yellow. It is arguably the best
golden variegated holly.
'**Hodginsii**'. A male with large dark green
leaves. One of the best varieties to plant in
industrial areas.
'**Wilsonii**'. A female with large green leaves
and a compact habit.

aquifolium *3–20m. (10–65ft)* *Whitish*
L. Spring E K S H A G

Europe (including Britain), western Asia. This
is the common holly, one of the few truly
native British evergreens. In gardens the wild
form is used mainly for hedging or as
windbreaks. For ornamental purposes it is
mainly the garden varieties that are planted.
The following are typical:

'**Argentea Marginata**'. A female with leaves
edged with white.
'**Argentea Medio-picta**'. Leaves with a splash
of creamy-white in the middle or towards the
base. It is often known as 'Silver Milkmaid'.
Male.
'**Argentea Pendula**'. Female with pendulous
branches. The leaves are mottled with
greyish-green in the centre and are broadly
edged with creamy-white. This variety is also
known as 'Perry's Weeping'.
'**Bacciflava**'. Leaves green, berries yellow.
'**Crassifolia**'. Both stems and leaves of this
very odd female variety are unusually thick. It
is popularly known as the Leather-leaf Holly.
'**Ferox**'. Another oddity, a male holly with
clusters of spines on the upper surface of the
leaves as well as around the edges. There are

white and yellow variegated varieties. These
are all known as Hedgehog Hollies.
'**Golden Queen**'. A male holly with
yellow-edged leaves.
'**Handsworth New Silver**'. A female holly
with white-edged leaves.
'**J C. van Thol**'. This variety, also known as
'Polycarpa', has dark green, sparsely spread
leaves and fine red berries. There is a
variegated variety named 'Golden van
Thol'.
'**Madame Briot**'. A female holly with yellow
variegation both around the leaf margins and
centrally.
'**Scotica**'. A female holly with smooth-edged,
spineless leaves. There are two yellow
variegated varieties, one called 'Scotica
Aurea', with the yellow around the edge of
the leaves, the other, 'Scotica Aureopicta',
with a central blotch of yellow.
'**Silver Queen**'. A male holly with purple
stems and a wide band of white around each
leaf.

cornuta *2.5–3m. (8–10ft)* *White* *Spring*
E K S H A

China and Korea. A distinctive species with
leaves that are roughly rectangular in shape
with a spine at each corner, a fifth, curved
downward at the apex and sometimes a few
smaller spines. The berries are large and red.

crenata *1.5–2.5m. (5–8ft)* *White*
L. Spring *E. Summer* E K S H A

Japan, Korea. A very variable species but
always slow-growing and relatively small.
The berries are black. Typical varieties are
'Convexa' with leaves convex above, *latifolia*
with small oval leaves, 'Mariesii' stiff in
growth and very dwarf and 'Variegata' with
leaves blotched with yellow.

opaca *3–12 m. (10–40ft)* *White*
E. Summer E K T S H A

Eastern and central USA. This is the American
Holly, a species rather like the common holly
but with duller leaves. The berries are

normally red but there is a variety named *xanthocarpa* with yellow berries. This species dislikes alkaline soils.

perado *3–12m. (10–40ft)   White   Spring*
E W K T S H A

Madeira, Canary Islands, Azores. This rather tender species is known both as the Madeira Holly and the Azorean Holly. It resembles the common holly and is chiefly of interest to gardeners as the parent, with that species, of the vigorous race of hybrids known as *I. x altaclarensis*.

pernyi *3–6m. (10–20ft)   Pale yellow*
L. Spring   E   K T S H A

China. The leaves of this species are very distinctive, more or less square at the base with a few spines on the sides and a very marked triangular tip. The habit is stiff and the whole effect rather architectural. The berries are red.

Illicium anisatum

verticillata *2–3m. (6–10ft)   White*
Summer   D T S H A

Eastern North America. A deciduous holly with berries that are red in the type but yellow in a variety named *chrysocarpa*. It can berry freely and a variety named 'Christmas Cheer' has been selected for this good quality.

ILLICIUM, Illiciaceae. Only two species are likely to be found in British gardens and then rarely for they are distinctly tender and even in the milder counties usually need the shelter of a wall. They are tolerant of some lime in the soil but thrive best in moderately acid, peaty soils. The only pruning necessary is to remove damaged or surplus growth in May. Increase is by layering in spring.

anisatum *2.5–3m. (8–10ft)*
Greenish-yellow   Spring   E   W T L

China and Japan. The leaves are broadly lance-shaped, the flowers curious, composed of numerous very narrow petals radiating around a central tuft of stamens. Both leaves and stems are aromatic when bruised.

floridanum *2–2.5m. (6–8ft)   Maroon*
L. Spring   E. Summer   E W T L

Southern USA. Rather like the last species but plants are shorter, leaves are narrower and the petals are maroon. It is similarly aromatic.

INDIGOFERA, Leguminosae. Like so many plants belonging to the pea family these are excellent shrubs for sunny, hot, even rather dry places in well-drained soils, which may be sandy and not particularly rich.
Unfortunately, most kinds are none too hardy and stems may be killed close to ground level in winter. All dead or damaged growth should be cut away in March and at the same time undamaged stems can be shortened considerably. Indigoferas can be raised from seed sown in a greenhouse in spring or by summer cuttings in a propagator.

amblyantha   *2m. (6ft)   Pink
Summer   E. Autumn   D W C S H*

China. This is one of the hardiest kinds,
capable of surviving quite a lot of frost
provided growth is well-ripened and drainage
is good. The small pale rose flowers are
carried in slender spikes like those of a vetch.

heterantha   *0.6–1.2m. (2–4ft)   Magenta
Summer   E. Autumn   D W C S H*

Himalaya. One of the most beautiful species,
with feathery leaves each composed of
numerous small leaflets and fine spikes of
magenta flowers, which continue into
autumn. Unfortunately it is not very hardy. In
gardens it is usually grown as *Indigofera
gerardiana*.

potaninii   *2–2.5m. (6–8ft)   Pink
Summer   D W C S H*

China. A species much like *I. amblyantha* and
the differences between the two are of more
significance botanically than horticulturally.

ITEA, Escalloniaceae. There are evergreen
and deciduous species of *Itea* and they require
rather different conditions. The two evergreen
kinds described below are both a little tender
and suitable only for planting fully in the
open in the milder parts of the British Isles.
Elsewhere they are best given the protection
of a south-facing wall. By contrast the
deciduous species described below prefers a
semi-shady place though it can be grown fully
in the open since it is hardier than the
evergreens. All species like good fertile soil
not liable to dry out badly in summer and
Itea virginica actually prefers a moist
situation. It can be pruned after flowering
when some of the older stems can be
removed. Some thinning of old stems is also
desirable with the evergreen species,
especially when wall-trained, but is best done
in April or May. All kinds can be increased by
late summer cuttings in a propagator and *I.
virginica* also by digging up suckers with
roots in autumn or winter.

ilicifolia   *2–3.5m. (6–12ft)   Greenish-white
L. Summer   E W T H*

China. A beautiful shrub with shining
holly-like leaves and tiny flowers borne in
long pendant chains.

Itea ilicifolia

virginica   *1–1.5m. (3–5ft)   Creamy-white
Summer   D O H V*

Eastern USA. A thicket-forming shrub which
flowers on stems made the previous year. The
small creamy-white flowers are scented and
are produced in slender erect spikes in July.

yunnanensis   *2–3m. (6–10ft)   White
Summer   E W T H*

China. A species very much like *I. ilicifolia*
but the leaves are narrower and not so
markedly toothed.

JASMINUM, Oleaceae. Jasmine. This is a big genus but many species are too tender to be grown outdoors in the British Isles. All like good soil and most grow best in warm sunny places, but *Jasminum nudiflorum* will thrive without direct sunshine provided the light is good. This winter flowering species is usually trained against a wall or fence and in such a position it is usually convenient to prune it immediately after flowering, cutting out most of the old flowering stems. Summer flowering jasmines can be cut hard back in spring or be allowed to grow naturally with no more than a little thinning out of old stems in spring or after flowering. All kinds can be increased by summer cuttings in a frame or propagator or by layering in spring or summer.

Jasminum mesneyi

beesianum   *2–2.5m. (6–8ft)   Rose-pink Summer*   D C O H L

China. In growth this is rather like the common jasmine, *Jasminum officinale*, but it is less vigorous and the sweetly scented rose-pink or carmine flowers are smaller.

fruticans   *1–1.5m. (3–5ft)   Yellow Summer*   ED O H

Southern Europe, North Africa, Asia Minor, Caucasus. An attractive dwarf semi-evergreen shrub with buttercup-yellow flowers. It grows well on alkaline soils.

humile   *2–2.5m. (6–8ft)   Yellow Summer*   E O H L

Afghanistan, Himalaya, Burma, China. A very variable species of which the best form for garden planting is 'Revolutum', often listed as *Jasminum revolutum*. It is a bigger shrub than *J. fruticans* and its bright yellow flowers are sweetly scented.

mesneyi   *1.2–2m. (4–6ft)   Yellow Spring   E. Summer*   E W F H L

China. This handsome species, known as the Primrose Jasmine, somewhat resembles *Jasminum nudiflorum* but the flowers are larger, often semi-double and the plant is much less hardy. It can only be grown fully in the open in the mildest parts of the British Isles and is unsuitable for cold gardens. It makes a wide, sprawling plant. It is often listed as *Jasminum primulinum*.

nudiflorum   *1–2m. (3–6ft)   Yellow Autumn   Winter*   D F H L

China. This is the Winter Jasmine, a favourite winter flowering shrub with green sprawling stems and bright yellow flowers. It is usually trained against a wall, in which situation it can eventually reach a height of 3m./10ft or even more.

polyanthum *3–6m. (10–20ft) White L. Spring Summer E W T H L*

China. This is one of the most tender species cultivated outdoors in the British Isles and is suitable only for the mildest localities, particularly maritime gardens of the south-west and west. It is also one of the most delightful in flower and scent, very free with its white flowers, which are pink outside, and casting its intensely sweet perfume a long way. It is a vigorous twiner.

x **stephanense** *3–6m. (10–20ft) Pink Summer D W T C H L*

A hybrid between *Jasminum beesianum* and *J. officinale*, with sweet-scented pale pink flowers. It needs a warm sunny place to do itself full justice.

JOVELLANA, Scrophulariaceae. Only one species is occasionally seen in British gardens and this needs a warm sunny position where there is little frost. It spreads by suckers and often sprouts up from the roots even when most growth above ground has been killed. It is not fussy about soil but prefers it to be well-drained. It can be hard-pruned each March or April and is readily increased by rooted suckers dug up in spring.

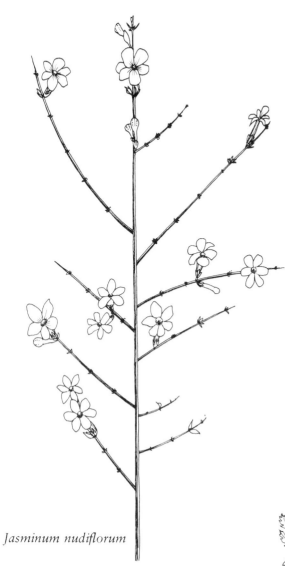

Jasminum nudiflorum

officinale *2–3m. (6–10ft) White Summer D W T C H L*

Caucasus, Iran, Afghanistan, Himalaya, China. The ever popular Common or Summer Jasmine with compound leaves and white sweetly scented flowers. Left to its own devices it will spread widely but it is usually trained on a fence, screen, arbour or wall and in such conditions can reach a height of 10m./33ft or more. It is not fully hardy in all parts of the British Isles and is unsuitable for very cold gardens. It climbs by twining.

Jovellana violacea

violacea   *1–2m. (3–6ft)   Mauve   Summer*
ED   W   C   S

Chile. A shrub of moderate height and dense growth spreading by suckers. The leaves are small and toothed, the little flowers shaped like scoops, and a rather pale violet-mauve in colour.

JUNIPERUS, Cupressaceae. Juniper. This large genus of evergreen conifers includes some species that are trees, some shrubs and a few that produce both trees and shrubs. All have two types of foliage, juvenile leaves that are small and pointed and adult leaves that are closely packed and scale-like. Most will thrive in all reasonably well-drained soils, including those containing chalk or lime. Pruning is, as a rule, both unnecessary and undesirable but if for any reason stems must be removed or shortened it is best done in May. Propagation of garden varieties is by summer cuttings in a propagator. Species can be raised from seed but it is slow to germinate unless first stratified by being kept moist for from three to five months at a temperature of 18 to 21°C./65 to 70°F. and then for a further three months at 3 to 4°C./38 to 40°F.

chinensis   *0.3–15m. (1–50ft)   Yellow*
E. Spring   E T H

Japan, Mongolia, China. It is the shorter or prostrate varieties of this very variable species that are useful as garden shrubs. Some authorities regard the following as not really varieties of this species but as hybrids between it and *J. sabina*, and so they list them under the name *J.* x *media*:

'Blaauw'. Makes a shuttlecock shaped bush, slow growing but eventually up to 2.5m. (8ft) high with blue-grey adult leaves. 'Globosa Cinerea' is similar but smaller and neater.
'Pfitzerana'. The branches of this remarkable variety grow out sideways, some horizontally, some ascending, but not steeply, though the bush can eventually become 2.5m. (8ft) high, by which time it will be much broader than

that. There are several yellow-variegated varieties including 'Aurea', with colour confined to the tips of the young stems, and 'Old Gold', in which the colour is more widely spread and longer retained.
'Plumosa'. Branches wide-spreading and with drooping plumy sprays of adult leaves. There are several variegated varieties including; 'Albovariegata', speckled with white; 'Aurea', yellow becoming bronzy with age; and 'Aurea Variegata', shorter in habit and yellow.

communis   *2–4m. (6–13ft)   Green*
L. Spring   E T H

Temperate Northern Hemisphere (including the British Isles). Another very variable species, with little pointed leaves crowded on the stems. The following varieties are specially recommended:

'Compressa'. A miniature tree growing very slowly into a dense narrow blue-green column about 45cm./18in. high. It is perfect for a rock garden or scree and is sometimes called Noah's Ark Juniper.
'Hibernica'. This is the Irish Juniper which could be described as resembling 'Compressa' on a much larger scale. An old specimen may be 3m./10ft high but no more than 60–75cm./2–2½ft in diameter.
'Hornibrookii'. A completely prostrate variety which will mould itself to anything that it encounters.
'Oblonga Pendula'. Branches spreading but ascending and then curling downwards at the tips.

horizontalis   *15–60cm. (6–24in.)   Green*
E. Summer   E T H

North America. A more or less prostrate species of which numerous forms have been selected for garden planting. Specially recommended are the following:

'Bar Harbor'. Quite prostrate, with tiny grey-green leaves.

'Douglasii'. Also prostrate and grey-green but becoming purple in winter.
'Glauca'. Blue-green with tiny leaves tight pressed to the prostrate stems.
'Wiltonii'. Grey-blue and mat-forming. It has been called 'Blue Rug'.

procumbens   *45–60cm. (18–24in.)   Green E. Summer   E T H*

Japan. This is known as the Creeping Juniper but in fact it is dwarf and spreading rather than actually carpet-forming and commonly builds up stems to a height of around 45cm./18in but extending over a good square metre of ground.

sabina   *1–2m. (3–6ft)   Green   E. Summer E T H*

Europe, West Russia. This is the species known as Savin, a low-growing mountain shrub with strongly aromatic grey-green leaves, mostly scale-like but some juvenile and pointed. The small rounded or top-shaped fruits are blue-black with bloom. There are numerous varieties of which by far the most popular is *tamariscifolia*, with horizontal branches packed closely one above another to make a low broadly dome-shaped bush.

squamata   *1–3m. (3–10ft)   Green E. Summer   E T H*

Himalaya, China. It is difficult to give dimensions for this species so variable is it in size and habit. Some forms actually make trees and some do not exceed 60cm./2ft in height but spread widely. The best variety for garden planting is 'Mayeri', which has arching stems and small pointed grey-green leaves. It is slow-growing but can eventually make a very big shrub.

KALMIA, Ericaceae. These very attractive North American evergreens enjoy conditions similar to those that suit rhododendrons except that they are even more susceptible to drought and prefer rather moist soil. It should also be acid and, for preference, peaty though this is not essential. Kalmias will grow in sun or partial shade but it should not be too dense. Little pruning is necessary but stems can be shortened or thinned after flowering if bushes become too large. Increase is by seed sown in moist peat and sand in spring. Late summer cuttings of some kinds will root in a propagator or under mist.

angustifolia   *15cm.–1.2m. (6in.–4ft)   Rose E. Summer   E O S H L*

Eastern North America. This shrub is known as Sheep's Laurel in America but not because it is of any use to sheep or other livestock since it is generally believed to be poisonous. It is an attractive shrub, varying greatly in height and habit and with the typical kalmia flowers, lantern-shaped in bud but much smaller than those of *K. latifolia*.

latifolia   *2–3m. (6–10ft)   Pink and White E. Summer   E O S H L*

Eastern North America. The most popular and decorative species, making a wide-spreading bush which, out of flower, looks rather like a rhododendron. The pink and white flowers are uniquely formed in bud and are saucer-shaped when open. They make a very attractive display.

KALMIOPSIS, Ericaceae. There is only one species and this grows in similar conditons to kalmia but appears to be more in need of a sunny place. Since it is naturally small, it requires no pruning. It can be raised from seed sown in peat and sand in spring or from summer cuttings in a propagator.

leachiana   *15–30cm. (6–12in.)   Rose-pink Spring   E S H*

Oregon, USA. A rare dwarf shrub with small leaves and little bell-shaped flowers well filled with protruding stamens.

KERRIA, Rosaceae. Jew's Mallow. The only species has two forms so distinct in habit that they really have quite different uses in the garden. The single-flowered form is thicket-forming and must be given plenty of space to spread, whereas the double-flowered form makes fewer but longer stems which can be readily spread out on a wall or over an arch or arbour. Both forms will grow in all reasonably fertile soils in sun or partial shade. Old stems, including those that have just flowered, can be cut out when the flowers fade. The single form is most readily increased by digging up rooted suckers in autumn or winter; the double-flowered form by layering in spring or autumn or by summer cuttings in a propagator.

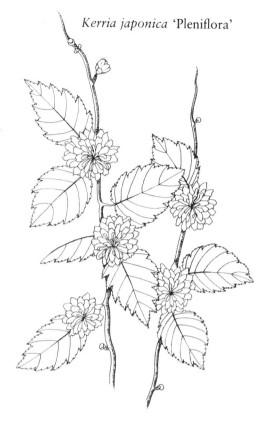

Kerria japonica 'Pleniflora'

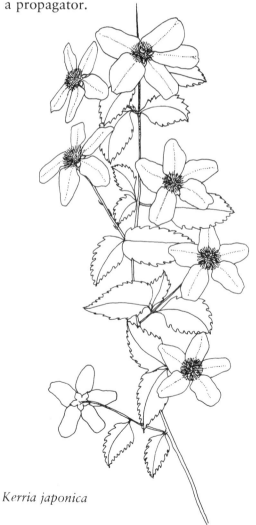

Kerria japonica

japonica *1.2–2m. (4–6ft) Yellow Spring D F H L V*

China. Despite its specific name this elegant shrub does not grow wild in Japan. Typically it makes a great many slender stems of moderate length bearing single yellow flowers. Variety 'Pleniflora' has longer stouter stems but far fewer of them so that, in the open, it can seem lanky but the stems are so flexible that they are ideal for training. The flowers are fully double, like little pompoms, and this is one of the plants popularly known at Batchelor's Buttons. There is also a white variegated form of the single-flowered kerria named 'Variegata'. It is quite a useful foliage plant and seldom exceeds 1m./3ft in height.

KOLKWITZIA, Caprifoliaceae. Beauty Bush. There is only one species and this thrives in all reasonably fertile soils including those overlying chalk or limestone. Old and weak stems, including some of those that have just flowered, can be cut out when the flowers fade. Increase is by seed sown in a greenhouse in spring, but seedlings may vary in quality, also by summer cuttings in a propagator and by suckers dug up with roots in autumn or winter.

amabilis *2.5–3m. (8–10ft) Pink
L. Spring E. Summer D F S H V*

China. In habit this is rather like a weigela but the pink, cream-throated flowers are smaller and more numerous and the display of a good form is very beautiful. Selected varieties with well-coloured flowers are 'Pink Cloud' and 'Rosea'.

LAPAGERIA, Philesiaceae. Chilean Bellflower. This very beautiful twiner is too tender to be grown outdoors in the British Isles except in the mildest and most sheltered places. Though it enjoys warmth it does not like strong sunshine and so, if trained on a wall, it is better to give it one facing west, or even north-west than south unless there is something else in front to shade it from the sun around midday. The soil should be lime-free with plenty of peat or leaf-mould to keep it cool and moist without impeding drainage in winter. Weak or damaged stems should be cut out in spring. Increase is by seed sown in a greenhouse in spring or by layering in spring.

rosea *3–4m (10–13ft) Crimson
Summer Autumn E W T S L*

Chile and Argentina. A slender twiner with rather thick undivided leaves and elegantly formed flowers like long bells with thick waxen-textured petals. The typical colour is light crimson but there are also pink varieties, of which one of the best is 'Nash Court', and a white-flowered variety named *albiflora*.

LAURUS, Lauraceae. Laurel. Bay tree. These are the true laurels, unconnected botanically with the cherry and Portugal laurels. There are only two species, both handsome

evergreens with aromatic leaves. In good conditions they will grow to tree size but they stand spring pruning and even summer clipping well and are frequently used as topiary specimens, particularly grown in tubs, in which they can be moved to a sheltered place in autumn and not returned fully to the open until the following spring. They like good loamy soil, will grow in sun or shade and must be well-watered in summer if growing in tubs or other containers. Male and female flowers are produced on separate trees and the males, with yellow stamens, are quite decorative. Increase is by late summer or early autumn cuttings in a propagator or frame or by seed sown under glass in spring.

azorica *3–15m. (10–50ft)
Greenish-yellow Spring E W K H S*

Canary Islands, Azores. This is the more tender of the two species, unlikely to survive prolonged or even moderately severe frost and so only suitable for planting in the milder parts of the British Isles, particularly near the coast. It differs from *Laurus nobilis* in having much larger leaves which are broadly lance-shaped.

nobilis *3–12m. (10–40ft) Greenish-yellow
Spring E W K H S*

Mediterranean region. This is the Bay Laurel used by ancient Greeks and Romans to honour their heroes. The aromatic leaves have culinary uses besides being decorative. This is an excellent town evergreen which survives polluted atmosphere well and benefits from the protection afforded by numerous buildings.

LAVANDULA, Labiatiae. Lavender. Grey-leaved aromatic evergreens much prized in gardens for their compact habit which makes them useful for forming small hedges for edging beds and terraces, and for their fragrant flowers, which can be cut when fully open and dried for use in sachets, pot-pourri etc. All lavenders like sun and warmth and enjoy alkaline soils though they will grow in almost any soils that are reasonably well-drained and not strongly acid. They benefit from clipping immediately the flowers fade since this improves their habit. All can be increased by late summer and autumn cuttings in a frame or propagator and the species also by seed sown in spring.

Lavandula dentata

angustifolia. *45–60cm. (18–24in.) Lavender Summer E F A H S*

Western Mediterranean region. This is the common lavender and, though it is such a well-known shrub, there is still dispute about its correct botanical name. Many gardeners still call it *Lavandula spica* but this name is also used for another species and botanists have discarded it as ambiguous. It is also

sometimes called. *L. officinalis*, an old name now discarded, and some forms or hybrids of it may appear in catalogues as *L. vera*. None of this is of much importance to gardeners were it not that the use of so many names for one plant sometimes causes confusion and may induce purchasers to obtain plants they already possess under the impression that they are getting something different.
L. angustifolia has narrow leaves and produces its flowers in slender spikes. It has produced numerous varieties and hybrids, the latter by being crossed with the broader-leaved species *L. latifolia*. It is difficult to disentangle varieties from hybrids and most convenient to lump them together, describing each individually under its varietal name. Among the best of these are 'Alba', not really a pure white since there is an undercurrent of pink; 'Folgate', very bushy, about 60cm./2ft high, purplish-blue; 'Grappenhall', sometimes over 1m./3ft high with lavender flowers; 'Hidcote', compact and fairly short with deep violet-purple flowers; 'Munstead', another compact variety, with blue-purple flowers; 'Nana Atropurpurea', so like 'Hidcote' that there is no need to have both; 'Nana Alba', white and no more than 30cm./1ft high, and 'Twickel Purple', up to 75cm./30in. high with purplish-lavender flowers.

dentata *45–90cm. (18–36in.)   Lavender Summer   Autumn   E   W   F   A   H   S*

Mediterranean region, Ethiopia, Arabia. In a warm, sunny place this can make quite a big bush which will continue to flower into the autumn but it is distinctly tender. The leaves are very distinctive since they are saw-edged.

latifolia *60–90cm. (2–3ft)   Purple Summer   E   W   F   A   H   S*

Western Mediterranean. This is less woody and has broader leaves than *Lavandula angustifolia* and is also less aromatic. The species is hardly ever seen in British gardens and is chiefly of interest as the other parent of the hybrid garden lavenders.

Lavandula stoechas

gales. *Lavatera olbia* grows well on chalk and limestone soils. All thrive by the sea, grow rapidly and often produce seed freely, which provides an easy means of increase. Plants can also be raised from summer cuttings in a frame or propagator. Habit is improved by shortening stems considerably each spring, and dead or damaged growth can be removed at any time.

maritima *1.2–1.5m. (4–5ft) Purple Summer Autumn E W C S H*

Western Mediterranean. A broad loosely-branched shrub with quite large downy leaves and the typical broadly funnel-shaped mallow flowers, lilac or mauve-veined with

stoechas *60–90cm. (2–3ft) Purple Summer E F H S*

South-western Europe. This is a most distinctive and attractive lavender, quite unlike any other in the way it crowds all its flowers into a short tightly-packed, rather stout spike, each with a little top-knot of coloured bracts. The colour is deep blue-purple. The plant is usually quite short and bushy and it loves a warm sunny place, sometimes seeding itself into crevices between rocks where it seems to be even happier and more permanent than in better soil. There is a white flowered variety named *leucantha*.

LAVATERA, Malvaceae. Tree Mallow. Many species are herbaceous and even those that are classed as shrubby have rather soft stems and are not usually very hardy or long-lived. Yet they are useful for their long flowering seasons and their ability to thrive in difficult places even when the soil is poor and shallow and they are exposed to

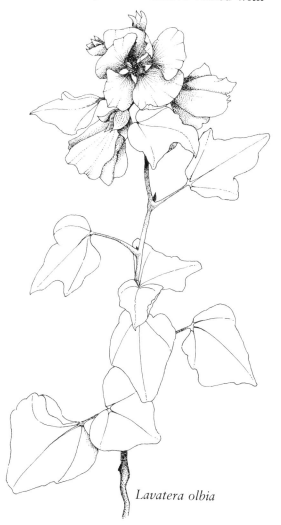

Lavatera olbia

deeper blue-purple. It is not very hardy and is really suitable only for permanent planting outdoors in the milder parts of Britain especially by the sea. The plant described as *Lavatera bicolor* is very like this and some botanists believe it to be no more than a variety of *L. maritima* with larger leaves and flowers. These make it a superior garden plant.

olbia *1.5–2.1m. (5–7ft) Carmine Summer Autumn E C S H*

Western Mediterranean. A hardier species than *Lavatera maritima*, but otherwise rather similar in appearance. The best variety is 'Rosea', which has clear pink flowers that are more attractive than the purplish-pink of the type.

LEIOPHYLLUM, Ericaceae. Sand Myrtle. There is only one species of *leiophyllum*, a small evergreen bush suitable for the peat garden or other places where the soil is acid and well supplied with humus. It is quite hardy, can be increased by seed in spring or cuttings in summer in a mixture of moist peat and sand and requires little pruning but can be cut back hard in June if it becomes straggly.

buxifolium *60–90cm. (2–3ft) Pink and White L. Spring E. Summer E O S H*

Eastern North America. As the specific name implies the leaves are box-like. The flowers are small, starry and crowded in little terminal clusters.

LEONOTIS, Labiatae. Lion's Ear. The semi-shrubby species described below is distinctly tender and only suitable for planting outdoors in Britain in the warmest sunniest places. It is most likely to succeed in maritime gardens of the west and south-west. It likes well-drained soil, can be raised from seed sown in a warm greenhouse in summer

or summer cuttings in a propagator, and stems can be thinned and shortened in March to prevent its becoming straggly.

leonurus *1m. (3ft) Orange-red Autumn ED W T S H*

South Africa. A handsome sub-shrub, a little like a phlomis in habit with whorls of showy hooded flowers which come at a time when there is a shortage of bright flower colour.

LEPTOSPERMUM, Myrtaceae. South Sea Myrtle. Manuka. These are highly attractive evergreen shrubs, mostly erect in growth but freely branched, with small leaves and flowers very freely produced. All are a little tender and require a warm sheltered sunny place. They dislike lime but will grow well in soils that are only marginally acid. Seed germinates readily and sometimes self-sown seedlings are produced, but selected varieties, including all those with double flowers, must be increased by late summer cuttings in a propagator. Little pruning is desirable but young stems can be shortened after flowering.

Leptospermum scoparium

humifusum   *15–20cm. (6–8in.)*   *White*
Summer   E W F S H

Tasmania. This prostrate species is often
listed as *Leptospermum scoparium
prostratum*. It is one of the hardiest kinds and
excellent for a sunny sheltered rock garden
since it will follow the contour of soil and
rocks.

lanigerum   *2.5–4m. (8–13ft)*   *White*
Summer   E W F S H

Australia and Tasmania. This species is so
variable that one form of it is often listed as a
separate species under the name
Leptospermum cunninghamii. It flowers a
good deal later in summer than the common
form, which is at its best in June. All have
leaves that are silky beneath, sometimes on
the upper surface as well.

scoparium   *0.3–3m. (1–10ft)*
White to Crimson   L. Spring   E. Summer
E W F S H

Australia, New Zealand. This is the species
known in New Zealand as Manuka.
Although probably slightly more tender than
L. lanigerum it is more frequently planted in
British gardens probably because it has
produced a number of beautiful varieties. One
of the most popular is 'Nichollsii' with
carmine flowers. 'Red Damask' is similar in
colour but the flowers are fully double and
make a great display. 'Keatleyi' has pale pink
flowers, nearly white at the edges and greyish
leaves. Both 'Nanum' and 'Nicholsii Nanum'
are dwarf, about 30cm./1ft high, the first with
pink, crimson-centred flowers, the second
carmine.

LESPEDEZA, Leguminosae. Bush Clover.
Sun-loving shrubs with short spikes of
vetch-like flowers and three-parted leaves.
The effect is similar to that of the shrubby
desmodiums. They flower late and freely and
enjoy hot dry places. They are quite likely to

be killed to ground level if there is much frost
but will usually sprout up again from the
roots in the spring. Dead and damaged
growth should be cut out then and stems that
have survived can be shortened considerably
to improve habit. Lespidezas will grow in all
reasonably well-drained soils and can be
increased by seed, by cuttings of young basal
shoots in spring in a propagator or by digging
up suckers or offsets with roots which may
need to be kept for a while in pots in a
greenhouse.

bicolor   *1–2m. (3–6ft)*   *Magenta*
L. Summer   E. Autumn   D W C S H V

China and Japan. The most attractive species,
very free-flowering and with long stems that
only just succeed in becoming woody in an
average British summer. It should be given the
warmest sunniest place available.

thunbergii   *1–2.5m. (3–8ft)*   *Magenta*
Autumn   D W C S H V

Manchuria, China, Japan. A rather sprawling
shrub with flower colour that needs careful
placing in the garden.

LEUCOTHOE, Ericaceae. These are good
shrubs for rather moist, acid, peaty soils.
They dislike being dried out in summer and
prefer dappled shade to full sun. Several make
an excellent dense undercover beneath trees
or taller shrubs. All are hardy and can be
increased by late summer cuttings in a
propagator or by layering in spring. Pruning
is usually unnecessary but old or weak stems
can be cut out in May.

fontanesiana   *0.6–2m. (2–6ft)*   *White*
L. Spring   E T H L

South-eastern USA. To many gardeners this
elegant evergreen will be more familiar as
Leucothoe catesbaei, a name which actually
belongs to another species. It has slender
arching stems, good lance-shaped leaves and
little close-packed trails of white

Leucothoe fontanesiana

pitcher-shaped flowers. There is a short variety named 'Nana' and another, named 'Rainbow', with cream variegated leaves and pink young stems.

racemosa *1.2–2m. (4–6ft) White E. Summer D T H L*

Eastern USA. This is a good deciduous shrub with paddle-shaped leaves and short slender spikes of white urn-shaped flowers very freely produced.

LEYCESTERIA, Caprifoliaceae. Deciduous shrubs with cane-like stems which grow up from the base and may not live for many years. It is wise to anticipate this natural death by cutting out old and weak stems each March leaving the strong young ones to flower. *Leycesteria* will grow in any reasonably fertile soil in sun or shade and usually spreads by self-sown seedlings.

formosa *2–2.5m. (6–8ft) White and Maroon Summer E. Autumn D T S*

Himalaya. It is presumably because it belongs to the honeysuckle family that this handsome sub-shrub is sometimes called the Himalayan Honeysuckle. In fact it is nothing like a honeysuckle but has long straight green stems, very leafy and bearing trails of white flowers almost enveloped in maroon bracts. These persist when the flowers themselves are succeeded by aubergine-purple berries.

LIGUSTRUM, Oleaceae. Privet. In addition to the common and broad-leaved privet, both much used for hedge-making, there are many other species and varieties several of which are highly decorative in leaf and flower. All are easily grown in any reasonably fertile soil, in sun or shade. All stand pruning well, anything from hard cutting back in spring, to reduce size or regenerate old plants, to clipping from May to August to maintain neat hedges. The more ornamental kinds are best lightly thinned in spring. All grow readily from summer cuttings in a frame or propagator and most from autumn cuttings in a frame.

delavayanum *2–2.5m. (6–8ft) White E. Summer E T K H A*

China. A very ornamental privet with small leaves and dense sprays of small, slightly unpleasantly scented white flowers. The fruits are black. It has been known by several names and may turn up in gardens and nurseries labelled *Ligustrum ionandrum* or *L. prattii*.

japonicum *2–3m. (6–10ft) White Summer E. Autumn E W T H*

China, Korea, Japan. A handsome evergreen with quite large dark green leaves and good cone-shaped sprays of white flowers rather like a small lilac. It is only moderately hardy. It has a curious slow-growing variety named 'Coriaceum', with stiff branches and smaller, thicker, more leathery leaves.

lucidum *3–5m. (10–16ft) White L. Summer E. Autumn E T H A*

China. One of the most handsome privets, much like L. japonicum but with larger lighter green leaves. In mild and favourable situations it can grow to small tree size. It is very decorative in flower.

ovalifolium *2–5m. (6–16ft) White Summer ED T K H A*

Japan. The broad-leaved privet, most popular of hedge-making shrubs particularly in its yellow-leaved variety 'Aureum', the Golden Privet. Another variety named 'Argenteum', has a narrow cream border to each leaf. In a hard winter L. ovalifolium will drop many of its leaves but in more favourable circumstances it is fully evergreen. In winter the Golden Privet is one of the brightest and most conspicuous of variegated shrubs.

quihoui *2–3m. (6–10ft) White Autumn D T H A*

China. This species has fairly small leaves and large sprays of white-scented flowers, making it a very decorative shrub in autumn.

sinense *3–6m. (10–20ft) White Summer ED T H A*

China. In favourable places this can make a small tree. It is expectionally free-flowering and it usually carries good crops of black berries. It has a variety named 'Variegatum', with grey-green and white leaf variegation.

vulgare *2–3m. (6–10ft) White Summer E T K H A*

Europe (including Britain). The common privet, a native plant which is sometimes used for hedging but is not as good for this purpose as L. ovalifolium since it is less branched. Its white flowers have a rather unpleasant scent but are decorative and followed by good crops of black berries.

Leycesteria formosa

LINDERA, Lauraceae. Spice Bush. Only a few species of this considerable genus of aromatic shrubs have found their way into British gardens but more may follow. The two that are most familiar are both hardy and easy to grow in lime-free soil that is reasonably fertile and well-drained. Male and female flowers are borne on separate plants. *Lindera* can be pruned quite severely, even into old wood if it is necessary to restrict their size, but otherwise pruning is unnecessary. Increase is by seed which needs to be kept moist at 4°C./39°F. for four months prior to sowing or by summer cuttings in a propagator.

benzoin   *2–3m. (6–10ft)   Greenish-yellow Spring   D T S H*

Eastern USA. This is the species to which the popular name Spice Bush is commonly applied. Its laurel-like leaves are strongly, and some would say rather unpleasantly, aromatic.

obtusiloba   *3–6m. (10–20ft)   Ochre L. Spring   D T S H*

China, Japan. The most ornamental species, with bright green leaves that are often three-lobed, for which reason it has been wrongly called *Lindera triloba.* They are distinctive and decorative, particularly in autumn when they turn yellow before falling. Round black fruits may be produced by female plants if there is a male nearby for fertilization.

LIPPIA, Verbenaceae. Lemon-scented Verbena. Only one species is cultivated in British gardens and that only in the mildest places since it is distinctly tender. It is a rather angularly branched deciduous shrub grown for its strongly lemon-scented leaves. It likes sun, warmth and good drainage and can be trained against a south-facing wall for protection. Even when severely damaged by frost it often shoots up again from the base in spring. Dead growth should be removed each

April at which time healthy stems can be shortened considerably, so encouraging strong new growth. Increase is by early summer cuttings in a propagator.

citriodora   *2–4m. (6–13ft)   Mauve Summer   D W C H*

Chile. The plant is not of great beauty, the flowers in multiple spikes being too small and pale to be effective, and the lance-shaped leaves rather undistinguished, but the scent liberated when they are bruised is strong and refreshing. A plant to place where it will be brushed against when passing.

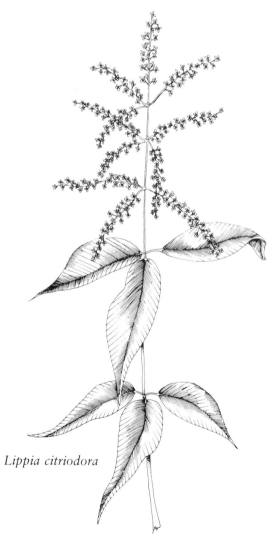

Lippia citriodora

LOMATIA, Proteaceae. In their native habitats in South America many of these are evergreen trees but in our colder climate they rarely exceed the dimension of large shrubs. They thrive best in the south and west in open woodland or other sheltered places, in acid or neutral soil. The only pruning necessary is to remove dead or damaged growth in the spring. Increase is by seed in a greenhouse in spring or some species by rooted suckers in spring.

ferruginea   *3–6m. (10–20ft)*
Chrome and red   Summer   E W T S

Chile, Argentina. Like other species this is grown primarily for its foliage. The leaves are large doubly-divided, dark green above but covered with rust-coloured down beneath. The small flowers are curious rather than beautiful.

tinctoria   *60–90cm. (2–3ft)*
Yellow and Green   Summer
E W T S V

Tasmania. This is a true shrub, spreading by suckers. The dark green leaves are variable in shape, simple, divided or doubly-divided and are decidedly decorative. The spikes of bloom are sweetly scented.

LONICERA, Caprifoliaceae. Honeysuckle. This very large genus includes shrubs as well as twiners, some deciduous, some evergreen, and differing greatly in hardiness. All the climbing species like good fertile soil well supplied with moisture in summer but not waterlogged in winter. Many are naturally woodland plants and enjoy some shade. In hot dry places they are often severely attacked by aphides, which not only do a great deal of direct damage but also spread virus diseases. The shrubby kinds also succeed best in fairly sheltered places, especially those that flower in winter or early spring. Pruning must be adapted to type of growth and time of flowering but a few, including *Lonicera*

japonica, are best pruned in spring. Bushy loniceras can be thinned by removing old stems and shortening younger ones in March or immediately after flowering if they are in bloom then. *Lonicera nitida* is often used as a hedge plant and can be clipped at any time between May and August inclusive. All honeysuckles can be increased by summer cuttings in a propagator, many also by layering in spring or autumn, and all species by seed sown in a frame or greenhouse in spring.

x americana   *4–8m. (13–26ft)*
Yellow and Purple   Summer   D O H L

A fine hybrid between *Lonicera caprifolium* and *L. etrusca*. It is a vigorous twiner with well-coloured, highly fragrant flowers freely produced. The effect is similar to that of *L. caprifolium* but usually superior to it.

x brownii   *3–6m. (10–20ft)   Scarlet*
L. Spring   L. Summer   E D O H L

Hybrids between *Lonicera sempervirens* and *L. hirsuta* often referred to as the Scarlet Trumpet Honeysuckles. All are moderately vigorous twiners, which retain many of their leaves in mild winters. The flowers are not scented. Several forms have been given distinguishing names but they do not really differ greatly.

caprifolium   *3–6m. (10–20ft)*
Creamy-white   L. Spring   E. Summer
D O H L S

Europe. A moderately vigorous twiner with very fragrant flowers. The leaves towards the ends of each shoot clasp the stems, which appear to grow through them, for which reason it is sometimes called the Perfoliate Honeysuckle.

etrusca   *4–8m. (13–26ft)   Yellow and red Summer   ED O H L S*

Mediterranean region. A vigorous and beautiful twiner which because of its mediterranean origin enjoys more sun and warmth than most species. The flowers are scented.

fragrantissima   *2–2.5m. (6–8ft)   Ivory Winter   E. Spring   ED T H L S*

China. A loosely branched shrub with small not very conspicuous flowers that are very sweetly scented. It closely resembles *Lonicera standishii*, which also starts to flower in mid-winter.

hildebrandiana   *5–10m. (17–35ft)   Yellow Summer   E W O H L S*

China, Burma, Thailand. The largest-flowered honeysuckle and also a very vigorous twiner but distinctly tender and so only suitable for planting outdoors in Britain in the mildest places. The flowers are cream when they open but deepen to rich yellow as they age. They are sweetly scented. This species is often incorrectly spelled *L. hildebrandtiana*.

japonica   *4–8m. (13–26ft) White to Yellow   Summer   E K H L S*

Japan, China, Korea. A very vigorous twiner with pale but exceedingly fragrant flowers. It has a fine variegated variety named 'Aureo-reticulata', in which the leaves are netted with yellow. Another variety, 'Halliana', does not appear to differ in any material way from the type described above.

nitida   *2–3m. (6–10ft)   Cream   Spring E K H L S*

China. This is the honeysuckle used for hedge-making. The round leaves are smaller than those of box but its stems are less rigid and it is more easily damaged by wind, rain and snow. It can be clipped to make a very narrow hedge but not a tall one. Its flowers are too small to make any effect. There are several good varieties including 'Baggesen's Gold', with yellow leaves, and 'Fertilis' and 'Yunnan', both more erect and stiffer in habit with slightly larger leaves.

periclymenum   *4–6m. (13–20ft) Cream and purple Summer   D O H L S*

Europe (including Britain) Asia Minor, Caucasus. This is the Common Honeysuckle or Woodbine, a native twiner of unimpeachable hardiness and a natural woodlander or hedgerow plant. The flowers are spicily fragrant. The two best forms are 'Belgica', known as the Dutch Honeysuckle, with flowers that are purplish-red outside and yellow within, and 'Serotina', the Late Dutch Honeysuckle, which is similar in colour but flowers for a longer period. Early (May-June) flowering honeysuckles sold as Dutch or 'Belgica' often prove to be forms, or maybe hybrids, of *L. caprifolium* the tell-tale indication being that the upper leaves are united around the stems.

sempervirens   *3–6m. (10–20ft)   Scarlet Summer   E. Autumn   ED O H L S*

Eastern and southern USA. This is known as the Trumpet Honeysuckle but the flowers are long and narrow, more tubular than trumpet-shaped. They are brilliant in colour but devoid of scent. In a warm sheltered place this vigorous twiner will retain most of its leaves in winter. 'Superba' is a particularly fine form.

standishii   *2–2.5m. (6–8ft)   Ivory Winter   E. Spring   ED T H L S*

China. A loosely branched bush closely resembling *Lonicera fragrantissima*. There is also a hybrid between the two named *L* x *purpusii* but any one of the three is really sufficient.

tatarica   *2.5–3m. (8–10ft)*
White to Rose-pink   L. Spring   E. Summer
D T H L S

Central Asia, Russia. A vigorous
well-branched shrub with small but numerous
flowers which may be anything from white to
quite a deep rose-pink. It is the well coloured
forms such as 'Arnold's Red', 'Hack's Red'
and 'Zabelii' that are most attractive.

x tellmanniana   *3–6m. (10–20ft)   Yellow*
Summer   D O H L

A fine hybrid between *Lonicera tragophylla*
and *L. sempervirens*. 'Superba' which
combines many of the best features of each is
a vigorous twiner with large well-displayed
flower clusters, bronzy-red in bud, deep
yellow when fully open but lacking scent. It
likes a cool shady root run.

tragophylla   *3–6m. (10–20ft)   Yellow*
Summer   D O H L S

China. A species notable for the size of its
flowers and their bright yellow colour but it
sadly lacks scent. Conditions as for
L x *tellmanniana*.

xylosteum   *2.5–3m. (8–10ft)   Yellowish*
L. Summer   D T H L S

Europe (including Britain), Asia Minor,
Siberia. A well-branched shrub with small
yellowish flowers which are not showy but
are followed by good crops of red berries. It is
known as the Fly Honeysuckle.

LUPINUS, Leguminosae. Lupin. The shrubby
lupins are all rather soft-stemmed and
short-lived but they grow readily from seed
and so can be quickly and cheaply replaced.
They thrive in sunny places, even if they are
hot and dry, and enjoy well-drained soils.
Faded flowers should be removed except for a
few to supply seed. Stems can be shortened in
spring to prevent plants becoming straggly.
Selected garden varieties must be increased by
summer cuttings in a propagator.

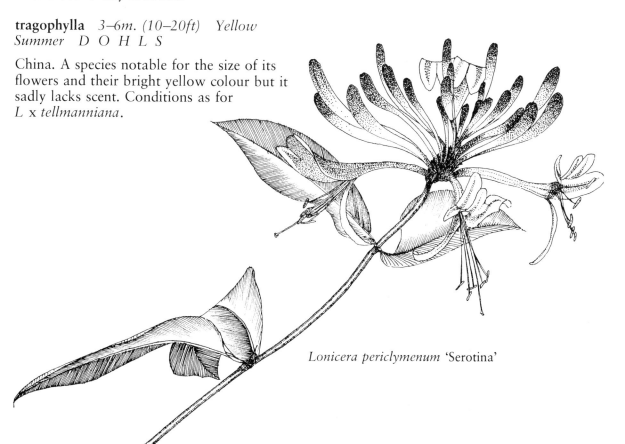

Lonicera periclymenum 'Serotina'

arboreus *1.2–2m. (4–6ft)* *Yellow*
Summer *E W F S H*

California. A loosely branched bush with the typical fingered leaves of the lupin family and spikes of flowers which are commonly a rather pale yellow but are variable. There is a good white-flowered variety named 'Snow Queen' and a deeper yellow one named 'Golden Spire'. Blue or purple varieties are occasionally seen but the yellows and whites are more attractive.

chamissonis *45–90cm. (1½–3ft)*
Purplish-blue *Summer* *D W F S H*

California. This small semi-shrubby plant is chiefly valued for its silvery leaves, which contrast with the purplish-blue or lilac flowers. It is usually short-lived even in a hot sunny place.

LYCIUM, Solanaceae. Box Thorn. These shrubs mostly make dense thickets of slender often arching stems, usually spiny and so providing good protection as an outer more or less untrimmed hedge. They thrive in quite poor dry soils including very sandy ones by the sea. Not much pruning is possible but plants can be thinned in winter or early spring by removing some of the older stems. Increase is by seed sown in a frame or greenhouse, by summer cuttings or by layering in spring or autumn.

barbarum *2–2.5m. (6–8ft)* *Pink or Purple*
Summer *D T S H L*

China. This is the species commonly grown, though often under other names, including *Lycium chinense* and *L. halimifolium*, since there has been considerable botanical confusion about it. Popularly it is known as the Chinese Box Thorn or Duke of Argyll's Tea Tree. It is wide-spreading with arching stems and small but abundant flowers, followed by little ovoid orange-red berries which can wreathe the stems in autumn when the shrub is at its most attractive.

MAGNOLIA, Magnoliaceae. Most of these are trees, many with magnificent flowers, but outside the scope of this book. Really only two kinds, *Magnolia liliiflora* and *M. stellata*, qualify as shrubs but a few others are included because in gardens they are often treated more as large shrubs than as trees. All like fertile soils, preferably lime-free, though a few will grow on chalk or limestone subsoils if there is plenty of readily available iron, manganese and magnesium in the surface soil. They will grow in full sun or dappled shade. Many roots are close to the surface so soil close to magnolias should never be dug or forked. It can with advantage be mulched occasionally with peat or leaf-mould. Though pruning is not essential, magnolias do recover well from cutting back and this can be used to prevent specimens growing too large. The best time to do this is in summer after flowering. Species can be raised from seed but seedlings vary so garden varieties are usually increased by layering in spring or by grafting onto seedlings.

denudata *4.5–9m. (15–30ft)* *White*
Spring *D F S L G*

China. This makes a much-branched, wide-spreading shrub or tree which as it gets old may layer itself by the weight of its branches bringing them down to soil level. The flowers are large, pure white, scented and freely produced. It is popularly known as the Yulan.

liliiflora *2.5–4m. (8–13ft)*
Purple and white *L. Spring* *E. Summer*
D F S L G

Japan. A richly coloured species though the colour is variable when it is raised from seed. One very deep reddish-purple variety has been named 'Nigra'. The flowers of the type species are purple outside and ivory flushed with purple inside.

x loebneri *4–8m. (13–26ft)* *White, Pink Spring* *D F L G*

A beautiful hybrid between *Magnolia kobus*, which is quite a large tree and *M. stellata*, which is a shrub. *M. x loebneri* is intermediate in size and variable in colour. One of the best forms, named 'Leonard Messel', has soft mallow pink flowers.

sieboldii *3–4.5m. (10–15ft)* *White and crimson* *L. Spring* *Summer* *D F S L G*

Japan, Korea. A beautiful species with cup-shaped white richly scented flowers each enclosing a central boss of crimson stamens. Although in the course of a season it can produce a lot of flowers they do not all come at one time and there is never the concentrated display characteristic of many spring flowering magnolias.

sinensis *3–6m. (10–20ft)* *White and crimson* *E. Summer* *D F S L G*

China. Another of the summer flowering species with richly scented cup-shaped flowers, white with a central boss of crimson

stamens. The flowers hang downwards and to be fully appreciated need to be viewed from below. This is one of the best magnolias to plant on chalk or limestone subsoils. *M. highdownensis* is said to be a hybrid between this species and the very similar *M. wilsonii* and, from a garden standpoint, there is not much to choose between them.

x soulangiana *4.5–9m. (15–30ft)* *White to Purple* *Spring* *D F L G*

A whole race of hybrids between *Magnolia denudata* and *M. liliiflora* varying in height, habit and the colour of their flowers. Typically plants are broad and open-branched in the manner of *M. denudata*, layering themselves where their branches touch the ground. The flowers are large, erect and very freely produced, anything from white to purple according to variety. A number have been given distinguishing names:

'Alba Superba' is white, scented and much like *M. denudata*.
'Alexandrina' is white flushed with purple.
'Brozzonii' has exceptionally large flowers, white with just a touch of purple at the heart of the bloom.
'Lennei' favours *M. liliiflora* but has larger flowers which are rose-purple outside, white flushed with purple inside.
'Rustica Rubra' is similar to the last but a little more rosy and less purple.

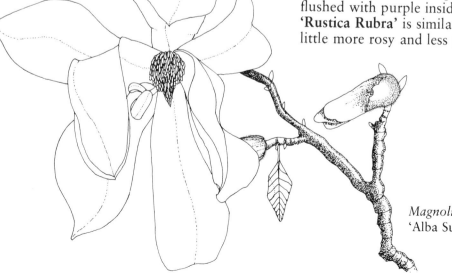

Magnolia x soulangiana
'Alba Superba'

stellata   *2.5–4m. (8–13ft)   White, Pink*
E. Spring   D   F   S   L   G

Japan. This popular species really deserves to
be called a shrub and, as it usually grows
quite slowly, it can be accommodated in small
gardens more easily than most. The flowers
are relatively small, with narrow tepals (what
most gardeners would call petals) but they are
very freely produced and make a fine display.
The type colour is white but the species varies
to soft pink and one of the best coloured
forms has been given the distinguishing name
'Rosea'. Another named 'Rubra' is slightly
deeper in colour but nowhere near red as the
name might imply.

wilsonii   *3–6m. (10–20ft)*
White and crimson   L. Spring   E. Summer
D   F   S   L   G

China. A spreading shrub or small tree much
like *Magnolia sinensis* but inferior to it for
general planting, since it is less tolerant of
chalk or lime and more susceptible to damage
by spring frosts.

MAHONIA, Berberidaceae. Evergreen shrubs
so closely related to berberis that at one time
they were merged in a single genus. However,
from a decorative standpoint they are very
distinct, for the mahonias all have quite large
leaves composed of a number of separate
leaflets individually not unlike those of holly.
Some kinds are rather tender but many can be
grown outdoors in most parts of Britain. They
are not difficult to please but thrive best in
fertile soils not liable to dry out severely.
Most kinds can be pruned in May if this is
necessary to restrict their size. Increase of
some kinds can be effected by digging up
rooted suckers or offsets in spring or early
autumn. All can be layered in spring or grown
from summer cuttings in a frame and species
also from seed sown outdoors or in a frame in
spring.

acanthifolia   *3–6m. (10–20ft)   Yellow*
L. Autumn   E. Winter   E   W   T   S   H   L

Himalaya. A very handsome but rather tender
species, with large leaves composed of up to
27 holly-like leaflets. The deep yellow flowers
are carried in clusters of slender spikes and
are followed by purple berries. It has been
much confused with *M. napaulensis*, which
resembles it but is even less hardy and flowers
in the spring.

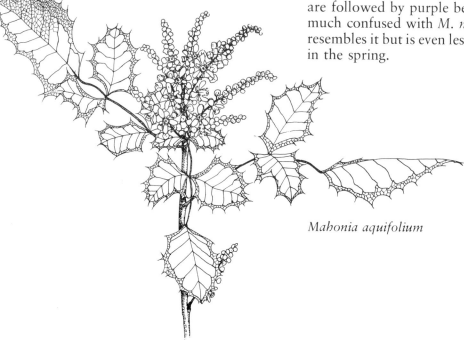

Mahonia aquifolium

aquifolium *1–2m. (3–6ft) Yellow L. Winter Spring E K S H L V*

Western North America. The most popular kind and a very easily grown shrub that will thrive in sun or shade. The small yellow flowers are borne in good clusters early in the year and are followed by black berries covered with grey bloom like grapes. It can be used as a small rather informal hedge.

bealei *2–3m. (6–10ft) Yellow Winter E T S H L*

China. Much confused with *Mahonia japonica* but *M. bealei* carries its flowers in shorter more erect clusters of spikes. It has become a fairly scarce plant, its place taken by *M. japonica* and its hybrids.

japonica *2–3m. (6–10ft) Yellow Winter E T S H L*

Japan. An exceptionally handsome evergreen with long leaves composed of numerous holly-like leaflets, which are shining green when young but may become red-tinted with age. The pale yellow flowers, scented like lily-of-the-valley, are carried in long slender spikes radiating outwards like the spokes of a wheel. It has produced a number of hybrids with *Mahonia lomariifolia*. See *M.* x *media*.

lomariifolia *2.5–4m. (8–13ft) Yellow Winter E W T S H L*

China, Burma. This species is as handsome in foliage as *M. japonica* and considerably more striking in flower since the colour is a much deeper yellow and the slender spikes are held up like a shuttlecock. However, it lacks scent, is not very hardy and it branches very little so that old plants become bare at the base. It crosses readily with *M. japonica* and these hybrids are described under *M.* x *media*.

x **media** *2.5–4m. (8–13ft) Yellow Winter E T H L*

The collective name given to hybrids between *Mahonia japonica* and *M. lomariifolia*. Most favour the latter in habit including the erect mode of carrying their flowers, but they have derived extra hardiness from *M. japonica* and can be safely planted outdoors in all but the coldest parts of the British Isles. One of the most popular forms is 'Charity' but this has no scent, whereas 'Buckland' and 'Lionel Fortescue' have even finer flower clusters and are scented, though not as powerfully as *M. japonica*.

pinnata *2–2.5m. (6–8ft) Yellow L. Winter Spring E K S H L*

California. It seems likely that the plants cultivated in Britain under this name are not usually the true species but hybrids between it and *M. aquifolium*, *M. repens* or other species. Be that as it may there are some fine garden shrubs among them including one, given an Award of Garden Merit as *M. pinnata*, which has lustrous green leaves and abundant clusters of yellow flowers in late winter. Another, listed as 'Undulata', is similar in character but the leaves have wavy edges and the flowers come in spring.

repens *30cm. (1ft) Yellow Spring E K S H L V*

Western North America. One of the shortest mahonias but very spreading and ideal for use as ground cover. It resembles *M. aquifolium* except in height and the mat texture of its leaves. A form or hybrid named 'Rotundifolia' has rounder spineless leaves and grows about 60cm./2ft tall.

MENZIESIA, Ericaceae. Small to medium size deciduous shrubs belonging to the heather family and suitable for rock gardens, peat beds and for shrub borders in lime-free soil with plenty of peat or leaf-mould. The position should be open and preferably sunny but the soil should not dry out in summer. Dead and thin growth can be removed in spring. Increase is by seed in moist peat and sand or summer cuttings in a propagator.

ciliicalyx *60–90cm. (2–3ft)*
Cream to Purple L. Spring D T S H

Japan. An attractive species with small bell-shaped flowers in little clusters. Colour is variable and the deeper reddish-purple shades, such as that of variety *purpurea*, are most decorative.

pilosa *1–2m. (3–6ft) Whitish L. Spring*
D T S H

Eastern North America. Though the flowers of this species are by no means showy they are charming and unusual, little greenish or yellowish bells flushed with red rather in the manner of *Enkianthus*.

MICROBIOTA, Cupressaceae. A prostrate conifer much like some cypresses in leaf and habit. It will grow in any reasonably fertile and well-drained soil in an open preferably sunny position and is suitable for use as ground cover or in fairly large rock gardens. Pruning is not normally necessary but stems can be thinned or shortened.

decussata *30cm. (1ft) Small cones*
Summer E T S H

Siberia. This attractive species, the only *microbiota* at present known, has not been in cultivation long and is a fairly scarce plant. It has somewhat the appearance of a prostrate cypress with more or less horizontal stems and plumy growth.

MUEHLENBECKIA, Polygonaceae. Creeping and twining shrubs with very slender but wiry stems and small evergreen leaves. They are not very hardy and the larger kinds can become uncomfortably invasive but in hot dry sunny places they make attractive cover for ground, walls, buildings and even unwanted trees or shrubs. They like well-drained soil, can be cut back in spring or summer and are easily increased by layering, which they do for themselves.

complexa *2–3m. (6–10ft) Whitish*
Summer E W K L

New Zealand. The wiry stems are black, the small rounded leaves shining green and the almost translucent flowers inconspicuous. In warm places it grows rapidly and is indestructible.

MUTISIA, Compositae. Evergreen plants climbing by slender tendrils. They are not hardy and are somewhat capricious, running wild in some places yet refusing to grow or dying suddenly and inexplicably in others. They like sun, warmth and good drainage and are suitable for planting close to south-facing walls or fences with trellis work or wires to which to cling. Detailed pruning is virtually impossible because of the dense tangle of growth but if plants become invasive they can be cut back at any time from May to August. Increase is by seed in a greenhouse in spring or by layering in spring, and sometimes by digging up rooted suckers or offsets in spring or early autumn.

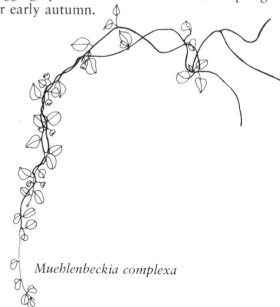

Muehlenbeckia complexa

clematis   *4–8m. (13–26ft)   Orange-red*
L. Spring   L. Autumn   E W K S L V

Columbian Andes. Probably the most reliable
species to grow provided the situation is
sufficiently mild to suit it. The compound
leaves are clothed in white wool, the quite
large daisy flowers are showy and produced
continuously for a very long time.

ilicifolia   *2.5–3m. (8–10ft)   Pink or mauve*
Summer   E W K S L V

Chile. Quite often this proves vigorous and
enduring but the flowers lack the warm
colour of some other species. The small
shining green leaves are spiny like holly.

oligodon   *1–1.5m. (3–5ft)   Salmon pink*
Summer   E. Autumn   E W K S L V

Chile, Argentina. Not as vigorous as most but
very beautiful and free-flowering.

MYRICA, Myricaceae. Gale. Bayberry.
Shrubs grown primarily for their aromatic
leaves. They are not fussy about soil but
prefer it to be acid. If plants become straggly
they can be cut hard back in spring. Increase
is by seed or by layering in spring.

gale   *0.6–1.2m. (2–4ft)   Brown*
L. Spring   E. Summer   D C S L

Northern Hemisphere (including Britain).
This species is known as Sweet Gale because
of the pleasant scent of the leaves when
bruised, and as Bog Myrtle for its liking for
boggy places. The flowers are produced in
little catkins and are not showy.

MYRTUS, Myrtaceae. Myrtle.
Free-flowering aromatic evergreen shrubs and
small trees which are none too hardy and only
suitable for planting outdoors in fairly mild or
sheltered, but preferably sunny, places. They
are not fussy about soil provided it is
reasonably well-drained and they will grow in
those that are moderately acid or alkaline. All

Mutisia ilicifolia

can be clipped or have their stems shortened
in summer if this is necessary to restrict them
but otherwise can be allowed to grow freely.
Increase is by summer cuttings in a
propagator or by seed in spring in a
greenhouse.

communis   *3–4m. (10–13ft)   White*
Summer   E W K H S

Western Asia. The Common Myrtle, with
neat, evergreen, aromatic leaves and small
white flowers each with a brush-like cluster of
stamens. They are followed by almost black
berries.

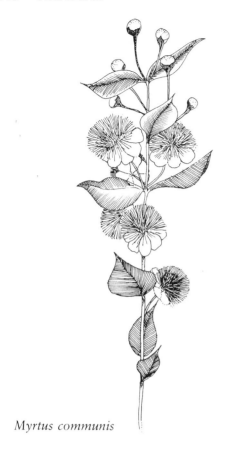

Myrtus communis

lechlerana *3–6m. (10–20ft)   Creamy-white*
L. Spring   E W K S H

Chile. A taller more tree-like species than *M. communis* and flowering earlier but just as freely. The flowers are scented and the berries become red before finally ripening to near black.

luma *3–15m. (10–50ft)   White*
L. Summer E. Autumn   E W K S H

Chile, Argentina. In some ways the most beautiful myrtle because of its light cinnamon-coloured, peeling bark, but for this to be fully developed it must be allowed to attain tree-like proportions. It produces seed freely, and when favourably situated there are usually abundant self-sown seedlings to be planted elsewhere or given away.

nummularia *Prostrate   White*
L. Spring   E. Summer   E K S H

Straits of Magellan, Falkland Islands. The hardiest as well as the shortest myrtle, a ground-hugging evergreen suitable for planting in rock gardens and on raised rock beds. The leaves are neat and rounded and the white flowers are followed by pink berries.

NANDINA, Berberidaceae. Heavenly Bamboo. It is quite a surprise to discover that this elegant plant, superficially so much like a bamboo, in fact belongs to the *Berberis* family. It is not very hardy and so is most suitable for sheltered gardens and the milder parts of the British Isles. It likes a warm sunny position and fertile soil that remains moist in summer without becoming very cold and waterlogged in winter, which really means a soil containing plenty of peat or leaf-mould. Old and weather-damaged stems should be cut right out in spring. Increase is by seed, sown in a warm greenhouse in spring, or by summer cuttings in a propagator with bottom heat.

domestica *2–2.5m. (6–8ft)   White*
Summer   E W T S H

China. An elegant plant with erect unbranched stems, bearing at the top long doubly or trebly compound leaves composed of narrow pointed leaflets. The clusters of small white flowers are not showy but are similar in character to those of *Berberis*. There are two useful garden varieties 'Nana Purpurea', dwarf and with purplish leaves, and 'Pygmata', compact and about 60cm./2ft. high.

NEILLIA, Rosaceae. Thicket-forming shrubs closely allied to *Spiraea* and as easily grown. They will thrive in all reasonably fertile soils in sun or partial shade, and can be increased either by summer cuttings in a propagator or by digging out suckers with roots in autumn or winter. Old stems can be cut out after flowering and at the same time the young stems can be shortened.

thibetica *2m. (6ft) Pink*
L. Spring E. Summer D O H V

China. The best species long known in garden
as *Neillia longiracemosa*. It makes long, more
or less erect stems direct from the roots with
oval toothed leaves and long slender
semi-pendant spikes of rose-pink flowers.

NOTOSPARTIUM, Leguminosae. These
are brooms from New Zealand, not very
hardy in Britain and suitable for planting
outdoors only in almost frost-free places.
They become hardier with age and one
recommendation is that they should be grown
in containers for the first two or three years
and planted out only when they have made
some good woody main stems. However,
brooms do not transplant well, least of all
when large, so this may not be a very good
idea. Apart from this they are not difficult
plants to grow in the warm sunny conditions
and well-drained soil that suit all brooms. The
only pruning necessary is to remove weak,
diseased or frost-damaged growth in spring.
Plants are best increased by seed.

carmichaeliae *1.2–3m. (4–10ft)*
Lilac pink Summer D W T S

New Zealand (South Island). A shrub with
slender arching and almost leafless green
stems with spikes of up to 20 small lilac-pink,
pea-type flowers along the length of the
younger stems.

OLEARIA, Compositae. Daisy Bush. A large
genus of evergreen shrubs, including also
some small trees, some of which are very
ornamental in leaf and flower. Few are
completely hardy in all parts of the British
Isles and all like warm, sunny places and
reasonably well-drained soils. All grow well
by the sea and some are used as windbreaks
or hedges in coastal areas. They respond to
pruning well and can be cut back quite hard
in May if necessary, or can be clipped or
shortened in summer. All grow readily from

late summer cuttings in a propagator and
species can also be raised from seed sown
under glass in spring.

avicennifolia *2.5–6m. (8–20ft) White*
L. Summer E. Autumn E C K H S

New Zealand (South Island). A handsome
shrub with lance-shaped leaves grey above
and covered with dense whitish wool beneath.
The small daisy flowers are borne in good
clusters. This is one of the hardiest species.
O. cheesmanii is much like it, very
free-flowering and almost as hardy.

x haastii *1.2–2.5m. (4–8ft) White*
Summer E C K H S

A hybrid between *Olearia avicennifolia* and
O. moschata and one of the best kinds for
general planting since it is almost completely
hardy. It makes a densely branched bush with
neat rounded leaves a little like those of box,
leathery and resistant to polluted atmosphere,
so that it thrives even in industrial areas. The
clusters of small white flowers are produced
very freely.

ilicifolia *2.5–3m. (8–10ft) White*
E. Summer E W C K H S

New Zealand. This might be described as a
smaller version of *Olearia macrodonta*, with
similar but narrower holly-like leaves and a
less vigorous habit. The white flowers are
produced in large flattish clusters and have a
distinctive musk-like scent. It is not very
hardy.

macrodonta *3–6m. (10–20ft) White*
Summer E W C K H S

New Zealand. One of the largest and most
handsome of the shrubby species. The leaves
are holly-like in shape, shining green above,
white-felted beneath. The flowers are
produced freely in large flat clusters and make
a fine display. The plant is large enough to
make a fine windbreak and is often used for
this purpose in maritime districts. It is not

very hardy but will withstand a lot of wind. A variety named 'Major' has even larger leaves and stronger growth and another, named 'Minor', has smaller and shorter leaves.

moschata   *1–2m. (3–6ft)   White Summer   E   W   C   K   H   S*

New Zealand (South Island). A compact free-flowering species with small leathery rounded grey-green leaves. The specific name refers to the musky scent of the flowers. The plant is not very hardy.

Olearia x *scilloniensis*

nummularifolia   *2–3m. (6–10ft)   Yellowish Summer   E   W   C   K   H   S*

New Zealand. A very distinctive shrub with small thick leaves closely packed on the stems, green above, yellow beneath. The small sweetly scented flowers vary in colour from near white to pale yellow. This is a fairly hardy species.

phlogopappa   *2–3m. (6–10ft) White, Pink or Blue   Spring E   W   C   K   H   S*

Tasmania, Australia. This is the first olearia to flower. The young stems are grey-felted and so are the undersides of the fairly small, toothed leaves. The flowers are carried in loose clusters and may be white, pink, mauve or blue according to variety. The whole plant is aromatic. The best coloured forms are usually grouped under the varietal name 'Splendens'. They are very attractive but even more tender than the more common white-flowered form. In gardens O. *plogopappa* is usually grown as O. *gunniana*, the name formerly used by botanists, and also sometimes as O. *stellulata*, a name which belongs to a similar but taller species with larger leaves and a less compact habit.

x scilloniensis   *2–2.5m. (6–8ft)   White L. Spring   E   W   O   K   L*

A hybrid between *Olearia phlogopappa* and the rather similar O. *lirata*. It resembles the former but is even more free-flowering and is probably the best of the small-leaved, medium size olearias considered primarily as flowering plants. It is rather tender but grows well in coastal regions and other places where frosts are neither severe nor prolonged. The leaves are green above, grey-green beneath.

traversii   *4–8m. (13–26ft)   Greyish E. Summer   E   W   O   K   S   H*

Chatham Islands. This is valueless as a flowering plant but quite good in foliage and excellent as a windbreak. The leaves are smooth-edged and broadly lance-shaped, silvery beneath, tough and wind resistant. The plant grows rapidly and in favourable places can reach tree-like proportions.

ONONIS, Leguminosae. Shrubby Rest Harrow. Most members of this genus are tough-stemmed perennials but a few are shrubby and are useful because they flower late and will grow in hot sunny places. They like reasonably fertile, well-drained soils, can be clipped with shears after flowering and are best increased by seed.

fruticosa *60–90cm. (2–3ft) Pale magenta Summer D K S H*

Southern Europe. A low but wide-spreading shrub with small three parted leaves set close to the stems and small sprays of vetch-like flowers. Useful for sunny banks, rock gardens and similar places.

Osmanthus x *burkwoodii*

OSMANTHUS, Oleaceae. Evergreen shrubs the best of which have small but very sweetly scented flowers. They will grow in all reasonably fertile and well-drained soils including those overlying chalk or limestone. They can be cut hard back in April if they become too large or are in need of regeneration. They can also be clipped in early summer and can be used for hedge-making. They prefer light places, preferably sunny. Summer cuttings root readily in a propagator or autumn cuttings in a frame.

armatus *2.5–4m. (8–13ft) Ivory Autumn E C T A H S*

China. This handsome species has long leaves which are sometimes much spined and sometimes smooth-edged. Sweetly scented flowers are produced in autumn.

x burkwoodii *2–3m. (6–10ft) White Spring E K C A H*

This is a hybrid between *Osmanthus delavayi* and *O. decorus*. It is densely branched, has small oval toothed leaves and small tubular sweetly scented flowers. At one time *Osmanthus decorus* was placed in another genus with the name *Phyllyrea decora*. This made the hybrid bi-generic and the name *Osmarea burkwoodii* was coined for it. Now that botanists have re-classified *P. decora* as a species of *Osmanthus* this special name is unnecessary but it is still in use in many gardens and nurseries.

decorus *1.5–3m. (5–10ft) White Spring E K C A H S*

Turkey. In gardens this useful evergreen with leathery leaves and small scented flowers followed by black berries is usually known as *Phillyrea decora*.

Osmanthus delavayi

delavayi *2–4m. (6–13ft)   White   Spring*
E K C A H S

China. A highly popular and beautiful shrub, densely branched, with small dark green glossy leaves and little tubular white flowers that throw their fragrance a long way. At one time it was known as *Siphonosmanthus delavayi* and may still be found in some gardens and nurseries bearing this name.

heterophyllus *3–6m. (10–20ft)   White*
Autumn   E C T A H S

Japan. Better known by gardeners as *Osmanthus ilicifolius*, a much more descriptive name for this large but slow-growing shrub with strikingly holly-like leaves. The small flowers are sweetly scented. There are several varieties: 'Aureomarginatus', also known as 'Aureus', with a yellow margin to each leaf;

'Variegatus', in which the marginal variegation is pale; 'Latifolius Variegatus', similar to the last but with broader leaves; 'Purpureus', with young shoots and leaves, very dark purple; and 'Myrtifolius' with smooth-edged leaves entirely lacking spines.

OSMARONIA, Rosaceae. Oso Berry. There is only one species and this is an easily grown, early-flowering shrub still known in many gardens and nurseries by a former name *Nutallia*. It is easily grown in any reasonably fertile soil including those overlying chalk or limestone. It forms thickets of suckers and if these are dug up with roots in autumn they can be used to propagate the plant. Old stems can also be cut out after flowering.

cerasiformis *2–2.5m. (6–8ft)   White*
E. Spring   D F V S

California. The leaves are lance-shaped, the flowers are small and unisexual, the sexes usually produced on separate plants. The male plant is better in habit and freer-flowering but cannot produce the small plum-purple fruits that have given this shrub its popular name. Female plants will do so only if there is a male near for pollination.

OZOTHAMNUS, Compositae. There has been considerable confusion as to the botanical classification of these evergreen shrubs and they are sometimes included in the genus *Helichrysum*. They are all natives of Australasia, not fully hardy and requiring warm sunny positions in well-drained soil. If they become straggly stems can be shortened in spring. Increase is by seed in a greenhouse in spring or by summer cuttings in a propagator.

rosmarinifolius *2–3m. (6–10ft)   White*
Summer   E W K S H

Australia, Tasmania. The rigidly erect stems and very small narrow leaves make this plant look rather like a tall heather until it produces its clusters of small chaffy flowers in summer.

In bud they are purplish-red but they open white and can make a notable display. In the wild this species is said to grow in moist peaty soil.

thyrsoideus   *2–3m. (6–10ft)   White Summer   E   W   K   S   H*

Australia, Tasmania. Much confused with *Ozothamnus rosmarinifolius* but slightly looser in habit and without the distinctive reddish buds. It flowers so freely that it has been called 'Snow in Summer'.

PACHYSANDRA, Buxaceae. Mountain Spurge. Prostrate evergreens of tufted habit much used in America as ground cover and also used for that purpose in Britain, though they do not always spread here as freely as expected. They thrive in shady places and reasonably good porous but rather moist soils. Increase is by summer cuttings in a frame or propagator. No pruning is necessary.

procumbens   *15–30cm. (6–12 in.) Greenish   Spring   E   H*

South-eastern USA. Popularly known as the Allegheny Spurge, this species makes fairly wide but low clumps of shining green leaves carried in clusters at the top of short stems. The flowers have no petals and do not contribute to the decorative effect.

terminalis   *15–20cm. (6–8in.)   Greenish Spring   E   H*

Japan. The general effect is much like that of *Pachysandra procumbens* but the leaves are a little smaller and narrower, the stems are even shorter and the habit more spreading. There is a variety with white variegated leaves named 'Variegata'.

PAEONIA, Paeoniaceae. Tree Peony. Though most peonies are herbaceous plants there are a few with woody stems though none which makes anything approaching a tree, which the popular name might suggest. All like rather rich, well-cultivated soil with plenty of peat or leaf-mould to keep it open and well-drained and yet allow it to retain adequate moisture in summer. Little pruning is required but some old stems can be removed after flowering. Increase of species is by seed sown outdoors as soon as ripe or in a greenhouse or frame in spring. Garden varieties are often grafted, sometimes on the roots of herbaceous peonies, which is not very satisfactory because the two types have totally different systems of growth. Such plants are best planted rather deeply, the union between stock and scion being covered with 8 to 10cm./3 to 4in. of soil so that the scion can in time form roots of its own. In gardens stems can be layered in spring, either in the soil or by the process known as air-layering. Cuttings of firm young growth, taken in July-August with a heel of older wood, may also be rooted in moist peat and sand in a propagator.

delavayi   *2m. (6ft)   Crimson   E. Summer D   O   S   L   H*

China. An open-branched shrub with doubly divided leaves and saucer-shaped flowers which are normally dark crimson. However, it hybridizes readily with *Paeonia lutea* and hybrids may have dark orange or orange-red flowers.

lutea   *1–2.5m. (3–8ft)   Yellow L. Spring   E. Summer   D   O   S   L   H*

China. This is a variable plant and the variety named *ludlowii* makes a much bigger bush, has larger flowers and produces them several weeks earlier than the type. All forms have handsome, three-parted leaves, the segments jaggedly toothed. The flowers are cup-shaped and bright yellow but tend to be rather hidden by the leaves, a fault less marked in variety *ludlowii* than in the type.

suffruticosa *1–2m. (3–6ft) Various*
L. Spring   E. Summer   D O S G L H

China. This is the species popularly known as Moutan and the one that has been most highly developed in gardens. The species has large bowl-shaped flowers, either white with a maroon blotch at the base of each petal or wholly magenta, but garden varieties are usually either fully double or semi-double and are available in a wide range of colours, including white, pink, carmine and purple. There are also hybrids with *Paeonia lutea* which bring in yellow, apricot and orange shades, These are sometimes listed separately under the botanical name *P.* x *lemoinei*. All these garden varieties are highly decorative, among the most sumptious of all flowers but sometimes so heavy that they need individual support. All forms of *Paeonia suffruticosa*, and the hybrids, tend to start into growth early and, since the young shoots are tender, may suffer as a result from frost damage. They are better not planted where spring frosts are likely to be severe or, if they are, should be protected during the danger period. Sometimes they actually succeed better in the colder parts of Britain, where they remain dormant much longer and so escape the spring frost danger.

PARAHEBE, Schrophulariaceae. A small genus closely allied to *Hebe* and *Veronica* and at one time included in the latter, so that some of the species listed below may be found in gardens or nurseries called 'veronica'. They are all small and only semi-shrubby; plants suitable for warm sunny rock gardens, raised rock beds, unmortared walls and similar well-drained places in fairly gritty soil. They do not normally require any pruning but if they become straggly stems can be shortened in spring. Increase is by summer cuttings in a propagator or by seed sown in spring under glass.

catarractae *20–30cm. (8–12in.)*
White and purple   L. Summer   E. Autumn
D K H S

New Zealand. A sprawling plant with many slender stems, small rounded saw-edged leaves and loose spikes of small white flowers veined with reddish-purple. A variety is available with pale blue flowers but this has no distinguishing name.

lyallei *15–20cm. (6–8in.)*
White and pink   L. Summer   E. Autumn
D K H S

New Zealand (South Island). This species is very similar to *Parahebe catarractae* and much confused with it in gardens and nurseries. It is a little more prostrate, the leaves are more coarsely toothed and the flowers are veined with rosy pink.

PARTHENOCISSUS, Vitaceae. Virginia Creeper. Boston Ivy. For many years most of the species in this genus were classified as 'ampelopsis' a name now discarded by botanists though it lives on in gardens. Some were also classified as vines, in the genus *Vitis*, and this name is also sometimes used in gardens and nurseries, causing further confusion. All are slender-stemmed but vigorous climbers, some supporting themselves by tendrils others by adhesive discs by which they can attach themselves to any firm surface. They will grow in all reasonably fertile soils and in sun or shade. If they spread too far they can be cut back as much as necessary in winter while they are at rest. Species can be increased by seed but selected varieties must be increased vegetatively by layering or by cuttings of firm young growth in summer in a propagator or ripe wood cuttings in late autumn under glass.

henryana *3–6m. (10–20ft) Green
Summer D W T S H A L*

China. The vine-shaped leaves of this slightly
tender species are naturally variegated with
white and pink on a dark green groundwork
which becomes purple in the autumn. Rather
against expectation this colouring occurs
most strongly when the plant is grown in a
light place but out of direct sunshine. It is not
sufficiently hardy for the coldest parts of
Britain but succeeds well in the south and
west and in many sheltered town gardens.

inserta *6–12m. (20–40ft) Green
Summer D T S H A L*

Eastern, central and south-western North
America. A plant much confused with *P.
quinquifolia* but differing from it in having
tendrils only and no adhesive discs. It can
climb up trellis work, over fences and into
trees but cannot attach itself to walls. It
colours magnificently in autumn.

quinquefolia *6–12m. (20–40ft) Green
Summer D T S H A L*

Eastern and central North America. This is
the true Virginia Creeper, a very vigorous
self-clinging climber that can climb high up
buildings or into trees. The leaves are large
and vine-like, green in summer but becoming
orange, scarlet and crimson in autumn.

tricuspidata *6–12m. (20–40ft)
Yellowish-green Summer D T S H A L*

Japan, China. This is the Boston Ivy or
Japanese Creeper, sometimes referred to as
the Small Leaved Virginia Creeper though it
has no connection with Virginia and the
leaves are variable in size. It is still known in
some gardens and nurseries as *Ampelopsis
veitchii* and is the plant most likely to be
indicated when gardeners simply speak of
'ampelopsis'. It is vigorous and self-clinging
and it colours brilliantly in autumn. It is the
small-leaved forms that are usually regarded
as most desirable; one of these has been
named 'Lowii'.

PASSIFLORA, Passifloraceae. Passion
Flower. Only one species of this very large
genus of climbers is at all commonly planted
outdoors in Britain and even this is by no
means reliably hardy. It requires a warm
sunny place on a wall or somewhere else that
will give it some protection from frost. It will
grow in any reasonably fertile soil. The
previous year's growths can be shortened
quite severely each spring. It climbs by
tendrils and so needs something for these to
cling to. Increase is by seed sown in a warm
greenhouse in spring, by layering in spring or
by summer cuttings in a propagator.

coerulea *3–6m. (10–20ft)
White and purple Summer E. Autumn
D W C S H L*

Brazil. Though this is often called the Blue
Passion Flower, the petals are whitish and it is
the broad ring of purplish-blue filaments
which lies around the central anthers and
stigmas that give the flower its blue
appearance. There is an all-white variety
named 'Constance Elliott'.

PENSTEMON, Scrophulariaceae. Most
species are herbaceous and even the shrubby
kinds are either rather soft-stemmed or so
small that they are better regarded as rock
plants than true shrubs. Nearly all are rather
tender and all like warm sunny places and
well-drained soils. The taller kinds can be
trained against south-facing walls. Most
make amends for these various difficulties by
flowering freely, often for a considerable
time, and being very attractive. The only
pruning necessary is to remove dead or
damaged growth in spring. All can be
increased by seed sown under glass in spring
but seedlings may vary a little and so selected
forms are increased by summer cuttings in a
frame or propagator.

cordifolius *1–2m. (3–6ft)   Scarlet*
Summer   E W T S H

California. A rather straggling shrub which is
all the better for being trained against a wall
or fence. The leaves are heart-shaped, the
tubular scarlet flowers are produced freely in
large broadly conical sprays.

corymbosus *30–45cm. (12–18in.)   Scarlet*
Summer   E W T S H

California. Much like *Penstemon cordifolius*
but smaller and with more compact clusters
of flowers.

fruticosus *15–60cm. (6–24in.)*
Mauve and purple Summer   D T S H

Western North America. A rather variable
sub-shrub usually cultivated in a low-growing
narrow-leaved variety named *scouleri* and
often listed as a separate species under that
name. The flowers of this form are
blue-mauve.

heterophyllus *30–45cm. (12–18in.)*
Amethyst to Blue Summer   E. Autumn
D T S H

California. A sprawling sub-shrub which
produces its tubular flowers freely for several
months. Poor forms have a lot of pink in the
colour but good forms are clear blue. A
selected form has been named 'True Blue'.

isophyllus *60–90cm. (2–3ft)   Scarlet*
L. Summer   Autumn   D W T S H

Mexico. Though not very hardy this
handsome plant will flower even on new
growth produced right from the base after all
top growth has been destroyed by frosts. The
tubular flowers are carried in erect spike-like
sprays.

PERIPLOCA, Periplocaceae. Silk Vine. The
species most likely to be found in British
gardens, *Periploca graeca*, is a vigorous
twiner which needs a sunny position but is
hardy and easily grown in any reasonably
fertile soil. Little pruning is desirable but
weak or old stems can be cut out in spring.
Increase is by seed or by division in spring.

graeca *6–9m (20–30ft)   Purple and Green*
Summer   D T S V

South-eastern Europe and the Near East. This
plant is more curious than beautiful with its
small clusters of starry brownish-purple and
greenish-yellow heavily scented flowers. Some
authorities believe that this scent is harmful
and the milky juice which flows out of the
smooth brown stems, if these are cut or
bruised, is certainly poisonous. The seed-pods
are also curious, long and slender, carried in
pairs and curved so that they are usually
joined at their tips.

PERNETTYA, Ericaceae. Evergreen shrubs
grown primarily for their marble-like berries
but also useful as foliage plants and quite
decorative in flower. Some species do not fruit
well unless a 'male plant', that is one chosen
for the characteristic of producing a high
percentage of male flowers, is growing among
them, and this is true even when plants are
not wholly unisexual. Pernettyas all require
lime-free soils, preferably well supplied with
peat, leaf mould or other humus-forming
material so that they remain moist in summer
without becoming waterlogged in winter.
They do not require pruning but will submit
to summer clipping and are occasionally used
to make low hedges. Increase is by seed sown
in peat and sand in spring, by summer
cuttings in a propagator or by digging up
rooted suckers or offsets in spring or autumn.

mucronata *0.6–1.5m. (2–5ft)   White*
L. Spring   E K S H V

Chile, Argentina. The most popular species, a plant which spreads freely by suckers and makes a low but dense thicket of growth. The leaves are small firm dark glossy green and sharp-pointed, closely placed on the slender but stiff stems. The flowers are small and bell-shaped, the berries which follow globe-shaped, red, crimson, pink, lilac or very deep purple. A variety named 'Thymifolia' produces male flowers freely but no berries. It is useful for pollination.

prostrata *30cm. (1ft)   White   E. Summer*
E K S H

Costa Rica, Chile. A more or less prostrate evergreen but variable in its characteristics. The form usually cultivated in Britain is known as *pentlandii* and has small leaves with bristle-like spines, small white globe-shaped flowers and the typical marble-shaped berries, normally dark purple but pink and white forms exist.

PEROVSKIA, Labiatae. At a short distance these grey-leaved shrubs look rather like tall, unusually stiff lavenders. Their stems are less woody than they at first appear and often suffer considerable damage in winter in the colder parts of Britain. However, the plant usually grows strongly from the base and also responds well to spring pruning, which can be used to get rid of all damaged or weak growth. *Perovskia* grows best in warm sunny places and reasonably good, well-drained soil. It resents root disturbance and should be planted from pots while still small. Propagation is by seed under glass in spring or root cuttings in winter.

abrotanoides *1–1.5m. (3–5ft)*
Lavender blue   L. Summer   E. Autumn
D C T S R

Russia, Iran. Much like *P. atriplicifolia* but less densely covered in grey down and with more deeply cut leaves, a feature which has

suggested to some gardeners that *P. atriplicifolia* 'Blue Spire' might really be a hybrid between the two species. However, most experts do not accept this.

atriplicifolia *1–1.5m. (3–5ft)   Lavender blue*
L. Summer   E. Autumn   D C T S R

Himalaya, Afghanistan. A semi-shrubby plant with stiffly erect stems covered in grey down, greyish toothed leaves which are aromatic when bruised and branched slender spikes of small lavender-blue flowers, the whole inflorescence grey with short down. This is a strikingly beautiful late-flowering shrub. There is a very distinctive variety named 'Blue Spire' in which the leaves are lobed and deeply slashed and the clusters of slender flower-spikes are particularly large.

PHILADELPHUS, Philadelphaceae. Mock Orange. Syringa. Deciduous shrubs mostly with white, sweetly scented flowers which are at their peak in June when they make a notable contribution to the garden. The popular name Syringa is unfortunate since it is the correct botanical name of the lilacs and so causes much confusion. The Mock Oranges are easily grown in most soils including those that are strongly alkaline. They can be pruned immediately after flowering, when the old flowering stems can be cut out and the bushes thinned if they are overcrowded. Increase is by summer cuttings in a frame or propagator or autumn cuttings in a sheltered place outdoors.

coronarius *2.5–3m. (8–10ft)*
Creamy-white   E. Summer   D F H A S

South-eastern Europe and Asia Minor. A well-branched shrub with clusters of good sized saucer-shaped flowers but the scent is heavy, pleasant in the open air but overpowering indoors. It has a fine yellow-leaved variety named 'Aureus', which is one of the best shrubs of its colour in spring and early summer though it becomes less bright as the leaves age.

delavayi *3–4m. (10–13ft)*
White or purple   E. Summer   D F H A S

China. A strikingly beautiful species in which white petals are contrasted with purple calyx segments. The colour is variable and one of the best forms is sold as 'Nymans Variety', though botanists would probably call it *melanocalyx*. All forms are richly scented.

inodorus *1.2–2m. (4–6ft)   White*
E. Summer   D F H A S

South-eastern USA. The least desirable of the familiar species since its flowers have no scent. It is a variable plant and it is the form known as *grandiflorus* that is usually planted, often listed simply as *P. grandiflorus* as if it were a species in its own right.

x lemoinei *1.5–2m. (5–6ft)   White*
E. Summer   D F H A

A group of hybrids between *Philadelphus microphyllus* and *P. coronarius*, mostly with rather small flowers but very freely produced and sweetly scented. 'Erectus' and 'Avalanche' have pure white single flowers and 'Manteau d'Hermine' is ivory and double.

mexicanus *1.2–2m. (4–6ft)   White*
E. Summer   D W F H A S

Mexico. This distinctly tender species is chiefly of interest because its flowers are rose-scented, and in some forms have a purple blotch on the base of each petal. One such blotched form is known as 'Rose Syringa' and it was a plant of this type that the French nurseryman Lemoine used to produce some of his fine purple blotched hybrids.

microphyllus *1–1.2m. (3–4ft)   White*
E. Summer   D F H A S

Colorado and Arizona. The smallest species in leaf, flower and ultimate height. This is a very attractive little shrub, immensely free-flowering and very sweetly scented.

pubescens *3–6m. (10–20ft)   White*
Summer   D F H A S

South-eastern USA. This is one of the largest species but there is some confusion between it and another American species named. *P. intectus*. Both grow very tall and produce great numbers of scented flowers which make a great display. In some gardens it is known as *P. grandiflorus* but this name really belongs to a variety of *P. inodorus*.

Philadelphus coronarius

Philadelphus Hybrids

In addition to the hybrids already mentioned under the species which were their parents, there are many more of more complex or unidentified parentage. They include some of the most popular and decorative varieties of *philadelphus*. The following are typical:

'Beauclerk'. A medium sized bush with arching stems bearing large broad-petalled fragrant white flowers sometimes stained with pinkish-purple at the centre.
'Belle Étoile'. One of the best varieties of medium size, about 2m./6ft high with clusters of large single white flowers blotched at the centre with purple and very sweetly scented.
'Burfordiensis'. A vigorous philadelphus up to 3m./10ft high, with large single white flowers which are not scented. It was one of the parents of 'Beauclerk'.
'Enchantment'. A moderately vigorous variety 2m./6ft or a little more in height with arching stems bearing double white sweetly scented flowers.
'Norma'. Grows to about 1.5m./5ft and has arching branches and moderately fragrant single pure white flowers.
'Purpureo-maculatus'. A low-growing variety not above 1m./3ft high with medium size white flowers conspicuously purple stained at the centre. It is sweetly scented.
'Sybille'. A fairly short but quite wide shrub with large single white flowers each with a large purplish-rose stain at the centre. The scent is strong but pleasant.
'Virginal'. The most popular double-flowered philadelphus, free-flowering and very sweetly scented and rather erect in habit.
'Voie Lactée'. Large broad-petalled white flowers on a well-shaped bush up to 1.5m./5ft high but not much scent.

PHILLYREA, Oleaceae. It is hard to realize now that there was a time when these relatives of privet were among the most popular of evergreen shrubs. Though seldom seen now they are still useful, especially as windbreaks or backgrounds for more showy plants. All are easily grown in all reasonably fertile soils and will stand clipping in spring and summer if this is deemed desirable to keep them tidy and restrict their size. They can also be cut back hard in May with good expectation that they will produce new growth even from quite old wood. Increase is by summer cutting in a propagator or seed in a greenhouse or frame in spring.

angustifolia   *2.5–3m. (8–10ft)*
Greenish-white   L. Spring   E. Summer
E   K   O   H   S

Portugal, North Africa. This makes a densely branched shrub with narrow leaves and clusters of inconspicuous but sweetly scented flowers. A variety named *rosmarinifolia* has even narrower leaves that are greyish-green rather than dark green.

Phillyrea

Phlomis fruticosa

latifolia *3–6m. (10–20ft)   Greenish-white Spring   E K O H S*

Southern Europe, North Africa, Asia Minor. This is a much bigger shrub than *P. angustifolia*, capable of developing into a tree. The leaves are broad and saw-edged, more or less oval in the type but rounder in variety *rotundifolia*, and more deeply toothed in variety *spinosa*.

PHLOMIS, Labiatae. Jerusalem Sage. The species cultivated in Britain are either herbaceous plants or sub-shrubs with rather soft stems that are liable to be cut back in cold winters. However, they usually produce new growth from lower down and this can be helped, and the habit of the bushes improved, by fairly hard pruning in spring. All love sun, warmth and good drainage but are otherwise not fussy about soil. They can be increased very easily from summer cuttings and also from seed sown under glass in spring.

chrysophylla *1.2–2m. (4–6ft)   Yellow Summer   E W C H S*

Lebanon. This species is not so well known as *Phlomis fruticosa*, which it much resembles except for the yellowish tinge of its leaves, particularly marked in spring and early summer.

fruticosa *1.2–2m. (4–6ft)   Yellow Summer   E W C H S*

Mediterranean. This is the familiar Jerusalem Sage, a bushy plant with sage-like leaves and whorls of hooded yellow flowers. It is a handsome free-flowering plant for a warm rather dry place.

PHOTINIA, Rosaceae. It is the evergreen species of this quite large and varied genus that are most useful in Britain as ornamental shrubs. They will grow in most soils, alkaline as well as moderately acid, but are not suitable for sites subject to late spring frosts since the young leaves, their most decorative feature in this country, are a little tender. They can be trained against south or west facing walls, in which case they can be pruned annually in early summer directly the young leaves lose their bronze or red colour, to keep growth tidy and within bounds. Increase is by summer cuttings in a propagator or the species by seed sown under glass in spring.

x fraseri *3–6m. (10–20ft)   White E. Summer   E W O H*

Hybrids between *Photinia glabra* and *P. serrulata* the best forms of which, such as 'Red Robin' which is moderate in size and 'Robusta' which is taller, are also the best photinias for widespread planting in Britain. The clusters of small rather heavily scented flowers are seldom produced in Britain and

Hydrangea 'Blue Wave'

above: *Rhododendron* 'Brocade'   below: *Actinidia kolomikta*

above: *Embothrium coccineum*   below: *Magnolia* x *soulangiana*

Datura sanguinea

these shrubs are grown for the fine bronzy-red colour of their young leaves shaped like those of the cherry laurel.

glabra   *2.5–3m. (8–10ft)   White and Pink E. Summer   E W O H S*

Japan. Chiefly of interest as one of the parents of *P.* x *fraseri*, because in most respects it is inferior as a decorative shrub to the other parent, *P. serrulata*, which it somewhat resembles though it is smaller in habit and leaf.

serrulata   *4–8m. (13–26ft)   White   Spring E W O H S*

China. A magnificent large shrub or small tree with large oblong, leathery leaves, very glossy and reddish-bronze when young, becoming dark green in summer. In warm countries the flattish clusters of small flowers are very freely produced but their scent at close quarters is rather overpowering. In Britain flowers are rarely seen and it is as a foliage shrub that the species is valued. Its only drawback in comparison with the *P* x *fraseri* hybrids is its greater size, which makes it unsuitable for small gardens.

villosa   *4–5m. (13–16ft)   White L. Spring   D T H S*

Japan, China, Korea. A variable species with quite large oval or broadly lance-shaped, sharply toothed leaves that colour brilliantly before they fall in autumn. The clusters of white flowers and the red berries that follow them resemble those of hawthorn.

PHYLLODOCE, Ericaceae. Small evergreen shrubs related to the heathers and suitable only for rather moist, peaty, lime-free soils. They are not very easy to grow and are apt to die suddenly and unexpectedly. They should have an open but not hot situation and straggling stems should be pegged to the soil, where they will soon form roots and so provide replacement plants should the main

plant die. Little pruning is required. Increase is by layering or summer cuttings in a propagator.

empetriformis   *30–40cm. (12–15in.) Magenta   Spring   E T H L*

North America. A mat-forming evergreen with narrow leaves and clusters of small magenta bell-shaped flowers.

glanduliflora   *10–20cm. (4–6in.) Pale yellow   Spring   E T H L*

North America. This species is distinguished by its narrow closely packed leaves and flowers closed in at the mouth so that they are almost globular.

x intermedia   *15–20cm. (6–8in.)   Magenta Spring   E T H L*

A natural hybrid between *Phyllodoce empetriformis* and *P. glanduliflora* with the strong colour of the former but the flower form of the latter. The best form is named 'Fred Stoker'.

nipponica   *10–20cm. (4–8in.) White and Pink   L. Spring   E T H L*

Japan. The most beautiful species, compact and tufted, with narrow leaves and bell-shaped flowers, white tinged with pink.

PHYSOCARPUS, Rosaceae. A small genus of deciduous shrubs closely allied to *Neillia* and occasionally listed under that name. They are all rather large, dislike lime, enjoy plenty of moisture and an open situation. They make much growth direct from the roots and may require drastic thinning or chopping back if space is limited. Rooted suckers, removed in autumn or winter, provide an easy means of increase and they can also be grown from cuttings in summer or seeds in spring.

opuliformis   *2–3m. (6–10ft)*
White and Pink   E. Summer   T H V S

Eastern North America. Quite a handsome
foliage plant with tree-lobed leaves like a
guelder rose and clusters of small white,
pink-tinted flowers. There is a variety named
'Luteus' with leaves that are yellow in spring
but become green in summer.

PIERIS, Ericaceae. Lily-of-the-Valley Bush.
These handsome evergreen shrubs are grown
both for their foliage and for their clusters of
slender spikes of small white, pitcher-shaped
flowers rather like those of lily-of-the-valley.
They all dislike lime and thrive best in
conditions similar to those that suit most
rhododendrons, that is, a moderately acid
humus-rich soil with plenty of peat or
leaf-mould to retain moisture in summer and
either dappled shade or not too much hot
sunshine. Also, like rhododendrons, they
usually make good new growth even when
hard-pruned but this should only be done
when essential to restrict size or rejuvenate
bushes, since it will restrict flowering the
following year. It is best done in May or early
June as soon as the flowers fade. Increase is
by seed in spring, by layering in spring or by
late summer cuttings in a propagator.

floribunda   *1–2m. (3–6ft)   White   Spring*
E O S L H

South-eastern USA. This is the smallest kind,
a compact evergreen with small white flowers
in short slender spikes themselves arranged in
small clusters. Its neat habit and slow growth
make it ideal for small gardens.

formosa   *2.5–5m. (8–16ft)   White*
L. Spring   E O S L H

China, Nepal, Burma, Assam. With such a
wide range of distribution it is not surprising
that this is a variable plant. The best variety is
forrestii, which has larger flowers carried in
clusters of slender spikes, and very often the
young shoots and leaves are brightly coloured

in spring when this fine plant is at its most
beautiful. In gardens it is usually represented
by a variety named 'Wakehurst' in which the
young growth starts by being bright red, fades
to a lighter shade and for a while becomes
nearly white before getting its final deep green
colour. Another variety named 'Charles
Mitchell' has even larger flowers but the
young growth is not quite so brilliant,
bronzy-red rather than near scarlet. *Pieris*
'Forest Flame' is a hybrid between some form
of *P. formosa* and *P. japonica* and has the
denser habit of the latter parent with the
young leaf and shoot colour of the former.

japonica   *2.5–3m. (8–10ft)   White*
E. Spring   E O S H L

Japan. A densely branched shrub producing
its flowers very freely in clusters of slender
semi-pendant spikes. As a flowering shrub it is
one of the most effective of the genus but it
starts to flower so early that it needs a place
where cold air does not collect, or the life of
the flowers may be brief. There are several
varieties, 'Christmas Cheer' and 'Flamingo'
have pink flowers, most deeply coloured in
the last named and opening extra early in
'Christmas Cheer'. 'Variegata' has rather
narrow leaves edged with cream and is an
excellent small, slow-growing variegated
evergreen shrub.

taiwanensis   *1.2–2m. (4–6ft)   White*
Spring   E O S H L

Formosa. Despite its country of origin this is a
hardy species for it grows wild at high
altitudes. It is compact and densely branched
and in the form usually seen in gardens,
carries its small flowers in clusters of more or
less horizontal or dependant spikes.

PILEOSTEGIA, Hydrangeaceae. Only one
species is likely to be found in British gardens
and this is a climbing 'hydrangea' with
evergreen leaves. Like *Hydrangea petiolaris*
and the two species of *Schizophragma*
cultivated, it climbs by aerial roots and so can

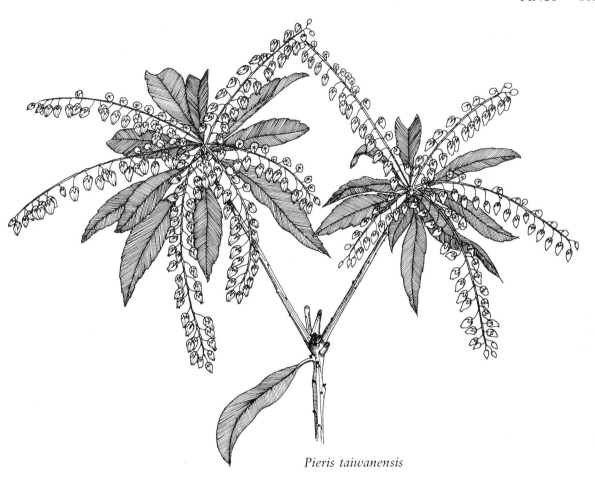

Pieris taiwanensis

be used to clothe a wall or tree trunk without further support, or it can be grown as ground cover. It prefers rather shady places and will thrive in any reasonably fertile soil but is sometimes slow starting. It can be cut back in spring as necessary to restrict it to the space available. Increase is by summer cuttings in a propagator or by layering in spring.

viburnoides *3–6m. (10–20ft)* *White Autumn* *E T C H L*

India, China, Formosa. The broadly lance-shaped leaves are leathery in texture and dark green in colour. The small flower clusters lack the showy bracts characteristic of *Hydrangea* and *Schizophragma* and their most conspicuous feature is the tuft of white anthers which each bears. This is not in any way a showy or even a particularly beautiful plant but it is interesting, and its dense growth of rather sombre foliage can be effective in the right place.

PINUS, Pinaceae. Pine. Only a few of the pines can be regarded as shrubs, all the rest being trees, many of considerable size. Those named here will thrive in any open place and well-drained soil. *Pinus mugo* will grow well in soils containing lime but *P. pumila* requires lime-free soil. Pruning of these dwarf kinds is usually undesirable but they can be branch-thinned a little in spring if necessary to restrict their size. Increase is by seed sown as soon as ripe or in spring. Seed may germinate more freely if kept moist at 4°C./39°F. for three months prior to sowing.

mugo *1.5–3m. (5–10ft)* *Purple*
E. Summer *E T S*

Europe. This species, known as the Dwarf Mountain Pine, is closely allied to *Pinus uncinata* and considered by some authorities to be a dwarf form of it. It is broad in proportion to its height, its leaves densely crowded so that it makes an excellent shelter shrub. There are several selected varieties including *pumilio*, which differ mainly in botanical details and 'Gnom' and 'Mops' both of which are smaller and even more compact.

pumila *1–1.5m. (3–5ft)* *Red*
E. Summer *E T S*

North-eastern Asia. This very hardy, semi-prostrate shrub is known as the Dwarf Siberian Pine. Some authorities regard it as a variety of *Pinus cembra* the Arolla Pine of the Alps, but from a garden standpoint it is very different. There are several varieties, including 'Compacta' and 'Dwarf Blue', both extra compact and with blue-grey leaves.

PIPTANTHUS, Leguminosae. Nepal Laburnum. Evergreen Laburnum. Only one species is at all commonly grown in British gardens and even this is not completely hardy except in the more favourable climates of the south and west. Otherwise it is not difficult to grow in any moderately fertile and well-drained soil and sunny position. It can be trained against a wall, and then it may be desirable to cut out quite a lot of the older stems each spring. However it is grown, weather-damaged and weak stems should always be cut out then. It is readily increased from seed and often produces self-sown seedlings. If transplanted this should be done while seedlings are still small, or they may be put singly into pots to grow on since they resent root breakage.

laburnifolius *2.5–4m. (8–13ft)* *Yellow*
L. Spring *ED W T S*

Himalayan. A distinctive shrub with rather soft green stems, many produced from the base and three-parted leaves. The bright yellow pea-type flowers are borne in short spikes and make a good display for a few weeks.

PITTOSPORUM, Pittosporaceae. Though none of these evergreens is completely hardy, many are very tolerant of wind even when salt-laden, and so are frequently used as shelter belts or hedges in mild but exposed coastal gardens. They are easily grown in most reasonably well-drained soils and prefer open sunny situations. The small-leaved kinds can be clipped any time from May to August if used as hedges, and all kinds can be thinned or even cut back quite severely in spring if it is necessary to reduce their size. All can be grown from summer cuttings in a propagator and all species, but not garden varieties, from seed sown under glass in spring.

crassifolium *4–5m. (13–16ft)* *Purple*
L. Spring *E W T K H S*

New Zealand (North Island). In New Zealand this is known as Karo. It has leathery leaves, smooth above, covered with brown or whitish felt beneath. The starry flowers are small and not very effective but this is an excellent shelter shrub for maritime gardens.

eugenoides *3–6m. (10–20ft)* *Yellowish*
Spring *E W T K H S*

New Zealand. This is a tree in its native land but in Britain is usually a rather tall but fairly narrow shrub especially when grown in its variety 'Variegatum', with creamy-white margin to the shining light-green leaf, since this is less vigorous. The flowers are small and unexciting in appearance, but are very sweetly scented.

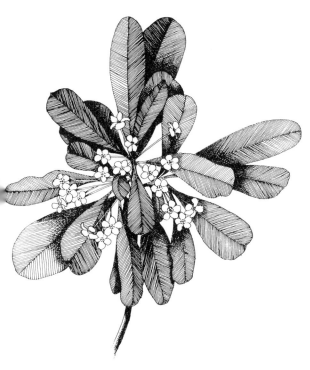

Pittosporum tobira

tenuifolium *3–6m. (10–20ft)*
Purplish-brown Spring E W T K H S

New Zealand. Another species that can make
a small tree but bears pruning well and is
often used as a hedge in mild places. It is one
of the most elegant species, with slender
stems, nearly black when young, neat light
green wavy-edged leaves and small, dull
coloured flowers that are very sweetly
scented. The cut stems are much in demand
by florists for foliage. There are numerous
varieties of which the most popular is 'Silver
Queen' with grey-green leaves edged with
white. Others are 'Garnettii' with
white-edged leaves becoming suffused with
pink in winter and believed by some to be of
hybrid origin; 'James Stirling', with small
grey-green leaves; 'Purpureum', with green
leaves becoming purplish-bronze with age;
and 'Warnham Gold', with leaves that
become progressively more yellow from
spring to autumn.

tobira *2.5–5m. (8–16ft) White Spring*
E W T C S H

Japan, Korea, China, Formosa. One of the
few species not native to New Zealand. It is a
very handsome foliage and flowering plant,
the leaves thick, narrow and lustrous green.
The bush branches widely and can in time
take up a lot of room though it can be
hard-pruned occasionally to prevent this. The
flowers are large and showy for a
pittosporum, looking and smelling rather like
orange blossom.

PODOCARPUS, Podocarpaceae. A large
genus of conifers, mainly trees but some kinds
are shrubs. Most are not fully hardy and so
suitable only for the milder parts of the British
Isles. Most will grow in all reasonably fertile
and well-drained soils but a few dislike lime.
Pruning is as a rule unnecessary. Increase is by
seed in spring or by nearly ripe cuttings in late
summer in a propagator.

alpinus *1–1.5m. (3–5ft) Green*
E. Summer E H S

Tasmania, New South Wales. A dense
dome-shaped bush of slender drooping
stems. The narrow leaves are small, green
above, greyish below. It is one of the hardiest
kinds.

macrophyllus maki *3–6m. (10–20ft)*
Green E. Summer E W H

China. The species is a tree but the variety
maki is a large shrub with quite long narrow
leaves, yellowish-green when young but
darker green as they age, grey-green beneath.
This is a species that dislikes lime. Opinions
differ as to its precise degree of hardiness but
it will certainly withstand quite a lot of frost if
other conditions are favourable.

nivalis *30–45cm. (1–1½ft)   Green*
E. Summer   E W H S

New Zealand. A low-growing,
wide-spreading evergreen with small narrow
stiff and sharp-pointed leaves. It has a wide
distribution in New Zealand, sometimes
growing at altitudes as high as
1600m./5000ft, and it is probable that there
is considerable difference in hardiness
according to the place from which the parent
plant or seed was obtained. It is popularly
known as the Alpine Totara.

POLYGALA, Polygalaceae. This is the genus
to which the milkworts belong though that
name seems more appropriate for the
herbaceous than for the shrubby species.
These are all tiny shrubs, more suitable for
rock gardens and raised rock beds than for
the company of other shrubs. They enjoy
rather moist peaty soil though in the wild
Polygala chamaebuxus is often found on
limestone mountains. It grows so close to the
soil that many shoots form roots into it and
can be dug up carefully in spring or autumn
and used for propagation. Plants can also be
raised from seed. No pruning is required.

chamaebuxus *15–30cm. (6–12in.)*
Yellow and Cream   Spring   E   V   S

Europe. This, the most popular kind, makes a
low mound of small rounded leaves
smothered in spring with little flowers that
look rather like those of the pea family. It is
most beautiful in a variety named *grandiflora*
in which the wing petals are wine-purple and
the keel is yellow. It is sometimes called
purpurea.

vayredae *7–10cm. (3–4in.)*
Purple and Yellow   E. Spring   E   V   S

Spanish Pyrenees. Rather like a smaller
P. chambaebuxus but the leaves are narrow
and each flower is terminated by a little crest.

POLYGONUM, Polygonaceae. Russian
Vine. Rampant twiners that will ascend tall
trees or clothe quite large outbuildings
rapidly. They will grow in all reasonably
fertile soils in sun or semi-shade though they
flower most freely if they can grow up into a
sunny situation. Because of the great tangle of
growth it is difficult to prune them but they
can be thinned or cut back in autumn or late
winter. Increase is by summer cuttings in a
propagator or by winter cuttings in a frame.

aubertii *6–12m. (20–40ft)*
White or Pinkish   L. Summer   E. Autumn
D T H A

China. A species so much like
P. baldschuanicum that even the experts seem
to find it difficult to tell which is which. As a
name it is less common in gardens than
P. baldschuanicum but as a plant it may well
be the more abundant as plants of *P. aubertii*
have almost certainly been distributed under
the other name. It matters little since they are
of equal decorative merit.

baldschuanicum *6–12m. (20–40ft)*
White or Pinkish   L. Summer   E. Autumn
D T H A

Russia. The leaves of this plant are unexciting
and it is when it comes into flower that its
decorative potentiality becomes apparent for,
though individually small, flowers are
produced in vast numbers covering the upper
parts of the plant with what looks at a short
distance like pink-tinted foam.

PONCIRUS, Rutaceae. Hardy Orange. There
is only one species and this is a very spiny
shrub which is hardy in the milder parts of the
British Isles, particularly near the coast, and is
sometimes used as a hedge to exclude
animals. It likes good fertile soil and a warm
sunny position. When grown as an isolated
specimen or in a shrub border it requires little
pruning beyond the removal of dead or
damaged growth in spring, but when planted
as a hedge it can be thinned at any time from

June to August. Plants can be raised from seed sown in a greenhouse in spring or from late summer cuttings in a propagator.

trifoliata   *2.5–5m. (8–16ft)   White L. Spring   E W O S H*

Korea, China. An angularly but densely branched shrub with usually three-parted, but occasionally five-parted, leaves and clusters of white strongly scented flowers followed by small orange fruits. It is, in fact, a member of the orange family and is sometimes known as *Citrus trifoliata*. The fruits are too bitter to eat raw but it is said that they can be made into marmalade.

POTENTILLA, Rosaceae. Cinquefoil. This very large genus is largely composed of herbaceous species but the few shrubby kinds have made up what they lack in numbers by the liberality with which they have produced garden varieties. All are easily grown in any reasonably well-drained soil. Though they will survive in shade they are happier and flower more freely in sunny places. Most tend to get overcrowded with growth in time and are improved by extensive thinning out of the weaker and older stems in spring, combined with some shortening of the sturdier young stems. Increase is by summer cuttings in a propagator or autumn cuttings in a frame but species can also be grown from seed. It has been suggested that poor flower production in some places, and particularly of some garden varieties, may be due to summer attacks by red spider mites, and if this is suspected plants should be sprayed occasionally from June to September with derris or malathion.

arbuscula   *45cm.–1.2m. (1½–4ft)   Yellow Summer   D T A H S*

Himalaya, Tibet, China. A very variable species, some forms of which closely resemble *Potentilla fruticosa* but those passing under this name in gardens are usually shorter, broader and have larger flowers. A variety named 'Beesii' has silvery leaves.

fruticosa   *1–1.2m. (3–4ft)   Yellow Summer   D T A H S*

Northern Hemisphere (including Britain). As grown in gardens this is usually a taller shrub, with more erect stems and slightly smaller flowers than *P. arbuscula*, but with its vast distribution in the wild it is not surprising that it varies greatly and some forms are actually prostrate or nearly so. A great many varieties are listed under this species though many are probably hybrids between it and other species, including *P. parvifolia* and *P. davurica*, a Russian and Chinese species, from both of which the pink and red-flowered varieties may, in part, stem. Examples of these cultivated varieties are included here:

'**Daydawn**' is of medium height with cream and pink flowers.
'**Elizabeth**' is about 1m./3ft high and has large soft yellow flowers.
'**Gold Drop**' is dwarf and compact, with small but numerous bright yellow flowers.
'**Jackman's Variety**' is tall and vigorous, about 1.2m./3ft with quite large bright yellow flowers.
'**Katherine Dykes**' is one of the tallest and can reach 1.5m./5ft. The flowers are of medium size and are light yellow.
'**Klondyke**' is dwarf and compact with deep yellow flowers.
'**Manchu**' is also known as 'Mandschurica' and is dwarf with greyish leaves and white flowers.
'**Moonlight**' is also known as 'Maanelys' and is tall with soft yellow flowers.
'**Primrose Beauty**' has arching stems, grey-green leaves and primrose-yellow flowers.
'**Red Ace**' is rather short and spreading with deep-coppery-red flowers.
'**Tangerine**' is short but broad with yellow and orange flowers not always freely produced.
'**Royal Flush**' is rose pink but pales in hot dry weather and is fairly dwarf.

'**Veitchii**' has white flowers, is rather tall and is considered by botanists to be a natural form of *P. davurica*.

'**Vilmoriniana**' is rather tall and erect, with silvery leaves and creamy white flowers.

parvifolia *1m. (3ft) Yellow Summer*
D T A H S

Central Asia, Siberia. Usually listed in catalogues as a variety of *P. fruticosa* but recognized by botanists as a distinct species. It is rather short and spreading, with small leaves and small flowers which are deep yellow in the form usually listed under this name but in the wild vary from white to orange. It is probable that the garden varieties with orange, red or pink flowers derive, at least in some measure, from this species.

PROSTANTHERA, Labiatae. Mint Bush. Rather tender Australasian plants of which only one species is much grown outdoors in Britain and that mainly in the mild coastal gardens of the west and south-west. Given freedom from frost it is not difficult to grow in any reasonably fertile and well-drained soil. It can be trained against a sunny wall. Old and weak stems can be cut out immediately after flowering and winter-damaged growth should be removed in spring. Increase is by early summer cuttings in a propagator or by seed in a warm greenhouse in spring.

rotundifolia *1.2–3m. (4–10ft) Purple Spring E W T O H S*

Tasmania. A very beautiful shrub with slender stems, small rounded aromatic leaves and innumerable small light heliotrope-purple flowers in April and May.

PRUNUS, Rosaceae. Cherry. Cherry Laurel. Almond. Peach. Plum. Apricot. This vast genus is composed mainly of trees, and the number of genuinely shrubby species is relatively small. All are unfussy about soil, thriving in most that are reasonably fertile and in some instances actually showing a preference for those that contain lime though they will also grow in neutral and moderately acid soil. In general the deciduous kinds can be pruned in autumn or winter but the almonds and peaches bloom principally on the young growth made the previous year and so as much as possible of this should be retained. By contrast the cherries, plums and apricots flower on spurs formed on the older stems, and young side-growths can be shortened to encourage the formation of spurs. All pruning of these kinds can be done in summer when the young shoots are shortened to a few leaves each as they complete their first flush of growth. This is a particularly good way to prune trained plants. Evergreen kinds are best pruned from May to August and can be trimmed as hedges if desired. Evergreens can be increased by summer or autumn cuttings but the deciduous kinds are mainly grown from seed or by grafting onto seedlings or vegetatively produced root-stocks of related kinds. Some kinds can also be layered in spring or autumn, or grown from cuttings in summer or autumn.

'**Cistena**' *1.2m. (3–6ft) White Spring*
D T K L A

A hybrid between *Prunus cerasifera* 'Pissardii', the Purple-leaved Plum, and *P. pumila*, the Sand Cherry. It has inherited the reddish-purple leaves of the former and the dwarf habit of the latter and is particularly useful as a short deciduous hedge plant.

glandulosa *1–1.5m. (3–5ft) White or Pink Spring D C A L*

China, Korea. Popularly known as the Chinese Bush Cherry this is a delightful shrub, with erect stems wreathed in bloom in spring. It is the double-flowered forms of the species that are almost always cultivated, either 'Alba Plena' with white flowers or 'Rosea Plena' with pink flowers. The latter is often called 'Sinensis' and may sometimes appear in catalogues as *Prunus japonica* 'Flore Roseoplena'.

incisa   *2–5m. (6–16ft)   White or Pink Spring   D P S A L*

Japan. This is known as the Fuji Cherry. It is very variable in habit, some forms growing to tree size. The flowers are small but numerous, white usually tinged with pink. There is a variety named 'Praecox', which starts to flower in winter and another named 'February Pink', which produces pale pink flowers in February or, in a mild winter, even earlier. It can be pruned in summer to keep it neat and compact and in this form makes an attractive deciduous hedge.

laurocerasus   *3–6m. (10–20ft)   White Spring   E K O S H L*

South-eastern Europe, Caucasus. This is the Cherry Laurel, a handsome strong-growing evergreen with sturdy oblong shining green leaves, slender spikes of white flowers and small cherry-like fruits which turn from red to near black. In its common form it can be used to form a large hedge or windbreak and it has produced a number of varieties which can be used as isolated specimens or in company with other shrubs. These include:

'**Angustifolia**' with narrow leaves and a relatively narrow but erect habit.
'**Magnoliifolia**' with very large leaves up to 30cm./1ft long.
'**Otto Luyken**' with narrow leaves and short but spreading habit.
'**Rotundifolia**' with leaves shorter and rounder than usual and an erect habit.
'**Schipkaensis**' with narrow leaves and wide-spreading habit coupled with great hardiness'.
'**Zabeliana**' with very narrow leaves and almost horizontal branches which make it useful as large ground cover.

lusitanica   *3–6m. (10–20ft)   White E. Summer   E K O H L S*

Spain, Portugal. This is the Portugal Laurel, an evergreen that is more densely branched, has smaller leaves and is hardier than the common form of the Cherry Laurel. It stands clipping well and is much used both for large hedges and topiary cones, mushrooms and other simple shapes. It is also a very handsome shrub in its own right, most striking of all when grown naturally and so allowed to cover itself in slender 'candle-stick' spikes of white flowers in early summer. It is susceptible to silver leaf disease which causes the leaves to become a distinctive metallic silvery green colour. Affected branches should be removed at once and wounds treated with a tree wound dressing.

pumila   *0.6–2.5m. (2–8ft)   White L. Spring   D T H L*

South-eastern USA. This is the Sand Cherry or Dwarf American Cherry, a species that is both variable in height and in the whiteness of its flowers, some being much purer than others. It is the rather short spreading forms with really white flowers that are most desirable for garden decoration. The flowers are small, single, but very numerous.

spinosa   *3–4m. (10–13ft)   White E. Spring   D O H S G V*

Europe (including Britain), Asia. This is the Sloe or Blackthorn, the first truly native shrub to make a big display in spring with its small but abundant white flowers. It is densely branched and very spiny and so makes a formidable hedge. The species is not usually used in any other way in gardens but there are two varieties that have a wider use; 'Plena' with double flowers and 'Purpurea' with reddish-purple leaves. Both are slow-growing and can be kept to a very reasonable size by pruning after the blossom falls.

Prunus tenella

tenella *0.6–1.5m. (2–5ft) Pink Spring*
D O L

Europe, Russia. This is known as the Dwarf Russian Almond and is a charming small shrub which flowers on young stems made the preceding year. The flowers are small but carried all along the stems. There are several varieties the most popular being those selected from a wild variety named *gesslerana*, which has deeper rose-pink or nearly red flowers. One of these, freely available, is 'Fire Hill'.

triloba *3–4m. (10–13ft) Pale pink*
Spring D F H A L

China. This beautiful species belongs to the almond section of the family but is not very hardy and in many places must be trained against a sunny wall to make it succeed. It is nearly always planted in its double-flowered variety, 'Multiplex', which has fully double flowers wreathing the previous year's stems like little pink rosettes in spring. It is much in demand as a cut flower.

PUNICA, Punicacae. Pomegranate. In warm countries the pomegranate grows to the size of a small tree and is much cultivated for its large many-seeded edible fruits. In Britain it must usually be trained against a sunny wall to keep it alive and it rarely produces, let alone ripens, any fruits. Nevertheless it is worth growing for ornament alone and there are dwarf varieties some of which appear to be hardier than the species. All like fertile well-drained soil and warm sunny places. Old and weak stems can be removed in spring. The species can be raised from seed sown under glass in spring, and so can at least one of the dwarf varieties. Other selected kinds may need to be increased by summer cuttings in a propagator to keep them true to type.

granatum *0.15–7m. (6in.–23ft) Scarlet*
L. Summer E. Autumn D T S H

Iran, Afghanistan. A densely branched bush
or small tree with shining green leaves and
scarlet flowers consisting of five petals
arranged in the form of a funnel emerging
from a funnel-shaped calyx. There are several
double-flowered varieties; 'Albopleno', also
known as 'Multiplex', with white flowers;
'Plena', also known as 'Flore Pleno', and
'Rubroplena', both with scarlet flowers; and
'Wonderful', orange-red. There are also
dwarf varieties though the name *nana* applied
to them seems to cover more than one form.
Typically they are miniature versions of the
species in some cases no more than 15cm./6in.
high and with single scarlet flowers.

PYRACANTHA, Rosaceae. Firethorn.
Stiff-stemmed and thorny evergreen shrubs
with clusters of white flowers followed by red,
orange or yellow berries. They grow well on
most reasonably well-drained soils and have a
particular liking for those containing lime.
They will grow, flower and fruit in sun or
open shade but are not suitable for planting
beneath trees. Although, if left to their own
devices, they make large bushes which may in
time become broader than high, they can be
trained against walls and fences and then it is
desirable to prune after flowering, shortening
all stems that are not carrying young fruits or
are not required for extension. Species can be
increased by seed sown in spring which
germinates more readily if first kept moist for
three months at 4°C/39°F., but selected
varieties must be increased by cuttings in a
frame or propagator in late summer or early
autumn. All kinds are susceptible to fireblight
which causes leaves to wither and stems to
die. This is a notifiable disease. They can also
be attacked by the scab disease that is
common on apples and pears but this, if it
becomes troublesome, can be controlled by
spraying with a fungicide, such as benomyl, a
few times from April to July.

angustifolia *3–4m. (10–13ft) White*
E. Summer E P S H A

China. This species is distinct in having leaves
that are dark lustrous green above but
covered with grey felt beneath. It is not an
effective flowering shrub but the deep yellow
berry-like fruits are not eaten by birds and so
usually remain all winter.

atalantioides *4–6m. (13–20ft) White*
L. Spring E. Summer E P S H A

China. A very strong-growing species which
can be used to clothe high walls or make a big
bush in the open. The scarlet fruits are rather
small but are freely produced and are usually
well retained. There is a variety named
'Aurea' (or 'Flava') with yellow fruits.

coccinea *3–4m. (10–13ft) White*
E. Summer E P S H A

Southern Europe, Asia Minor. Probably the
most familiar species and a very good one.
The flowers are freely produced and
decorative and are followed by fine crops of
bright red fruits. It has a highly popular
variety, named 'Lalandei', which is
stronger-growing and has slightly larger
orange-red fruits.

crenato-serrata *3–5m. (10–16ft) White*
E. Summer E P S H A

China. From a garden standpoint this species
is so much like *P. atalantioides* that it does
not seem necessary to plant both. 'Knap Hill
Lemon', with light yellow fruits, is said to be a
variety of it.

rogersiana *2.5–3m. (8–10ft) White*
E. Summer E P S H A

China. This species has smaller leaves than
most, flowers very freely and decoratively and
has fruits which may be any shade from
orange-red to yellow. In gardens two forms
are distinguished as 'Aurantiaca', orange
berries and 'Flava', yellow berries.

Pyracantha Hybrids

In addition to these species and the garden varieties associated with them there is now an increasing number of hybrids with garden names. These include 'Buttercup', with yellow berries; 'Mohave', orange-red berries; 'Orange Glow', orange-red berries; 'Shawnee' deep yellow berries which start to colour early; and 'Watereri', with red berries. It is claimed that some of these are more resistant to disease than the species.

RHAMNUS, Rhamnaceae. Buckthorn. A large genus of trees and shrubs of which a few are worth planting for their foliage. All are easily grown in any even moderately fertile soil. Little pruning is required or is desirable except to remove dead or damaged growth in spring and to thin out a little where overcrowded. All species can be grown from seed and garden varieties from layers pegged down in spring.

alaternus   *2.5–3m. (8–10ft)*
Yellowish-green   Spring   E T S L

Portugal, Morocco, Mediterranean region, Crimea. This well-branched bush covers itself with broadly lance-shaped shining green leaves but it has little else to win the gardener's esteem. It is rather tender, its flowers are small to the point of being inconspicuous and its black fruits are not exciting. However, it has produced a good variety named 'Argenteo variegata', with narrower leaves that have a wide creamy white margin.

frangula   *3–5m. (10–16ft)*
Yellowish-green   E. Summer   D T S L

Europe (including Britain), Russia, Siberia and North Africa. The Alder Buckthorn with leaves rather like those of alder in shape, dark green and shining, turning yellow before they fall in autumn. The flowers are inconspicuous but the small fruits, which change from green to red and then black, can be freely produced.

It has a variety named 'Asplenifolia', with leaves so narrow as to be little more than a midrib.

RHAPHIOLEPIS, Rosaceae. Little known evergreen shrubs which are attractive in foliage and flower and sufficiently hardy to be grown outdoors in all but the coldest parts of the British Isles. They like reasonably fertile and well-drained soil and a warm sunny position. In April badly placed stems can be shortened or cut out and all dead or damaged growth should be removed. Increase is by seed under glass in spring or by summer cuttings in a propagator.

umbellata   *2–3m. (6–10ft)   White*
E. Summer   E W T S H

Japan, Korea. The best species to plant. It has rather leathery, oval dark green leaves and scented white flowers rather like those of some of the large-flowered thorns (*Crataegus*). They may be followed by small blue-black fruits. It can be trained against a wall if there is not a suitably warm and sheltered place for it in the open. It is sometimes called *R. japonica*.

RHODODENDRON, Ericaceae. It is not possible to deal with this vast genus adequately in a general book on shrubs for it needs at least one large volume to itself to cover it in any detail. There are at least 800 species distributed in many parts of the world, though with a concentration of some of the most beautiful hardy kinds in and around the Himalaya. In addition there are innumerable hybrids since many of the species can be interbred and the resultant hybrids will then interbreed with each other or with species. For over a hundred years professionals and amateurs have been busy breeding rhododendrons and they have transformed garden-making as a result, giving an enormous impetus to woodland gardening since many rhododendrons thrive best in the cool semi-shady conditions of thin woodland.

Botanists still include the shrubs which gardeners call Azalea in the genus *Rhododendron* though in gardens they do serve rather different purposes and some require slightly different treatment. But with such a huge and varied genus it is difficult to generalize about anything and many species and hybrids do require special conditions. Some are fully hardy and others show varying degrees of tenderness. Of all it can be said that they thrive best in moderately acid, peaty soils that hold moisture well in summer without becoming waterlogged in winter. They dislike lime, which deprives them of necessary iron and manganese unless these are supplied in special chelated (sequestrated) forms which prevent immediate chemical reaction with the lime making them insoluble and therefore unavailable. By using iron and manganese sequestrols it is possible to grow rhododendrons in soils containing free lime but it is an expensive and time-consuming task which it would be unwise to attempt on any large scale.

Rhododendrons make dense masses of fine, fibrous roots so that even quite old and large bushes can be transplanted without loss. They suffer quickly from drought and are unsuitable for hot dry places though the deciduous azaleas will take a lot more direct sunshine than most of the evergreen rhododendrons, with the exception of the Hardy Hybrids. Pruning is generally undesirable since it reduces the flower production but even old rhododendrons can be cut back severely with a good prospect that they will recover and make strong new growth. The best time to do this is May, with loss of at least one year's flower, but it can be a useful way of rejuvenating old plants or restoring them to manageable size.

Suckers from grafted plants must be removed. Rhododendrons can be raised from seed but the seed is very small and needs to be sown on the surface of a moist peat compost and barely covered. It takes several years for a seedling to reach flowering size. Seedlings of species reproduce all the characteristics of their parents but seedlings from hybrids may vary considerably. Selected garden varieties are often propagated commercially by grafting but in private gardens they may be increased by layering in spring or by cuttings of firm young growth in late summer or autumn in a propagator or frame. Cuttings of evergreen azaleas and of the small-leaved rhododendrons root more readily than those of deciduous azaleas or of the large-leaved evergreen rhododendrons, which may require mist treatment and may root more readily in early autumn.

albrechtii *1–1.5m. (3–5ft) Magenta Spring D S L H*

Japan. A deciduous azalea with clusters of small but numerous flowers which make a fine display at a time when there is little strong colour about.

arboreum *6–12m. (20–40ft) Red Spring E W S L H A*

Himalaya. This magnificent species grows to tree size and is a splendid sight in March and April when covered with its dense rounded clusters of long bell-shaped flowers. It is itself rather tender and mainly of use in the milder maritime gardens of the west and south-west but it has had an enormous effect in the breeding of hybrid rhododendrons many of which are completely hardy. In addition to the typical blood-red form of R. *arboreum* there are crimson, rose, pink, and white-flowered forms mainly associated with a sub-species named *campbelliae*, which grows at higher altitudes and is therefore hardier and more suitable for widespread planting in Britain. Yet another sub-species is named *cinnamoneum*, usually with white or pink flowers spotted with purple or yellow, and this is also hardier than the blood-red type. In nursery catalogues it is unlikely that these botanical sub-divisions will be listed as such and the variously coloured forms will simply appear as 'Album', white; 'Blood Red' and 'Roseum', pink.

argyrophyllum   *3–6m. (10–20ft)*
White or Pink   L. Spring   E S L H A

China. A large wide-spreading shrub with long rather narrow leaves that are silvery beneath. The funnel-shaped flowers are carried in large rather loose clusters and may be either white, with some suffusion of pink, or pink with deeper spots. This is a handsome and hardy species.

augustinii   *1.2–3m. (4–10ft)   Blue*
L. Spring   E S L H

China. This is the rhododendron from which some of the best blue has come but it is a very variable plant in height, habit and colour and by no means all have anything approaching blue flowers. They can be quite objectionable mauves and purplish pinks or amethyst and the clearer truer blues must be sought carefully and then increased vegetatively since seedlings are always likely to vary. Typically *R. augustinii* is rather tall in proportion to its breadth, not very densely branched and with leaves of medium size, giving it no great merit as a foliage plant. The flowers are of medium size, widely funnel-shaped and carried in small clusters of three or four but freely produced, so that a good plant can be well covered with them in May when, at its best, this species can be outstandingly beautiful. When purchasing plants it is wise to select while they are in flower so that really well-coloured forms, which may be anything from light lavender to deep violet, can be secured. Alternatively the variety 'Electra' can be obtained, which has larger clusters of violet-blue flowers and was produced by crossing *R. augustinii* with its own natural variety *chasmanthum*.

auriculatum   *3–9m. (10–30ft)*
White or Pink   Summer   E S L H A

China. This is the latest-flowering species and it can still be carrying its loose trusses of long funnel-shaped flowers in August long after most rhododendrons have finished. It is usually white but sometimes pink and always sweetly scented. It is hardy provided it has time to ripen its young growth, but if autumn comes early this may not be possible. The leaves are large and handsome, the bush large and open-branched. It should be grown in thin woodland.

barbatum   *3–9m. (10–30ft)   Scarlet*
Spring   E S L H A

Himalaya. No species has brighter scarlet flowers than this and they are carried in good, closely packed trusses which make a magnificent display. However, though hardy in stem and leaf, its flowers are at risk from frost and come in April when they are unlikely to survive long in cold places. The bush is also rather tall and gaunt but the peeling yellowish and blue-grey bark is pleasing. It is the parent of numerous fine hybrids.

calendulaceum   *2–3m. (6–10ft)*
Red to Yellow   L. Spring   E. Summer
D S L H

Eastern North America. A striking azalea with good-sized trusses of funnel-shaped flowers in fine colours which include many shades of red, orange and yellow. It has been used by hybridists to give these colours to garden varieties.

calophytum   *3–9m. (10–30ft)*
White or Pink and crimson   Spring
E S L H A

China. A very large bush or even wide tree with big leaves, up to 30cm. long, and broadly bell-shaped flowers which may be white or pink but are always crimson-blotched at the centre. They are carried in large but rather loose and wide clusters.

calostrotum *0.6–1.2m. (2–4ft)* *Magenta L. Spring* E S L H A

Burma. A striking dwarf rhododendron, compact in habit with rounded leaves, grey-green above and brownish beneath, and saucer-shaped flowers carried in ones and twos in various shades of magenta from light to dark.

campanulatum *2–3m. (6–10ft)* *Purple Spring* E S L H A

Himalaya. A vigorous open-branched shrub with loose clusters of bell-shaped flowers. The colour is variable, from pale mauve to rosy purple, purple-spotted inside. Selected forms are available including 'Knap Hill', which is near to lavender in colour and 'Album', white.

campylocarpum *1.2–3m. (4–10ft)* *Yellow Spring* E S L H A

Himalaya. A fine yellow-flowered species with rounded leaves that are green above blue-grey beneath. The flowers are widely bell-shaped carried in loose clusters and are variable in colour, from cream to sulphur yellow. It is wise to select plants of this variety while in bloom so that the best colours can be picked out.

campylogynum *4–40cm. (2–15in.)* *Purple L. Spring E. Summer* E S L H A

Himalaya, China, Burma. A variable species but in its best forms dwarf and compact with small rounded leaves, blue-grey beneath, and nodding bell-shaped dark crimson flowers carried singly or in small clusters. There are white and pink flowered forms and also several botanically recognized variants including *myrtilloides*, which is virtually prostrate and has small flowers, and *cremastum*, which has been recorded as tall as 1.2m./4ft in the wild but does not appear to attain as much in gardens.

catawbiense *2–3m. (6–10ft)* *Purple E. Summer* E S L H A

South-eastern USA. This is not itself a particularly desirable species since the flowers are of poor quality but it has been an extremely valuable parent of hybrids, passing on to them its very dense habit, good dark green rather broad leaves and great hardiness. Typically the flower colour is light magenta but there are deeper coloured and also white variants.

caucasicum *0.6–1m. (2–3ft)* *Pale yellow L. Spring* E S L H A

Caucasus, Armenia, Turkey. A low compact bush with pale yellow flowers spotted and sometimes flushed with pink, narrowly bell-shaped and in closely packed trusses. This wild form appears to be scarce in gardens and the plants grown under this name are usually taller, up to 3m./10ft and may well be hybrids. Certainly this species, which is very hardy, was used in the breeding of the Hardy Hybrids.

chaetomallum *1.2–1.5m. (4–5ft)* *Crimson E. Spring* E S L H A

China. A handsome plant with leaves that are covered beneath with brown down and clusters of bell-shaped deep crimson flowers. Because it flowers early it needs a sheltered situation.

ciliatum *1–1.2m. (3–4ft)* *Pink E. Spring* E S L H

Himalaya. A charming species, dwarf but spreading, with small clusters of bell-shaped flowers that are rose-red in bud but gradually pale as they open until with age they become white or nearly so. The specific name refers to the short stiff hairs around the edges and on the upper surface of the leaves.

cinnabarinum *2–3m. (6–10ft) Red*
L. Spring E. Summer E S L H A

Himalaya. An exceptionally beautiful and
distinctive species which carries its long
slenderly funnel-shaped cinnabar-red flowers
partly drooping in a loose truss. The leaves
are of medium size, oval and a shining
greyish-green above. There are numerous
forms including *blandfordiiflorum*, with
flowers that are red outside and yellow
within, and *roylei*, plum-red. It is also the
parent of some delightful hybrids which
resemble it in flower form, such as 'Lady
Chamberlain', orange-red and 'Lady
Rosebery', various shades of pink.

concatenans *2–2.5m. (6–8ft) Apricot*
Spring E S L H A

Tibet. A species allied to *R. cinnabarinum* but
the bell-shaped flowers are not so long and
narrow and are a distinctive apricot yellow
colour. It is a hardy and attractive
rhododendron of medium height and it has
produced some fine hybrids such as 'Alison
Johnstone', 'Conroy' and 'Trewithan
Orange'.

dauricum *1.2–2m. (4–6ft) Magenta*
Winter ED S L H A

Russia, Mongolia, China, Korea, Japan. The
flowers of this semi-evergreen species are
rather small and flat but are brightly coloured
and open at a time when such colour is scarce.
A variety named 'Midwinter' retains its leaves
better and has phlox-purple flowers.

davidsonianum *2–3m. (6–10ft) Rose*
Spring E S L H

China. This species makes a loosely branched
bush with rather small leaves and flowers, the
latter always some shade of pink but varying
considerably from pale phlox-pink to quite a
deep rose or magenta. It is wise to select
plants in flower.

decorum *3–6m. (10–20ft) White or Pink*
Spring E. Summer E S L H A

China. This is a very variable plant but the
best forms are extremely beautiful, with
widely funnel-shaped white or shell-pink
scented flowers carried in well formed trusses
in late May or early June. Good forms are
also well-branched and make shapely bushes.
This is another rhododendron to select when
in flower.

Rhododendron cinnabarinum hybrid

dicroanthum *0.6–1.5m. (2–5ft) Orange L. Spring E. Summer E S L H A*

China. Valuable for its colour, which is usually some shade of orange though this may be variously suffused with pink or red. The flowers are long bell-shaped and carried in loose trusses and the leaves are covered beneath with white or grey down.

discolor *3–5m. (10–16ft) White Summer E S L H A*

China. A very beautiful species which has passed on its late-flowering habit to some excellent hybrids. It makes a big well-branched bush with quite large but rather loose trusses of funnel-shaped, scented flowers which are usually white but may be tinged with pink.

elliottii *2.5–3m. (8–10ft) Scarlet L. Spring E. Summer E W S L H A*

Assam. The habit of this species is not good and it is not very hardy but the scarlet colour of its flowers is brilliant and so it has been used by breeders to produce fine red-flowered hybrids such as 'Billy Budd', 'Fusilier' and 'Grenadier'.

eriogynum *2–3m. (6–10ft) Red E. Summer E W S L H*

China. Another distinctly tender species which has nevertheless been a valuable parent of late-flowering red hybrids such as 'Romany Chai' and 'Tally Ho'.

falconeri *3–9m. (10–30ft) Cream and purple Spring E S L H A*

Himalaya. A magnificent species which makes a very large, open-branched shrub or broad many-stemmed tree with large leaves, wrinkled above and covered with rusty-coloured down beneath. The big bell-shaped flowers, creamy-white or very pale yellow with a central blotch of purple, are packed into large trusses of twenty or even more. It likes moisture in soil and air and grows particularly well in woodland near the sea.

ferrugineum *0.6–1.2m. (2–4ft) Rose E. Summer E A H L S*

Alps. This European species makes a neat densely branched bush with quite small leaves and clusters of small rose or rosy-scarlet flowers. It likes cool moist air and plenty of moisture in the soil, especially in summer. There is a white-flowered variety.

fictolacteum *3–9m. (10–30ft) White and crimson Spring E A H L S*

China. One of the big tree-like rhododendrons, widely branched and with large leaves which are covered in reddish-brown down beneath. The bell-shaped flowers are packed in large trusses and may be white, cream or pink-tinged always with a crimson blotch at the centre. It can be variable in flower quality and so it is important to obtain plants propagated from good forms with large well-shaped flowers. *R. rex* closely resembles this species but the down on the undersides of the leaves is lighter in colour.

forrestii *15–30cm. (6–12in.) Crimson Spring E H L S*

China, Tibet, Burma. A variable species, sometimes quite prostrate, sometimes making low dome-shaped bushes and occasionally climbing. The very prostrate forms are usually regarded as a separate variety distinguished as *repens*. This is often shy-flowering and not a very satisfactory plant except in some favourable places where the soil is moist, the air cool and there is some shade but not excessive. However, the real garden value of *R. forrestii* is as a parent of low-growing crimson, scarlet or red hybrids such as 'Elizabeth' and 'Jenny'.

fortunei   *2.5–3m. (8–10ft)   Pink*
L. Spring   E S L H A

China. A very beautiful species, open-branched and wide-spreading with well-formed sweetly scented pale pink flowers carried in quite large loose trusses. It is hardy and an excellent garden plant besides being a prolific parent of fine hybrids, including 'Gladys, 'Loderi' and 'Naomi'.

fulvum   *3–6m. (10–18ft)*
White, pink and crimson   Spring
E S L H A

China, Burma, Tibet. This species is cultivated mainly for its foliage and, as this differs quite a lot in effectiveness, it is necessary to choose plants with care. The leaves are always large and dark green above. Below they are covered with down, which may be any shade from fawn to cinnamon, and it is the richly reddish-brown forms that are most attractive. The flowers are also variable; white, pink or rose with a central blotch of crimson.

grande   *4–8m. (13–26ft)*
Ivory and crimson   Spring
E W S L H A

Himalaya. One of the most breath-taking rhododendrons, a noble bush of tree-like proportions, widely but openly branched, with very large leaves that are smooth and green above and closely covered with down beneath, which is usually silvery but in some forms is tawny. The bell-shaped flowers are also large, ivory white but crimson-blotched inside and packed into huge, upstanding trusses sometimes containing as many as thirty flowers. It is distinctly tender and quite unsuitable for cold inland gardens but it thrives well in coastal gardens of the south-west and west right up into Scotland, where it is very happy in the moist and relatively equable climate.

griersonianum   *2–3m. (6–10ft)   Scarlet*
E. Summer   E S L H A

China. Like some other red-flowered and slightly tender rhododendrons this handsome plant with long narrow leaves and loose trusses of scarlet flowers is more important to gardeners as a parent of splendid hybrids, many of them red or rose and late-flowering, than as a garden plant in its own right. It needs sunny but sheltered conditions and is most suitable for planting in the maritime counties of the west and south. Among its offspring are 'Elizabeth', 'Fabia', 'Fusilier', 'Laura Aberconway', 'Matador', 'May Day', 'Romany Chai', 'Tally Ho' and 'Vanessa'.

griffithianum   *3–6m. (10–20ft)   White*
L. Spring   E W S L H A

Himalaya. At its best this is a very beautiful rhododendron with widely bell-shaped, perfectly formed flowers carried in loose trusses. Unfortunately it is one of the more tender species and so only suitable for planting outside in mild places especially in the west and south. However, it has been mainly used by breeders to get its flower size and quality into hardier hybrids. The very popular 'Pink Pearl' is a second generation hybrid from *R. griffithianum*, and among the many notable first generation offspring are 'Angelo', 'Beauty of Tremough', 'Cornish Cross', 'Loderi' and 'Penjerrick'.

haematodes   *1–3m. (3–10ft)   Red*
L. Spring   E. Summer   E S L H A

China. A species variable in height and colour but it is the shorter forms with deep scarlet flowers that are most highly regarded for garden decoration. The leaves are of medium size and covered with reddish-brown down beneath. The plant is completely hardy but is sometimes shy-flowering especially for the first few years. One of the best hybrids raised from it is 'May Day'.

hanceanum   *0.30–1m. (1–3ft)*
Cream or Yellow   Spring   E S L H

China. A variable species most attractive in its small-leaved, hummock-forming varieties, of which one of the shortest and most distinctive has been named *nanum*. This seldom exceeds 30cm./1ft in height and has clear yellow flowers in scale with the rest of the plant. Excellent for a rock garden and quite hardy.

hippophaeoides   *1–1.5m. (3–5ft)   Blue*
Spring   E S L H

China. In habit, leaf size and flower this species somewhat resembles the evergreen azaleas but is botanically quite distinct from them and belongs to another group, or series, of the rhododendron family called *lapponicum*. It is variable in colour, never a true blue but in its best forms an attractive lavender-blue. A good form of this colour is named 'Inshriach'.

impeditum   *15–30cm. (6–12in.)*
Blue-purple   Spring   E S L H

China. A species very close to R. *fastigiatum* and much confused with it. The best forms are very dwarf and compact, with quite small dark green leaves and little clusters of small blue-purple flowers. Excellent for a rock garden and very hardy.

indicum   *0.30–2m. (1–6ft)   Red*
E. Summer   E W S L H

Japan. One of the two species (the other is R. *simsii*) commonly known as Indian azaleas though neither has any connection with India. Both are tender but R. *indicum* less so than R. *simsii* and it can be grown outdoors in the milder parts of the country. It makes a well-branched bush with fairly small leaves and quite large, funnel-shaped flowers carried singly or in pairs. In the species they are always some shade of red but there are garden varieties differing in flower colour and form. 'Balsaminiflorum' has double salmon-pink flowers and is around 30cm./1ft high.

'Crispiflorum' has rose flowers, and 'Double Rose' is exactly what its name implies. The garden varieties named 'Gumpo', all dwarf and compact with quite large flowers having frilled petals, are also connected with this species. 'Gumpo' itself is white sometimes flecked with red; 'Pink Gumpo' is peach-pink with deeper pink markings and there are other colours.

intricatum   *15–30cm. (6–12 in.)   Blue*
Spring   E S L H

China. A very dwarf and compact species belonging to the *lapponicum* series, which includes many rhododendrons suitable for rock gardens. This is one of the best, neat and rounded in habit with very small leaves and clusters of small flowers, which in the best forms are lavender-blue. 'Bluebird' is a good violet-blue hybrid from it.

irroratum   *2.5–3m. (8–10ft)*
White or Cream   Spring   E S L H A

China. This species can make a very large bush. The flowers are narrowly bell-shaped, packed into large trusses and rather variable in colour, white or cream but sometimes with a suffusion of pink and often with purple spotting. One form has been picked out for this last feature and named 'Polka Dot'.

japonicum   *1.2–2.5m. (4–8ft)*
Red or Rose   L. Spring   E S L H

Japan. This species is a parent of one of the big families of garden-raised azaleas, the Mollis Hybrids. It is not itself much planted in gardens though it is a strong-growing plant, with large flowers produced in good clusters in a variety of shades from soft rose to orange-red.

Rhododendron johnstoneanum

johnstoneanum   *1.5–3m. (5–10ft)*
White or Primrose   L. Spring
E W S L H

Assam. A beautiful but rather tender species
with leaves of medium size, fringed with hairs
when young, and small clusters of quite large
funnel-shaped flowers that are either white or
very pale yellow and may sometimes be a little
spotted or flushed with purple or crimson.
They are always sweetly scented and some
forms have double flowers, one of these
having been named 'Double Diamond'.

kaempferi   *1.5–3m. (5–10ft)   Red, Pink*
L. Spring   E. Summer   ED S L H

Japan. This is one parent of many of the
evergreen garden azaleas, including the
small-leaved Kurume varieties and the large
Kaempferi Hybrids. It does not always retain
all its leaves in winter, tending to drop those

formed in spring and to retain only those
towards the ends of the stems that were
formed in summer, and this is a characteristic
that it has passed on to some of the hybrids.
The flowers are widely funnel-shaped, carried
singly or in small clusters, usually in some
shade of red or pink though this can vary
greatly from strong orange-scarlets to quite
pale shades of pink. There are also white
forms as well as semi-doubles. All are best in
semi-shade which preserves the rather thin
petals from sun-scorching. One of the most
beautiful forms is named 'Eastern Fire' and
has single camellia rose flowers. See also *R.
kiusianum*.

keiskii   *0.15–2m. (½–6ft)   Yellow   Spring*
E S L H

Japan. A very variable species some forms of
which are prostrate, others dwarf but bushy
and yet others erect. The light yellow flowers
are widely funnel-shaped and carried in small
clusters. The short forms are to be preferred
and one of these has been named 'Yaku
Fairy'.

keysii   *2–3m. (6–10ft)   Red and yellow*
E. Summer   E S L H A

Himalaya. Many people seeing this plant for
the first time might not recognize it as a
rhododendron, for its flowers are very
distinctive, quite small and tubular,
orange-red tipped with yellow. It is not a
spectacular plant but it is an attractive
curiosity. 'Cinnkeys' is a good hybrid from it
with *R. cinnabarinum* as the other parent.

kiusianum   *60–90cm. (2–3ft)*
Purple to pink and white
L. Spring   E. Summer   ED S L H

Japan (Kyushu). This is very close to
R. kaempferi and by some authorities has
been regarded as no more than a regional
variation of it. The leaves and flowers are
small, the plants twiggy and densely
branched, the flower colour variable and
including white. The very popular garden

azalea 'Amoenum', with small deep magenta flowers produced with immense freedom, is now regarded as a variety of *R. kiusianum*, and *R. obtusum*, once regarded as the species to which 'Amoenum' belonged, is also now reduced to a mere variety, or maybe a hybrid, for nobody seems very certain, of *R. kiusianum*. None of this matters greatly to gardeners except that it confuses nomenclature in catalogues. What is important is that these are all highly decorative garden plants retaining all or most of their small leaves in winter and bringing a lot of bright, though sometimes rather crude, colour to the garden in May and June.

lacteum   *3–9m. (10–30ft)   Pale yellow Spring   E S L H A*

China. This very beautiful species, with medium size broadly bell-shaped primrose-yellow flowers carried in good clusters, is both difficult to propagate and to grow. So it remains a prestige rhododendron giving great joy to those who can grow it but always likely to remain a scarce plant. It is seen at its best in the mild and moist west coast gardens in markedly acid soil.

leucaspis   *30–60cm. (1–2ft)   White L. Winter   E. Spring   E S L H*

Himalaya. A low-growing plant with fairly small oval leaves and quite large flat flowers, white or creamy with a central tuft of chocolate-coloured anthers. The plant is fairly hardy but the flowers are not and, since they are likely to start opening in February, this is a plant that needs a sheltered place if its considerable beauty is to be enjoyed. It is the parent of some good hybrids including 'Bric-a-Brac', which resembles it closely but is more bushy, less prostrate in habit.

lutescens   *1–2m. (3–6ft)   Pale yellow L. Winter   E. Spring   E S L H*

China. The stems of this species are long and rather slender and the not very large lance-shaped leaves are bronze when young becoming green later. The flowers are quite small, pale yellow, carried singly or in pairs and not making a spectacular display but very attractive in a quiet way. Its fault is that it starts to flower too early so that it is at risk from bad weather, which can ruin its flowers in a few hours. Best grown well sheltered in woodland.

luteum   *2.5–3m. (8–10ft)   Yellow L. Spring   E S L H*

Caucasus. This is the common yellow azalea, a plant so sturdy and so much at home in Britain that in many places it naturalizes itself, spreading by self-sown seedlings. It is an open, rather stiffly branched bush with bright yellow flowers of medium size carried in clusters. It is spicily fragrant and its scent is carried a long way on a mild, still, rather damp day. As an additional attraction its leaves colour richly before they fall in autumn. It is one of the parents of the Ghent Hybrid azaleas.

macabeanum   *4–9m. (13–30ft)   Yellow Spring   E S L H A*

Assam. This is another of the big 'tree' rhododendrons in the style of *R. falconeri*, with sturdy branches spreading widely, large leaves covered in grey or white down beneath and large deeply bell-shaped flowers packed into dense trusses of up to thirty. The colour is variable, from pale to quite deep yellow with a purple blotch at the centre of the bell. This species is moderately hardy but needs the shelter of thin woodland and is happiest in the milder and moister climate of west and south-west coastal gardens.

maximum   *2.5–5m. (8–16ft)   Magenta Summer   E S L H A*

Eastern USA. This American species is seldom planted for ornament since its flower trusses are relatively small and open after the plant has made a good deal of growth, so that they are partially obscured by leaves. However, it is very hardy and was available in Britain very early, long before the finer Asiatic species began to arrive, and it was one of the parents used in the nineteenth century to produce the Hardy Hybrids.

molle   *0.6–1.5m. (2–5ft)*
Yellow or Orange   L. Spring   D S L H

China. This sturdily branched azalea is closely allied to R. *japonicum* but its leaves are much more downy. It has given its name to one of the most showy races of garden hybrids, the Mollis Azaleas, but is not itself much planted in gardens.

moupinense   *0.6–1.2m. (2–4ft)*
White or Pink   L. Winter   E. Spring
E S L H

China. A charming early-flowering species, dwarf and compact, with quite large, widely funnel-shaped flowers which may be white or pink and are carried singly or in clusters of no more than three. Yet there are enough of them to make a fine display, but if this is not to be prematurely terminated by frost or rain the plant must have a sheltered place.

x mucronatum   *1.2m. (3–6ft)   White*
L. Spring   E L H

The precise botanical status of this fine azalea has been much argued about but it is almost certainly a garden hybrid originating a long time ago in Japan. It is one of the most attractive of white evergreen azaleas, with numerous widely funnel-shaped scented flowers produced on a well-branched plant. Another popular white hybrid azalea, 'Palestrina', is closely allied to it.

mucronulatum   *2–2.5m. (6–8ft)   Magenta*
Winter   D S L H

China, Russia, Korea, Japan. This very hardy deciduous rhododendron flowers in mid-winter, and since its flower buds open successively it is capable of keeping up a display even if the weather is very patchy. The flowers are of medium size, widely funnel-shaped and a deep and effective magenta. Most of the stems are erect and there is not a lot of branching. The effect in January or February can be heart-warming.

neriiflorum   *2–3m. (6–10ft)   Red*
Spring   E S L H A

China, Burma, Himalaya. A distinctive species with medium size oval leaves that are milky white beneath, and narrowly bell-shaped flowers that are rather fleshy in texture and always in some shade of red often a bright scarlet or rich crimson. A rather tall, loosely branched form with light crimson flowers is distinguished as variety *enchaites*. At one time this was regarded as a separate species.

niveum   *3–4m. (10–13ft)   Light purple*
Spring   E S L H A

China. The name, meaning snowy, refers to the white down which covers the young leaves, and has no connection with the flowers which in the best forms are a muted lilac-purple. Poor varieties can be slatey and dull. The truss is also distinctive, very rounded and neat, with closely packed deeply bell-shaped flowers. The plant is open-branched and sturdy and it is quite hardy, though frost will destroy the flowers which can be opening in April.

nuttallii   *3–6m. (10–20ft)*
Ivory and yellow   Spring   E W S L H

Himalaya, Tibet, Burma. Despite a rather straggly habit this is one of the most beautiful of rhododendrons because of the great size of its widely funnel-shaped lily-like flowers. They are ivory white suffused with yellow inside and are very richly scented. However, it is very tender and only suitable for planting outdoors in nearly frost-free places. Elsewhere it must be given the protection of a greenhouse in winter.

occidentale *2–2.5m. (6–8ft)*
Cream and yellow E. Summer D S L H

Western North America. This is a
late-flowering deciduous azalea with sweetly
scented flowers. It is a very attractive species
and it has also been used in the breeding of
garden azaleas, especially in the Knap Hill
Hybrids and the Occidentale Hybrids. It is
quite hardy and a very satisfactory garden
plant.

orbiculare *2–3m. (6–10ft) Pink Spring*
E S L H A

China. A fine species making a well-branched,
dome-shaped bush with distinctive rounded
leaves, heart-shaped at the base. The
rose-pink flowers are widely bell-shaped,
carried in a quite large but rather loose truss.

oreotrephes *3–6m. (10–20ft) Mauve*
Spring ED S L H

China, Burma, Tibet. A rather variable
species which produces its widely
funnel-shaped flowers very freely. They vary
greatly in colour from a rather pale mauve to
magenta, often with crimson or brown
spotting. The best forms are mauve, pink or
rosy purple and they make a fine display if
their colours are acceptable. In cold winters
the bushes may lose a lot of their leaves.

pemakoense *30cm. (1ft) Mauve Spring*
E S L H

Tibet. A charming dwarf rhododendron
making low, dome-shaped mounds covered in
small rounded leaves and disappearing in
spring beneath widely funnel-shaped flowers
produced singly or in pairs from almost every
branch end. Colour is rather variable, always
some shade of mauve but ranging from the
rather wishy-washy to stronger and more
effective blue or purplish lilacs.

ponticum *3–6m. (10–20ft) Purple*
E. Summer E S L H A

Black Sea region. It is probably a good thing
that this is the only rhododendron that has
become so much at home in Britain that it has
spread unaided over large tracts of country. It
makes a fine, dome-shaped bush,
well-branched, with laurel green leaves and
making excellent cover for game. On top of
that the colour of its flowers is never harsh,
always some shade of mauve, lilac or purple
that fits well in our often misty and seldom
glaring light, so that it has readily been
accepted as if it were a truly native plant.
However, the very virtues which make it
acceptable in the countryside tell against it in
the garden, where the demand is usually for
more outstanding plants with better flower
quality and stronger or more clearly defined
colour. Here R. *ponticum* is chiefly of value to
form shelter belts and give protection to more
delicate species. It is itself indestructably
hardy, and will even tolerate some lime in the
soil.

quinquefolium *2–3m. (6–10ft) White*
Spring D S L H

Japan. An exquisite azalea very distinctive in
its foliage, the little rounded diamond-shaped
leaves being always arranged in whorls of five
and being light green, often with a
reddish-purple margin. The flowers are fairly
small and funnel-shaped, gleaming white with
some green spots which heighten the cool
effect, and carried singly or in small clusters.
It is a species which stands apart and does not
appear to have been used in any of the big
azalea breeding programmes.

racemosum *1–2m. (3–6ft) Pink Spring*
E S L H

China. A species distinct in the manner in
which it carries its small pink or rose flowers
all along the stems so that these are wreathed
in bloom. It is variable in habit, sometimes
quite dwarf and compact, sometimes

considerably taller, with the stems red when young, held stiffly erect. Several forms have been selected and given distinguishing names. 'Forrest's Dwarf' is one of the best, dwarf and compact with cerise flowers. 'Glendoick' grows quite tall and erect and has deep pink flowers. 'Rock Rose' is of medium height and has bright pink flowers.

russatum *1–1.2m. (3–4ft)* *Purple*
Spring *E S L H*

China. In colour this is one of the best of the small 'blue' species, a really deep and clear blue-purple which makes a fine effect in the garden. The plant is densely branched, the leaves small and numerous and the little funnel-shaped flowers are carried in tightly packed clusters of up to ten. This fine species, admirable for a rock garden or the front of a border, was long known as *R. cantabile* and may still be found under that name in some gardens and nursery catalogues.

schlippanbachii *2–3m. (6–10ft)* *Pink*
Spring *D S L H*

Korea, Russia, China. This is one of the most delightful azalea species, with soft pink flowers which have the elegance of butterflies. The flowers open almost flat and have prominent stamens and they are carried in small trusses scattered all over the well-branched bush. It has the reputation of being rather difficult, partly because it often commences to unfold its leaves too early and they then get destroyed by frost, but I have had no trouble with it in a cold Sussex garden in only very slightly acid soil and with a light cover of trees which do not completely exclude direct sunshine.

scintillans *0.6–1m. (2–3ft)*
Purple or Blue *Spring* *E S L H*

China. One of the very good small-leaved rhododendrons, which makes a densely branched, twiggy bush and covers itself in April or May with little clusters of small, widely funnel-shaped flowers, which may be any shade from quite a light lavender to deep purplish-blue or occasionally purplish-rose. It is completely hardy and suitable for planting in a rock garden or towards the front of a border.

Rhododendron schlippanbachii

simsii *1–2.5m. (3–8ft) Red L. Spring E W S L H*

China, Taiwan, Burma, Thailand. This is the parent of the greenhouse or Indian azaleas (it was at one time called *Rhododendron indicum*) and is too tender to be planted outdoors in Britain except in the mildest maritime gardens where frosts are light and of short duration. It has fairly large widely funnel-shaped flowers in some shade of red but the garden varieties and hybrids have been extended to include many shades of pink and crimson, often with white markings as well as some that are wholly white. Semi-double and fully double varieties are also available. Two varieties 'Queen Elizabeth', white edged with rose, and 'Queen Elizabeth White' wholly white, are reputed to be hardier than most.

sinogrande *4–9m. (13–30ft) Cream or pale yellow Spring E W S L H A*

China, Burma. A species closely allied to *R. grande* and resembling it in many respects but the leaves, silvery beneath, are even larger and in some forms the flowers are more distinctly yellow, always with red blotches at the centre of the bell. It is a magnificently handsome shrub but opinions differ as to its suitability for planting in any but the milder and moister parts of Britain. It seems probable that some forms are hardier than others as there are records of plants surviving very low temperatures.

souliei *1.5–3m. (5–10ft) Pink and white L. Spring E S L H A*

China. A very beautiful but relatively little known rhododendron which makes a good bush of medium size, well clothed in rounded leaves and with quite large saucer-shaped flowers carried in small clusters in May. They may be wholly pink or pink and white, like apple blossom. The plant is completely hardy, growing and flowering well even in the colder parts of Scotland away from the coast.

sutchuenense *2.5–3m. (8–10ft) Pink L. Winter E. Spring E S L H A*

China. A very handsome species with long rather narrow leaves and trusses of large widely bell-shaped lilac-pink flowers. It has sturdy stems and makes a wide open-branched bush which is itself quite hardy, but the flowers start to open so early that they are at risk except in the mildest places.

tephropeplum *0.3–1.2m. (1–4ft) Magenta Spring E S L H*

China, Burma. A very distinctive small shrub with rather small bell-shaped flowers produced very freely in small clusters. It is variable in height, habit and colour and is one that should be selected when it is in bloom because the purplish-pink of some plants can be displeasing. The best forms are heather-pink.

thomsonii *3–4m. (10–13ft) Blood-red Spring E S L H A*

Himalaya. Arguably this is the finest deep red species, a magnificent shrub with sturdy stems, rounded leaves, bluish-white or greyish beneath, and large bell-shaped flowers richly blood-red in colour. Its flowers and young shoots can be damaged by frost so it needs a sheltered position to ensure a regular display but otherwise it is hardy. It has been much used by breeders, and among the many notable hybrids raised from it are 'Ascot Brilliant', 'Barclayi', 'Cornish Cross', 'J.G. Millais', 'Luscombei' and 'Sir John Ramsden'.

vaseyi *2.5–4m. (8–13ft) Pink Spring D S L H*

North Carolina. A charmingly light and elegant azalea with slender but stiff stems, narrow leaves which colour well in autumn and loose clusters of small pink flowers like tiny lilies with swept-back petals and prominent stamens and pistil. There are deeper rose-pink and white-flowered forms.

viscosum   *2–2.5m. (6–8ft)*
White or Pink   Summer   D S L H

Eastern North America. This azalea is known
in America as the Swamp Honeysuckle
because of the colour, form and sweet
perfume of its flowers. It was one of the first
rhododendrons to be introduced and was
used by breeders in the early nineteenth
century but does not appear to have had
much influence on the modern races of hybrid
azaleas. The flowers are distinctive, narrow
and tubular at the base, expanding at the
mouth and sticky all over. It is the last azalea
to flower.

wardii   *3–6m. (10–20ft)   Yellow*
L. Spring   E S L H A

China, Tibet. A fine yellow-flowered species
much like *R. campylocarpum* in leaf and
habit but the flowers are more widely open,
saucer-shaped rather than bell-shaped and in
some forms a deeper yellow. It is variable in
habit, some being relatively dwarf and
compact others considerably taller and more
openly branched. Many fine hybrids have
been raised from it including 'Cowslip' and
'Hawk'.

williamsianum   *1–1.5m. (3–5ft)   Pink*
Spring   E S L H

China. A captivatingly beautiful small
rhododendron making a neat, dome-shaped,
densely branched bush with rounded leaves,
heart-shaped at the base and light bronze
when young, eventually becoming dark
shining green above and milky green beneath.
The flowers are perfect bells, quite large, in
small nodding clusters, a very soft and
pleasing rose-pink. It enjoys a more open,
sunny position than most evergreen
rhododendrons, for in shade it often fails to
produce flower buds. It has been much used
by breeders to produce hybrids of similar
character, among the best being 'Bow Bells',
'Brocade', 'Cowslip', 'Humming Bird',
'Moonstone' and 'Temple Belle'.

xanthocodon   *2.5–4m. (8–13ft)   Yellow*
L. Spring   E S L H A

Tibet. This species is allied to *R.
cinnabarinum* and *R. concatenans*. Its leaves
are milky green, beneath the flowers are
narrowly bell-shaped, hanging in small
clusters, always in some soft shade of yellow.

yakushimanum   *1–1.2m. (3–4ft)*
White and pink   L. Spring   E S L H A

Japan (Island of Yakushima). One of the
shortest and most compact species, bearing
flowers in large trusses. It has fairly long
leaves that seem narrower than they are
because they roll downwards and inwards at
the edges. The flowers are bell-shaped of good
size and closely packed in upstanding trusses,
apple-blossom-pink in bud but opening pale
pink and eventually fading to white. A whole
new race of dwarf but large-flowered
rhododendrons has been raised by crossing it
with other species and hybrids.

yunnanense   *2.5–3m. (8–10ft)*
White, Mauve or Lavender
L. Spring   ED S L H

China, Tibet. The habit of growth and the
small clusters of widely open flowers scattered
all over the bush might suggest that this was
an azalea but in fact its true affiliation is with
such species as *R. augustinii* and
R. oreotrephes. It makes a fine display but it is
very variable in colour and should be selected
when in flower. The most desirable forms are
light lavender, blush-pink and white.

Rhododendron Hybrids

The number of rhododendron hybrids is now legion and it is clearly impossible for nurserymen to stock more than a very small percentage of them. It is convenient to consider the 'azalea' hybrids separately from those of other groups of the Rhododendron family and to sub-divide these azaleas into evergreen and deciduous sections. The remaining rhododendrons can also be conveniently split into two major groups, the Hardy Hybrids specifically bred to flower rather late, in May and June, when the danger of flowers being destroyed by frost is low, and the rest, sometimes referred to as Pedigree Hybrids, since their precise parentage is usually known, which is not always the case with the Hardy Hybrids. To these major groups must be added another, the Azaleodendrons, produced by crossing azalias and rhododendrons but they are of far less garden importance, since they are almost all rather difficult to grow.

Taking the evergreen rhododendrons first the Hardy Hybrids are of most importance to ordinary, non-specialist gardeners since they have been bred to be tough, showy and easy to grow. Most make big, dome-shaped bushes and carry their bell-shaped flowers closely packed in erect beehive-shaped trusses. Colours vary from white, cream, pale-pink and pale mauve to fairly good yellows (but not so good as in some of the Pedigree Hybrids) pinks, carmine, scarlet, crimson, lavender and purple, Often the flowers are blotched or speckled in some attractive way and they are always freely and regularly produced. Hardy Hybrids put up with polluted atmosphere much better than most of the species, with the notable exception of *R. ponticum*, and so they make better town garden shrubs. Their fault is a lack of variety in style of growth, and rather dull, laurel-like foliage which is all they can offer for about eleven months out of the twelve. The Pedigree Hybrids are infinitely more varied in every way, running the whole gamut of the race and offering choice from prostrate ground cover to large shrubs with leaves and flowers of

vastly differing size. Sometimes they have hybrid vigour which makes them tougher and easier to grow than the species but this cannot be guaranteed.

If seed is saved from complex hybrids the resultant seedlings are likely to differ greatly both from each other and from their parents since they will be the outcome of random pairing between a great assortment of genes. It is quite otherwise with hybrids between two species since those receive one set of genes from one parent, another from the second parent. Not only are the seedlings likely to be closely alike (though probably notably different from either parent) but the same cross can be repeated time and again with similar results. Hybrid rhododendrons such as 'Loderi' (*fortunei* x *griffithianum*), 'Alison Johnstone' (*concatenans* x *yunnanense*) and 'Cowslip' (*wardii* x *williamsianum*) are of this kind and it is possible to raise these from seed by repeating the original cross, though in practice this is seldom done. Even so there is always some variation with seed-raised plants and so if particularly desirable forms appear they are set aside and propagated vegetatively by layers, cuttings or grafting. Such plants are not new individuals, like seedlings, but simply extensions of the original plant and together they constitute an identical clone. Such clones are usually given distinguishing names, for example, a particularly fine white-flushed pink clone of *R.* x '*Loderi*' is known as 'King George'.

THE MAIN AZALEA GROUPS

With azaleas there has been a greater tendency to build up groups based on known or presumed relationships. Also with the deciduous azaleas there has been much greater readiness to raise particular strains or related hybrids from seed and offer the resultant seedlings more cheaply than vegetatively propagated plants. Good strains produce a high proportion of excellent plants but even so, since there will be a lot of variation, it is desirable to pick out the plants one requires while they are in flower.

DECIDUOUS HYBRID AZALEAS

Ghent Hybrids. Relatively small flowers in a good range of colour. They are hardy, flower freely and are often very sweetly scented.

Rustica Hybrids. Closely allied to the Ghent azaleas but with double flowers.

Mollis Azaleas. Much larger flowers than the Ghent hybrids and extending the colour range to include some vivid scarlets but nearly always lacking scent.

Knap Hill Hybrids. The result of interbreeding Ghent and Mollis hybrids and bringing in other species as well to preserve the fine flower size, extend the colour range still further and bring back some of the scent lost in the quest for size.

Exbury Azaleas. A step on from the Knap Hill Hybrids with yet more species brought in to improve both quality and variety. The best seed strains are available here.

Occidentale Hybrids. Varieties bred from *R. occidentale* with other azaleas. Most have delicately coloured, pink or cream, sweetly scented flowers opening in both May and June.

EVERGREEN HYBRID AZALEAS

Kurume Azaleas. Small-leaved, much branched, twiggy bushes with small but abundant flowers.

Kaempferi Hybrids. Flowers mostly larger than those of the Kurume race and including many that have semi-double flowers.

Malvaticum Hybrids. These are closely akin to the Kaempferi Hybrids, since they were produced by interbreeding azaleas of that type with a variety named 'Malvaticum', itself a hybrid of uncertain origin, possibly between the pink Kurume azalea 'Hinodigiri' and white *R.* x *mucronatum*. 'Malvaticum' has large mauve flowers and the Malvaticum Hybrids tend also to be large-flowered.

Indian Azaleas. These are the tender varieties raised by crossing *R. simsii* with *R.* x *mucronatum* and possibly other kinds. Many flower in winter or early spring and have large, often semi-double or fully-double flowers mainly in shades of pink and red plus white. In Britain they are mainly useful as pot plants for frost-proof greenhouses and conservatories and for winter and spring decoration in the house.

American Hybrids. Several races distinguished by the name of their raisers, for example, Gable Hybrids, or by the place in which they have been raised: for example, Glen Dale Hybrids, have been raised in the eastern states of America. They are of fairly complex parentage but are for the most part fairly large-flowered and they have a very wide colour range. In hardiness they differ considerably and individual assessment of varieties is therefore necessary to determine their value in British gardens.

RHODOTHAMNUS, Ericaceae. In the wild this plant grows in limestone areas but in gardens it is often said to grow best on moderately acid, peaty soil. Yet there is disagreement even about this and there are reports of it thriving in soil mixtures containing mortar rubble. What seems certain is that this is not a very easy plant to grow and that it requires good winter drainage combined with plenty of moisture in a rather porous soil in summer. It also likes a sunny but not very hot situation. Increase is by seed sown in peat and sand in a frame without shading, also by cuttings in similar compost in a close frame in late summer. No pruning is necessary.

chamaecistus *15–30cm. (6–12in.)   Rose*
Spring   E S H

Eastern European Alps. A charming
semi-prostrate evergreen with small leaves
edged with bristles and clusters of small
rose-pink flowers, which in favourable
conditions can be produced very freely.

RHODOTYPOS, Rosaceae. There is only one
species and this is easily grown in any
reasonably fertile soil either in sun or in
partial shade. It flowers on stems produced
the previous year and should be pruned
immediately after flowering, when much of
the old flowering growth can be cut out,
leaving all good young stems to grow on and
flower the following year. Increase is by
summer cuttings in a warm propagator.

scandens *2m. (6ft)   White*
L. Spring   Summer   D F H S

China. This shrub, with long flexible stems, is
closely allied to kerria and rather like it in leaf
and habit but the small single rose-like
flowers are white.

RHUS, Anacardiaceae. Sumach. These are
grown mainly as foliage shrubs and
particularly for their fine autumn colour,
which is most fully developed in warm sunny
places and in soil that is not too rich. Most
kinds sucker freely and, unless some suckers
are required for propagation, it may be
necessary to chop them out with a sharp
spade to prevent the plants encroaching too
far. Those kinds with finely divided leaves
may be pruned quite hard each February or
March to limit the amount of growth and
secure the maximum size of leaf. Apart from
increase by digging up rooted suckers in
autumn or winter, *Rhus* can be increased by
seed sown under glass in spring or by root
cuttings in winter.

aromatica *1–1.5m. (3–5ft)   Yellowish*
Spring   D T S R V

Eastern North America. This species is known
as the Fragrant Sumach because its leaves,
each composed of three leaflets, are aromatic
when bruised. The greenish-yellow flowers
make a better display than is usual with
species of *rhus* and they are followed by
clusters of red hairy fruits.

copallina *1–1.2m. (3–4ft)*
Greenish-yellow   Summer   D T S R V

Eastern North America. This species is known
as the Shining Sumach or the Dwarf Sumach
because its compound leaves are glossy green
and it is exceptionally low-growing. The
leaves colour well in autumn and again there
are red hairy fruits to add to the very
distinctive display at that season.

glabra *1.2–2m. (4–6ft)   Greenish*
L. Summer   D C S R V

North America. This is known as the Smooth
Sumach because its stems and its large
compound leaves are smooth not downy as in
some other species. The tiny flowers are
tightly packed in erect, spindle-shaped
clusters and are followed by fruits similarly
arranged and covered in a plush-like crimson
down. The long leaves can have as many as 29
leaflets and they colour brilliantly before they
fall in the autumn. In variety 'Laciniata' each
leaflet is deeply cut so as to give the whole leaf
an almost fern-like appearance.

radicans *2.5–9m. (8–30ft)* *White*
Summer   D S R

North America. This is the plant known as
Poison Ivy because the yellow, viscid sap can
cause severe skin damage. There are both
climbing and sprawling forms, the climbers
supporting themselves on any firm surface by
means of aerial roots like those of ivy. The
leaves are compound, each composed of three
leaflets, and they colour well in autumn, but
because of its poisonous character this is not a
species that can be recommended for garden
planting.

typhina *3–4m. (10–13ft)* *Greenish*
Summer   D C T S R V

Eastern North America. The Stag's-horn
Sumach, so called because of the supposedly
antler-like appearance of the erect flower and
fruit clusters. The fruits are more conspicuous
than the flowers because of their dense
covering of crimson hairs. The very long
leaves are composed of up to 25 leaflets and
are very handsome, especially when they turn
to orange and crimson in the autumn. There is
a beautiful but less vigorous cut-leaved form
often known as 'Laciniata', though it should
really be called 'Dissecta'. Both species and
variety can spread widely by suckers and may
become a nuisance if not kept well in hand.
The species can be pruned to form a small tree
or it can be cut back annually in
'February-March to form a widely branched
and suckering shrub with leaves of even
greater size.

RIBES, Grossulariaceae. Currant.
Gooseberry. The genus which has supplied
gardens with some of their most popular soft
fruits has also produced a number of highly
ornamental shrubs. All are easy to grow in
almost any reasonably fertile soil and in full
sun or semi-shade. They respond well to
pruning and the currants can have most or all
their flowering stems cut down to a few
centimetres immediately after flowering. The
gooseberries can be pruned in winter and it is

the oldest branches that should be removed,
leaving the younger growth to carry on.
Species can be raised from seed but the garden
varieties must be propagated vegetatively,
either by summer cuttings in a propagator or
by autumn cuttings outdoors or in a frame.

laurifolium *1–2m. (3–6ft)*
Greenish-white   L. Winter   E. Spring
E O S H

China. One of the few evergreen species and a
most attractive shrub, with shining green
leaves and compact trails of small
greenish-white flowers which commence to
open very early in the year. It deserves to be
better known.

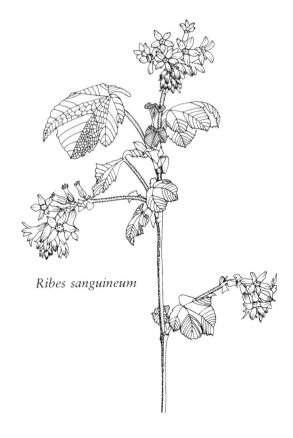

Ribes sanguineum

odoratum *2–2.5m. (6–8ft)   Yellow
Spring   D F S H A*

Central USA. This attractive yellow-flowered species is much like *Ribes aureum*, with which it is much confused, but it is a better garden plant with larger flowers in similar little trails and equally fragrant. It makes smooth, whippy stems and is popularly known as the Buffalo Currant.

sanguineum *2–2.5m. (6–8ft)   Red
Spring   D F S H A*

Western North America. This is the American Currant or Flowering Currant and is by far the most popular ornamental species. It makes many long erect stems which produce flowers the following spring. The flowers are borne in short trails all up the stems and make a fine display. The colour is somewhat variable, typically carmine but a deeper purer red in 'Pulborough Scarlet', crimson in 'King Edward VII', and pink in 'Carneum'. A pink-flowered variety named 'Brocklebankii' has yellow leaves, the colour well retained in a moderately shady place.

speciosum *2–2.5m. (6–8ft)   Red Spring
D T S H A*

California. The best of the ornamental gooseberries and a very distinctive plant. It has been called the Fuchsia-flowered Gooseberry, presumably because of the tubular form of the deep red flowers and its long exerted stamens but the analogy is not very apt unless one is thinking of a very small-flowered species such as *Fuchsia microphylla*. The bush is well-branched and spiny.

ROBINIA, Leguminosae. False Acacia. Most of the robinias are trees but a few are rather large open-branched shrubs. They like warm sunny places and reasonably well-drained, not over rich, soils. They do not respond well to pruning but badly placed branches can be removed after flowering. It is possible to train the shrubby robinias against walls and the extra warmth can be of considerable benefit to them. The best method of increase is by seed, if available, sown under glass in spring, but suckers can sometimes be dug up with roots in autumn or winter. This method is useless if plants have been grafted. It is also said that root-cuttings will succeed.

hispida *2–2.5m. (6–8ft)   Rose
L. Spring   E. Summer   D O S V R*

South-eastern USA. This species is known as the 'Rose Acacia'. It is a freely suckering shrub with rather lax stems and an awkward habit, but the elegant leaves, composed of numerous light green leaflets, and short trails of quite large, bright rose, pea-type flowers make ample amends for such deficiencies and, where it will thrive, this is a very desirable shrub.

kelseyi *2.5–3m. (8–10ft)   Pink
E. Summer   D O S V R*

North Carolina. A species similar to *R. hispida* but taller, always completely smooth-stemmed, and the flower colour is more variable though equally good in the best forms.

ROSA, Rosaceae. Rose. Of ornamental shrubs only rhododendron has so captivated the imagination and engaged the skill of gardeners as *Rosa*. And whereas rhododendron is a relative newcomer, the rose has been a favourite since ancient times though, as with so many plants, the rate of development has increased greatly since the early nineteenth century. Much breeding during the last hundred years has been concerned with improving the quality of the rose as a bedding plant by making it flower more continuously for a longer period and to carry its blooms on rather flat-topped plants so that all are the same height and the plants can be grown close together to produce solid sheets of colour. Such plants, though still shrubs in the technical sense, are scarcely shrubs in any decorative manner and so are outside the scope of this book.

Genuinely shrubby roses in the sense that they make well-branched bushes bearing flowers at various levels and looking good even when grown as isolated specimens must be sought in three major areas: the species, the old garden roses and the modern hybrid shrub roses. To these can be added all climbing roses but particularly those sufficiently vigorous to be grown among shrubs or allowed to scramble up into trees. There is plenty to choose from in all these groups.

Nearly all roses like good rich soil and open sunny places. Nearly all also bear their best flowers on the current year's growth, and these are most freely and sturdily produced from the younger stems left over from former years. In the wild, roses often allow old growth that has become woody and unproductive to die. Since this is unsightly in gardens it is anticipated and prevented by annual pruning to remove old wood and retain the best young growth. With bedding roses it is sometimes necessary to delay this pruning until early spring, since the young shoots are often tender and so one does not want to stir into early growth those that are most essential to the maintenance of the plant. Shrub roses are, with a few exceptions, hardier and less dependent on rather severe pruning, and it is usually quite safe to prune them either in autumn, when their leaves have dropped, or in late winter. Pruning is largely a thinning operation to get rid of old growth and prevent the bushes from becoming overcrowded.

Species can be increased from seed, which germinates best if exposed to cold for several months. Traditionally it is sown outdoors as soon as ripe but it is often possible to get even better results with less risk of loss through pests or diseases by keeping the seed moist for three or four months at a temperature of 3–4°C./37–39°F, about the temperature at the bottom of a domestic refrigerator, before sowing it outdoors in February or March. Garden varieties and hybrids cannot be raised true to type from seed and must be propagated vegetatively. Nurserymen usually do it by budding (a form of grafting) on to rose root-stocks raised from seed or cuttings. This requires a certain amount of skill, which comes with practice, and home gardeners are likely to find it easier as well as more satisfactory to raise plants from summer cuttings in a propagator or by layering in spring or autumn. Such plants will have root systems of their own kind and suckers growing from them can be retained or, if dug up, can be replanted elsewhere since they will resemble the parent plant in every particular. By contrast when plants are budded, suckers will have the character of the root-stock, usually a wild species, and they must be removed as soon as they are observed because they can quickly take over and starve out the garden rose which the root-stock is supposed to maintain.

Species and shrub roses in general suffer less from pests and diseases than bedding roses but they are not immune, and if trouble does occur they should be sprayed with whatever is appropriate for the cause, an aphicide to kill greenflies, a more general insecticide for other pests or a good fungicide to check mildew, black spot or rust.

x **alba**   2–2.5m. (6–8ft)   *White or Pink*
E. Summer   D T H A V

The parentage of this very old hybrid is uncertain but is generally thought to be some form of *Rosa canina* crossed with *R. damascena*. Growth is strong, erect and thorny, leaves are a very distinctive grey-green and the flowers are white or pale pink. There are many garden varieties and hybrids including: 'Semi-plena' with semi-double white flowers, the traditional White Rose of York; 'Incarnata', also known as 'Great Maiden's Blush' with blush-pink flowers; 'Königin van Dänemark' ('Queen of Denmark'), fully double soft pink; and 'Celestial', double pale pink. All are sweetly scented.

banksiae   *3–6m. (10–20ft)*
White or Yellow   L. Spring   E. Summer
ED W T H A L

China. This is the Banksian Rose and it is the
double-flowered forms that are usually seen in
gardens since they are more effective than the
single-flowered species. 'Alba Plena' has
clusters of small, fully double white flowers
and 'Lutea', the Yellow Banksian, has similar
clusters of light yellow flowers. All are
pleasantly scented. The leaves are a rather
light green and in warm sheltered places may
be retained all winter. Stems are slender but
long and these are roses that can be trained
very effectively against sunny walls. They are
not repeat-flowering.

x borboniana   *1.2–2m. (4–6ft)*
Red or Pink   Summer   D T H A G

These are the Bourbon Roses, old hybrids
between *Rosa chinensis* and either
R. damascena or *R. gallica*. They have large
double flowers often scented and usually in
shades of red or pink, but also white, and they
are to a limited extent repeat-flowering.
Typical varieties are 'Boule de Neige', white;
'Zigeuner Knabe' ('Gypsy Boy'),
crimson-purple; 'Mme. Isaac Pereire',
purplish crimson; 'Mme Pierre Oger', cream
flushed with rose; and 'Souvenir de la
Malmaison', blush white.

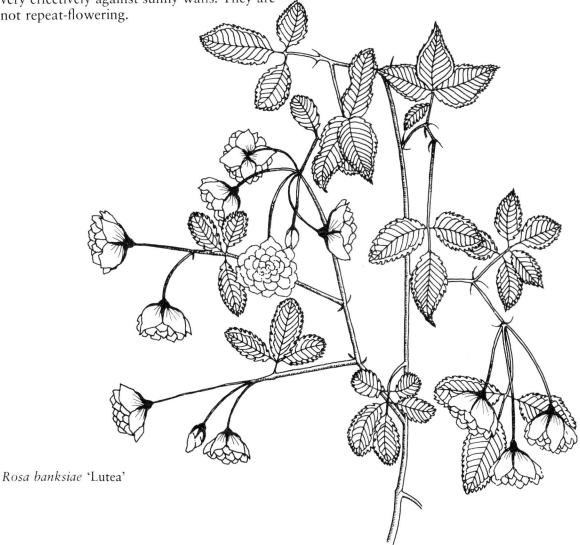

Rosa banksiae 'Lutea'

bracteata   *3–6m. (10–20ft)   White
Summer   E W T S H A L*

China. A handsome but rather tender
climbing rose which should be given a warm
sheltered sunny place. The single white
flowers are exceptionally large and
distinctively scented. The leaves are deep
shining green and retained all winter.

brunonii   *6–12m. (20–40ft)   White
Summer   D W T S H A L*

Himalaya. This very vigorous climbing
species is known as the Himalayan Musk
Rose and is often wrongly labelled *Rosa
moschata*. The clusters of white flowers with
conspicuous yellow anthers are very sweetly
scented and freely produced, but this is not a
very hardy rose and it needs a warm sunny
position. The light green softly downy leaves
are rather thin. A variety named 'La Mortola'
has larger flowers even more freely produced.

Rosa 'Canary Bird'

californica   *1.5–2.5m. (5–8ft)   Pink
E. Summer   D T S H A L*

Western North America. In gardens it is
usually the semi-double-flowered variety,
'Plena', that is grown. It makes a thorny bush
of pleasing arching habit and the pink flowers
are very freely produced.

x 'Canary Bird'   *2–2.5m. (6–8ft)   Yellow
L. Spring   E. Summer   D T H A L*

A beautiful early flowering hybrid of
uncertain parentage but probably *Rosa
hugonis* x *R. xanthina*. It makes a thicket of
erect very spiny stems and covers itself in May
with light-yellow single flowers. The leaves
are composed of small leaflets.

x cantabrigiensis   *2–2.5m. (6–8ft)   Yellow
L. Spring   D T H A L*

Another hybrid probably from *Rosa hugonis*,
this time with *R. sericea* as the presumed
other parent. The habit is similar to that of
'Canary Bird' and the soft yellow flowers pale
to cream as they age. It has some scent.

centifolia   *1.2–2m. (4–6ft)
Rose pink   E. Summer   D T H A L*

The origin of this very ancient rose is
unknown. It has very large, fully double,
rose-pink flowers for which reason it is
known as the Cabbage Rose, and it is richly
scented. It is closely allied to *Rosa gallica* and
may be a hybrid between that species and
R. x damascena. The Moss Roses ('Muscosa')
are varieties of it, distinguished by the bristly
glands covering the calyx and flower-stems,
making them appear as if covered in moss. In
another form, known as 'Cristata', 'Crested
Moss', or 'Chapeau de Napoleon', the calyx
segments are not only glandular but are split
to give the flower bud a crested appearance.
There are also many other garden varieties of
both Cabbage and Moss roses. Typical of the
former are 'De Meaux', dwarf with small
rose-pink flowers; 'Fantin Latour', pale pink,'
and 'Tour de Malakoff' carmine and lilac.

Typical Moss roses are 'Nuits de Young', maroon-purple; 'Old Pink Moss', rose-pink; and 'William Lobb', purple fading to blue-grey.

chinensis *1–3m. (3–10ft)   Pink, Red Summer   D T S H A L*

China. This is the 'China Rose', a fairly small bush with rather slender stems, sparse foliage, reddish-brown when young, and flimsily built flowers produced over a long season, hence the name Monthly Rose often applied to one of the early garden varieties, 'Old Blush', which has double, pink, pleasantly scented flowers. A remarkable variety named *mutabilis* has the typically fragile single flowers of the species but they start as orange buds, open to soft yellow flowers and then change first to coppery pink and finally to crimson. Another strange variety, 'Viridiflora' has green flowers tinted with brown and is known as the Green Rose, 'Cecile Brunner' is a perfect minature China rose with small leaves and perfectly shaped double pink flowers in clusters. It has a climbing sport which will cover a considerable area and there is another sport, named 'Bloomfield Abundance', which has identical miniature flowers but makes quite a large bush up to 2m./6ft high. 'Comtesse de Cayla' is rather similar but only about 1.2m./4ft high and the small double flowers are yellow flushed with orange and pink. Other notable forms or hybrids of the China rose are 'Cramoisie Supérieur', deep crimson; 'Hermosa', lilac-pink, and 'Madame Laurette Messimy', salmon-pink.

There are even smaller varieties of the China rose than 'Cecile Brunner' of which 'Pamela', raised early in the 19th century, is probably the original and the better known. 'Rouletii' is a later descendant. It grows to about 23cm./9in and has small double pink flowers. It is one of the parents of an ever-increasing race of miniature roses. Another miniature, said to have been introduced from Mauritius in 1810, was named 'Minima' and became known as 'Miss Lawrence's Rose', and

was later given the name *Rosa lawrenceana*. Miniature roses are still sometimes referred to as Fairy Roses and may be listed as such in seed catalogues.

damascena *2–2.5m. (6–8ft)   Pink to Red E. Summer   D T S H A L*

The origin of this very ancient Damask Rose is uncertain. It may be a hybrid but if so its parentage is unknown. It carries its double flowers in clusters, they are commonly in some shade of pink or red and they are very sweetly scented. A variety named 'Trigintipetala' with semi-double pink flowers is cultivated in Bulgaria to produce attar of roses. Another variety, 'Versicolor', has white flowers heavily flaked with rose and is known as the York and Lancaster rose. Other garden varieties listed as Damask Roses include 'Celsiana', semi-double pale pink; 'Madame Hardy', fully double white; and 'Omar Khayyam', with a very full, flat-topped light pink flower.

ecae *1–1.2m. (3–4ft)   Yellow L. Spring   E. Summer   D T S H A L*

Afghanistan. A densely branched very prickly species with slender arching stems bearing small buttercup-yellow flowers. It has the reputation of being rather difficult, which is not surprising in view of the extreme climatic conditions of Afghanistan. It certainly needs a sunny place and will probably flower more freely if trained against a south-facing wall. 'Helen Knight' is a hybrid of this species, probably with *R. spinosissima altaica* as its other parent. It also bears small deep yellow flowers very freely.

eglanteria *2–2.5m. (6–8ft)   Pink Summer D T S H A L*

Europe (including Britain). The Sweet-briar or Eglantine, the first name referring to the scented foliage which makes it so distinctive. In other respects it is much like the common briar or dog rose, *R. canina*, with erect, very thorny stems making a thicket of growth and single pink flowers followed by scarlet heps. It makes an excellent deciduous hedge, impenetrable because it is so dense and prickly, and it fills the garden with delicate perfume, especially on a damp warm day. Many hybrids are related in some manner to this rose. They include 'Amy Robsart', 2.5m./8ft semi-double, rose-pink; 'Lady Penzance', 2m./6ft coppery-pink, single, and 'Meg Merrilees', 3m./10ft crimson, single.

elegantula *2m (6ft)   Pink   E. Summer*
D   T   S   H   A   L

China. This very distinctive and graceful species has been known as the Threepenny-bit Rose because of the small size of its flowers, but that is a name that must soon lose its significance for a generation unfamiliar with the old coinage. The stems are slender and arching, the little single mauve pink flowers, though often carried singly, are produced with great profusion and the leaves and leaflets are also small in keeping with the elegant character of the plant. The form usually grown is named *persetosa* and was selected for the smallness of its flowers and leaves. The species itself has long been known as *R. farrerii*

filipes *9–12m. (30–40ft)   White*
Summer   D   T   S   H   A   L

China. A very vigorous climber with long stems and large clusters of small creamy-white flowers with yellow stamens. The form usually grown in British gardens is known as 'Kiftsgate', and is distinguished by its very strong stems and extra large, well-branched flower clusters. Where it does well it is one of the most sturdy and floriferous of all climbing roses, but it does not succeed everywhere and it is difficult to pinpoint exactly what it is that makes it so good in some places and so disappointing in others. It often seems to take several years to get fully established and it also sometimes only makes one or two stems

at the base through which all sap must rise to feed the leaves above. It would probably help to prune rather severely the first February-March after planting to ensure a greater number of foundation stems.

foetida *1–1.5m. (3–5ft)   Yellow*
E. Summer   D   T   S   H   A   L

Asia Minor, Iran, Afghanistan. This beautiful rose is known as the Austrian Yellow or Austrian Briar apparently because it is naturalized in Austria, but it is not a true native and must have been brought there from south-western Asia. It has rather slender stems, very prickly and freely branched though not making a very tidy bush. In the type the single flowers are deep yellow but in variety 'Bicolor', known as the Austrian Copper rose, they are coppery-red inside and yellow outside, and in variety 'Persiana', known as the Persian Yellow rose they are yellow and double. They have a rather heavy scent which some find unpleasant. All may require fairly frequent spraying from April to September with a good fungicide, such as benomyl, to check black spot disease to which all forms of *R. foetida* are very susceptible. The rose known as 'Harrison's Yellow' or *R. x harrisonii* is a hybrid between *R. foetida* and *R. spinosissima*. It makes a well-shaped bush about 2m./6ft high with bright yellow semi-double flowers. Much of the yellow colour in modern hybrid roses as well as the bicolor red and yellow colouring of some varieties comes from cross-breeding with *Rosa foetida* and its varieties.

gallica *1–1.2m. (3–4ft)   Pink to Red*
E. Summer   D   T   S   H   A   L   V

Europe and western Asia. This is the French Rose, parent of many of the early garden roses. The species suckers freely and can be increased by digging up rooted suckers in autumn or winter. The stems are erect and armed with small prickles, the leaves matt-green above and downy beneath, the flowers

deep rose-pink and richly scented. There are
several well defined forms of the species.
'Officinalis', known as the Apothecaries Rose
or the Red Rose of Lancaster, has
semi-double rose-pink flowers, and
'Versicolor', also known as 'Rosa Mundi', has
rose-red flowers striped with lighter pink and
white. Among the numerous hybrid roses
classed as Gallicas are 'Belle de Crécy' with
double flowers combining purple-rose and
mauve; 'Belle Isis', pink; 'Cardinal de
Richelieu', deep purple; 'Charles de Mills',
plum-crimson; 'Tuscany', deep maroon, and
'Tuscany Superb' with extra large
crimson-purple flowers. 'Complicata' is a
particularly fine form of the species with large
single rose-pink flowers and plentiful golden
anthers.

gigantea *6–12m. (20–40ft)   Creamy-white*
E. Summer   ED W T S H A L

China, Burma. In warm sheltered places this
is a very vigorous climber, with large creamy-
white flowers that are delicately and
distinctively scented. In such places it will also
retain most of its leaves all winter. Unhappily
it is not very hardy and so is only suitable for
planting outdoors in the milder parts of
Britain. It was a parent of the Tea Roses
which, when crossed with the Hybrid
Perpetuals, gave rise to the modern Hybrid
Tea or large-flowered bedding roses.

glauca *2–2.5m. (6–8ft)   Pink   Summer*
D T S H A L

Central Europe. A delightful shrub, rather
stiff and erect in its main stems but branching
well at the top. The leaves are purplish-grey,
quite distinct from those of any other rose and
perfectly matched by the little single flowers
which are a purplish shade of pink. Even the
stems are purple and for good measure in
autumn there are fine crops of globular bright
red heps. It is one of the quite indispensible
species roses and it associates well with other
shrubs. In gardens it has long been known as
R. rubrifolia.

helenae *4–6m. (13–20ft)   Creamy-white*
E. Summer   D T S H A L

China. A vigorous climbing rose producing
single creamy-white flowers in dense clusters.
They are very sweetly scented and are
followed by abundant crops of small
orange-red heps which are highly decorative.
This is a good rose to send up into a tree or
allow to ramble over an outbuilding.

hugonis *1.2–2m. (4–6ft)   Yellow*
L. Spring   D T S H A L

China. One of the most beautiful of the
yellow-flowered species, this makes a
spreading bush with long arching stems, small
leaves and abundant flowers carried singly
and followed by nearly black heps. Its stems
are liable to die back in winter and care
should be taken to remove all dead growth
even if this means a second pruning in April
or May.

laevigata *4–5m. (13–16ft)   White*
L. Spring   E. Summer   ED T S H A L

China. This handsome semi-evergreen
climbing rose has become naturalized in the
southern states of America and is known
there as the Cherokee Rose. The leaves are
glossy green and composed of three leaflets
only. In a warm situation they are retained all
winter. The flowers are large, single and
sweetly scented and there are several garden
forms including *anemonoides*, also known as
the 'Anemone Rose', with large single silvery
pink flowers with deeper pink shadings, and
'Ramona', which is similar in every respect
except that the colour is carmine. All forms
have golden anthers. This fine species used to
be called *Rose sinica* and may still be found
under that name is some gardens and
nurseries.

longicuspis *4–9m. (13–30ft) Milky-white Summer ED T S H A L*

China. Another of the very vigorous climbing roses in the style of *Rosa filipes* and *R. sinowilsonii*, and much confused with the latter from which it differs in its slightly smaller, smoother, less handsome leaves and less markedly red-tinted young growth. It is a fine rose with large clusters of flowers distinctly cream-tinted in bud but opening nearly white apart from the conspicuous centre of yellow stamens. The rather strong scent is unusual and not all people find it to their liking. It can be carried considerable distances on a warm rather damp day. The long stems are more flexible than those of *R. filipes* 'Kiftsgate'.

macrantha *1.5m. (5ft) Pink Summer D T H A L V*

A rose of uncertain origin, most likely a hybrid from *Rosa gallica*, which makes a densely branched wide-spreading, very prickly bush. The well-scented flowers are single, produced in clusters, pink in bud but paling on opening to almond pink and becoming almost white with age. Each bloom has a conspicuous central tuft of golden stamens. This is a very beautiful, thicket-forming rose.

moschata *3–4m. (10–13ft) Cream L. Summer Autumn D T S H A L*

This is the Musk Rose, so called from its presumed musky perfume though not all would agree about this. It is not known in the wild in any of the types that have been described in gardens. Indeed there are few roses about which there is so much confusion, since the roses that are usually cultivated as *Rosa moschata* are much more vigorous than the above description, may reach a height of 12m./40ft and are very sweetly scented. Some experts say that most of these are really forms of *R. brunonii*, others that they are a form of *R. moschata* known as *major*. There is also a double-flowered form of true *R. moschata* which appears to have been lost, or almost so, and then to have reappeared spontaneously as a sport from the single type. In addition to all these confusions, *R. moschata* is frequently said to be one of the parents of the Hybrid Musk roses which bear its name, but this is in no way directly true. Such musk rose genes as the Musk Hybrids possess came to them tenuously through an early parent named 'Trier', which was already several generations removed from any breeding directly involving *R. moschata*. Because of this it would really be much better to forget the term Hybrid Musk altogether, since it has no real meaning, and simply call all these varieties Shrub Roses. Among the best of them are 'Buff Beauty', 1.5m./5ft double apricot-yellow flowers; 'Cornelia', 1.5m/5ft coppery-pink fading to shell-pink; 'Felicia', 1.5m/5ft, apricot-pink. fading to light pink; 'Moonlight', 2m./6ft, white, semi-double; 'Pax', 2–2.5m./6–8ft, creamy-white; 'Penelope', 2m./6ft, creamy-pink fading almost to white; 'Prosperity', 2m/6ft, ivory white, and 'Vanity', 2.5m./8ft, rose-pink and nearly single.

moyesii *2–3m. (6–10ft) Crimson Summer D T S H A L*

China. A plant of strong erect growth, angularly branched and apt to get bare at the base. The single crimson flowers are striking and are followed by even more remarkable heps, large and waisted, like bottles, and shining orange-red. In fruit it is probably the most handsome of all roses but the common form needs space to display itself fully. A variety named 'Geranium' is not quite so tall or wide-spreading at the top, and is superior for garden decoration though its flower colour is a little less pleasing, bright red rather than crimson.

multibracteata *2m (6ft) Pink*
Summer D T S H A L

China. A very prickly, stiff-stemmed shrub
with ferny leaves and small lilac-pink flowers
followed by small, egg-shaped bristly
orange-red heps. It has a longer flowering
season than most species and, as it is also
attractive in foliage and in fruit, it ranks high
in merit as a garden shrub.

multiflora *3–6m. (10–20ft) White*
Summer D T S H A L V

Japan, Korea. This very vigorous species can
either be grown as a big bush, in which case it
will spread widely by suckers and also by
layering itself wherever its flexible stems
touch soil, or it can be used as a climber to
scramble up into a tree or cover an
outbuilding. As its name implies it flowers
very freely, the small white very sweetly
scented flowers carried in broadly
cone-shaped clusters. There are numerous
forms of it including one, named *simplex*,
which is thornless and much used by
nurserymen as a root-stock on which to bud
hybrid roses. 'Cathayensis' has pink flowers,
'Carnea' is similar in colour but flowers are
double and 'Platyphylla', also known as
'Seven Sisters Rose', is another double form in
which the flowers open a deep magenta but
fade to mauve or even ivory white before they
fall. There was also, at one time, a class of
hybrid garden climbers known as Multiflora
Ramblers from their supposed relationship
with *Rosa multiflora*, but it never made a
great deal of sense as most were of fairly
mixed parentage and the term is seldom used
today except in a historical way.

nitida *45–60cm. (1½–2ft) Rose-red*
D T S H A L V

Eastern North America. This is a dwarf but
freely suckering shrub which will in time
make dense thickets covering quite a lot of
ground if not chopped back periodically with
a spade, a process which also allows the plant

to be increased very easily. The rose-red
flowers are single and freely produced but the
real decorative value of this rose resides in its
very shining green leaves, which turn red and
then crimson before they fall in autumn.

x odorata *3–5m. (10–16ft)*
Pink, Red or Yellow Summer
D T H A L

Hybrids between *Rosa chinensis* and
R. gigantea known as 'Tea Roses' because
their delicate perfume was supposed, rather
misleadingly, to resemble that of tea. The
class grew rapidly in size during the
nineteenth century, becoming more hybrid in
the process and eventually producing, by
interbreeding with the Hybrid Perpetual race
an entirely new race of large-flowered,
recurrent flowering roses which were for long
called Hybrid Teas and are now known
simply as large-flowered bush roses. A variety
of *R.* x *odorata* named 'Pseudindica' or
'Fortune's Double Yellow' is a climber about
3m/10ft high, with semi-double flowers that
are coppery-yellow flushed with
coppery-scarlet. It is a little tender and best
trained against a sunny wall.

'Paulii' *60–90cm. (2–3ft) White*
Summer D T H A L

A sprawling hybrid between *Rosa rugosa* and
R. arvensis which resembles the former in leaf
and makes long trailing stems. The large
single flowers are white in the type but there is
a deep-pink-flowered variety named 'Rosea'
Both these roses make excellent if rather
rampant ground cover, but if weeds do
establish themselves their removal among the
dense low dome-shaped mat of very prickly
stems can be painful.

pimpinellifolia *10–90cm. (4–36in.)*
Creamy white L. Spring E. Summer
D T S H A L V

Europe (including Britain) to north-western
Asia. This is the Scots or Burnet Rose, a
species found in a variety of habitats in

Britain, deep-rooted in sand dunes, finding sustenance in seemingly solid limestone and in many other unpromising places. Under these conditions it is rarely more than a few centimetres high but in better soil it makes a densely branched thicket up to about a metre. Its leaves are always small, its stems slender, wiry and intensely prickly. Botanists have disagreed about its name and in gardens it is frequently grown as *R. spinosissima*. It has many varieties including *altaica*, with primrose-yellow flowers and making a much bigger bush, to 2m./6ft, with fewer spines; *lutea*, 1m./3ft, buttercup-yellow; 'Double White', 1.5m./5ft, double white flowers; 'Double Yellow' like the last but yellow; and 'William III semi-double, light crimson. 'Stanwell Perpetual' is a hybrid with

R. damascena and has semi-double flowers, pale pink on opening but quickly paling to white.

x polliniana   *60–90cm. (2–3ft)*   *Pink Summer*   *D T H A L*

There has been considerable confusion about the correct name of this very attractive rose, and in gardens it is usually labelled *Rosa sancta* which is really a synonym for a species correctly known as *R. richardii*. This rose is a hybrid between *R. arvensis* and *R. gallica*. There is no doubt whatsoever about its beauty. It makes a low but rather wide-spreading bush covered in quite large saucer-shaped, clear pink flowers each with a tuft of golden anthers in the centre.

Rosa pimpinellifolia

primula *2–2.5m. (6–8ft) Pale yellow*
L. Spring D T S H A L

Turkestan. This is yet another of the central Asiatic yellow roses, a very attractive one with light primrose-yellow flowers carried singly on long arching stems. The flowers are slightly scented but the doubly divided leaves are strongly aromatic, and this incense-like perfume can be borne a long way on a still damp warm day.

roxburghii *2–2.5m. (6–8ft) Pink*
Summer D T S H A L

China, Japan. The species is known as the Burr Rose or Chestnut Rose because the heps are covered in prickles. The whole plant is heavily armed with thorns, has stiff, often twisted branches and leaves with an exceptional number of leaflets, up to fifteen in some instances. The flowers are pale pink with golden stamens.

rugosa *2–2.5m. (6–8ft) Magenta*
Summer D T S H A L V

China, Japan, Korea. This vigorous, thicket-forming rose makes erect, intensely spiny stems which eventually fall outward under the weight of their abundant distinctively wrinkled leaves, large single magenta sweetly-scented flowers, and quite large, rounded scarlet heps. It is much used as a root-stock for garden roses but is not desirable for that purpose because it produces suckers so freely. As a decorative garden shrub it is best planted in one of its selected forms such as 'Rubra', with deep magenta flowers; 'Scabrosa', with even larger crimson-magenta flowers followed by extra large heps; 'Alba', single white; 'Blanc Double de Coubert', double white; 'Frau Dagmar Hastrup', pale pink flowers, large heps and a rather dwarf, spreading habit, and 'Roseraie de l'Hay', deep magenta double flowers richly scented.

sericea *2.5–3m. (8–10ft) White*
L. Spring D T S H A L

China. A variable species but always making a big wide-spreading spiny plant. Some forms have been called *R. omiensis* but this name is no longer valid. The most remarkable variety, named *pteracantha*, has such wide thorns that they run together to form what appear to be spiky wings running the length of the stems. As they are crimson and semi-transluscent, they are strikingly decorative – more so than the rather starry four-petalled white flowers. The plant benefits from hard pruning after flowering to ensure a succession of strong young stems on which the best coloured thorns are produced.

setigera *1–2m. (3–6ft) Rose-pink*
L. Summer D T S H A L

Eastern USA. This is known in America as the 'Prairie Rose' and its natural habit is to sprawl its slender trailing stems over a considerable area of ground. In gardens it can be used as ground cover and is distinctive in its three-parted leaves. The single flowers are sweetly scented, rose-pink when they open but paling with age and produced later than those of most species.

setipoda *2.5–3m. (8–10ft) Rose and white*
Summer D T S H A L

China. A handsome shrub with sturdy stems, rather long leaves which have the sweet-briar perfume especially if bruised, and deep lilac-pink flowers with white centres. These are followed by bottle-shaped red heps similar to those of *R. moyesii* but smaller.

sinowilsonii *6–12m. (20–40ft) White*
Summer D W T S H A L

China. Some authorities regard this vigorous climbing rose as synonymous with *R. longicuspis* but G.S. Thomas considers it not only quite distinct but the most handsome in leaf of all roses. The young stems and thorns are red-brown, the leaves are dark green and shining above and purple beneath. The flowers are white but not, in Mr Thomas' opinion, in the first rank for beauty. The plant is rather tender and needs a sheltered place.

soulieana *2.5–4m. (8–13ft)* *White* *Summer* D T S H A L

China. This species can be grown as a large shrub or a moderate climber. In growth it resembles our own Dog Rose, with sturdy stems well armed with spines. The leaves are grey-green, the flowers pink in bud but white when fully opened followed by small egg-shaped red heps. It is a rose well able to look after itself and where there is space for it there is no need to prune at all.

villosa *1.5–2.1m. (5–7ft)* *Rose-pink* *Summer* D T S H A L

Europe, western Asia. Many experts call this species *Rosa pomifera* and its popular name is the Apple Rose because of its globular red heps rather like little red crab apples. It has bluish green downy leaves, and quite large single flowers which are pink when fully open but carmine in bud, and it makes a very shapely bush. This is an excellent rose for a mixed shrub border and so is the variety or hybrid 'Duplex', sometimes called 'Woley-Dod's Rose', with semi-double flowers.

virginiana *1–2m. (3–6ft)* *Pink* *Summer* D T S H A L V

Eastern North America. A very attractive rose, especially in foliage because the leaves are shining green all summer and then turn to yellow, orange and crimson in the autumn. The flowers are pink, single and not very large but they are produced rather late, mainly in July and August. The almost globular bright red heps usually remain for a long time. As a rule the plant is fairly short but it spreads freely by suckers and so can make quite a wide thicket in time if not chopped back periodically with a sharp spade.

wichuraiana *3–6m. (10–20ft)* *White* *Summer* E D F S H A L

Japan, Korean archipelago. This vigorous rose is a parent of many of the popular rambler roses and, like them, it can be allowed to scramble up into trees or be trained over arches, pergolas, screens, etc. However, its natural habit is to sprawl, covering large areas with its slender flexible stems and making excellent ground cover. The small white flowers are carried in large clusters in July and August and are richly scented. Among the many garden varieties associated with it are 'Alberic Barbier', with double creamy-white flowers and nearly evergreen leaves; 'Albertine', coppery-pink, sweetly scented and very thorny; 'Emily Gray', buff yellow with very good glossy leaves; 'François Juranville', salmon-pink and light rose, sweetly scented; and 'Leontine Gervaise', much like the last but a more coppery pink. 'Max Graf' is a hybrid between *R. wichuraiana* and a garden variety of *R. rugosa*, and it is one of the best of these roses to be used as ground cover. Its flowers are single, bright pink and white with golden stamens.

willmottiae *2–2.5m. (6–8ft)* *Lilac pink* *E. Summer* D T S H A L

China. A graceful rose with ferny leaves, arching stems and lilac or purplish-pink single flowers followed as a rule by good crops of small egg-shaped, orange-red heps.

xanthina *2m. (6ft)* *Yellow* *L. Spring* *E. Summer* D T S H A L

China, Korea. A species much like *R. hugonis* and differing from it mainly in botanical details of no decorative importance. An oddity about this rose is that botanists first described it from a double-flowered garden variety imported from China. The single-flowered wild form was not introduced until later so the name *R. xanthina* belongs to the double-flowered form and the wild type is known as *R. xanthina spontanea*.

ROSMARINUS, Labiateae. Rosemary. These aromatic evergreen shrubs have been grown for so many centuries in British gardens that one is apt to forget that they are natives of the warmer parts of Europe and of Asia Minor and are therefore not fully hardy. They enjoy warm sunny places and they like really well-drained soil. A certain amount of dryness is far less likely to damage them than excess moisture especially in winter. Bushes can be lightly pruned or trimmed with shears in late spring after flowering, and the erect forms of rosemary make excellent small hedges. All kinds can be increased by summer cuttings in a propagator and species also by seed sown in a greenhouse or frame in spring.

officinalis   *0.15–2m. (½–6ft)*   *Blue*
Spring   E   W   K   H   S

Southern Europe, Asia Minor. A shrub that is very variable in habit but in all its forms has narrow aromatic leaves, dark green and glossy above, grey beneath, and clusters of little violet-blue flowers. There is a white-flowered variety named 'Albus' and a number that differ in habit or the intensity of the blue colour. 'Miss Jessup's Upright', also known as 'Pyramidalis' and 'Fastigiatus' is narrowly erect in habit and can readily be clipped to form a neat column. 'Prostratus' by contrast, spreads out almost flat and is ideal for a rock garden or the top of a terrace retaining wall. It is rather more tender than most and is considered by some experts to be a distinct species which should be known as *R. lavandulaceus*. 'Angustifolius' has even narrower leaves than the type, 'Severn Sea' is dwarf but not prostrate and has deeper violet-blue flowers, and 'Tuscan Blue' also has deep-coloured flowers and leaves a little broader than average.

Rosmarinus officinalis 'Prostratus'

RUBUS, Rosaceae. Bramble. This family has provided gardens with some useful soft fruits, including the blackberries and raspberries, and also with a few interesting ornamental shrubs and climbers. All are easy to grow and some will survive even in quite poor soils and in sun or shade. All are amenable to pruning, the best method being to cut out older growth in the autumn or, in the case of kinds grown for winter stem colour, in the early spring. Some kinds sucker freely and can be increased by digging up suckers with roots in autumn or winter. The climbing kinds can be layered by burying the tips of young canes in the soil in summer. Some kinds grow fairly readily from summer cuttings in a propagator and all species can be increased by seed in spring.

cockburnianus   *2.5–3m. (8–10ft)*   *Purple*
Summer   D   T   S   H   L

China. This species makes an open-branched bush consisting of long stems covered in white blooms, which give it a white-washed appearance. This is most striking in autumn but the plant needs plenty of room to be really effective. It is sometimes called the Whitewash Bramble.

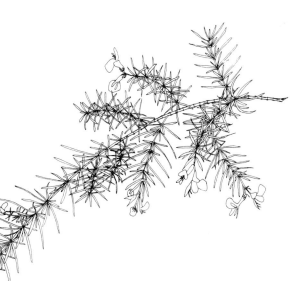

deliciosus *2–3m. (6–10ft)   White
L. Spring   E. Summer   D F S L*

Rocky Mountains. A very loosely branched
shrub with long stems carrying quite large
white flowers like single roses. It is one parent
of a fine hybrid named 'Tridel' (the other
parent is *Rubus trilobus*) which is very similar
in appearance.

henryi *4–6m. (13–20ft)   Pink Summer
E C S L*

China. A vigorous climber with long slender
stems and quite large three-lobed leaves
which are smooth and dark green above and
white with felt-like down beneath. The
flowers are too small to be effective. A variety
named *bambusarum*, is similar except that
each leaf is composed of three distinct leaflets.
Both are handsome foliage plants but have no
other beauty.

illecebrosus *30–45cm. (12–18in.)   White
Summer   D T S H V*

Japan. A dwarf suckering shrub chiefly
remarkable for its fruits which resemble
strawberries, though they are almost tasteless.
It is sometimes known as the Strawberry
Raspberry which may lead some people to
suppose that it is a hybrid between the two
but this is not so. It is more of an oddity than
a beauty but in fruit it is quite decorative.

laciniatus *3–4m. (10–13ft)   White
Summer   D T S L*

Though this bramble is named as a species it
has not been found in the wild and its origin is
unknown. It is a blackberry with much
divided leaves and is popularly known as the
Fern-leaved or Cut-leaved Blackberry. It
crops well and its fruits are sweet and
well-flavoured so that it is both a decorative
and a useful plant. The old fruiting stems
should be cut right out when the crop has
been gathered and the young canes trained in
their place.

odoratus *2–2.5m. (6–8ft)
Magenta   Summer   E. Autumn   D T S V*

Eastern North America. A rather rampant
free-suckering shrub that is more suited to the
wild garden than to mixed borders but in the
right place can be very effective. The single
magenta flowers are quite large and effective
and are sweetly scented. The plant needs to be
chopped back with a sharp spade occasionally
and rooted suckers can be replanted
elsewhere if desired.

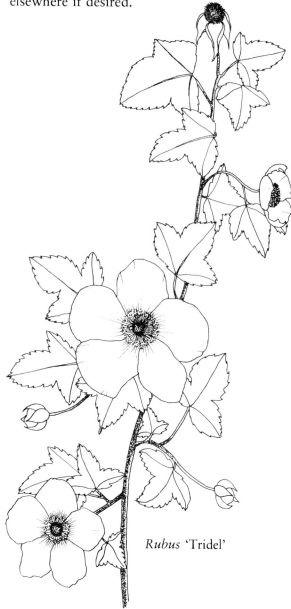

Rubus 'Tridel'

phoenicolasius   *2.5–3m. (8–10ft)   Pink*
Summer   D   T   S   L

Japan. A handsome shrub best treated as a
climber, the long flexible stems spread out on
a trellis or screen so that their dense covering
of purple bristles can be fully appreciated.
The red loganberry-like fruits are edible but
are not well-flavoured despite the enticing
popular name Japanese Wineberry.

spectabilis   *1.2–2m. (4–6ft)   Magenta*
Spring   D   T   S   V

Western North America. This is another of
the freely suckering, thicket-forming species
with showy magenta flowers. It can become a
nuisance but in a wild garden or rough corner
it can be very effective. The orange-yellow
fruits are edible.

trilobus   *2–2.5m. (6–8ft)   White*
L. Spring   Summer   D   T   S   L

Mexico. A loosely branched shrub with large
white, rose-like flowers. It closely resembles
Rubus deliciosus but its leaves are larger and
more sharply lobed. It is the parent, with
R. deliciosus, of the popular, free-flowering
hybrid *R.* 'Tridel', and a vegetatively
increased selection of this is named
'Benenden'.

ulmifolius   *2.5–3m. (8–10ft)   Pink*
Summer   D   T   S   L

Europe (including Britain). It is the
double-flowered variety, named 'Bellidiflorus',
of this native blackberry that is recommended
as a sprawling or semi-climbing decorative
plant. The flowers are fully double, pink and
very attractive, but the plant needs a lot of
room and is really only for rough places and
wild gardens. Old flowering stems can be cut
out when the flowers have faded but the great
tangle of prickly stems makes this difficult.

Ruscus aculeatus

RUSCUS, Liliaceae. Butcher's Broom. A
peculiarity of these small thicket-forming
shrubs is that what appear to be evergreen
leaves are in fact flattened stems performing
the duties of leaves. The flowers and berries
are borne in the centres of these false leaves or
cladodes. Species of *Ruscus* are useful because
they will grow in densely shady places
including those most awkward of sites that
are both shady and dry. They spread by
offsets which can easily be split away from the
parent plant, so division in early spring or
autumn is the simplest method of increase.
Pruning is not necessary except for the
removal in spring of dead or damaged stems.

aculeatus *45–90cm. (1½–3ft)   Greenish*
Winter   E. Spring   E   T   V   S

Europe (including Britain). This is the true
Butcher's Broom, a dense-growing plant with
sharp-pointed 'leaves', dark green and glossy,
insignificant flowers and quite large shining
red globular berries. Plants usually produce
flowers of one sex; only those with female
flowers can produce berries and then only if a
male is in the vicinity to ensure pollination.
Nurserymen rarely seem to know what sex
their plants are and though it is fairly easy to
make certain of obtaining females by
purchasing those plants that are actually
carrying berries one cannot be equally certain
that those without berries are males. These
need to be chosen while in flower, the males
having stamens in each flower, whereas the
females have a little cup in place of stamens.

hypoglossum   *20–45cm. (8–18in.)*
Greenish   Spring   E   T   V   S

Europe. A shorter plant than the foregoing
with narrow longer leaves that are not
spine-tipped. The red berries are seldom seen
in Britain, and again there is segregation of
the sexes and both males and females are
required if there is to be any possibility of
plants fruiting.

RUTA, Rutaceae. Rue. The species cultivated
was originally valued as a medicinal herb but
is now grown mainly as an ornamental shrub.
It will grow in most well-drained soils but
prefers those that contain chalk or lime. It
likes sunny open places. Habit is improved by
removing weak stems in spring and
shortening the rest a little. The plant can be
raised from seed but seedlings may vary, so
selected varieties are increased by early
autumn cuttings in a frame.

graveolens   *30–90cm. (1–3ft)   Yellow*
Summer   E   K   A   S

Southern Europe. A shrub of variable habit
with doubly divided ferny bluish-green leaves
and sprays of small dull yellow flowers.
'Jackman's Blue' is a variety usually planted
since it is compact and has specially
well-coloured leaves. There is also a variety,
named 'Variegata', with leaves variegated
with ivory-white.

SALIX, Salicaceae. Willow. This huge family
contains both trees and shrubs and is made
yet more complex by the freedom with which
some species hybridize. Nearly all are easy to
grow, especially if the soil is moist and not
liable to dry out severely at any time. The
flowers are produced as catkins, males and
females on separate plants, and sometimes
they differ considerably in beauty. All
withstand pruning well and those that are
grown primarily for their coloured bark are
usually cut back hard each spring, since this
produces a good crop of young stems on
which the best colour is produced the
folowing winter. All willows can be increased
easily by late summer or autumn cuttings in
moist soil outdoors or in a frame.

acutifolia   *3–4m. (10–13ft)   Silvery*
L. Winter   E. Spring   D   T   A

Finland, Russia, Siberia, Central Asia. This is
closely allied to *Salix daphnoides* and
considered by some authorities to be a
narrow-leaved and smaller variety of it. The
young stems are dark purple covered with a
white bloom, rather like a plum.

aegyptiaca   *3–4m. (10–13ft)   Yellow*
L. Winter   E. Spring   D   T   A

Russia. The young stems of this species are
covered with grey down and the male flowers
are yellow like those of the Goat Willow,
Salix caprea. It can be in flower by January
and there are several varieties the most
vigorous and decorative being that which
received an R.H.S Award of Merit in 1925.

apoda *Prostrate Yellow E. Spring*
D A L

Caucasus. A completely prostrate plant moulding itself to the form of soil or rocks. The catkins are silvery becoming yellow in the male plants as the anthers develop. A fine male form received an R.H.S. Award of Merit in 1948 but has not been given a distinguishing name.

elaeagnos *2.5–4m. (8–13ft) Grey Spring*
D T A

Europe, Asia Minor. The leaves of this willow are exceptionally narrow, grey-downy all over at first but later coming green above the down remaining on the under surface. It is often listed as *Salix incana*.

fargesii *2.5m. (8ft) Silvery Spring*
D T A

China. The stems are sturdy and shining red-brown and the winter buds, which are large and similarly coloured, enhance the display before the leaves and slender silvery catkins appear.

gracilistyla *1.2–2m. (4–6ft) Yellow*
E. Spring D T A

Japan, Manchuria, Korea. The young shoots and leaves are grey with down and the catkins come before them. The males are particularly good, silvery at first but becoming yellow as they expand and the stamens emerge.

hastata *1.2–2m. (4–6ft) Yellow Spring*
D T A

Europe, Asia. The best variety of this species for planting is 'Wehrhahnii', a well-branched rather wide-spreading bush with narrow green leaves and quite long silvery grey catkins which become yellow in the male form.

herbacea *Prostrate Grey Spring*
D A L V

North Temperate Zone (including the British Isles). This is one of the smallest of willows, a ground-hugging plant which roots as it goes. It is in no way spectacular but it is attractive and interesting and makes good ground cover in a moist spot in a rock garden or beside a pool.

irrorata *2–2.5m. (6–8ft) Red and yellow*
E. Spring D T A

South-western USA. The stems of this species start green but become purple with a white bloom. The male catkins also undergo a colour change, grey to begin with then reddish as the anthers develop but finally yellow. The lance-shaped leaves are green above greyish below.

Salix hastata 'Wehrhahnii'

lanata   *60–90cm. (2–3ft)   Yellow*
L. Spring   D T A

Arctic and sub-Arctic Europe (including
Scotland) and Asia. The young leaves of this
stout-branched bush are densely grey-silky all
over but as they age the upper surface
becomes smooth. The large catkins, both
male and female, are golden yellow and very
attractive. There is a variety, or more
probably a hybrid with *S. lapponum* named
'Stuartii' which has even larger female
catkins.

purpurea   *1.5–3m. (5–10ft)   Grey*
E. Spring   D T A

Europe (including Britain), Asia, North
Africa. The 'Purple Willow' is so-called
because of the purple colour of the young
stems but they become yellowish or olive
green as they age. The grey male catkins
become reddish-purple as they expand. From
a garden standpoint it is most useful in a
variety named 'Pendula', which has hanging
stems. If grafted on top of a straight willow
stem it makes an attractive small weeping
'tree' which need not be more than 2m./6ft
high.

repens   *0.3–1.5m. (1–5ft)   Grey   Spring*
D T A

Europe (including the British Isles), Asia. A
shrub of very variable habit but in its best
forms almost prostrate. The leaves are
covered with silvery down when young but
become smooth above as they age. The male
catkins have yellow anthers.

SALVIA, Labiatae. Sage. The ornamental
shrubby salvias are all rather soft-stemmed
plants suitable for warm sunny places and
well-drained soils, but not very hardy and
unsuitable for outdoor planting where
winters are severe or prolonged. In other
respects they are easy to grow in most soils,
alkaline or acid. They can be grown in the
open or be trained against sunny walls, and it

helps to protect the lower parts of the plants
in winter with bracken, straw or fine-mesh
netting. The previous year's growth can be cut
back quite severely each spring and at the
same time dead, damaged or weak stems
should be removed. Summer cuttings root
readily in a propagator and plants can also be
grown from seed sown in a greenhouse in
spring.

coerulea   *1–1.5m. (3–5ft)   Blue*
L. Summer   Autumn   E W C H S

South America. An attractive late-flowering
species with softly downy heart-shaped leaves
and slender spikes of light blue flowers. It is
likely to die back almost to the base each
winter except in the mildest places.

Salvia microphylla

fulgens *1–1.2m. (3–4ft)   Red*
L. Summer   Autumn   E W C H S

Mexico. Known as the Cardinal Salvia. It is
only semi-shrubby and its deep red flowers
are carried in small well-spaced clusters.

greggii *1–1.2m. (3–4ft)   Scarlet*
Summer   E W C H S

Mexico, Texas. This is much like the
following species in decorative effect but the
colour of the flowers is even brighter.

microphylla *1–1.2m. (3–4ft)   Scarlet*
Summer   E W C H S

Mexico. A useful shrub because of its long
flowering season, which can extend into the
autumn in favourable conditions. There are
seldom sufficient flowers at any one time to
make a spectacular display but they are very
brightly coloured and cheerful. The leaves are
strongly aromatic when bruised. A vigorous
form of this species is often grown as
S. grahamii. Another variety, named *neurepia*
carries its flowers in slender spikes. It is often
listed as a separate species.

officinalis *30–60cm. (1–2ft)   Purple*
Summer   E C H S

Southern Europe. This is the common sage
grown primarly as a seasoning herb but there
are several varieties with decorative leaves. In
'Icterina' they are splashed with yellow, in
'Purpurascens' they are reddish-purple
throughout and in 'Tricolor', the most
handsome of all, they are green, purple, pink
and cream. There is also a variety 'Alba', with
white flowers.

SAMBUCUS, Caprifoliaceae. Elder. If these
vigorous shrubs were less familiar or more
difficult to grow they would doubtless be held
in much greater regard, for they can be quite
spectacular in flower, they have good berries
and there are some excellent foliage shrubs
among them. All can be grown in all soils that
are not very dry and they will thrive in places
much too wet for most shrubs. They should

be pruned in late winter or early spring when
some of the older stems can be cut out and the
younger ones shortened a little. They can be
increased by summer or autumn cuttings or,
the species only, by seed.

canadensis *2.5–3m. (8–10ft)   White*
Summer   D T H A S

Eastern North America. This fine species
makes long erect stems and really needs to be
placed behind something shorter that will
screen its rather bare lower parts. The small
white flowers are produced in large plate-like
clusters and are followed by small almost
black berries. There are several varieties.
'Aurea' has yellow leaves and red berries. In
'Maxima', the compound leaves and
flower-heads are extra large and this is the
most handsome variety for garden planting.

nigra *3–6m. (10–20ft)   White*
E. Summer   D T H A S

Europe (including Britain). The species itself
is such a common shrub in Britain that it
scarcely seems necessary to include it in
garden planting except in wild gardens, but it
has several varieties which are well worth a
place. 'Laciniata' has much divided leaves;
'Albo-variegata' has leaves edged with
ivory-white; 'Aurea' is light yellow becoming
deeper as the summer advances; and
'Purpurea' has purple leaves and flower buds.

racemosa *2.5–3m. (8–10ft)   Yellowish*
Spring   D O H A S

Europe, Asia Minor, western Asia. This
species is known as the Red-berried Elder
because its fruits are scarlet instead of the
usual elder black. It also has some very
attractive foliage variations, most notably
'Plumosa Aurea', with leaves that are both
deeply cut and yellow, and 'Tenuifolia', in
which the leaf divisions are as fine as those of
the most dissected forms of Acer palmatum,
which it also resembles in its low
dome-shaped habit. It lacks vigour and is
rather difficult to grow from cuttings.

SANTOLINA, Compositae. Lavender Cotton. These bushy mound-forming plants are only semi-woody and they need to be grown in sunny places and well-drained not over-rich soil to keep them reasonably hard and so able to withstand the combination of frost and damp so typical of British winters. Otherwise they are easily grown and they can either be trimmed with shears in summer to keep them tidy or can be cut back a good deal more severely in early spring to rejuvenate them with young growth. Early autumn cuttings root readily in a frame.

chamaecyparissus   *30–60cm. (1–2ft)*
Yellow   Summer   E K C A

Southern Europe, North Africa. This is the most popular kind. It has small silvery grey leaves which are strongly (some think unpleasantly) aromatic. The flowers consist of the pad-like central disc of the daisy family without ray petals, like a tansy. It is an excellent plant to use for bold silver edgings, as groundwork in formal parterres or to make small hedges. A variety named 'Nana' or 'Corsica' is shorter and more compact.

neapolitana   *30–60cm. (1–2ft)*
Light yellow   Summer   E K C A

Italy. Very similar to *S. chamaecyparissus* and by some experts considered a variety of it but in fact it is probably a sub-species of *S. pinnata*. The leaves are a little longer, the growth looser and the flowers a lighter yellow to the point of becoming nearly white or sulphur-yellow in varieties 'Edward Bowles' and 'Sulphurea'.

rosmarinifolia   *30–60cm. (1–2ft)*
Light yellow   Summer   E K C A

Mediterranean region. This differs most obviously from the two preceding species in having bright green leaves. The flowers are light yellow, primrose in the variety 'Primrose Gem'. It is often grown as *S. viridis*.

SARCOCOCCA, Buxaceae. Christmas Box. These small evergreen shrubs are allied to the box but, unlike box, are grown as much for their flowers as for their foliage. Not that the flowers are in the least spectacular, they are too small and hidden among the leaves for that, but they are sweetly scented and they come in winter when they are especially welcome. The plants succeed in sun or shade in all reasonably fertile soil and have a special liking for those containing lime. All can be pruned in spring, dead or untidy growths being cut out but the natural rather graceful habit of the plants should be preserved. Increase is by early autumn cuttings in a frame.

confusa   *1–2m. (3–6ft)   White   E. Spring*
E T A S

China. This plant makes quite a dense bush with slender stems, long pointed shining green leaves and very sweetly scented flowers followed by black berries.

hookeriana   *1–2m. (3–6ft)   White*
Winter   E. Spring   E T A S V

Himalaya. The leaves of this species are narrow and lance-shaped, particularly attractive in the variety named *digyna*. Both species and variety spread by rhizomes, forming dense thickets in time, and it is possible to increase them by division. The kind often listed as *S. humilis* appears to be a short variety of *S. hookeriana*.

ruscifolia   *1–2m. (3–6ft)   White*
Winter   E. Spring   E T A S

China. The leaves of this species are variable in shape but long and narrow in the variety most commonly cultivated, which is called *chinensis*. This is so much like *S. confusa* that there is little point in planting both except for botanical interest.

SCHIZOPHRAGMA, Hydrangeaceae. This is another of the 'climbing hydrangeas' differing from *Hydrangea petiolaris* in having one large bract to each sterile flower instead of the four smaller sepals of that species. Like *H. petiolaris*, schizophragmas climb by aerial roots and can easily succeed in ascending a wall or tree trunk without additional help. They like good fertile rather moist soil and will grow in sun or shade. They are very vigorous but if they extend too far long stems can be shortened in winter. Increase is by seed, by summer cuttings in a propagator or by layering at almost any time.

hydrangeoides   *6–12m. (20–40ft)*   *Cream Summer   D T S H L*

Japan. This is the less desirable of the two genera commonly listed in Britain because the bracts which make the flat flower clusters effective are not so large as those of *S. integrifolium*.

Senecio greyi

integrifolium   *6–12m. (20–40ft)*   *Cream Summer   D T S H L*

China. This is the species to obtain and for effectiveness it is by far the best of all the 'climbing hydrangeas'. The bracts are long and pointed and the clusters of small fertile flowers around which they hang can be as much as 30cm./1ft across. This is a very handsome self-clinging climber which always attracts a lot of attention when in flower.

SENECIO, Compositae. The genus which has given us groundsel and ragwort, both pernicious weeds, has also provided some fine ornamental shrubs though none can be regarded as completely hardy in all winters throughout the British Isles. They are plants for warm sunny places and well-drained even rather dry soils. They do well by the sea and do not mind some salt in the air. Some, including *R. reinoldii*, make good windbreaks in mild maritime gardens. A little thinning out of old growth and shortening of young stems in spring will keep them tidy and increase their life span. Increase is usually by summer cuttings in a propagator but plants can also be raised from seed.

compactus   *60–90cm. (2–3ft)*   *Yellow Summer   E W T H S*

New Zealand. This species is much like the far better known *S. greyi* and is often confused with it. Differences are that *S. compactus* is more compact, has shorter leaves with wavy edges and is even more tender but in sheltered places it is the better plant for small gardens.

greyi   *1–2m. (3–6ft)*   *Yellow Summer E W T H S*

New Zealand. There has been a great deal of confusion between this species, *S. compactus* and *S. laxifolius*, the plants commonly grown as *S. greyi* being hybrids of these species now referred to as Dunedin Hybrids. The form usually seen is 'Sunshine'. It is a fairly loosely branched, wide-spreading shrub with leathery oval leaves densely covered when young with white down but becoming smoother and grey-green above as they age. The bright yellow daisy flowers are produced in large clusters in summer but are not as showy as those of *S. greyi*.

laxifolius *1–1.2m. (3–4ft)* *Yellow Summer* E W T H S

New Zealand. The third of the trio of species which have caused botanists and gardeners a great deal of confusion. *S. laxifolius* has narrower leaves than those of *S. greyi* and is not so neat in habit as *S. compactus*. It is probably more tender than either but that may depend upon where the original plants were collected, since this is a mountain species and plants growing at high altitudes are likely to be hardier than those lower down.

monroi *1–1.2m. (3–4ft)* *Yellow Summer* E W T H S

New Zealand. Another rather variable species but in its best forms highly decorative, compact and well-branched, with wavy-edged leaves, these and the stems covered with felt-like white down. It is on the border line of hardiness but usually grows well in maritime gardens.

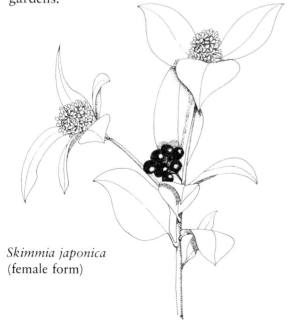

Skimmia japonica
(female form)

reinoldii *1.2–2m. (4–6ft)* *White Summer* E W T H S

New Zealand. This species used to be called *S. rotundifolius*, which is a good descriptive name since the quite large and very leathery leaves are almost completely round. It makes a dense dome-like bush and is able to withstand a great deal of salt-laden wind but not much frost.

SKIMMIA, Rutaceae. These useful evergreen shrubs have many virtues including good foliage, attractive and sometimes sweetly scented flowers and brightly coloured berries which are retained for a long time. They will thrive in sun or shade and in most reasonably fertile soils that do not dry out badly, though one species, *Skimmia reevesiana*, objects to lime. They are mostly so compact in habit that pruning is normally unnecessary but if some plants do get bare at the base a few stems can be cut hard back in spring to encourage new growth from low down. Increase is by autumn cuttings in a frame or by seed sown as soon as ripe in a greenhouse or frame.

japonica *1–1.2m. (3–4ft)* *White Spring* E A S

Japan. The most popular species and one that has produced several excellent garden varieties. Typically it is a well-branched bush with shining green leaves, short spikes of white flowers and scarlet berries. The flowers are of two sexes and are segregated on separate bushes. Only the females can produce berries and then only if a male is growing nearby for pollination but this is no hardship since the males usually make the best flower display and have the most sweetly scented flowers. Varieties include 'Fragrans', a male with very sweetly scented flowers; 'Rubella', a male notable for its reddish-purple flower buds which make an attractive display all autumn and winter and 'Fructu-albo' with ivory white berries. 'Nymans' is a good red-berried variety.

SOLANUM, Solanaceae. Potato Vine. The two climbing species of *Solanum* cultivated in British gardens are very different in character. One, *S. jasminoides*, is a true climber with elongating twining petioles, the other, *S. crispum*, is really a shrub, with very long flexible stems which look best when trained to a wall or other support but have no means of climbing of their own accord. Both require wires, trellis or something else to hold them up but the stems of *S. crispum* will have to be tied to this, whereas those of *S. jasminoides* will support themselves without assistance. Both are rather tender, *S. jasminoides* more so than *S. crispum*, and both succeed best in warm sunny places and reasonably good and well-drained soil. Weak and damaged stems of both kinds should be cut out in April-May and at the same time stems that are growing too far can be shortened. Increase is by layering or by seed sown in a warm greenhouse in spring.

crispum   *2.5–4m. (8–13ft)   Blue*
Summer   E. Autumn   ED W T H L S

Chile. The stems are long and flexible, the lance-shaped semi-evergreen leaves plentiful but not particularly beautiful. It is the abundant flowers that make this a spectacular plant. Individually they resemble those of the potato, purplish-blue with a cone of yellow anthers in the centre, and they are produced freely in good-sized clusters over a long period. This last quality is most marked in a variety named 'Glasnevin'.

jasminoides   *4–8m. (13–26ft)*
Blue or White   Summer   E. Autumn
E W T H L S

Brazil. The slender but quite wiry stems of this fine climber can cover a considerable area but they are much more tender than those of *S. crispum*. A variety named 'Album', with white, yellow-centred flowers, is to be preferred to the common wild form, which has rather dull, slaty-blue flowers.

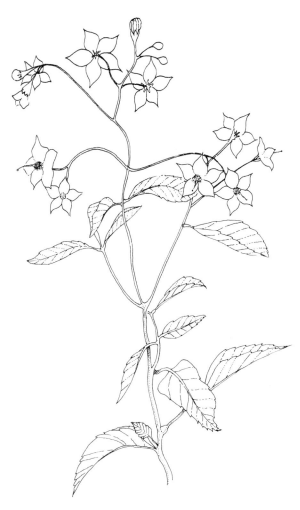

Solanum jasminoides

'Foremanii' and 'Rogersii' are names of doubtful validity probably belonging to hybrids between *S. japonica* and *S. reevesiana*.

reevesiana   *60–90cm. (2–3ft)   White*
Spring   E A S

China. This is a much shorter, more horizontally branched shrub than *S. japonica* and its flowers are bisexual, which means that every plant is capable of producing scarlet berries whether growing alone or with others. The small white flowers are scented.

SOPHORA, Leguminosae. Kowhai. This is an example of the Pea family producing one of its strange variations on its normal flower shape. The flowers are tubular and a little curved, almost like a claw, each capped by a bell-shaped calyx of the same colour, the whole hanging in clusters. They are shrubs which always attract attention and they are attractive in foliage as well as in flower. Unfortunately they are not very hardy, suitable only for planting fully in the open in the mildest parts of the British Isles but capable of being grown against a sunny wall in many places. They will grow in most reasonably fertile and well-drained soils. In the open they need little or no pruning but when trained, badly placed or surplus growth should be cut out in early spring. Increase is by seed sown in a warm greenhouse in spring or by summer cuttings in a propagator.

microphylla *3–5m. (10–16ft)   Yellow*
L. Spring   D W T H S

New Zealand. The leaves of this species are compound, composed of numerous small rounded leaflets, the whole effect being almost lace-like. The flowers are buttercup-yellow. This is the best kind for training.

tetraptera *4–8m. (13–26ft)   Yellow*
L. Spring   D W T H S

New Zealand. This differs from the foregoing in being larger in all its parts. In very mild places it will eventually become a tree.

SORBARIA, Rosaceae. False Spiraea. Very vigorous suckering shrubs with handsome compound leaves and great plumes of tiny white flowers like those of the herbaceous astilbes. Unfortunately they do not last long but while they are there they are spectacular. They will grow in most places but are best in fairly rich rather moist soil. Pruning is usually necessary to prevent plants becoming too large and overcrowded. It can be done in winter, when some of the oldest stems can be cut out altogether and the young stems shortened by a third or half. At the same time suckers that are extending the plant too far

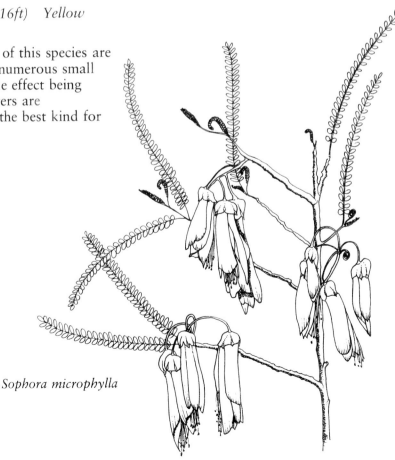

Sophora microphylla

can be chopped out. If dug up with roots they can be planted elsewhere or plants can be increased by autumn stem cuttings or by root cuttings in winter.

aitchisonni *2.5–3m. (8–10ft)* *White* *Summer* *D T A R V*

Western Asia. One of the less rampant kinds. The leaves are composed of numerous lance-shaped leaflets and the flower plumes are broadly conical.

arborea *4–6m. (13–18ft)* *White* *Summer* *D T A R V*

China. Much like *S. aitchisonii* but larger. This is a very handsome shrub where there is room for it but it is definitely not for small gardens.

sorbifolia *1.2–2m. (4–6ft)* *White* *Summer* *D T A R V*

Japan. The smallest and least spreading species and therefore the best for small gardens. Apart from its size it resembles the others.

tomentosa *4–5m. (13–16ft)* *White* *Summer* *D T A R V*

Himalaya. Another of the big kinds, much like *S. aitchisonii* in effect. It is often known as *Sorbaria lindleyana*.

SPARTIUM, Leguminosae. Spanish Broom. There is only one species of spartium and it is an excellent shrub for an open sunny place in soil that can be well-drained to the point of becoming really dry. It also withstands sea gales well, appearing to be more or less impervious to salt-laden wind. It is apt to get top heavy with all new growth at the top and bare stems at the base, but this can be checked by shortening all the previous year's growth to within 2–3cm./1–2in. of the old stems each spring. It is best raised from seed, which it produces freely, but summer cuttings can also be rooted in a propagator.

junceum *2.5–3m. (8–10ft)* *Yellow* *Summer* *E. Autumn* *D C S H*

Southern Europe. The stems of this broom are bright green, smooth and rush-like and the sweetly scented yellow pea-type flowers are carried in slender spikes. If cut they last quite well in water. There are virtually no leaves and in any case they are so small as to pass almost unnoticed. They fall off in autumn but the young stems remain green and smooth giving the bushes an evergreen appearance.

SPIRAEA, Rosaceae. This is one of the big genera of shrubs, with something like a hundred species distributed around the North Temperate Zone, many of them sufficiently attractive to be worth planting in gardens. A few are invasive, making rapidly spreading thickets by means of suckers which can be quite hard to chop out. Most are more discreet, forming well-branched shrubs, and some are short and very suitable for small gardens or even for planting in rock gardens. All are easily grown in most soils, alkaline or moderately acid, though most of the thicket-forming kinds with narrow bottle-brush flower clusters dislike lime. For pruning they fall into two distinct groups, those such as *S. x arguta* and *S. thunbergii*, which flower on, or from, the previous year's stems, and those such as *S. douglasii* and *S. menziesi*, which flower on the current year's growth. With the first group pruning is a thinning operation best done as soon as the flowers fade, when old and weak stems can be cut out and the rest shortened a little if it seems desirable to do so. The second group is also thinned but in late winter or early spring when most stems that flowered the preceding year (they will probably still have dead flowers on them) can be cut out at soil level. The suckering kinds can be increased by digging out rooted suckers in autumn or winter, the rest by summer cuttings in a propagator.

'Arguta'   *2–2.5m. (6–8ft)   White   Spring*
D O H

This is one of the shrubs commonly known as
Bridal Wreath, because its slender arching
stems are wreathed in small white flowers. It
is very attractive in the garden and is also
excellent for cutting. It is a hybrid between
S. multiflora and *S. thunbergii*

x billiardii   *1.2–2m. (4–6ft)   Magenta
Summer   D T V H*

Another hybrid, this time between
S. douglasii and *S. salicifolia*. It is
thicket-forming and carries its magenta
flowers close-packed in a short spike like a
bottlebrush. The best form is named
'Triumphans' and neither this nor the parent
really enjoy lime in the soil.

canescens   *3–4m. (10–13ft)   White
Summer   D O H*

Himalaya. An elegant shrub with long slender
arching stems from which come short
side-shoots, each terminated by a cluster of
small white flowers.

cantoniensis   *1.2–2m. (4–6ft)   White
E. Summer   D O H*

China. It is the beautiful double-flowered
form of this species, variously named 'Flore
Pleno' or 'Lanceata', that is commonly
cultivated in gardens. It is not suitable for
planting in places subject to severe late spring
frosts because its young growth is tender. The
flowers are produced along the length of
slender arching stems.

douglasii   *1.2–2m. (4–6ft)   Magenta
Summer   D T V H*

Western North America. This is a
thicket-forming species with the bottlebrush
type of flower spike. It does not like lime but
it enjoys moisture and is excellent for lakeside
planting.

japonica   *1.2–2m. (4–6ft)   Pink
Summer   D T H*

Temperate eastern Asia. This makes a dense
bush of mainly erect stems and carries its
small flowers closely packed in flat clusters. It
has produced a number of useful varieties
such as 'Alpina', also known as 'Nana', very
dwarf and compact; 'Bullata', another dwarf
with dark green puckered leaves and magenta
flowers; and 'Little Princess' also known as
'Nyewood' just a little looser in growth than
'Bullata', with carmine flowers. However the
most popular of all is 'Anthony Waterer'
often listed as *S. x bumalda* 'Anthony
Waterer'. It is of medium height with fine
carmine flowers and leaves which, especially
when young, are often variegated with cream
and pink. 'Goldflame' is similar but has leaves
that are copper-yellow when young but
becoming greener in summer.

nipponica   *2–2.5m. (6–8ft)   White
E. Summer   D O H*

Japan. A most decorative shrub particularly
in its variety 'Rotundifolia', which has larger
and rounder leaves than the type and is the
form most commonly seen in British gardens.
Its small clusters of flowers are carried all
along the arching branches in June. Another
variety, named 'Snowmound', is much
smaller and denser but at least equally
free-flowering. It is sometimes wrongly listed
as *S. nipponica tosaenis* which is similar but
inferior in flower as a garden plant.

prunifolia   *1.2–2m. (4–6ft)   White
Spring   D O H V*

China. This is one of those plants that first
became known in a garden form to which the
name *S. prunifolia* belongs. It has fully double
flowers carried all along the arching branches
in spring, and is another of the spiraeas to be
known as Bridal Wreath. The true wild
species came later and is distinguished as
variety *simpliciflora*. From a decorative
standpoint it is inferior.

thunbergii *1–1.5m. (3–5ft)   White Spring   D O K H*

China. Usually the first spiraea to flower and a very pretty plant in April when every slender stem is wreathed in small white flowers. It is rather like *S. arguta* but even earlier and more slender, and since it can be clipped in summer it makes quite a nice small hedge.

x vanhouttei *2m. (6ft)   White E. Summer   D O H*

A fine hybrid between *S. cantoniensis* and a compact Asiatic species named *S. trilobata*. From this is inherits a tendency to produce three-lobed leaves but its beauty lies in its long arching stems wreathed in tight clusters of white flowers. It grows very densely and can need quite a lot of thinning out of old stems after flowering.

veitchii *2.5–3m. (8–10ft)   White Summer   D O H*

China. One of the most beautiful of the summer-flowering species with quite large, flattish clusters of white flowers standing up from the arching stems in late June or July. It needs space to do it justice as it grows both tall and wide.

STACHYURUS, Stachyurus. These unusual but very attractive early flowering shrubs produce their flowers in very slender quite stiff trails which hang straight down. Apart from the fact that frost may spoil the flowers, the plants are quite hardy and they will grow in all reasonably fertile soils. Little pruning is necessary unless plants are trained against walls, in which case it will probably be necessary to cut out some of the older branches each year after flowering to make way for the young stems. Increase is by seed or summer cuttings in a propagator.

Spiraea x vanhouttei

salicifolia *1–2m. (3–6ft)   Pink   Summer D T H V*

Europe, Asia. Another of the freely suckering species with the narrowly cylindrical bottlebrush type of flower cluster. Like most of this kind it does not like markedly alkaline soil.

chinensis   *2.5–3m. (8–10ft)   Pale yellow*
E. Spring   D   O   H   S

China. This makes an open-branched shrub and the flower buds are almost globular, hanging like strings of primrose yellow beads. The flowers are cup-shaped.

praecox   *2.5–3m. (8–10ft)   Pale yellow*
L. Winter   E. Spring   D   O   H   S

Japan. This is the more familiar of the two species most likely to be seen in British gardens. It closely resembles *S. chinensis* but flowers about a fortnight earlier.

STAPHYLEA, Staphyleaceae. Bladder Nut. These are easily grown shrubs thriving in most reasonably fertile soils, including those overlying chalk or limestone. Some kinds tend to sucker, and rooted suckers dug up in autumn provide one means of increase. Others are by seeds, which are produced inside the large bladder-like seed capsules, which have suggested the popular name, and also by summer cuttings in a propagator. Old and weak branches and suckers can be removed in winter.

colchica   *2.5–3m. (8–10ft)   White*
L. Spring   D   T   H   V   S

Caucasus. A rather stiffly branched shrub with compound leaves having either three or five leaflets and little erect clusters of bell-shaped white flowers.

holocarpa   *4–8m. (13–26ft)*
White or Pink   Spring   D   T   H   S

China. A larger plant than the foregoing, sometimes making a small tree. The leaves are three-parted and the flowers, which are pink in bud, hang in little trails. The pink colour is retained in the open flower in variety 'Rosea' but the common form becomes white.

pinnata   *3–4m. (10–13ft)   White*
L. Spring   E. Summer   D   T   H   V   S

Europe. This species is less decorative than the two fore-going and it differs in having more leaflets to the compound leaves. The flowers hang in little trails.

STAUNTONIA, Lardizabalaceae. A small genus of twining plants allied to *Holboellia* and, like it, evergreen. They are not very hardy but can be grown easily enough in the mild maritime gardens of the west and south west and on sheltered walls (they need not be sunny) in many other places. They will thrive in most fertile soils and require little pruning though old or weak growths can be cut out in the spring. The fruits are quite large and edible and plants can be raised from their seeds sown in a warm greenhouse in spring, though the more usual method of propagation is by summer cuttings in a propagator.

hexaphylla   *5–10m. (16–33ft)*
White and Violet   L. Spring   E   W   T   H   S

Japan, China. A vigorous climber which produces both male and female flowers in separate clusters on the same plant. The compound leaves are quite large and leathery, composed of several leaflets, and the egg-shaped fruits are purple-tinged. This is an interesting rather than an outstandingly beautiful plant.

STRANVAESIA, Rosaceae. These handsome evergreen shrubs deserve to be better known for they are good in leaf, flower and berry, they are fully hardy and extremely easy to grow. They have no fads about soil, which can be alkaline or moderately acid, well-drained or rather moist and they will thrive in full sun or in light shade. Plants can be trained against a wall, in which case they will probably need to be spur-pruned in summer, but if grown in the open little pruning is necessary beyond an occasional thinning out of old wood in spring. Increase is by seed sown in spring, by summer cuttings in a propagator or by layering in spring or summer.

davidiana *3–6m. (10–20ft)* *White*
E. Summer   *E T P S H L*

China. This is the best species, a tall but not wide-spreading shrub with lance-shaped dark green leaves, which may be broad or narrow according to variety, clusters of small white flowers like those of a cotoneaster followed by holly-red berries. There is an excellent yellow-berried variety named 'Fructulutea', and a much shorter, wider-growing variety named *undulata* because the leaves are wavy at the edge.

STUARTIA, Theaceae. These lime-hating plants are mainly small trees but a few make large shrubs. All are grown for their late flowering, fine autumn leaf colour and handsome peeling bark. They grow best in thin woodland in the kind of conditions that suit camellias and rhododendrons well. Little pruning is desirable but the main branches should be kept free of small side-growths so that the beauty of the bark is fully revealed. Seeds provide one means of increase, sown in peat and sand as soon as ripe. Layering and late summer cuttings are other methods of propagation. The name is often spelled *stewartii* but *stuartia* is correct.

malacodendron *3–4m. (10–13ft)* *White*
L. Summer   *D S L A*

South-eastern USA. A wide-spreading open-branched shrub with white flowers like small camellias but they have blue anthers.

sinensis *4–8m. (13–26ft)* *White*
L. Summer   *D S L A*

China. A larger plant than the foregoing capable of making a sizeable tree under favourable conditions. The bark is smooth yet peeling, pumice-grey or pink-tinged, and the autumn leaf colour is rich.

Symphoricarpos albus

SYMPHORICARPOS, Caprifoliaceae. Snowberry. Coral Berry. Densely twiggy shrubs chiefly of value for their crops of marble-like berries in autumn. All are hardy, will grow in sun or shade and in most soils that do not dry out badly in winter. They make excellent undergrowth in woodlands and do not mind if the soil is alkaline. Because of their thicket-forming habit they are difficult to prune in any detailed way but they can be trimmed to shape in late winter and suckers can be chopped out at any time. If done in autumn or winter the suckers with roots can be used as propagating material. Plants can also be increased by autumn cuttings outdoors or by seed sown in spring.

albus *60–90cm. (2–3ft)   Pink   Summer D T A V S*

Eastern North America. This is the species popularly known as Snowberry because its berries are shining white. It is usually grown in a variety correctly known as *laevigatus* though this name is unlikely to be used in gardens and nurseries. It differs from the common type in being taller and making an even denser thicket of growth and it is the kind that has become widely naturalized in Britain and is often call *S. rivularis*.

x chenaultii *60–90cm. (2–3ft)   White Summer   D T A V*

An attractive hybrid between *S. microphyllus* and *S. orbiculatus*, which has purple and pink berries, the colour being most developed on the sunny side.

'Doorenbos Hybrids' *1.2–2m. (4–6ft) Pinkish   Summer   D T A V*

This is a series of good hybrids between *S. x chenaultii, albus laevigatus* and *S. orbiculatas*. There are several selected forms of this including 'Erect' and 'White Hedge', both more upright in growth than most, the first with lilac the second with white berries, and also 'Mother of Pearl', with pink and white berries. These are probably the best kinds for general ornamental planting in gardens.

orbiculatus *1.2–2m. (4–6ft)   White L. Summer   E. Autumn   D T A V S*

Eastern USA. This is the species known as Coral Berry or Indian Currant because of the magenta colour of its berries. It has a good variety with yellow-edged leaves named 'Variegatus'.

SYRINGA, Oleaceae. Lilac. The lilacs that everyone knows are varieties of *Syringa vulgaris* which can make big bushes or small trees, but there are many other less well known species, some quite small shrubs, and mostly highly attractive. All are easily grown in most reasonably fertile soils and have a particular liking for those overlying chalk or limestone. They like open sunny places. Little pruning is desirable beyond the removal of faded flower-heads but if plants do become too large whole branches can be removed in winter, or stems may be shortened as necessary after flowering though this will entail some loss of flower the following year. Nurserymen often graft garden varieties onto common lilac root-stocks, and then all suckers must be removed as they will have the character of the stock. If lilacs are raised from layers or seeds suckers can be retained, if there is room for them, or can be dug up with roots in autumn or winter and replanted elsewhere. However, seedlings of garden varieties are likely to show considerable variations from the parent plants. Late summer cuttings can be rooted in a propagator. Seed will germinate better if kept moist at a temperature of 4°C./39°F. or less for two months prior to sowing.

x chinensis *3–4m. (10–13ft)   Lilac L. Spring   D T L H*

This is known as the Rouen Lilac and is a very attractive hybrid between *Syringa x persica* and *S. vulgaris*. It is smaller and more densely branched than the common lilac and has long rather loose sprays of scented flowers that are the usual lilac-mauve in colour. There are several varieties, including 'Alba', white; 'Metensis', lilac-pink; and 'Saugeana', purplish-red.

emodi   *3–4m. (10–13ft)*
White or purplish   E. Summer
D T H L S

Himalaya. A sturdy bush with rather unpleasantly scented conical sprays of flowers, which are purple in bud and may retain some of this colour when they open or become white. There are two varieties with coloured leaves; 'Aurea', pale yellow all over, and 'Aureo Variegata', edged with yellow.

x **hyacinthiflora**   *3–4m. (10–13ft)   Purple*
Spring   D T H L

A race of hybrids between *S. oblata* and *S. vulgaris azurea plena* useful for flowering early. There are numerous varieties. The first to be raised by the French breeder Victor Lemoine in 1876 had double violet-purple flowers and is now known as 'Plena'. Others are 'Alice Eastwood', double reddish-purple; 'Buffon', single lilac-pink; 'Clarke's Giant', single, lilac-blue; 'Esther Staley', single, lilac-pink; and 'Lamartine', single blue-lilac.

x **josiflexa**   *3–4m. (10–13ft)   Purple*
L. Spring   E. Summer   D T H L

A race of hybrids between *S. josikaea* and *S. reflexa*, distinguished by rather long drooping sprays of flowers which curl back at the mouth of the tube. They are freely produced and are scented. Several forms have been named one of the best being 'Bellicent', with reddish-purple flowers.

josikae   *2.5–3m. (8–10ft)   Lilac*
E. Summer   D T H L S

Europe. This is the species often known as the Hungarian Lilac. It has slender but solidly packed sprays of lilac flowers which have a little scent.

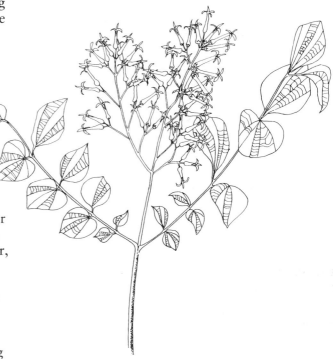

Syringa meyeri 'Palibin'

julianae   *1.2–2m. (4–6ft)   Lilac*
L. Spring   E. Summer   D T H L S

China. A useful species for small gardens because of its moderate size. The flowers are scented and freely produced in slender but not very large sprays that are held erect.

meyeri   *2m. (6ft)   Lilac*
L. Spring   E. Summer   D T H L S

Korea. The variety of this species commonly grown is named 'Palibin'. It is a delightful shrub which grows so slowly that it can be accommodated in a small space for several years. It makes a densely branched, dome-shaped bush with small usually rounded leaves and little sprays of sweetly scented lilac flowers in May and early June. It has suffered from a surfeit of names and may turn up in catalogues as *Syringa palabiniana*, *S. velutina* or *S. patula*.

microphylla *1–1.5m. (3–5ft) Lilac*
E. Summer D T H L S

China. This is very different from the popular image of a lilac, a small bushy plant with small leaves and short erect sprays of scented flowers. The main display is in June but there may be some more flowers in September. A particularly good form has been named 'Superba'.

x persica *1.2–2m. (4–6ft) Lilac*
L. Spring D T H L

The Persian Lilac was for long regarded as a true species, native to Afghanistan, but is now regarded as a hybrid between *S. afghanica* and *S. laciniata*. Whatever its true botanical status, it is a charming garden plant, a medium size shrub of rounded habit with privet-like leaves and small loose sprays of scented lilac flowers. There is a white-flowered form named 'Alba'.

x prestoniae *2.5–3m. (8–10ft)*
Lilac to Purple L. Spring E. Summer
D T H L

A race of hybrids between *S. reflexa* and *S. villosa*, notable for their hardiness and for the graceful drooping sprays of closely clustered flowers. There are a number of varieties including 'Audrey', pink; 'Elinor', lavender; 'Isabella', light rose; and 'Royalty', purple.

reflexa *2.5–3m. (8–10ft) Pink*
L. Spring E. Summer D T H L S

China. A distinctive species with narrowly conical drooping sprays of purplish-pink flowers which lack scent. It is free-flowering and attractive in appearance but as a garden plant is probably surpassed by some of its hybrid offspring such as *S x josiflexa* and *S. x prestoniae*.

sweginzowii *2.5–3m. (8–10ft) Pink*
L. Spring E. Summer D T H L S

China. An attractive species with loose sprays of sweetly scented flowers. Typically these are pale pink but a white variety named 'Albida' is known. 'Densiflora' has more closely packed flowers and 'Superba' has flower sprays of increased size.

villosa *2.5–3m. (8–10ft) Lilac pink*
L. Spring E. Summer D T H L S

China. This fine species closely resembles *S. josikae* but its flowers are much more loosely arranged in the sprays. It has no scent but it does make a very good display which continues well after the common lilacs have faded.

vulgaris *3–6m. (10–20ft) Lilac*
L. Spring D T H V L S

Eastern Europe. This is the common lilac, a well-loved large shrub or small tree which suckers freely and produces conical sprays of sweetly scented flowers in May. In cultivation it has proved a very variable plant, producing double-flowered as well as single-flowered forms in a range of colour from pale mauve to deep reddish-purple and also white and pale primrose yellow. Hundreds of these varieties have been named, of which the following is a selection of some of the best that are freely available in Britain:

'Charles Joly'. Double, deep reddish-purple.
'Charles X'. Single, deep reddish-purple.
'Congo'. Single, reddish-purple.
'Katherine Havemeyer'. Double, lavender-purple.
'Madame Antoine Buchner'. Double, rosy-mauve.
'Madame Lemoine'. Double, white.
'Massena'. Single, reddish-purple.
'Maud Notcutt'. Single, white.
'Michel Buchner'. Double, pale rosy lilac.
'Mrs Edward Harding'. Double, reddish-purple.

'Paul Thirion'. Double, magenta.
'President Grevy'. Double, blue-lilac.
'Primrose'. Single, pale primrose-yellow.
'Sensation'. Single, reddish-purple flowers with white edge.
'Souvenir de Louis Spaeth'. Single, deep reddish-purple.
'Vestale'. Single, white.

yunnanensis   *2.5–3m. (8–10ft)   Lilac pink*
E. Summer   D T H L S

China. A fast-growing but not always very long-lived species which produces plenty of narrow sprays of lilac-pink or purplish flowers which have not got a very pleasant scent. It is one of the easiest lilacs to grow from seed and it does not produce any suckers.

TAMARIX, Tamaricaceae. Tamarisk. These shrubs have been designed by nature to grow in dry or exposed places, and some tender species live in deserts. The hardy kinds with which we are concerned here are all excellent seaside shrubs, able to withstand severe storms and capable of surviving in sandy soils. None of this means that in gardens they will not make fine specimens and produce more beautiful flower sprays if given better conditions; richer soil (though it must be well-drained) and sheltered though sunny places in which they can grow into well-balanced bushes. For pruning they may be grouped in two classes; the spring flowering kinds which can have the old flowering stems removed or shortened after flowering, and the summer flowering kinds which can be cut back quite a lot in February or March. Increase of all is by late autumn cuttings in a frame.

gallica   *2–3m. (6–10ft)   Pink*
Summer   E. Autumn   D C T A

South-western Europe. An open branched shrub with tiny leaves on slender stems, giving it a feathery appearance. The small pink flowers are crowded on the current year's growth in very slender spikes. It is one of the best species to plant as a windbreak in exposed coastal regions. It is sometimes called *T. anglica.*

ramosissima   *3–4m. (10–13ft)   Pink*
L. Summer   E. Autumn   D C T A

Western and Central Asia. The most beautiful species because of its elegant habit and rose-pink flowers very freely produced in August and September. In gardens and nurseries this species is usually called *T. pentandra.* A variety named 'Rubra' has deeper coloured flowers.

parviflora   *2–3m. (6–10ft)   Pink*
L. Spring   D O A

South-eastern Europe. The effect is similar to that of *T. gallica* but the stems are purple and this species flowers on the previous year's growth and should not be pruned until the flowers fade. They are quite a deep rose-pink.

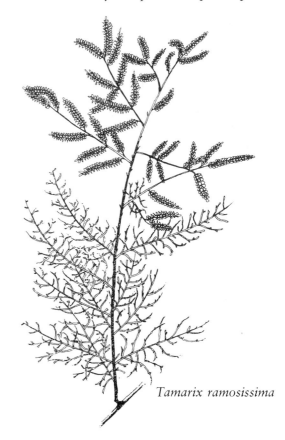

Tamarix ramosissima

Teucrium fruticans

TAXUS, Taxaceae. Yew. Left to its own devices common yew can in time make a broad tree but it grows slowly, responds well to pruning or clipping and has also produced so many varieties of restricted habit that gardeners usually regard it as a shrub. It will thrive in all soils including those containing a lot of lime, in sun or shade even if it is quite dense and also in soils that are distinctly dry. The wild type can be raised from seed but this needs a period of at least five months moist at a temperature of 20°C./68°F. or more, followed by a second period of at least three months at a temperature of 4°C./39°F. or less before it will germinate. Garden varieties are increased by late summer cuttings in a propagator or autumn cuttings in a frame or sheltered place outdoors.

baccata *3–12m. (10–40ft)   Greenish Spring* E K H A S

Europe, north-eastern Africa, western Asia. The common yew is too well known to require description and its narrow dark green leaves make it an ideal background for light-coloured plants and ornaments, particularly when it is clipped as a hedge plant or topiary specimen, for both of which purposes it is ideally suited. It has produced numerous garden varieties including: 'Fastigiata', the 'Irish Yew', which is broadly columnar in habit; 'Standishii', which is more narrowly columnar much slower growing and has yellow leaves; 'Aurea', normal in habit and with yellow leaves; 'Dovastoniana' with horizontal branches and pendulous branchlets also available in a golden leaved variety; 'Repandans', almost prostrate; 'Fructo-luteo' with yellow instead of red fruits; and 'Semperaurea' with golden yellow leaves.

TELOPEA, Proteaceae. Waratah. A curious very primitive genus related to embothrium and with rather similar clusters of narrowly tubular flowers with long protuding curved styles. The plants are not very hardy and they require lime-free soil, preferably peaty and not liable to dry out in summer. They are most suitable for the warm maritime gardens of the west and south-west in thin woodland, but may survive in especially sheltered places elsewhere or trained against sheltered walls that are not too hot and dry. Little pruning is likely to be required except for the removal of dead or damaged growth in spring. Increase is by summer cuttings in a propagator.

truncata *2–2.5m. (6–8ft)   Crimson E. Summer* E W T H

New Zealand. A rather stiffly erect shrub with stout stems, leathery dark green leaves and tight clusters of crimson flowers terminating the stems.

TEUCRIUM, Labiateae. Germander. This is a big genus but only two shrubby species are of great importance for gardens. One is *Teucrium fruticans*, which thrives in warm sunny places and well-drained soils. It is not fully hardy but it does well in most coastal gardens of the south and west, in sheltered places inland and trained against sunny walls. The other species, *T. chamaedrys*, is much smaller and hardier and suitable for planting in unmortared walls or rock gardens or as ground cover in a sunny place. Both species can be increased by summer cuttings in a propagator or by seed, that of *T. fruticans* sown in a greenhouse in spring and *T. chamaedrys* can also be divided in spring. *T. fruticans* can have old or surplus stems cut out in April or May and *T. chamaedrys* can be clipped with shears at the same time to keep it tidy.

chamaedrys *15–20cm. (6–9in.)* *Purple Summer* *E. Autumn* *E K H V S*

Europe. This small spreading plant is really only semi-shrubby. It has small aromatic leaves and little spikes of purple or rose flowers.

fruticans *1m. (3ft)* *Lavender* *Summer* *E W T H S*

Southern Europe, northern Africa. An excellent grey-leaved shrub for warm sunny places, angularly and densely branched and with quite large lavender-blue flowers carried in short terminal spikes over a long period. Occasional clipping in summer will make it much neater in habit but will check flower production. There is a variety with bluer flowers named 'Azureum'.

THUJOPSIS, Cupressaceae. There is only one species of this handsome conifer and it thrives in all reasonably fertile soils including those overlying chalk or limestone. It will grow in sun or semi-shade. It is really a broad tree though it is variable in habit. If it is required to make a wide-spreading shrub any erect stems should be cut out each May. Increase is by seed sown in spring after at least two months moist at a temperature of 4°C./39°F. or less, or by early autumn cuttings in a frame.

dolobrata *3–12m. (10–40ft)* *E T S A*

Japan. The feature of this plant is that the broad scale-like leaves arranged on flattened branches are dark glossy green above, grey-banded beneath. It can make a very handsome foliage shrub but it needs a lot of space.

Trachelospermum jasminoides

TRACHELOSPERMUM, Apocynaceae. Rather tender evergreen twiners valuable for their good foliage and richly scented flowers. They will grow in all reasonably fertile soils but require warm sheltered and preferably sunny places. They are excellent for training against walls but will require trellis or wires round which to twine. Not much pruning is possible but dead, damaged or weak stems should be cut out in April or May. Increase is by layering in spring or by late summer cuttings in a propagator.

asiaticum *3–6m. (10–20ft)*   *White*
Summer   E   W   T   H

Japan, Korea. This is the best species to plant
since it is the hardiest and in no way inferior
to *T. jasminoides* in beauty. The medium size
oval leaves are leathery and dark green. The
small white flowers are produced in little
clusters but tend to be partly hidden by the
leaves. It is their scent, carried far and wide,
that makes them so desirable.

jasminoides *3–6m. (10–20ft)*   *White*
Summer   E   W   T   H

China. In all respects, except a slight extra
tenderness, this so closely resembles
T. asiaticum that there is no need to plant
both in their green-leaved forms. However,
T. jasminoides has an excellent variety named
'Variegatum', in which the leaves are heavily
splashed with cream.

ULEX, Leguminosae. Gorse. No native shrub
contributes more to the gaiety of the British
countryside than gorse but, just because it is
so common in the wild, few people would
want to plant it in their gardens except,
possibly, as an impenetrable hedge. However,
it has varieties that are worth planting and
these, like their parent, thrive in all
well-drained not over-rich soils and open
sunny places. Gorse can be clipped in May
after the main flush of flowers is over.
Increase of garden varieties is by summer
cuttings in a propagator.

europaeus *1.2–2m. (4–6ft)*   *Yellow*
Spring   D   K   H

Europe (including the British Isles). This
intensely spiny shrub has produced a variety
with double flowers, named 'Plenus', which is
even more effective as a decorative shrub,
and, since it does not produce any seed does
not spread itself by self-sown seedlings where
it is not wanted.

VACCINIUM, Ericaceae. Blueberry.
Cranberry. Whortleberry. These shrubs not
only dislike lime in any form but will actually
grow in the most acid soils, some of them
even in acid bogs. This is a big genus of
something like 400 species, some of
commercial importance for their berries but
none of outstanding decorative value. Most
can have old and weak stems cut out in
spring. All can be increased by seed sown in
moist peat and most also by late summer
cuttings in a propagator.

arctostaphylos *2–3m. (6–10ft)*
White and Purple   E. Summer   D   T   S   H

Caucasus. This is known as the Caucasian
Whortleberry and is quite an attractive shrub
with broadly lance-shaped leaves that turn
purplish-red before they fall in autumn. The
sprays of small urn-shaped flowers are white
more or less tinged with purple.

corymbosum *1.2–3m. (4–10ft)*
White or Pink   L. Spring   D   T   S   H

Eastern North America. This is the Swamp
Blueberry, a thicket-forming shrub with
clusters of urn-shaped white or pale pink
flowers followed by black berries covered
with blue bloom. The leaves colour well
before they fall.

cylindraceum *2.5–3m. (8–10ft)*
Green and red   L. Summer   Autumn
ED   T   S   H

Azores. One of the most decorative species,
with slender spikes of tubular flowers that are
yellowish-green tipped with red, followed by
black berries with a blue bloom.

vitis-idaea *15–30cm. (6–12in.)*
White and Pink   Summer   E   H   V   S

Europe (including Britain), Asia and North
America. This is the Cowberry, a creeping
evergreen with short drooping spikes of
bell-shaped pink and white flowers followed
by red edible berries. The leaves are small,

rounded and shining green, and the plant makes good ground cover in suitably moist and acid soil.

VESTIA, Solanaceae. This attractive evergreen is not very hardy but grows well in maritime gardens of the west and south west or it can be trained against sunny walls. It grows in all fertile, reasonably well-drained soils and requires little or no pruning beyond the removal of dead, damaged or weak stems in spring. Summer cuttings root readily in a propagator.

foetida　*1.2–1.5m. (4–5ft)　Yellow Spring　Summer　E　W　T　H*

Chile. This is the only species and it grows like a cestrum, to which it is related, making slender stems, mainly from the base, with small shining green leaves which smell unpleasant when bruised, and tubular pendant bright yellow flowers produced over a long period. It is often known as *V. lycioides*.

VIBURNUM, Caprifoliaceae. Guelder Rose. Snowball Tree. Wayfaring Tree. This is a big genus rich in good garden plants most of which can be grown in all reasonably fertile and well-drained soils whether alkaline or moderately acid. Pruning, when necessary, is usually a thinning-out operation to get rid of old weak or overcrowded growth and is best done in late winter for the deciduous kinds and in spring for the evergreens. *Viburnum tinus* can be clipped in summer as a hedge. Some kinds spread by offsets or layer themselves and it may be necessary to chop them back occasionally to prevent them extending too far. Rooted offsets or layers can be planted elsewhere if required. Most kinds can also be increased by summer cuttings in a propagator and some also by autumn cuttings in a frame. Seeds of many species germinate best if kept moist for five months at a temperature of at least 20°C./68°F. and then for a further three months at 4°C./39°F. or less.

betulifolium　*3–4m. (10–13ft)　White E. Summer　D　T　H　A　S*

China. A magnificent fruiting shrub making very long rather slender stems bending in autumn beneath the weight of large clusters of berries like small redcurrants. The flowers come in flat clusters.

bitchiuense　*2–2.5m. (6–8ft) Pink and white　Spring　D　O　H*

Japan. An open-branched bush with tightly packed clusters of pink and white flowers which are richly scented. It is much like *V. carlesii* but taller and looser in habit. It can vary in flower quality.

x bodnantense　*2.5–3m. (8–10ft)　Pink Winter　D　T　H　A　S　L*

A hybrid between *V. farreri* and *V. grandiflorum*, which more closely resembles the latter in its stiff stems, angular branching and quite large clusters of very fragrant pink flowers. The two best varieties are 'Dawn', which is rose-pink and 'Deben', which is pink in bud but opens white.

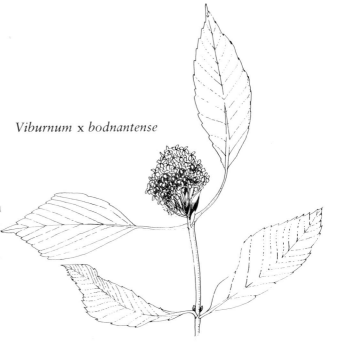

Viburnum x *bodnantense*

x burkwoodii   *1.5–2m. (5–6ft)   White*
L. Winter   E. Spring   E O H

A fine hybrid between *V. carlesii* and *V. utile*, much like the former in its tight clusters of white richly scented flowers but evergreen and taller. Easily propagated and in every way a very satisfactory shrub.

x carlcephalum   *2–2.5m. (6–8ft)   White*
L. Spring   D O H

A hybrid between *V. carlesii* and *V. macrocephalum* with large, almost globular, clusters of white scented flowers. It is the largest flowered of these early flowering scented viburnums but not the sweetest.

carlesii   *1.2–1.5m. (4–5ft)*
Pink and White   Spring   D O H S

Korea. A favourite spring flowering shrub, excellent itself and parent of several fine hybrids. The leaves of this species are rounded, slightly downy and fall in autumn. The white pink-flushed flowers are packed into tight dome-shaped clusters and are richly scented. There are several selected varieties such as 'Aurora', with red flower buds, and 'Diana', with pink flowers and a rather more compact habit.

davidii   *60–90cm. (2–3ft)   White*
E. Summer   E T H S

China. This is primarily grown as a foliage plant for its quite large, deeply veined shining green leaves. The white flowers, borne in flat clusters, are sometimes followed by good crops of small turquoise blue berries but some plants seem to berry much more freely than others. *V. cinnamomifolium* is, from a decorative standpoint, a large version of *V. davidii* but the latter is the better species for small gardens and makes a very dense bush excellent as ground cover.

dilatatum   *2–3m. (6–10ft)   White*
L. Spring   E. Summer   D T H A S

Japan. A good deciduous species with clusters of white flowers followed by bright red berries, which remain for a long time. There is a yellow-berried variety named 'Xanthocarpum'.

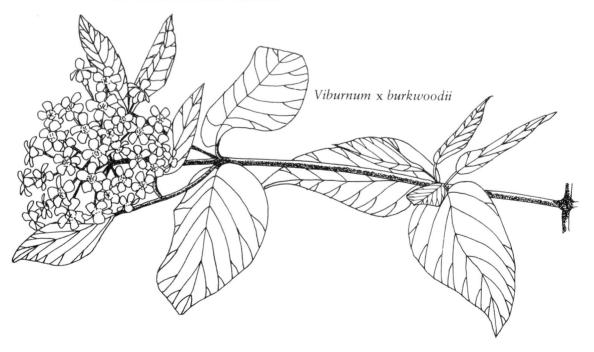

Viburnum x *burkwoodii*

farreri *2.5–3m. (8–10ft)* *White* *Winter*
D O H L V

China. This is the sweetly scented
winter-flowering viburnum which most
gardeners know as *V. fragrans*. It makes an
ever expanding thicket of erect stems. The
flowers are carried in small tightly packed
clusters and are pink in bud but white when
fully open.

grandiflorum *2.5–3m. (8–10ft)* *Pink*
Winter *D O H L S*

Himalaya. This fine winter flowering species
differs from *V. farreri* in its much stouter
stems, stiffer more angular branching and
larger flowers and flower clusters. The colour
is also deeper, carmine in bud and quite a
deep rose when the flowers first open though
they pale later. It does not form thickets as
freely as *V. farreri*.

henryi *2–3m. (6–10ft)* *White*
E. Summer *E T H L S*

China. A very distinctive evergreen species,
open and erect in habit, with long shining
green leaves and cone-shaped sprays of small
white flowers which are followed by berries,
at first red but later becoming black. This is a
handsome June-flowering shrub.

x juddii *2–2.5m. (6–8ft)* *White* *Spring*
D O H L

This is one of the best deciduous hybrids from
V. carlesii, with *V. bitchiuense* as the other
parent. It makes a larger bush than *V. carlesii*
with more slender stems and in some gardens
it succeeds better. The flower clusters, pink in
bud but opening white, are freely produced
and very fragrant.

lantana *3–4m. (10–13ft)* *White*
L. Spring *E. Summer* *D T H A L S*

Europe (including Britain). This is the
Wayfaring Tree, an attractive large shrub
with broadly heart-shaped leaves, slightly

domed clusters of small creamy-white flowers
followed by berries which are first red but
soon change to black. The leaves often colour
attractively before they fall. This is an
especially good shrub for limy and chalky
soils.

macrocephalum *2–3m. (6–10ft)* *White*
L. Spring *ED O H A L*

China. The form cultivated in gardens is
sterile and so has the 'snowball', type of
flower-head entirely composed of
white-petalled sterile flowers. It is a
handsome plant but not, unfortunately, a very
hardy one and in many places it needs to be
trained against a wall to preserve it from frost
damage. It has handed on some of its flower
quality to the hybrid *V. x carlcephalum*,
which also has the advantage of some
fragrance.

opulus *3–4m. (10–13ft)* *White*
E. Summer *D T H A L*

Europe (including Britain), Asia, N. Africa.
This is the native 'Guelder Rose', a fine shrub
that, were it not so common in the
countryside, would certainly be highly
esteemed in gardens. It makes a large,
angularly branched bush with maple-like
leaves, flat heads of 'lace-cap' flowers
followed by shining red berries and, as an
additional bonus, the leaves usually colour
pleasantly before they fall in autumn. There is
a much shorter, bushier form named
'Compactum' and another, named
'Xanthocarpum', with yellow berries. The
most popular garden form is 'Sterile', the
Snowball Tree, so called because all the
flowers are sterile and have white petals so
that they abandon their flat formation and
become ball-like clusters.

plicatum *2.5–3m. (8–10ft)   White*
E. Summer   D T H A L

China, Japan. This is one of those plants that first became known in a garden form, one with all-sterile flowers forming balls of white. It is to this form, known as the Japanese Snowball Tree, that the name *V. plicatum* belongs, and the wild type with 'lace-cap' flowers, in flat clusters, small and bead-like in the centre surrounded by a circle of white sterile flowers, came later and is distinguished as variety *tomentosum*. It is as beautiful as the sterile form, its large clusters being held erect along the mainly horizontal branches. Specially good forms are 'Mariesii', 'Lanarth' and 'Rowallane', and really there is little to choose between them.

rhytidophyllum *3–4m. (10–13ft)   Cream*
L. Spring   E O H A S

China. Most gardeners will be content to grow this as a foliage plant for its very large deeply-veined leaves not unlike some of the large-leaved rhododendrons, and with the advantage that this is a shrub that will thrive in limy soils. However, the flowers are moderately effective, more so in variety 'Roseum' in which they are a rather dull pink, and if several bushes are planted fairly close together for cross-pollination there will also be crops of berries, at first bright red, later black.

sargentii *2.5–3m. (8–10ft)   White*
Summer   D T H A S

Asia. A big shrub much like *V. opulus* but possibly a little superior to it in decorative merit. Its berries are normally currant-red but there is a yellow-berried variety named 'Flavum'.

tinus *2–3m. (6–10ft)   White*
Winter Spring   E O K H A S L

Mediterranean region. This is the shrub popularly known as Laurustinus, a favourite evergreen in the nineteenth century but

somewhat neglected in recent years. It makes a densely branched, dome-shaped bush, well covered in leaves and bearing clusters of small flowers which are reddish in bud but white when they open. The buds are already there in autumn and some will start to open directly there are a few warm days. The main flowering is in March and April and the variety *lucidum*, which has glossier leaves than the species, scarcely ever opens any of its flowers before March. *V. tinus* grows well by the sea, makes a good windbreak and can be clipped as a hedge. A variety named 'Eve Price' has pale pink flowers and an even denser habit than the species. There is also a variety with cream-splashed leaves named 'Variegatum'.

utile *1.2–2m. (4–6ft)   White   L. Spring*
E O H A S

China. This is the parent, with *V. carlesii*, of *V. burkwoodii* and it is from *V. utile* that the hybrid gets its more open habit and evergreen leaves. For some reason *V. utile* itself does not appear to have become so popular but it is a very decorative shrub, with tightly packed clusters of sweetly scented flowers typical of this spring flowering group.

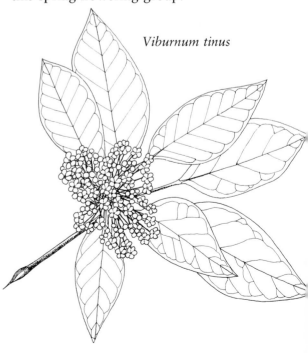

Viburnum tinus

VINCA, Apocynaceae. Periwinkle. Sprawling evergreens with long slender runners, more like those of a herbaceous perennial than a shrub, which root wherever they touch the soil. In this way periwinkles spread rapidly and make splendid ground cover where there is room for them. They will grow in all kinds of soil, in sun or shade. They do not require any pruning but they may need to be chopped back with a spade from time to time to prevent them spreading where they are not wanted. Any pieces dug up with roots can be replanted elsewhere, if required.

major   *Trailing   Blue*
Spring   E. Summer   E   V

Europe, North Africa. This is the Greater Periwinkle, so called because it is bigger in all its parts than *V. minor*. Its leaves somewhat resemble those of privet and its flowers are quite large star-shaped and violet-blue. There is an excellent cream-variegated variety named 'Variegata'.

minor   *Trailing   Blue*
Spring   E. Summer   E   V

Europe, western Asia. The Lesser Periwinkle is a more manageable plant than *V. major* since it does not spread so far nor so fast. It is smaller in leaf and flower and it has produced a number of good varieties. 'Alba' has white flowers and 'Gertrude Jekyll' is a specially good selection of it. 'Azurea Flore Pleno' has double blue flowers, 'Bowles' Variety' is single, and clear blue, and 'Multiplex' has double purple flowers. There are also two varieties with variegated leaves, 'Aureovariegata', leaves splashed with yellow, and 'Variegata', splashed with ivory white.

VITEX, Verbenaceae. Chaste Tree. The only species likely to be seen in British gardens requires the protection of a south-facing wall in most places. It will grow in most fertile well-drained soils but needs sun and warmth to ripen its growth. It can be pruned quite hard in March, the previous year's stems

shortened to 3–4cm./1–2in. and dead, damaged or weak growth cut out. The new growth that follows this pruning can be spread out fanwise if it is to be trained against a wall. Increase is by summer cuttings in a propagator.

agnus-castus   *3–4m. (10–13ft)   Violet blue*
Autumn   D   C   H

Mediterranean region. An open-branched bush with five-parted leaves and slender spikes of tubular violet-blue flowers which are sweetly scented. It is valuable for its late flowering. There is a white-flowered variety named 'Alba'.

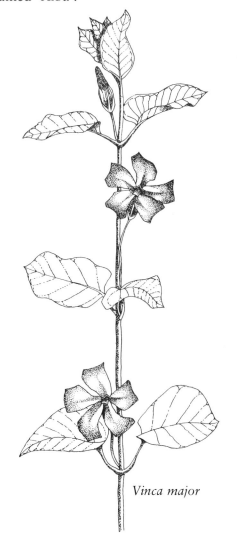

Vinca major

VITIS, Vitaceae. Vine. Grape vines are themselves often planted for ornament but in addition there are several species that are solely of value as decorative climbers. All climb by means of tendrils, which must have some fairly slender support such as wires, trellis work or the twigs of a tree. Most will grow in any reasonably well-drained soil and have a special liking for those containing lime or chalk. They can be allowed to go their own way or can be restricted to a few main stems carrying side-growths which are then considerably shortened, even to as little as 3 or 4cm./1–2in. each winter. Stems that are growing too far can also be shortened a little in summer. Vines can be increased by cuttings of ripened growth in a frame in the autumn. Single growth buds, cut with a few centimetres of stem, will also root in peat and sand in autumn or winter. Vines can also be layered in autumn.

coignetiae   *6–12m. (20–40ft)   Green Summer   D C H L*

Japan. Not only is this species extremely vigorous but it has exceptionally large leaves, rounded and not deeply lobed like most vines and up to 30cm./1ft in diameter. In autumn they turn red and crimson before they fall and this vine is then among the most spectacular of all climbing plants.

vinifera   *3–6m. (10–20ft)   Green E. Summer   D C H L*

Caucasus. This is the grape vine cultivated mainly for its fruit and with a great many commercially important varieties. Those most suitable for use as decorative climbers are 'Apifolia', also known as 'Laciniosa', with deeply cut leaves; 'Brandt', really of hybrid origin, which produces good crops of black grapes and has leaves that become crimson and purple before they fall in autumn; 'Incana', leaves covered with grey down; and 'Purpurea', known as the 'Teinturier Grape', with reddish-purple leaves that become even darker as they age.

Weigela florida 'Variegata'

WEIGELA, Caprifoliaceae. Easily grown deciduous shrubs flowering in late spring and early summer. They are not at all fussy about soil and will grow in shade but will flower more freely in full sun. They are all excellent town garden shrubs little affected by air pollution. Pruning should be done after flowering when old stems, including those that have flowered, can be cut out to make room for the young growth that will flower the following year. Increase is by summer or autumn cuttings.

floribunda   *1.2–2.5m. (4–8ft)   Red L. Spring   E. Summer   D F H A*

Japan. A slender-stemmed shrub with funnel-shaped, deep red flowers in clusters along the previous year's branches.

florida   *1.2–2.5m. (4–8ft)   Pink*
L. Spring   E. Summer   D F H A

China, Korea. Much like W. *floribunda* but very variable in habit and with mainly pink flowers. There is a variety named 'Foliis Purpureis', which is relatively dwarf and compact and has purplish leaves, and a very good variegated variety named 'Variegata', which makes a large upstanding bush and has a wide creamy-white border to every leaf.

praecox   *1.2–2m. (4–6ft)   Pink   L. Spring*
D F H A S

Korea. Shorter than the two foregoing species and flowering a week or so earlier.

Weigela Hybrids

There are many of these derived from the three species named above and showing all their characteristics in various combinations. Typical of these are 'Abel Carriere', a rather large shrub with pink flowers; 'Bristol Ruby', 'Eva Rathke' and 'Newport Red', all deep carmine; 'Mont Blanc', white; and 'Looymansii Aurea', pink flowers and light yellow leaves.

WISTERIA, Leguminosae. Wistaria. Twiners with fine trails of small pea-type flowers in late spring and early summer. The very vigorous kinds, such as W. *sinensis*, are impossible to prune if allowed to ascend trees or otherwise extend to their full extent but when trained on walls, pergolas or screens it is almost essential to restrict them. This can be done by shortening all side-growths to above five leaves in July and, if time permits, cutting them back still more to 4 or 5cm./ 2–3in., in autumn or winter. Increase is by seeds (but seedlings can sometimes give poorly flowering plants), by late autumn cuttings in a frame or by layering in spring or autumn.

floribunda   *3–6m. (10–20ft)   Violet blue*
L. Spring   E. Summer   D P S A L

Japan. This is the least rampant of the species and by spur-pruning almost from the outset it can be made into a wide-spreading, almost self-supporting bush or a tree-like standard. The scented flowers are carried in long trails which in the variety 'Macrobotrys' (also known as 'Multijuga') may measure as much as 1m./3ft. There are several other varieties including 'Alba', white; 'Rosea', lilac-pink; and 'Violacea Plena', double violet-blue. Newer varieties introduced from Japan are 'Pink Ice', dark rosy-pink; 'Peaches and Cream', rosy-pink in bud opening nearly white; 'Snow Showers', white and late-flowering; 'Reindeer', white; 'Purple Patches', violet-purple and 'Domino', lilac-blue.

sinensis   *10–30m. (33–100ft)   Violet*
L. Spring   D P A L S

China. The most rampant of all the wistarias and one that can easily mount to the top of a tall tree. Its vigour can be embarassing in a garden and though it is often planted on house walls this is not really wise because its long stems choke gutters and find their way under tiles and into lofts. It varies a good deal in quality of colour, some forms being a rather pale slatey-blue. There is a white variety named 'Alba', a double pinkish variety named 'Plena' and a magnificent double, deep blue-purple variety named 'Black Dragon'. All forms are scented.

venusta   *5–9m. (16–30ft)   White*
L. Spring   D P A L S

China. The notable feature of this species is the size of the individual flowers but they are not carried in very long trails nor are they strongly scented. Though this white-flowered form carries the specific name it is not the wild species, which is violet-coloured and is distinguished as variety *violacea*.

YUCCA, Liliaceae. Adam's Needle. Not even the palms give a more immediately exotic appearance to a garden than the yuccas, with their fine rosettes of sword-shaped leaves and stiffly upstanding flower-stems bearing quite large drooping flowers. Several are much hardier than they appear and most succeed in town gardens as well as by the sea. They like warm sunny places and well-drained soils but are not otherwise fussy. No pruning is possible other than the removal of dead flower stems. Plants can be raised from seed, by root cuttings and some kinds by removing rooted offsets or 'toes' in spring.

filamentosa   *1m. (3ft)   Creamy-white Summer   E S R V*

South-eastern USA. One of the hardiest kinds, stemless and spreading by offsets, with flower spikes up to 2m./6ft in length and leaves edged with thread-like filaments. There is a variety with cream-variegated leaves named 'Variegata'.

flaccida   *1m. (3ft)   Creamy-white Summer   E S R V*

South-eastern USA. Much like *Y. filamentosa* and much confused with it. The most obvious difference is in the leaves, which are not held stiffly but bend downwards about mid-way. There is a specially fine-flowered variety named 'Ivory'.

gloriosa   *1.2–2.5m. (4–8ft) Creamy-white   Summer   E. Autumn E S R V*

South-eastern USA. This handsome species forms a short main stem or trunk on which several rosettes of leaves may be carried. The leaves themselves are spine-tipped and this is the species commonly called Adam's Needle in Britain, though in America the name appears to be applied to *Y. filamentosa*, and *Y. gloriosa* is called the Spanish Dagger or Palm Lily. It is not as hardy as the two foregoing species. It has a cream-variegated variety named 'Variegata'.

whipplei   *1m. (3ft)   Cream and purple L. Spring   E. Summer   E S R V*

California. Arguably the most handsome of all the yuccas that can be grown outdoors in Britain but it is suitable only for the mildest places since it will not survive much frost. It is stemless and spreads by offsets. The stiff leaves are very sharp-pointed and the flower-stems can tower to a height of around 3m./10ft. The flowers may be creamy-white throughout or purple-flushed and are always scented.

ZENOBIA, Ericaceae. A beautiful evergreen shrub for acid soils. It thrives under precisely the same conditions as those that suit rhododendrons and can be pruned after flowering by cutting out the old flowering stems and also any weak growth. Increase is by seed in peat and sand, by late summer cuttings in a propagator or by layering in spring.

pulverulenta   *1.2–2m. (4–6ft)   White E. Summer   ED F S H L*

South-eastern USA. A shrub with rather slender arching stems, shallowly toothed grey-green leaves and bell-shaped white flowers in small clusters along the stems. There is a variety named *nuda* with green leaves.

10 Plants for special purposes

Various Kinds of Climbers

Self-clinging Plants. These can attach themselves to any firm surface, such as a wall or tree trunk, by aerial roots or adhesive pads.

Campsis radicans
Ercilla volubilis (may require some extra
    assistance)
Euonymus fortunei radicans
Hedera canariensis and varieties
    colchica and varieties
    helix and varieties
Hydrangea petiolaris
Ficus pumila
Parthenocissus henryana
    quinquefolia
    tricuspidata
Pileostegia viburnoides
Schizophragma hydrangeoides
    integrifolia

Twining Plants. These wind themselves around branches, poles, pillars, trellis, strained wires or any other support that is not too thick.

Actinidia chinensis
    kolomikta
    moupinense
Akebia quinata
    trifoliata
Aristolochia heterophylla
    macrophylla
Berberidopsis corallina
Billardiera longiflora
Celastrus orbiculatus
Holboellia coriacea
    latifolia

Jasminum officinale
Lapageria rosea
Lonicera x *americana*
    x *brownii*
    caprifolium
    etrusca
    hildebrandiana
    japonica
    periclymenum
    sempervirens
    x *tellmanniana*
    tragophylla
Muehlenbeckia complexa
Periploca graeca
Polygonum baldschuanicum
Trachelospermum asiaticum
    jasminoides
Wisteria floribunda
    sinensis
    venusta

Tendril Climbers. These plants have thin tendrils which wind themselves around suitably slender supports such as twigs, wire and trellis.

Bignonia capreolata
Clematis alpina
    armandii
    chrysocoma
    durandii
    flammula
    florida
    grata grandidenta
    x *jackmanii*
    x *jouiniana*
    lanuginosa
    macropetala
    montana

orientalis
paniculata
patens
rehderana
tangutica
texensis
vitalba
viticella
many garden hybrids.
Eccremocarpus scaber
Mutisia decurrens
oligodon
Parthenocissus inserta
Passiflora coerulea
Solanum jasminoides
Vitis coignetiae
vinifera

Shrubby Climbers. These plants are not natural climbers but can be readily trained against walls, fences, etc. and in some cases may be almost entirely self-supporting because of the rigid nature of their stems. Others may require a few ties to hold them back and place their stems where they are required.

Abutillon x suntense
vitifolium
Acacia pravissima
riceana
Azara integrifolia
microphylla
Camellia reticulata
Ceanothus arboreus
dentatus
griseus
impressus
rigidus
thyrsiflorus
x veitchianus
most evergreen garden hybrids
Cestrum elegans
newellii
parqui
Chaenomeles speciosa
x superba
Chimonanthus praecox

Cotoneaster horizontalis
microphyllus
Crinodendron hookeranum
pantagua
Cytisus batandieri
x Fatshedera lizei
Forsythis suspensa
Garrya elliptica
Jasminum mesneyi
nudiflorum
Magnolia delavayi
grandiflora
Pyracantha angustifolia
atalantioides
coccinea
crenato-serrata
rogersiana
all garden hybrids
Sophora microphylla
tetraptera
Vitax agnus-castus

Thrusters. These push their long stems through other shrubs or trees, often holding on by thorns.

Rosa anemoniflora
banksiae
bracteata
brunonii
filipes
gigantea
helenae
laevigata
longicuspis
moschata
multiflora
sinowilsonii
wichuraiana
hybrid climbers and ramblers
Rubus laciniatus
phoenocolasius
Solanum crispum

Shrubs to Grow as Individual Specimens

Acer japonicum and varieties
    palmatum and varieties
Aralia elata and varieties
Berberis darwinii
    jamesiana
    x *stenophylla*
Camellia japonica varieties
    williamsii varieties
Clerodendron trichotomum
Clethra alnifolia
Cornus alternifolia 'Argentea'
    florida
    kousa
Corylopsis sinensis
    spicata
    willmottiae
Cotinus coggygria and varieties
Cotoneaster conspicuus
    dielsianus
    franchetii
    frigidus
    henryanus
    lacteus
    pannosus
    salicifolius
Elaeagnus pungens 'Aurea' and 'Maculata'
Embothrium coccineum and varieties
Fatsia japonica
Genista aetnensis
Hamamellis mollis
Hoheria glabrata
    lyallii
Hydrangea aspera
    sargentiana
Ilex (all kinds)
Kalmia latifolia
Laurus azorica
    nobilis
Magnolia denudata
    liliiflora
    loebneri
    sieboldii
    sinensis

    x *soulangiana*
    stellata
    wilsonii
Mahonia acanthifolia
    bealei
    japonica
    lomariifolia
    x *media*
    pinnata
Olearia macrodonta
Paeonia delavayi
    lutea
Philadelphus coronarius 'Aureus'
    delavayi
    'Beauclerk'
    'Belle Étoile'
    'Burfordiensis'
    'Enchantment'
    'Virginal'
Photinia x *fraseri*
    serrulata
Pieris formosa and varieties
    japonica
Pittosporum eugenoides and varieties
    tenuifolium and varieties
Rhododendron arboreum
    auriculatum
    calophytum
    decorum
    discolor
    falconeri
    fictolacteum
    grande
    macabeanum
    orbiculare
    sinogrande
    sutchuenense
    williamsianum
Spiraea canescens
    cantoniensis 'Flore Pleno'
    prunifolia
    x *vanhouttei*
    veitchii
Stachyurus colchica
    holocarpa
Stuartia melacodendron
    sinensis

Styrax japonica
    obassia
Viburnum betulifolium
    plicatum
    tomentosum
    rhytidophyllum

Ground Cover Shrubs

Calluna vulgaris varieties
Ceratostigma willmottianum
Cotoneaster adpressus
    dameri
    horizontalis
    microphyllus and varieties
    salicifolius 'Herbstfeur',
        'Parkpeppich' and 'Repens'
Cytisus purpureus
Daboecia cantabrica
Daphne laureola
    pontica
Erica carnea and varieties
    ciliaris and varieties
    cinerea and varieties
    x *darleyensis*
    tetralix and varieties
    vagans and varieties
    x *watsonii*
Euonymus fortunei radicans
Gaultheria procumbens
Genista sagittalis
    tinctoria and variety 'Plena'
Hebe pinguifolia 'Pagei'
Hedera canariensis and varieties
    helix and varieties
Helianthemum nummularium and varieties
Hypericum calycinum
Juniperus horizontalis and varieties
    procumbens
Mahonia repens
Microbiota decussata
Ononis fruticosa
Pachysandra terminalis and varieties
Parahebe cataractae
    lyallii
Pernettya prostrata
Rhododendron forrestii repens

Rosa x *paulii*
    'Max Graf'
    setigera
Salix herbacea
    repens
Vaccineum vitis-idaea
Vinca major
    minor

Variegated shrubs

White or Cream

Actinidia kolomikta
Aralia elata 'Variegata'
Buddleia davidii 'Harlequin'
    'Variegated Regal Red'
Buxus sempervirens 'Argentea'
    'Elegantissima'
Cornus alba 'Elegantissima'
    alternifolia 'Argentea'
Coronilla glauca 'Variegata'
Euonymus fortunei 'Silver Queen' and
    'Variegatus'
    japonicus 'Albo-marginatus'
Fatsia japonica 'Albo-marginata'
Fuchsia magellanica 'Variegata'
Hebe x 'Andersonii variegata'
    x *franciscana* 'Variegata'
Hedera canariensis 'Gloire de Marengo'
    helix 'Adam', 'Glacier' and
    'Marginata elegantissima'
Hydrangea macrophylla 'Maculata'
Hypericum x *moserianum* 'Tricolor'
Ilex aquifolium 'Argenteo marginata',
    'Argentea medio-picta'
    'Argentea pendula', 'Handsworth
    New Silver' and 'Silver Queen'
Juniperus chinensis 'Plumosus albovariegata'
Kerria japonica 'Variegata'
Leucothoe fontanesiana 'Rainbow'
Ligustrum ovalifolium 'Argentea'
Ligustrum sinense 'Variegatum'
Pachysandra terminalis 'Variegata'
Pieris japonica 'Variegata'
Pittosporum eugenoides 'Variegatum'
    tenuifolium 'Silver Queen'

Prunus lusitanica 'Variegata'
Rhamnus alaternus 'Argenteo variegata'
Sambucus nigra 'Albo variegatus'
Viburnum tinus 'Variegatum'
Vinca major 'Variegata'
 minor 'Variegata'
Weigela florida 'Variegata'

Yellow or Yellow and Green

Abutilon megapotamicum 'Variegatum'
Acer palmatum 'Aureum'
Aralia elata 'Aureovariegata'
Aucuba japonica 'Crotonifolia'
 'Sulphurea'
Buxus sempervirens 'Aurea pendula', 'Aureo
 variegata' and 'Gold Tip'
Calluna vulgaris 'Aurea', 'Gold Haze' and
 'Serlei aurea'
Cassinia fulvida (natural colour)
Cornus alba 'Spaethii'
Daphne odora 'Aureo-marginata'
Erica cinerea 'Golden Drop'
Elaeagnus pungens 'Aurea' and 'Maculata'
Euonymus japonicus 'Aureus', Duc d'Anjou'
 and 'Ovatus Aureus'
Griselinia littoralis 'Variegata'
Hebe x *andersonii 'Variegata'*
 ochracea (natural colour)
Hedera colchica 'Dentata variegata'
 helix 'Buttercup' and 'Goldheart'
Ilex x *altaclarensis 'Golden King',*
 aquifolium 'Golden Queen'
 and 'Madame Briot'
Juniperus chinensis 'Old Gold' and 'Plumosa
 aurea'
Ligustrum ovalifolium 'Aureum'
Lonicera japonica 'Aureo-reticulata'
 'Baggesen's Gold'
Philadelphus coronarius 'Aureus'
Pittosporum tenuifolium 'Warnham Gold'
Ribes sanguineum 'Brocklebankii'
Sambucus canadensis 'Aurea'
 nigra 'Aurea'
 racemosa 'Plumosa Aurea'
Spiraea x *japonica 'Goldflame'*
Symphoricarpos orbiculatus 'Variegatus'
Vinca minor 'Aureovariegata'

Grey and Silver-Leaved Shrubs

Atriplex canescens
 halimus
Buddleia crispa
 fallowiana
 x *'Lochinch'*
Caryopteris x *clandonensis*
 incana
 mongolica
Cistus albidus
 creticus
 crispus
 x *pulverulentus*
 x *skanbergii*
Convolvulus cneorum
Coronilla glauca
Cytisis battandieri
Elaeagnus angustifolius
 x *ebbingei*
 macrophylla
 umbellata
Erica tetralix 'Con Underwood'
Erinacea anthyllis
Euonymus fortunei 'Variegatus'
Euryops acreus
Fuchsia magellancia 'Versicolor'
Hedera helix 'Glacier' and 'Marginata
 elegantissima'
Helianthemum nummularium (some
 varieties)
 Helichrysum splendidum
Hippophae rhamnoides
Helichrysum splendidum
Hippophae rhamnoides
Juniperus chinensis 'Blaauw' and 'Globosa
 cinerea'
 communis 'Compressa' and
 'Hibernica'
 horizontalis 'Bar Harbour', 'Douglasii',
 'Glauca', and 'Wiltonii'
 sabina 'Tamariscifolia'
Lavandula angustifolia
 dentata
 latifolia
 stoechas
Leonotis leonurus
Lycium chinense

Olearia avicennifolia
   moschata
   phlogopappa
   x *scilloniensis*
Perovskia atriplicifolia
Phlomis chrysophylla
   fruticosa
   samia
Pittosporum tenuifolium 'James Stirling' and
   'Silver Queen'
Potentilla arbuscula 'Beanii'
   fruticosa 'Vilmoriniana'
Rosa alba
   rubrifolia
Rubus cockburnianus (stems)
Salix acutifolis (stems)
   aegyptiaca (stems)
   elaeagnos (young leaves)
   lanata (young leaves)
   repens (young leaves)
Santolina chamaecyparissus
   neapolitana
Senecio compactus
   greyii
   laxifolius
   monroi
Teucrium fruticans
Vitis vinifera 'Incana'
Zenobia pulverulenta

Pink, Red, Purple and Bronze-Leaved Shrubs

Acer palmatum 'Atropurpureum',
   'Dissectum atropurpureum' and
   'Heptalobum rubrum'
Actinidia kolomikta
Berberis thunbergii 'Atropurpurea',
   'Atropurpurea nana', 'Bagatelle',
   'Erecta' and 'Rose Glow'
   vulgaris 'Purpurea'
Coitinus coggygria 'Foliis purpureis',
   'Notcutt's Variety' and 'Royal Purple'

Hypericum x *moserianum* 'Tricolor'
Leucothoe fontanesiana 'Rainbow'
Photinia x *fraseri* (young leaves)
   serrulata (young leaves)
Pieris formosa 'Wakehurst' and
   'Charles Mitchell' (young leaves)
   x 'Forest Flame' (young leaves)
Pittosporum tenuifolium 'Purpureum'
Prunus 'Cistena'
Sambucus nigra 'Purpurea'
Vitis vinifera 'Purpurea'
Weigela florida 'Foliis purpureis'

Berries and Other Ornamental Fruits

Akebia quinata
   trifoliata
Arbutus unedo
Aronia arbutifolia
   melanocarpa
Aucuba japonica (female forms)
Berberis aggregata
   buxifolia
   candidula
   x *carminea*
   concinna
   darwinii
   empetrifolia
   gagnepainii
   glaucocarpa
   hakeoides
   hookeri
   jamesiana
   julianae
   linearifolia
   prattii
   pruinosa
   x *rubrostilla*
   sargentiana
   temolaica
   thunbergii
   vulgaris
   wilsoniae

Callicarpa bodinieri
    japonica
Celastrus orbiculatus
Chaenomeles japonica
    speciosa
    x *superba*
Clematis flammula
    orientalis
    tangutica
Clerodendrum trichotomum
Colutea arborescens
    x *media*
    orientalis
Cotinus coggygria
Cotoneaster adpressus
    buxifolius
    congestus
    conspicuus
    dammeri
    dielsianus
    franchetii
    frigidus
    henryanus
    horizontalis
    lacteus
    microphyllus
    pannosus
    prostratus
    salicifolius
    simonsii
Daphne mezereum
Decaisnea fargesii
Euonymus europaeus
    latifolius
    planipes
    yedoensis
Garrya elliptica (female form)
Gaultheria miqueliana
    procumbens
Hedera colchica (adult form)
    helix (adult form)
Hippophae rhamnoides (female form)
Hypericum androsemum
    x *inodorum*
Ilex x *altaclarensis* (female forms)
    helix (female forms)
    cornuta (female forms)
    crenata (female forms)

    opaca (female forms)
      perado (female forms)
      pernyi (female forms)
      verticillata (female forms)
Leycesteria formosa
Ligustrum vulgare
Lycium chinense
Magnolia sieboldii
    sinensis
    wilsonii
Mahonia aquifolium
    pinnata
    repens
    undulata
Pernettya mucronata
    prostrata
Prunus spinosa laurocerasus
Pyracantha angustifolia
    atalantioides
    coccinea
    crenato-serrata
    rogersiana
    garden hybrids
Rhus aromatica
    corallina
    glabra
    typhina
Rosa eglanteria
    helenae
    hugonis
    moyesii
    mutibracteata
    multiflora
    rubrifolia
    rugosa
    setipoda
    soulieana
    villosa
    virginiana
    willmottiae
Rubus illecebrosus
    laciniatus
    phoenicolasius
    spectabilis
Ruscus aculeatus (female forms)
Sambucus canadensis
    nigra
    racemosa

Skimmia japonica (female forms)
      reevesiana
Stransvaesia davidiana
Symphoricarpos albus
      x *chenaultii*
      'Doorenbos hybrids'
      orbiculatus
      rivularis
Vaccineum corymbosum
      cylindraceum
      vitis-idaea
Viburnum alnifolium
      betulifolium
      davidii
      dilatatum
      henryi
      lantana
      opulus
      rhytidophyllum
Vitis vinifera

Shrubs for Autumn Colour

Acer japonicum
      palmatum
Amelanchier canadensis
      laevis
      lamarckii
      ovalis
      stolonifera
Aronia arbutifolia
      melanocarpa
Berberis jamesiana
      thunbergii
      wilsoniae
Callicarpa bodinieri
      japonica
Calluna vulgaris 'Aurea' and 'Robert
      Chapman'
Cotinus coggygria
      obovatus
Cotoneaster horizontalis
      franchetii sternianus
Disanthus cercidifolius

Euonymus alatus
      europaeus
      latifolius
      planipes
      yedoensis
Fothergilla major
Hamamelis x *intermedia*
      japonica
      mollis
      vernalis
      virginica
Lindera obtusiloba
Parthenocissus henryana
      inserta
      quinquefolia
      tricuspidata
Rhododendron luteum and many hybrid
      azaleas
Rhus copallina
      glabra
      radicans
      typhina
Vaccineum arctostaphylos
      corymbosum
Vitis coignetiae

Bibliography

Bailey, L.H., *Hortus Third*. Macmillan, 1976.

Bean, W.J., *Trees and Shrubs Hardy in the British Isles*. 8th edition, John Murray, 1970–80.

Brown, George E., *The Pruning of Trees, Shrubs and Climbers*. Faber and Faber, 1972.

Flora Europaea, Vols 1–3. Cambridge University Press, 1969–72.

Harrison, Richmond E., *Trees and Shrubs for the Southern Hemisphere*. Reed, 1967.

Hay, Roy and Synge, Patrick M. *The Dictionary of Garden Plants in Colour*. Ebury Press and Michael Joseph, 1969.

Hillier, H.G., *Hillier's Manual of Trees and Shrubs*. David and Charles, 1972.

Makins, F.K., *The Identification of Trees and Shrubs*. Dent, 1967.

Mitchell, Alan, *A Field Guide to the Trees of Britain and Northern Europe*. Collins, 1974.

Royal Horticultural Society, *Dictionary of Gardening*. Oxford University Press. 1951. Supplement 1969.

Royal Horticultural Society, *Rhododendron Handbooks*, Parts 1 and 2, 1969.

Thomas, Graham Stuart, *Shrub Roses of Today*. Dent, 3rd edition 1967.

Thomas, Graham Stuart, *The Old Shrub Roses*. Dent, revised edition 1979.

Thomas, Graham Stuart, *Climbing Roses Old and New*. Dent, revised edition 1978.

Willis, J.C., *A Dictionary of the Flowering Plants and Ferns*. Cambridge University Press, 1966.

Wyman, Donald, *Wyman's Gardening Encyclopaedia*. Macmillan, 1971.

Index

Abelia 22
Abutilon 23
Acacia 24–5
   False 191
Acanthopanax 25–6
   spinosus, see *A. sieboldianus* 25
Acer 26–7
   palmatum 2, 26
Acidity, Rectification of 3
Actinidia 27
Adam's Needle 234
Aerial roots 2, 46, 113, 120, 162, 211, 235
Aesculus 27
Age of growth, Estimating 14
Air layering 19
Akebia 28
Albizzia 28
Alexandrian Laurel 78
Alkaline soil 3
Alkalinity, Rectification of 3
Allspice 43
Almond 168, 170
Amelanchier 28–9
   x *grandiflora*, see *A. lamarckii* 29
   vulgaris, see *A. ovalis* 29
American Currant 191
American Witch Hazel 99
Andromeda 29
Angelica Tree 29
Apple Berry 38
Apricot 168
Aralia 29–30
   Japanese 96
Arbutus 30
Aristolochia 30–1
   durior, see *A. macrophylla* 31
   sipho, see *A. macrophylla* 31
Aronia 31
Aster 31
Atriplex 31–2
   halimus as windbreak 9
Aucuba 32–3
Azalea 3, 173
   'Balsaminiflorum' 179
   'Crispiflorum' 179
   Exbury Hybrids 188
   flower bud formation 15
   Gable Hybrids 188
   Ghent Hybrids 188
   Glen Dale Hybrids 188
   'Gumpo' 179
   Indian 179, 185, 186
   Kaempferi Hybrids 180, 188

   Knaphill Hybrids 183, 188
   Kurume 180, 188
   Malvaticum Hybrids 188
   Mollis Hybrids 179, 182, 188
   Occidentale Hybrids 183, 188
   Rustica Hybrids 188
   seed, time of sowing 16
Azara 33

Balling 5–6
Bamboo, Heavenly 148
Barberry 34
Bayberry 147
Beauty Bush 130
Beech for hedges 9
Bellflower, Chilean 131
Bell-heather 89
Benomyl 7
Berberidopsis 33–4
Berberis 34–8
   aristata, see *B. glaucocarpa* 35
   'Barbarossa' 35
   'Buccaneer' 35
   for hedges 9
   'Pirate King' 35
   polyantha, see *B. prattii* 37
   'Sparkler' 35
Bignonia 38
Billardiera 38–9
Blackberry, Fern-leaved or
   Cut-leaved 204
Black spot 7
Blackthorn 169
Bladder Nut 218
   Senna 65
Blueberry 226
Blue Spruce 48
Bog Rosemary 29
Bootlace fungus 7
Boston Ivy 2, 154–5
Bottle Brush 42
Box 40
   Christmas 210
   for hedges 9
   Thorn 142
   Trimming 15
Bramble 2, 203–5
Bridal Wreath 216
Broom 75, 103
   Montpelier 76
   Mount Etna 104
   Spanish 215
   Warminster 77
   White Spanish 76

Buckthorn 172
Buddleia 39–40
   davidii, Pruning 15
   'Lochinch' 40
   seed, Time of sowing 16
Buffalo Currant 191
Bupleurum 40
Buplever 40
Bush Clover 135
Butcher's Broom 205–6
Butterfly Bush 39
Buxus 40–1
   sempervirens for hedges 9

Caesalpinia 41
Calcium carbonate 3
Californian Allspice 44
   Lilac 2, 50
Callicarpa 41
   giraldii, see *C. bodinieri* 41
Callistemon 42
Calluna 3, 42–3
Calycanthus 43–4
Camellia 1, 2, 3, 44–6
   'Captain Rawes', see
     C. reticulata 45
Campsis 46
Capsid bugs 7
Caragana 47
Carolina Allspice 43
Carpentaria 47–8
Carpinus betulus for hedges 10
Caryopteris 48–9
   x *clandonensis*, Pruning 15
   mastacanthus, see *C. incana* 48
Cassia 49
Cassinia 49
Cassiope 49–50
Ceanothus 2, 50–2
   coeruleus, see *C.* x *delilianus* 50
   x *pallidus*, see *C.* x *delilianus* 51
Celastrus 52
Cephalotaxus 52
Ceratostigma 53
Cestrum 53–4
Chaenomeles 2, 54–5
   lagenaria, see *C. speciosa* 54
Chalk 3
Chamaecyparis lawsoniana for
   hedges 10
Chaste Tree 231
Cherry 168–9
   Laurel 168
   for hedges 10

Chilean Bellflower 131
  Hazel 105
Chimonanthus 55
Chinese Witch Hazel 108
Chionanthus 55–6
Choisya 56–7
Chokeberry 31
Christmas Box 210
Cinquefoil 167
Cistus 57–9
  incanus, see *C. creticus* 57
  'Blanche' 58
  hirsutus 106
  'Paladin' 58
  'Pat' 58
  psilosepalus 106
  C. villosus, see *C. creticus* 57
Clematis 2, 59–64
  'Ascotiensis' 64
  'Barbara Dibley' 63
  'Belle of Woking' 61
  'Comtesse de Bouchard' 61
  'Daniel Deronda' 63
  'Duchess of Albany' 63
  'Duchess of Edinburgh' 61
  'Ernest Markham' 64
  'Gravetye Beauty' 63
  'Henryi' 62
  'Lady Betty Balfour' 64
  'Lasustern' 64
  'Madame Boisselot' 63
  'Nelly Moser' 62
  'Perle d'Azure' 61
  'The President' 63
  'Ville de Lyon' 64
  'Vyvian Pennell' 63
Clerodendrum 64
Clethra 64
  seed, Time of sowing 16
Clianthus 64
Climbers, Shrubby 20
  Use of 2
  Method of ascent 2
Clover, Bush 135
Colletia 65
Colutea 65
Container grown plants 5–6
Convolvulus 66
Coral Berry 220
  Plant 33
Cornus 4, 66–7
  controversa 'Variegata' 67
Corokia 67–8
Coronilla 68
Correa 68–9
Corylopsis 69–70
Corylus 70–1
Cotinus 71
  americanus, see *C. obovatus* 71
Cotoneaster 71–4
  'Cornubia' 73
  for hedges 9–10
  horizontalis 2, 73
  'John Waterer' 73
  microphylla 2, 74
  'Rothschildiana' 73

rotundifolius, see *C. prostratus* 74
  x *watereri* 73
Cowberry 226
Cranberry 226
Crataegus monogyna for hedges 12
Crinodendron 74–5
Cross-leaved Heath 90
Cross Vine 38
Cupressocyparis for hedges 10
Cupressus for hedges 10
Currant 190–1
  Indian 200
Cuttings, Leaf 18
  Root 18
  Stem 17–8
Cydonia japonica, see Chaenomeles
  speciosa 54
Cypresses for hedges 10
  Trimming 15
Cytisus 75–8
  'Burkwoodii' 78
  'Donard Seedling' 76
  'Dorothy Walpole' 76
  'Johnson's Crimson' 76
  prostratus, see *C. scoparius* 77
  racemosus, see *C.* x *spachianus* 78
  stenopetalus 78

Daboecia 3, 78
  polifolia, see *D. cantabrica* 78
Daisy Bush 149
Danae 78–9
Daphne 79–81
  x *neapolitana*, see *D. collina* 79
Daphniphyllum 81
Datura 81
Decaisnea 81–2
Dendromecon 82
Desfontainea 82
Desmodium 82
Deutzia 82–4
  seed, Time of sowing 16
Dimethoate 7
Dipelta 84
Disanthus 84
Disease, Pruning out 13
Division 19
Dogwood 4, 66
Dorset Heath 89
Drainage 4
Drimys 84–5
  aromatica, see *D. lanceolata* 85
Dutchman's Pipe 30
Dyer's Greenweed 104

Eccremocarpus 85
Edgeworthia 85
Elaeagnus 86–7
Elder 4, 209
Elsholtzia 87
Embothrium 87–8
Enkianthus 2, 88
  seed, Time of sowing 16
Ephedra 88
Ercilla 88
Erica 3, 88–91

erigena, see *E. mediterranea* 90
  herbacea, see *E. carnea* 89
  seed, Time of sowing 16
Erinacea 91
Escallonia 91–2
  for hedges 10
  punctata, see *E. rubra* 92
  sanguinea, see *E. rubra* 92
Euonymus 92–4
  fortunei, 2, 93
  japonicus for hedges 10
  Trimming 15
Eupatorium 94
Euryops 94
Evergreens, Planting 6
Exochorda 95

Fabiana 95
Fagus sylvatica for hedges 9
Fatshedera 96
Feeding shrubs 6
  hedges 8
Feijoa 97
Ficus 97–8
Fig 97
  Climbing 98
Figleaf Palm 96
Filbert 70
Fireblight 71
Fire Bush 87
Firethorn 172
Flower buds, Time of formation 14–5
Flowering Currant 191
  season 4
Forsythia 98–9
Fothergilla 99
  monticola, see *F. major* 99
Foundation planting 2
Fremontia, see Fremontodendron 100
Fringe Tree 55
Fuchsia 100–2
Fuchsia-flowered Gooseberry 191
Fuchsia, Hardy Hybrids 102
  magellanica for hedges 10

Gale 147
Garrya 103
Gaultheria 103
Genista 103–4
  Florists' 76, 78
  fragrans 78
Germander 225
Gevuina 105
Glory Flower 85
  Pea 64
Golden Balls 98
Gooseberry 190–1
Gorse 226
  Spanish 104
Grafted shrubs, Pruning 13
Greenflies 7
Grevillea 105–6
Griselinia 106
  for hedges 10
Ground cover 3, 238
Guelder Rose 227, 229

Hakea 106
x Halimiocistus 106
Halimium 106–7
   commutatum, see *H. libanotis* 107
Hamamelis 107–8
Hazel 70
   Chilean 105
HCH 7
Heath 88–90
   St. Dabeoc's 78
   Tree 89–91
Heather 3, 42, 88
Heavenly Bamboo 148
Hebe 108–13
   armstrongii, see *H. ochracea* 111
   'Compacta', see *H. propinqua* 111
   for hedges 10
   lavaudiana, see *H.* x 'Fairfieldii' 110
   Garden Hybrids 112–3
   'Midsummer Beauty', see
      H. salicifolia 112
   salicornoides 'Aurea', see
      H. propinqua 111
Hedera 113–5
Hedgehog Broom 91
Hedge trimmers 15
Hedges 3, 8–9
   Informal 9
   of mixed shrubs 9
   Trimming 8–9
Hedysarum 115
Helianthemum 115
Helichrysum 115–6
Hercules Club 29
Hibiscus 116–7
Himalayan Honeysuckle 136
Hippophae 117
Hoheria 117
Holboellia 117–8
Holly 122–4
   for hedges 10
Honey fungus 7
Honeysuckle 139–41
   Dutch 140
   Fly 141
   Himalayan 136
   Perfoliate 139
   Scarlet Trumpet 139
   Trumpet 140
Hornbeam for hedges 10
Horse Chestnut 27
Hydrangea 118–20
   Climbing 2, 120, 163, 211
   macrophylla 2, 119
   paniculata, Pruning 15
   seed, Time of sowing 16
   villosa, see *H. aspera* 118
Hypericum 121–2
   hircinum, see *H.* x *inodorum* 122
   seed, Time of sowing 16

Ilex 122–4
   aquifolium for hedges 10
Illicium 124
Indian Currant 220
Indigofera 124–5

Island beds 3
Itea 125
Ivy 2, 113
   Boston 154–5

Japanese Aralia 96
   Maples 2, 26
   Quince 2, 54–5
   Wineberry 205
   Witch Hazel 108
Japonica 54
Jasmine 126–7
Jasminum 126–7
Jerusalem Sage 160
Jew's Mallow 130
Jovellana 127–8
Juniper 128–9
Juniperus 128–9

Kalmia 3, 129
   seed, Time of sowing 16
Kalmiopsis 129
Kangaroo Thorn 24
Karo 164
Kerria 130
Kolkwitzia 130–1
   seed, Time of sowing 16
Kowhai 214

Laburnum, Nepal 164
Lapageria 131
Laurel 131
   Alexandrian 78
   Cherry 169
   for hedges 10
   Portugal 169
Laurus 131
Laurustinus 230
   for hedges 10
Lavandula 131–2
   officinalis, see *L. angustifolia* 132
   spica, see *L. angustifolia* 132
Lavatera 133–4
Lavender 131
   Cotton 210
   for hedges 11
Layering 19
Leiophyllum 134
Lemon-scented Verbena 138
Leonitis 134
Leptospermum 134
Lespedeza 135
Leucothoe 135–6
   catesbaei, see *L. fontanesiana* 135
   seed, Time of sowing 16
Leycesteria 136
Ligustrum 136–7
   for hedges 11
Lilac 221–2
Lily of the valley Bush 162
Lime haters 3
Lime, Hydrated 3
Lindera 138
Ling 42
Lippia 138
Lobster Claw 64

Lomatia 139
Lonicera 139–41
   nitida for hedges 11
   trimming 15
Lupin 141
Lupinus 141
Lycium 142

Magnolia 142–4
   flower bud formation 15
   highdownensis, see *M. sinensis* 143
Mahonia 144–5
Mallow, Tree 135
Manuka 134
Maple 26
Mechanical trimmers 15
Menziesia 145–6
Mexican Orange Flower 56
Mice 16
Microbiota 146
Mimosa 24
Mint Bush 168
Mist propagation 17
Mock Orange 157
Moisture 4
Mountain Spurge 153
Moutan 154
Muehlenbeckia 146
Mutisia 146–7
Myrica 147
Myrobalan for hedges 11
Myrtle 147
   Sand 134
   South Sea 134
Myrtus 147–8

Nandina 148
Neillia 148–9
Notospartium 149
Nutallia, see Osmaronia 152

Old Man's Beard 60
Olearia 149–51
   cheesmanii 149
   gunniana, see *O. phlogopappa* 150
   stellulata, see *O. phlogopappa* 150
Oleaster 86
Ononis 151
Open ground plants 5–6
Orange, Hardy 166
Osmanthus 151–2
   x *burkwoodii* for hedges 11
   ilicifolius, see *O. heterophyllus* 152
Osmaronia 152
Oso Berry 152

Pachysandra 153
Paeonia 153–4
   x *lemoinei*, see *P. suffruticosa* 154
Parahebe 154
Parrot's Bill 64
Parthenocissus 2, 154–5
Passiflora 155
Passion Flower 155
Pea Tree 47
Peach 168

Penstemon 155–6
Peony 153
    Tree 153
Periploca 156
Periwinkle 231
Perlite 17
Pernettya 156–7
Perovskia 157
pH 3
Philadelphus 157–9
    grandiflorus, see *P. inodorus* and
        P. pubescens 158
    seed, Time of sowing 16
Phillyrea 159–60
    decorus, see Osmanthus *decorus* and
        O. x *burkwoodii* 151
Phlomis 160
Photinia 160–1
Phyllodoce 161
Physocarpus 161–2
Pieris 2, 3, 162–3
    seed, Time of sowing 16
Pileostegia 162–3
Pine 163–4
Pinus 163–4
Piptanthus 164
Pittosporum 164–5
    for hedges 11
Planting hedges 7
Plum 168
    Yew 52
Podocarpus 165–6
Poison Ivy 190
Polygala 166
Polygonum 166
Polythene bags for cuttings 17
Pomegranate 170
Poncirus 166–7
Poppy, Tree 82
Portugal Laurel 169
Potato Vine 213
Potentilla 167–8
    davurica, see *P. fruticosa*
        'Veitchii' 168
    seed, Time of sowing 17
Privet 136–7
    for hedges 11
    Trimming 15
Propagators 17
Prostanthera 168
Protection after planting 6
Pruning deciduous shrubs 14
    evergreens 14
    for mature growth 15
    hedges 7–8
    to preserve flower buds 14–5
    to prevent overcrowding 13
    to restrict size 14
Prunus 168–70
    cerasifera for hedges 11
    'Cistena' for hedges 11, 168
Punica 170–1
Pyracantha 2, 171–2
    for hedges 11

Quince, Japanese 54

Raphiolepis 172
Refrigerating seeds 16
Rhamnus 172
Rhododendron 1, 2, 3, 172–88
    'Alison Johnstone' 176, 187
    'Amoenum', see *R. kiusianum* 180–1
    'Angelo' 178
    'Ascot Brilliant' 185
    'Barclayi' 185
    'Beauty of Tremough' 178
    'Billy Budd' 177
    'Bric a Brac' 181
    'Cinnkeys' 180
    'Conroy' 176
    'Cornish Cross' 178, 185
    'Cowslip' 186, 187
    'Elizabeth' 177, 178
    'Fabia' 178
    flower bud formation 15
    'Fusilier' 177, 178
    'Gladys' 178
    'Grenadier' 177, 179
    'Gumpo' 179
    Hardy Hybrids 2, 187
    'Hawk' 186
    'Jenny' 177
    'J. G. Millais' 185
    'Lady Chamberlain' 176
    'Lady Rosebery' 176
    'Laura Aberconway' 178
    'Loderi' 178, 187
    'Luscombei' 178, 187
    'Matador' 178
    'May Day' 178
    'Naomi' 178
    'Palestrina' 182
    'Penjerrick' 178
    rex, see *R. fictolacteum* 177
    'Romany Chai' 178
    seed, Time of sowing 16
    'Sir John Ramsden' 185
    'Tally Ho' 178
    'Trewithen Orange' 178
    'Vanessa' 178
Rhodothamnus 188–9
Rhodotypos 109
Rhus 189–90
Rhus *cotinoides*, see Cotinus
        obovatus 71
    R. cotinus, see Cotinus
        coggygria 71
Ribes 190–1
Robinia 191
Rock Rose 57
Root forming hormones 17–8
Root-stock 13
Rosa 191–202
    x *harrisonii* 196
    lawrenceana, see *R. chinensis* 195
    pomifera 202
    richardii 200
    'Rouletii' 195
    sancta 195
    sinica, see *R. laevigata* 197
    spinosissima, see *R.*
        pimpinellifolia 200

Rose 191–202
    'Alberic Barbier' 202
    'Albertine' 202
    'Amy Robsart' 196
    Anemone 197
    Apothecaries 197
    Apple 202
    Austrian Copper 196
    'Belle de Crécy' 197
    'Belle Isis' 197
    'Bicolor' 196
    'Blanc Double de Coubert' 201
    'Bloomfield Abundance' 195
    'Buff Beauty' 198
    Burnet 199
    Burr 198
    Cabbage 194
    'Cardinal de Richelieu' 197
    'Carnea' 199
    'Cathayensis' 199
    'Cecile Brunner' 195
    'Celsiana' 197
    'Chapeau de Napoleon' 194
    'Charles de Mille' 197
    Cherokee 197
    Chestnut 201
    China 195
    'Comtesse de Cayla' 195
    'Cornelia' 198
    'Cramoisie Supérieur' 195
    'Crested Moss' 194
    'Cristata' 194
    Damask 195
    'De Mieux' 194
    'Emily Gray' 202
    Fairy 195
    'Fantin Latour' 194
    'Felicia' 198
    'Fortune's Double Yellow' 199
    'François Juranville' 202
    'Frau Dagmar Hastrup' 201
    Green 195
    'Helen Knight' 195
    'Hermosa' 195
    Himalayan Musk 194
    Hybrid Musk 198
        Perpetual 197
        Tea 197, 199
    'Kiftsgate' 196
    'Lady Penzance' 196
    'Leontine Gervaise' 202
    'Madame Laurette Messimy' 195
    'Madame Hardy' 195
    'Max Graf' 202
    'Meg Merrilees' 196
    'Minima' 195
    'Miss Lawrence's Rose' 195
    Monthly 195
    'Moonlight' 198
    Moss 194
    Musk 198
    'Nuits de Young' 195
    'Old Pink Moss' 195
    'Omar Khayyam' 195
    'Pamela' 195
    'Pax' 198

'Penelope' 198
'Persiana' 196
'Persian Yellow' 196
'Platyphylla' 199
Prairie 201
'Prosperity' 198
'Pseudindica' 199
'Ramona' 197
'Rosa Mundi' 197
'Roseraie de l'Hay 201
'Scabrosa' 201
Scots 199
'Seven Sisters' 199
'Stanwell Perpetual' 200
Tea 197, 199
'Tour de Malakoff' 194
'Tuscany' 197
'Tuscany Superb' 197
'Vanity' 198
'William III' 200
'William Lobb' 195
'Woley-Dod's Rose' 202
Rosemary 203
for hedges 11
Roses for hedges 11
Rosmarinus 203
Rubus 2, 203–5
'Tridel', see R. deliciosus 204
Rue 206
Ruscus 205–6
Russian Vine 166
Ruta 206

Sage 208–9
Bush 31
Jerusalem 160
St Dabeoc's Heath 78
St John's Wort 121
Salix 4, 206–8
'Stuartii', see S. lanata 208
Salvia 208–9
Sambucus 4, 209
Sand Myrtle 134
Santolina 210
pinnata, see S. neapolitana 210
viridis, see S. rosmarinifolia 210
Sarcococca 210
humilis, see S. hookeriana 210
Savin 129
Scion 13
Scramblers 2
Sea Buckthorn 117
Secateurs 15
Seed dormancy 16
germination 16
protection 16
Seedling variation 16
Seeds to sow as soon as ripe
16–7
Senecia 211–2
Serviceberry 28
Shears 15
Sheep's Laurel 129
Shrubs as background 3

specimens 2
Silk Tree 28
Vine 156
Siphonosmanthus delavayi, see
Osmanthus delavayi 152
Skimmia 212–3
'Foremanii' and 'Rogersii', see
S. japonica 212
Sloe 169
Smoke Tree 71
Snowball Tree 227, 229
Japanese 230
Snowberry 220
Snowy Mespilus 28
Soil preparation 6
for hedges 7
warming 17
Solanum 213
Sophora 214
Sorbaria 214–5
South Sea Myrtle 134
Spanish Broom 215
Gorse 104
Spartium 215
Spartocytisus nubigenus 78
Spice Bush 138
Spindle Tree 92–3
Spiraea 215, 217
Blue 48
False 214
seed, Time of sowing 17
thunbergii for hedges 11
trilobata 217
Spotted Laurel 32
Stachyurus 217–8
Staking 6
Staphylea 218
Stauntonia 218
Stranvaesia 218–9
Stratification 16
Strawberry Raspberry 204
Tree 30
Stuartia 219
Suckers as propagating material 19
Removal of 13
Sulphur 3
Sumach 189–90
Venetian 71
Sun Rose 115
Swamp Honeysuckle 186
Symphoricarpos 220
rivularis, see S. albus 220
Syringa 157, 220–3
palabiniana see S. meyeri 221
patula 221
velutina 221

Tamarisk 223–4
Tamarix 223–4
anglica, see T. gallica 223
pentandra, see T. ramosissima 223
Taxus 224
baccata for hedges 12
Telopea 224

Tendrils 2, 235–6
Teucrium 225
Thinning 14
Thorn hedges 12
Thujopsis 225
Thuya plicata for hedges 12
Tick-trefoil 82
Topiary 1, 3
Trachelospermum 225
Traveller's Joy 60
Tree Mallow 135
Peony 153
Poppy 82
Triforine 7
Trumpet Vine 46
Tutsan 121
Twiners 2, 235

Ulex 226

Vaccineum 3, 226
Venetian Sumach 71
Verbena, Lemon-scented 138
Vermiculite 17
Vernalisation 16
Veronica traversii, see Hebe
brachysiphon 109
Vestia 227
Viburnum 227–30
cinnamonifolium, see
V. davidii 228
tinus for hedges 10
Vinca 231
Vine 2, 232
Russian 166
Virginia Creeper 2, 154–5
Vitex 231
Vitis 232
Voles 16

Waratah 224
Watering hedges 8
Wattle 24
Wayfaring Tree 227, 229
Weigela 232
seed, Time of sowing 17
Whortleberry 226
Wig Tree 71
Willow 4, 206–8
Windbreaks 3, 8–9
Wineberry, Japanese 205
Wistaria (Wisteria) 233
Witch Hazel 107
American 99
Woodbine 140
Woodland gardens 3

Yew 224
for hedges 12
Trimming 15
Yucca 234
Yulan 142

Zenobia 234

Date Due		
MAR 6 1983		
APR 3 1983		
MAY 2 7 1983		
JUN 2 2 1983		
SEP 1 0 1983		
MAR 1 7 1987		
JUN 5 1987		
NOV 1 0 1992		
DEC 1 8 1996		
JAN 2 3 1998		
MAY 2 5 1999		
Jun. 19, '99		
DEC 1 9 1999		

FORM 109